THE ENGLISH HOUSE

1000 YEARS OF
DOMESTIC ARCHITECTURE

Frontispiece. Anderson Manor, Dorset

THE ENGLISH HOUSE

1000 YEARS OF DOMESTIC ARCHITECTURE

Weatherboarded cottage in Chapel Street, Steeple Bumpstead, Essex

John Steel and
Michael Wright

ANTIQUE COLLECTORS' CLUB

PUBLISHER'S NOTE

Michael Wright died in June 2006, still working on the final proofs of this book.
It is a great sadness that neither he, nor John Steel, lived to see its publication.

ISBN 10: 1-85149-523-1
ISBN 13: 978-1-85149-523-8

British Library Cataloguing-in-Publication Data
A catalogue record for this book is available from the British Library

Printed in China
for the Antique Collectors' Club Ltd., Woodbridge, Suffolk

CONTENTS

FOREWORD

In one sense, my involvement with this book can be expressed simply as an act of friendship. John Steel and I were close friends for many years and it was through writing and publishing that we were brought together. I knew that John was writing a book on domestic architecture in this country and we discussed and argued about the coverage of the book and debated the merits of individual houses to be included on the evidence of the many photographs that he had taken.

John's untimely death in 1998 led to my taking a much closer interest in the work that he had done and it soon became clear that, while the framework for the book and a substantial part of the earlier chapters had been completed, quite a lot of writing remained to be done, especially on the nineteenth and twentieth centuries, if John's own plan was to be adhered to. One alternative was to let the text stand as he left it, incomplete, rather like the torso of a Greek statue, but John's own introduction to the book made clear what a loss this would represent. The alternative, of finishing the book, was fraught with its own difficulties, especially as it was the work of a friend, and, although I cannot claim that John ever asked me to do so, the fact that we discussed the subject so frequently, when he knew that he had only a limited time left to him, might suggest that he was not adverse to my doing so.

What made me want to complete *The English House*, however, was the similarity of our views on the history of domestic architecture. I too feel that there is a gap in the coverage of this subject between the books produced by social and economic historians and those written by architectural ones, while both addressed an audience interested primarily in the technical detail. And, if you wanted the general architectural picture, the Pevsner books were not arranged for easy reference. What both John and I were aware of was how similar the objectives of the occupants of the medieval castle and of the modern semi-detached house were. The lord of a Norman castle might be interested primarily in defence, but he was also a wealthy and influential man in a local area for whom comfort, convenience and beauty were as important as his own security and that of his family.

He was also clear about the signals that his great building was sending out to neighbouring magnates and to the population at large, just as the owner of a semi-detached house is conscious of the effect that a new porch or an extension will have both on his neighbours and on the value of his property. Moreover, there is a striking similarity between the rooms and how they were used from the medieval period through, perhaps, to the country houses of the Edwardian period, built by architects such as Sir Edwin Lutyens. Thereafter the story is a rather different one, as the chapter on twentieth century houses makes clear.

There is another reason why John's book has especial merit. William Morris, when he started the Society for the Protection of Ancient Buildings in 1877, said that you should be able to read the history of a building in its exterior appearance, and that changes made in earlier times should be welcomed for that reason. Taking a building back to a notional date in its past, as is occasionally done today, often for financial as well as conservation reasons, was to him an act of vandalism. In this respect, therefore, the ability to isolate the dates, however approximate they might be, of window- and roof-lines, of doorcases, and of the proportions of a façade, is valuable evidence for the social historian, as well as being fascinating to the general reader, enabling a picture to be built up of a community in previous times.

Michael Wright, 1936-2006

INTRODUCTION

The genesis of this book was my own interest, stretching over thirty years, in the seemingly endless variation in the houses that are to be found in England. Nowhere else in the world are there so many different types built in a small space over 1,000 years. As a publisher it irritated me that this rich inheritance had not persuaded anybody to produce an intelligent introduction. To be sure there are books galore on specialist aspects of domestic architecture, but nothing at a serious level for the person coming new to the subject.

So I started thinking about the subject from two directions, that of photographing the houses that I thought interesting and reading as many books as possible. That was all I had time to do until I retired in the mid-1990s, but even by that time it was obvious that the two were not going to be an easy match: a good proportion of what I photographed merited very little attention in books; and the houses that the books talked about were, in general, pretty thin on the ground. There were dozens of different types that got very little coverage. I say types because it seems obvious that, while every house is different from every other house in some way, they do tend to fall into broad categories, sometimes by type, sometimes by date. It is these categories which I have attempted to define and discuss.

There are more than three hundred house types, most of which are illustrated. I have tried to select the more typical examples. The dates that appear after each heading are approximately those between which the features highlighted are most frequently to be found. Often an idea starts some time before it is taken on generally and isolated examples tend to turn up long after the idea has gone out of fashion. Dating a house is far from an exact science and one gets better at it as one sees more houses. What I hope

I have done is to put into the hands of the reader material which will enable him to improve the accuracy of his dating, and also to make a preliminary judgement about how successful a particular house is within its type. Too much respect is given blindly to art in general, just as if age or monetary value confer aesthetic quality. How often do you see 'experts' on television condemn as of poor quality the objects they describe? The crowds that shuffle around National Trust houses all too often do so with uncritical church-like solemnity and they only come to life in the nurseries and the kitchens. Yet common sense tells us that not everything made in the past was of top quality, any more than everything made today is bad. If the occasional reservations or condemnations in the text irritate, please bear in mind that they are an attempt to stimulate the reader's critical faculties and are not just the comments of a querulous and elderly writer.

Had I only listed house types, something which has not been done before, this might have been useful, but I have tried to go one step further and group them by period, starting with the largest properties and making my way down through the economic scale and mentioning regional differences within a period. This has proved an interesting exercise, because it seems that, apart from the Middle Ages, changes take place every twenty-five to forty years; in other words, each generation moves away from what their predecessors have done. So, for each of the divisions I have adopted, there is an introduction which attempts to outline what is happening in the country at large and what are the main trends in house design.

At this point I expect there will be objections that Pevsner's 'Buildings of England' series, which is published by county, does just that. It does not. They are superb books, and you should certainly have the ones that cover the counties in which you travel, but they are essentially a catalogue of the most important architecture, of which houses are only one part, and it is the important houses that get the most attention. Pevsner provides some fifty different lists. What is offered here is a single history of the progression. This is the same cake but cut the other way, and is probably best thought of as an introduction to Pevsner's more erudite text. I also assume that the reader has no pre-knowledge; at times Pevsner seems to be talking only to his fellow architectural historians.

It is tempting to think that the thousand years covered by this book comprise the whole history of English domestic architecture, as it seems likely that, at the lower economic levels, boxes decorated with pastiches of earlier styles will become the norm. The section on the twentieth century, however, shows that this is unduly pessimistic, and further up the economic scale some very exciting things are happening. Of course, many better-off people buy old houses and, while it is not difficult to find horrors, careful conservation of old features has become much more the norm than it was, say, thirty or forty years ago.

In order to be comprehensive within a reasonable compass, I have in the main restricted myself to considering the outside of a house and then usually only the front. But, where the elevation is affected by the plan, this has also been discussed. Such an approach has merit because, just like the human face reveals character, you can tell a great deal about a house from looking at its appearance. At the end of the book there are credits for the books I have consulted, not only to acknowledge my debt, but also to lead the reader on to a new level of enquiry. About half a dozen of the more expert works by modern authors are very informative and readable, and these I have concentrated on, making the list of authorities quoted quite short. I do not wish to imply that the old is bad and the modern good, for some writers from the past, like Pugin, are most enjoyable to read, and so too is Ruskin, if you can bear his rather orotund style.

As we are discussing house types, there are fewer architects mentioned than might have been expected in a book of this kind. Some created house types, however, and refuse to be subsumed in the process of general development and appear in the text in their own right.

Finally, a word on definitions. I define 'domestic' as anything that is, or can be, made suitable for living in regardless of its original use; and 'architecture' as the result of money and effort spent on a house over and above the minimum needed to provide a sound weather-proof box for living in. So, 'architecture' identifies the way people spend money unnecessarily on extras that they consider important, not just for their own pleasure but as statements they wish to make to their contemporaries about themselves.

Thirty years' publishing have taught me to have a clear view of my reader. I have in mind an educated, professional person who is used to looking up references whether they are tax or legal precedents, computer programmes or medical journals; someone in a hurry, used to the careful abstraction of information, who has begun to look at houses for the first time, perhaps because he or she is about to buy one; or, perhaps,

> …someone will forever be surprising
> A hunger in himself to be more serious.

Accordingly I have tried to provide information without waffle, spiced with the occasional aesthetic comment. I hope the book is sufficiently interesting to draw you on to the next stage of more specialist reading where the house and its relationship with its creator are explored more fully.

John Steel, 1934-1998

CHAPTER 1

1000-1300

1.0 INTRODUCTION

The domestic part of the medieval castle was essentially a group of smaller rooms surrounding three greater spaces accommodating the Great Hall, the chapel and the kitchen. It seems likely that this arrangement derived from separate huts in a defensive enclave encircled by a wooden wall and it was the requirements of security that first brought them together in the same building. But, coupled with this, both domestic convenience and aesthetics played a part and from the earliest times design both of the arrangement of the rooms and the way they

were embellished reflected the sophistication of the owner of the castle and the status he was anxious to secure for himself and his family among his peers.

The life of the lord of the castle was to begin with largely dominated by the Great Hall and by the quasi-religious ceremonial surrounding the eating of the main meal of the day. In the twelfth century Bishop Grosseteste, who drew up the rules of conduct for the household of the Countess of Lincoln, made clear the importance that should be attached to the presence of the Countess in her Hall eating amongst her tenants. Ironically, this centralisation was soon to give way to the human need of the wealthy for privacy and greater comfort, and the following excerpt from William Langland's *The Vision of Piers Plowman*, written in about 1362, shows that the Hall had had its day by 1400:

Wretched is the hall…each day in the week
There the lord and lady liketh not to sit,
Now have the rich a rule to eat by themselves
In a privy parlour… for poor men's sake,
Or in a chamber with a chimney, and leave the chief hall
That was made for meals, for men to eat in.

From that time the lord of a great castle, and soon also that of a more modest manor house, ate and entertained his guests in the Great Chamber, once a bedchamber. Although this room was smaller than the Great Hall, there was no diminution in ceremonial and the arrangement and decoration of the Great Chamber continued to follow the requirements of the feudal system and to have a religious significance. Both Great Hall and Great Chamber would normally be two storeys high and the lord would sit, either on his own or with his main guest or his wife, on a dais at the opposite end from the doorway, looking down on his tenants or lesser guests seated at trestle tables running the length of the room. On his right-hand side a bay window, often elaborately carved, would cast light both on the lord, emphasising his continued good health, and on his 'cupboard', literally a board, on which was displayed his most precious plate, symbolising his financial health.

2. Penshurst Great Hall with the central hearth

The Great Hall was originally heated by a central hearth with a smoke hole in the timber roof and a fine example of this can still be seen in the Barons' Hall at Penshurst Place, in Kent *(Plates 1 and 2)*. Although this hearth is thought to date from about 1340, I think that, in this regard, Penshurst must have been rather behind the times, as wall-mounted chimneys were installed in John of Gaunt's Great Hall at Kenilworth Castle *(Plate 3)* in the 1380s as a matter of course. It was certainly the practice to place the fireplace closer to the lord on the dais than to the Hall's entrance.

Opposite. 1. The Barons' Hall, Penshurst, Kent

Right. 3. Great Hall of Kenilworth Castle, Warwickshire with wall-mounted fireplace

The approach to the Hall, originally from the courtyard, might be used ceremonially by the lord and was accordingly provided with a carved stone doorway; the lobby to the Hall was also sometimes frescoed. It was usual to raise the floor of the Hall as a further security precaution and at Stokesay Castle, for instance, it can be seen that the earliest practice was to approach the Great Hall by an outside wooden staircase which could be removed in an emergency *(Plate 4)*. At the entrance end of the Hall three archways would give access to the kitchen, the buttery and the pantry, a carved wooden screen cut down the draughts which must have plagued the occupants of the Hall, while the staircase giving access to the Great Hall on the first floor, and the lord's private apartments opening from it, would rise from the dais end of the Hall and would also be elaborately decorated to reflect the status of the building's owner.

Gradually, during the thirteenth and fourteenth centuries, the lord's private apartments took on an established pattern. In a reasonably grand house with a Great Chamber his suite of rooms would include a closet for work and prayer, a bedchamber, a wardrobe usually with a chimney where his clothes were stored and mended, and a privy *(Plate 6* overleaf). Very often, and Broughton Castle, Oxfordshire, is a case in point, the closet would have a balcony from which the lord could look down into the sanctuary of the chapel, thus attending the mass without sitting among his tenants. As the nation became more secure in the Middle Ages, so Great Chamber, chapel and closet windows became more ornate, proclaiming the importance of the person occupying the lodgings.

4. Stokesay Castle, Shropshire

5. *The Abbot's Kitchen, Glastonbury, Somerset*

The construction of the Great Chamber on the first floor of a building behind the wall at the dais end of the Great Hall left a void beneath it and this was usually filled by a privy parlour. Langland mentions them in about 1400 and they were used by the family to dine in privately when State was not being kept. But, again, great care was taken over the decoration of these rooms and window frames were usually of carved stone. The arrangement of the rooms in castles and great houses was followed on a smaller scale by the owners of more modest properties, and what was suitable for the secular lords was equally appropriate for the ecclesiastical magnates like the abbots of the great monasteries.

Kitchens were originally built away from the lodgings because of the fire risk *(Plate 5)*, but, when they were

13

incorporated in the structure, they were usually of stone and of two storeys to enable heat and smells to be vented. It is interesting that the same arrangement of the lord's lodging was adopted whether it was in a curtain-walled castle, as at Bodiam Castle in Sussex, or in the keep of a castle, as at Tattershall, Lincolnshire (**Plate 7**), or in a gatehouse tower, as is the case at Layer Marney in Essex.

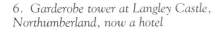

7. *The Keep of Tattershall Castle, Lincolnshire*

6. *Garderobe tower at Langley Castle, Northumberland, now a hotel*

8. Fairfield, Eastry, Kent

1.1 THE AISLED HALL 1100-1300

When it came to designing the early Great Hall, the best precedent that house builders could follow was that of the church. This was mainly an Anglo-Saxon rather than a Norman practice. The use of aisles enabled the huge weight of the roof to be at least partly borne by the pillars which formed the aisle posts, while the narrow aisles could be used for sleeping or storage. The large space in the middle, open to the roof, served as a communal room for the lord and his extended family and servants, but it was also used to conduct manorial business. The lord would sit in his chair (itself a status symbol) on the dais, often under a canopy, while he gave judgement on disputes and legal matters relating to the manor. The central hearth would be fed with dry wood and allowed to die down to charcoal to minimise the smoke which made its way out of special vents in the roof. There would probably be no glass in the windows and shutters would be closed on the weather side of the building.

In these very early times, the owner of the hall and his wife would sleep in a small room, probably at the dais end, while at the other, beyond a cross passage leading to the open air, would be the kitchen and store rooms. Fairfield, at Eastry, in Kent, was the secondary manor house built in the late thirteenth century for Christ Church Priory and consists of an aisled hall with a three-part plan *(Plate 8)*. Here there are no projecting wings and the ground-floor rooms at each end of the building only rise as high as the tops of the two aisle walls. To overcome the difficulties posed by the downward-sweeping roof, the jettied upper rooms in the cross wings at the two ends are independently roofed making them look like hipped dormers. As a result, the aisled hall is really no longer than it is wide.

Aisled hall houses continued to be popular in the south of England until about 1480, but they gradually descended the social scale. In the north of England, particularly around the prosperous wool centre of the Upper Calder Valley, they provided, in addition to status for their owners, extra working and storage space, and continued to be built into the sixteenth century. Today, survivors often nestle between heavily beamed, two storeyed wings built at right angles. It is difficult from the outside to spot the existence of an aisled hall, or to distinguish it from a later extension or outshut. One indication is that the roof sweeps down closer to the ground than usual. Because of the resulting poor lighting there might be only one aisle. Essex has a large number of those remaining.

1.2 FIRST-FLOOR HALL HOUSES 1100-1300

The other design which could be followed, in miniature, was the castle. Built in stone, with an eye to protecting the owner and his goods, the window-less ground floor might be dug into the ground with pillars and arches of great strength to support the upper floor, creating an undercroft or stone cellar. Here merchandise was stored and the public was admitted through strong ground-floor doors which could be firmly barred at night. However, the undercroft often did not have direct access to the upper floors, which suggests that, in these cases, either the two parts of the building were in different ownerships or that it was more important to protect the lord and his family on the first floor than to save the goods. Most medieval towns like Chester and Norwich have undercrofts of this kind, but they are not found where flooding was likely, as it was in York. The first floor, where later the Great Hall was situated, was often divided into two, and had a fireplace on the longer wall and a well-tiled roof.

Saltford Manor House *(Plate 9)*, between Bristol and Bath, has strong claims to be the oldest, continuously occupied house in Britain, and, on stylistic grounds, was recently dated by John Goodall to 1150. Approaching the house from the High Street, it is clear that the entrance front is seventeenth century, but inside there are two substantial ceiling beams and a round-headed Norman arch on plain impost blocks with a similarly plain moulding. From the garden it is at once apparent that the living hall was on the first floor and a Norman window can be seen with a carved zig-zag frieze under a semi-circular hood moulding.

Inside there are two Norman windows, the one which is blocked having very sophisticated window-seats *(Plate 10)* below the east gable, which is decorated on the exterior with a stone beast. The open window in the north wall has two orders of colonnettes with scallop capitals and a frieze, and it seems likely that there must once have been a northern wing to the house projecting from the east end of the structure. On the second floor there are traces of wall painting of the end of the twelfth century depicting a seated Virgin and a Wheel of Fortune *(Plate 11)*. Saltford Manor House has been carefully restored by the present owners, Mr and Mrs James Wynn, and stylistic details would seem to suggest that the same masons who worked on Hereford Cathedral were also responsible for Saltford and the original builder most probably had the responsibility of administering the Cathedral's estates in the north Somerset area.

10. Window seat in Norman window-opening at Saltford

11. Wall painting showing the Virgin seated

9. *The Manor House, Saltford, near Bristol*

12. Boothby Pagnell Manor House, Lincolnshire: the entrance front

13. The west front of Boothby Pagnell

Just as important is the Manor House at Boothby Pagnell, Lincolnshire *(Plates 12 and 13)*. Built in about 1180 by the descendants of Theodoric and Lezelina de Botheby, it stood within a moat, traces of which can still be seen today to the west of the early nineteenth century Boothby Pagnell Hall. It is clear that the rectangular stone building was a chamber block for the accommodation of the lord and his family built at right angles to, and at the dais end of, a single-storeyed Great Hall. Archaeology has revealed the foundations of such a hall and the layout at Boothby Pagnell marks, therefore, the first stage in the development of the medieval English house which was to be completed when a further chamber block was built at the service end of the hall achieving the H-shaped structure which was to become familiar in the fifteenth century.

Indeed, research in Normandy would suggest that, where land for building was unrestricted, the hall and the chamber would stand alongside each other, the undercroft of the chamber being used for storage. It also seems more than possible that the influence leading to the construction of chamber blocks where the lord could eat privately but still keep his 'State' travelled from this country to France, rather than the other way about, and might have originated here before the Conquest. More physical evidence is needed before this problem can be solved.

At ground level the undercroft has quadripartite rib-vaulting, but the only access to the lord's hall above was by an external stone staircase, much of which has been rebuilt, doubtless in the original manner. At the top the doorway has a round head with a simple hood moulding, carved stops and chamfered jambs, and this originally led straight into the main hall. The most striking feature of the hall today is the fireplace with its flat stone hood supported on brackets and corbels and with a lintel of interlocking blocks. The presence of a wall-mounted fireplace is a remarkably early survival, though there is evidence of such sophistication in the White Tower of the Tower of London in the eleventh century, but that was a royal palace, of course. The cylindrical chimney which can be seen on the west front is also a fine feature.

Beyond the hall a doorway decorated with a stone arch leads into the solar and here the round-headed, two-light window facing east has fitted stone seats and a channel to collect rainwater that might penetrate the original wooden shutters. From the outside it is clear that the ground-floor windows have been recut and the main hall window on the first floor is most likely to date from 1500. Boothby Pagnell is not only a remarkable survival of a

14. Norman window at Hemingford Grey Manor House, Huntingdonshire

highly sophisticated house, but it offers valuable clues as to how the medieval house developed in this country.

The Manor House, Hemingford Grey, in Huntingdonshire, is also of particular interest as most of the centre of the building is a mid-twelfth century hall, the main living space being once again on the first floor. On the west, south and east façades two-light Norman windows can still be seen *(Plate 14)* and it seems at least possible that there was a chapel block attached at the east. The doorway is on the south and must have been approached by an external wooden staircase. Inside the Manor House there is a great chimneypiece flanked by two Norman columns surmounted by scalloped capitals. A moat surrounds the house on three sides, while the river provides defence on the other side.

The Manor House, Donington le Heath, in Leicestershire, was built in about 1280 **(Plate 15)**. As might be expected, the Hall faces south and on the other side there is a thirteenth century block which houses an interior staircase, although the masonry holes on the south face suggest that the first-floor hall was originally approached by means of an external stair. Passing through the two-centred-arched door, the visitor would have found himself either in a screens passage or in one of the service rooms, perhaps the buttery, separated from the Hall itself by a wooden partition, the mortice holes for which can still be seen. Interestingly, there is evidence of a stair up from the undercroft which was perhaps added after the original construction period. In the Hall are two open trusses with collars and chamfered ties and a fireplace in the north wall closer to where the dais must have been.

Sometimes, as at The Jew's House, Well Lane, Lincoln, of the late twelfth century, there is no undercroft and the ground floor is at street level **(Plate 16)**. The reason in this instance is perhaps the fall of the land and the presence of what used to be round-headed openings for shops, that are now rectangular. The doorway has shafts with an arch above decorated with chain links, and two of the first-floor windows have double-arches, all of which is Norman work, and there is a similar house

15. Manor House, Donington le Heath, Leicestershire

nearby called 'The Norman House'. A scene in the Bayeux Tapestry shows knights eating in a first-floor castle *(Plate 17)* and another early example of the use of the first-floor hall is the Hall built by William Marshall in his keep at Chepstow Castle, in Wales.

17. King Harold feasting on the upper floor of his manor at Bosham, Sussex: from the Bayeux Tapestry

16. The Jew's House, Well Lane, Lincoln

21

1.3 ENGLISH WOOL HOUSES

> I praise God and ever shall
> It is the sheep hath paid for all

These words can be found engraved on the glass window of a wool merchant's house and they underline the importance of sheep to architecture as well as to medieval society in England, not least because of the rarity and the expense of having glass windows. In 1353 wool was described as 'the sovereign merchandise and jewel of this realm of England', making up as it did eighty per cent of the nation's exports. From the eleventh until the fourteenth centuries the two great centres of cloth production were the Low Countries and Florence, and wool from the Spanish peninsula, Burgundy, and especially England was of a much higher quality than that from elsewhere. Buyers travelled to England to buy directly from the great estates, with those from Italy doubling as papal tax gatherers from the monasteries.

The finest English wool came from the Shropshire and Herefordshire borderland, roughly the area between the Severn and the Welsh Marches. Next in preference was wool from Lindsey, in Lincolnshire, as well as the large output of the Cotswolds, which grew steadily in importance in the fifteenth century. These three areas produced the best quality export wools, while Yorkshire, Derbyshire and the Midlands produced a middle grade, the chalk of the south and East Anglia a coarser, but still exportable wool, and the produce of Devon and Cornwall was considered to be too poor to be sent abroad.

While many villagers had substantial herds, the pattern before the Black Death of the 1350s was that vast estates, both religious and secular, maintained tens of thousands of sheep. After the disaster of the plague the shortage of labour encouraged even bigger herds, as they needed less tending than crops, and as the fourteenth century drew to its close land was rented out by the richer families who dissociated themselves from farming, just as the rich factory owners of the nineteenth century became gentlemen and shunned the industry that provided their money. This broadening of wealth gave opportunities for middlemen to buy and sell and to lend money against future purchases, taking as interest sacks of wool, enabling them and those further down the economic ladder to build solid houses.

The need for money to finance the Hundred Years War resulted in 1363 in the establishment of a monopoly or 'Staple' in the then English town of Calais. In this way a limited number of merchants controlled the export of English wool to the Low Countries and they paid a heavy tax to the king for the privilege. Naturally, they passed on as much of this tax as they could by reducing the price they paid to the producers and increasing that to be paid by foreigners. The result was cheap wool for the English cloth industry which expanded rapidly at the expense of weavers in Europe, so that, despite many ups and downs and a general levelling out of wealth, by the time of the Dissolution of the Monasteries in about 1535-1540, this country was a major producer of cloth with a sheep population of some ten million. Then, by the end of the sixteenth century, the level of cloth exports declined as the taste of the rich turned to silks and other luxury fabrics. To aid the industry, the export of raw wool was prohibited in 1614.

Periods of prosperity for growers, profits for middlemen and merchants provided the funds to build houses, but the usury on lent money, the discounting of bills and the legal arguments that surrounded the industry were also highly advantageous to others than the merchants, as were the profits from supplying arms and from funding and serving the king. A section of society quickly grew up between the new super rich, who themselves rapidly joined the aristocracy, and the lower orders of society, and they constituted a large middle class. There has always been an ambitious, intelligent or at least greedy group of individuals, and the fifteenth century offered them an especially lucrative opportunity. They needed to reinforce their standing, and what better way to do so than to build, confirming to the world the high opinion they had of themselves. Not all made it, and some lost it, but they began a middle stratum of society which has left us with some wonderful houses.

There are many timber-framed and stone houses in the important wool areas that might illustrate the wealth that clothiers enjoyed in the medieval period. An outstanding example is Grevel House, in the High Street of Chipping Campden, in Gloucestershire **(Plate 18)**. William Grevel, the wool merchant himself, died in 1401. His house is built of Cotswold stone with a striking Perpendicular bay window stretching over two storeys with six five-headed lights, a traceried panel in between the storeys and gargoyles above. There is also an entrance doorway of the late fourteenth century with a moulded pointed arch and, inside the house, a contemporary chimneypiece.

Opposite: 18. Grevel House, High Street, Chipping Campden,
Gloucestershire

19. Vicars' Close, Cathedral Precinct, Wells, Somerset

1.4 GROUND-FLOOR HALLS IN TOWNS

From the earliest times the church had need for buildings in towns in which to house priests, servants, schoolchildren and travellers. The large number of chantry chapels in cathedrals and in the large urban churches meant that there were always some priests without official accommodation, while associated with the cathedrals themselves the Vicars, who were subordinate members of the cathedral either in orders or in minor orders, also needed to be at least modestly housed. The Vicars acted as vice-prebendaries and sang the services in the cathedral on behalf of the often absent prebendaries themselves. Their cottages were normally built in rows end on to the street to save space, as they are in Vicars' Close in the cathedral precinct at Wells *(Plate*

19). Although they had existed as a group since the reorganisation of Wells Cathedral, it was Bishop Ralph of Shrewsbury who established them as a college and gave them their quarters in 1348. It is intriguing to see what amounts to a planned street of the mid-fourteenth century and, although many changes have been made to the street in the intervening centuries, No. 22, which has been restored, gives an impression of how these ground-floor halls must originally have appeared. The street itself tapers in a manner which must have been a deliberate device to create perspective, and is closed by the chapel.

A similar arrangement of street houses for chantry priests is to be found in York. Alongside the arch leading to Holy Trinity there is a group of low timber-framed cottages at 64-

20. 64-72 Lady Row, Goodramgate, York

72 Lady Row, Goodramgate *(Plate 20)*. Dating from about 1320, these houses have what is perhaps the earliest overhang in the country and the timbers are exposed. In the fourteenth century these small buildings would consist of a ground-floor living room open to the roof with a single bedroom beyond a cross-passage at one end, and an open hearth in the living space. The cottages in York are timber-framed, though in some areas stone might be used for the ground floor, and by the middle of the fourteenth century they are thought to have been jettied and the ground floor living space ceiled, presumably to provide more accommodation. Just off Goodramgate, in a lane called Bedern, there was Bedern Chapel which belonged to the premises of the Vicars Choral.

21. The Clergy House, Alfriston, Sussex

1.5 MEDIEVAL OPEN-HALL HOUSES

Although the Alfriston Clergy House in East Sussex **(Plate 21)** is typical of many timber-framed 'Wealden' houses built in the late medieval period, it is also remarkable as it was the first historic building to be acquired and restored by the fledgling National Trust in 1896. It was most probably built by a yeoman farmer who had flourished in the aftermath of the Black Death in 1350 when more than a quarter of the population had died, including eight out of the thirteen Augustinian canons at the nearby Michelham Priory. In the fifteenth century the Priory acquired the house and it remained church property for five centuries.

The oak frame of the Clergy House is filled in with strips of chestnut or oak, covered with daub and lime washed. Two storeys high, the house has a thatched roof, which is hipped at both ends, and at the eastern end the upper floor is jettied out. The interior is simple, with a central communal hall open to the rafters, and the family rooms are at the eastern end consisting of a Parlour and garderobe on the ground floor and a Solar, or living room, above. At the other, western, end there were two floors of humbler accommodation where the food was prepared and the servants slept.

This part was demolished in the mid-sixteenth century and replaced by a new two-bayed wing projecting to the rear of the building, and at that time the Parlour was moved. This space, with the two chambers above, was warmed by fireplaces joined to a single brick chimney set against the west end of the house. The difference between the fourteenth and sixteenth century work can be clearly seen in the main elevation, where the later close studding can be contrasted with the diagonal foot and head bracing in the central and eastern part.

Many of the medieval window openings have survived; they were originally covered either by shutters or sacking until they were glazed at the end of the sixteenth century. Although the building was socially modest, the Parlour was, in the Middle Ages, two rooms – the buttery and the pantry – as if it was much grander. The Hall roof is supported on timbers forming a central vertical crown-post and the remains of the first hearth has been found in the centre of the room, smoke from it escaping through the windows and through the roof. The floor is made of chalk compressed and sealed with sour milk.

Tickenham Court, near Nailsea, in north Somerset, is also a fine survival, but less well known **(Plates 22-24)**. The Great Hall of about 1400 is remarkably complete and a two-storeyed solar wing was added in the 1480s at the west end and running south. The Hall has two-light windows on both sides, its front and back doors are preserved at either end of a screens passage, the grooves for which can still be seen, and there are two blocked doorways in the east wall with elaborate four-centred heads which must have led to the kitchen and other service rooms. A third archway, in the north-east corner of the

22. Tickenham Court, near Nailsea, Somerset

Hall, has the beginnings of a spiral stair which might have given access to a first-floor suite of rooms occupied by a principal household officer. This too is now blocked.

Today the ceiling of the Hall is boarded, but above the roof has collar beams and arched braces, while at the western end of the Hall, where the High Table would have stood, there is a blocked arch probably giving access to a withdrawing room in the 1400 house. Curiously, there are corbels high up on each of the long walls, the purpose of which can only be guessed at. One possibility is that they held flambeaux added to improve lighting on large formal occasions during Tickenham's early Tudor period. The upper-floor room of the solar wing is an especially fine space and was most probably the Great Chamber of the 1480 house. Open to the rafters, the room has a splendid roof with collar-beams, arched braces and three levels of wind-braces.

The present owner's mother, an architect, was responsible for much-needed restoration about fifty years ago when she and her husband lived at Tickenham Court, and English Heritage takes the view that this work was so well done that it has formed part of the history of the house. Certainly, in the nineteenth century, Tickenham was part of the Ashton Court estate, owned for many generations by the Smyths, a merchant family from Bristol. It is almost certain that there was a building on the site before the present house and it is thought that one of its flanking walls might have run east-west on the north side of the 1400 Hall, but whether there was in those early times a further wing on the line of the present kitchen and other domestic offices is a matter for the archaeologist. These are questions, however, which make the detailed study of early houses like Tickenham Court so fascinating.

A variation of the open-hall house is the aisled structure, mainly to be found in Essex and in parts of Kent. As the name suggests, the roof is supported by aisle posts before finishing its downward sweep on at least one of the low outside walls of the Hall. One such house is Nurstead Court, near Meopham Station, in Kent. In spite of its fame as an important medieval house, part of the original structure was lost in the nineteenth century when a new house was built. What can still be seen, however, is half of an aisled Great Hall. Only 29ft. (8.8m) across, the Hall is constructed of timber and must date from about 1320. The aisle arches rest on responds, while the roof arch cuts into the underside of the tie-beam and there is a short crown-post. Although this arrangement is rare in houses, it was common in churches. The fact that the distribution of the plan is mainly in the east of the country suggests an Anglo-Saxon origin, while, by the beginning of the fifteenth century, it had lapsed altogether.

23. The Great Hall, Tickenham Court, looking to the service end
24. Roof structure of the Great Chamber at Tickenham Court

25. Interior of the Great Barn, Lacock, Wiltshire

26. Exposed cruck truss in Church Street, Lacock

1.6 CRUCK HALLS 1250-1450

If you can find two trees bent to a similar angle, they can be cut down and leant together to form an arch or cruck, and a number of similar arches placed in line and stabilised by ridge timbers form the structure of the cruck hall. Of course, the blade or inclined curved timber can also be cut to the triangular specifications of the frame. There are various forms of the cruck, but the full or true cruck has two blades forming the triangular principals of the roof rising from a cill beam near the ground to the ridge and supporting both the roof and the walls of the Hall. The base cruck rises from just above the ground to the first transverse timber or tie-beam, while the raised cruck has the lower part of the cruck timbers set on solid walls and rising to the ridge.

These structures tend to be found in the western rather than in the eastern counties and were originally built by rich peasants rather than by the gentry. The origins of the cruck are obscure, but were probably developed in pre-Norman times, their heyday being in the fourteenth and early fifteenth centuries, although isolated examples of full cruck construction are even found in the eighteenth century.

In form the structure was rather like an upturned boat and difficult to extend unless you add more crucks. The alternative box-frame method of construction was easier to enlarge and was more readily adapted to awkward sites. More importantly still, the box-frame allowed more space on the upper floors and for those who could afford it this was always going to be the preferred method of building. In East Street, Lacock, Wiltshire, there is a fourteenth century barn originally belonging to Lacock Abbey which has eight bays with cruck trusses and a four-bay wing where the roof-structure can be clearly seen (Plate 25), but, as part of the street scene, No. 3 Church Street has a cruck truss exposed on its east face (Plate 26).

27. *Little Wenham Hall, Suffolk*

1.7 THE KNIGHT'S HOUSE 1270-1350

Whereas the first-floor Hall House had a single hall on two levels, the Knight's House was a mini castle with a tower as its main defence and accommodation or storage provided on several floors. It might also have a moat and was easier to defend and more prestigious than a first-floor Hall House. Because of the frequency of rebellion in the thirteenth and fourteenth centuries, it was necessary to obtain a royal licence to crenellate before building battlements. As times became more secure and prosperity increased, a hall and other rooms, such as a chapel, could be added, an arrangement which tended to produce a rather haphazard plan which appealed to later Romantic tastes.

Little Wenham Hall, in Suffolk, is a good example of these early Knight's Houses *(Plate 27)*. Dating from about 1280, it was probably built for Sir John de Vallibus and is remarkable both for the local brick in which it is built and also because it is halfway between a keep and a fortified manor house, in a

similar category, therefore, to Stokesay Castle. The structure is L-shaped with a spiral stair and, like Stokesay, the entrance is on the first floor, with a rib-vaulted ground floor in brick supporting the Hall and chapel. The Hall has four windows with plate tracery including trefoils and quatrefoils and, unlike the chapel, is not vaulted. The chapel vault rests on corbels, two of which date from the Early English period of stiff-leaf capital carving contemporary with the window tracery in the Hall. Above the chapel is the Solar, and the battlements, differing building heights of the Hall and chapel ranges and the spiral stair make for a wonderfully varied skyline. Little Wenham Hall evokes the early fourteenth century Knight's House recalling Chaucer's Prologue to the *Canterbury Tales*, where it is said about the Knight's son, the Squire:

Polite, modest, willing to serve, and able
He carved before his father at their table.

CHAPTER 2

1300-1450

2.0 INTRODUCTION

Although there are many regional variations in houses during the fourteenth century, their general layout continued to follow the style discussed in the first chapter. What was different was the greater security of rural life and a consequential emphasis on comfort and decoration rather than defence. Even where moats, drawbridges and portcullises were introduced, there is little evidence of them being used and in some cases elements of this kind were introduced as *jeux d'esprit* in the nineteenth century.

The manor house was a legally defined sub-division of land administered by the lord of the manor whose house was, therefore, the seat of local administration. Most manor houses started life as simple rectangles, their width being determined largely by the timber available to roof the hall and by the wealth of the lord. The usual span of the most important space was accordingly 17ft. (5m) to about 30ft. (9m), and this upper dimension is the width of the fine fourteenth century Banqueting Hall of Haddon Hall, Derbyshire *(Plate 28)*. At the lower end of the Hall a cross passage, soon known as the screens passage because of the function of the wooden screen as a draught excluder, stretched across the house from front to back door, and beyond were the service rooms – kitchen, buttery and pantry. The late medieval kitchen at Haddon Hall still evokes the atmosphere of the time and possesses

cupboards, chopping blocks, bread ovens and butchery equipment dating from these early times.

The Hall itself served as living room, courthouse, and sleeping chamber. The dais, from which the lord would administer justice, would be lit by a large bay window which emphasised the status of the house, while the long oak tables standing on the dais were at this time often only carved on the hall side. From the middle of the fourteenth century cross wings at right angles to the dais end of the house were built to overcome the inconvenience of these living arrangements, and these extensions provided a Parlour where the family could entertain in more privacy, and a further living room upstairs, a Solar, which might be used as a bedroom.

Clevedon Court, the manor house of Clevedon, near Bristol, in north Somerset, is one of the most complete houses of its time to have survived *(Plate 29)*. Built in about 1320 for Sir John de Clevedon, it is entered from the south through a two-storeyed porch opening into a stone-flagged screens passage which provides the spine of the house. Each porch has a portcullis groove in its inner doorway, and the gates were operated by windlasses in the rooms above. The south porch has a spiral stair leading to the roof, while that on the north side terminates at the first floor.

28. *Great Hall of Haddon Hall, Derbyshire, looking to the dais*

29. *Clevedon Court, Somerset: the entrance front*

The Great Hall at Clevedon Court *(Plate 30)* underwent some changes in both the sixteenth and eighteenth centuries, but the most unusual aspect of the Hall is the deep alcove at the dais end. Approached through a magnificent chamfered stone arch, the recess is unusual for the fourteenth century and anticipates not only the oriels of the Tudor period, but the little rooms in sixteenth century manor houses such as that at Lytes Cary in Somerset.

At Clevedon the purpose of the alcove is to support the hanging chapel on the first floor, dedicated to St Peter, patron saint of fishermen, and the patron's connection with the sea is echoed in the beautiful rectangular window filled with reticulated tracery A newel stair, now blocked at ground-floor level, led to the roof, connecting the alcove to the chapel. In medieval times the church and the manor house were usually built alongside each other, but the Norman church of St Andrew's, Clevedon, stands on Wain's Hill, two miles away.

The probable reason for this unusual siting is that floods in the winter frequently cut the church off from manor house, and it was more important for Sir John de Clevedon to be able to travel dry-shod to Bristol, from which direction all the supplies for the house would come, than to have contact with the church, especially as he had his own chapel at Clevedon Court. Just as intriguing is the fourteenth century window in the interior wall of the chapel with a view down into the Great Hall. I suspect that this had two purposes: to enable the household below to participate in the Mass with a degree of retirement for the owner and to allow the lady of the manor to keep an eye on what was going on in the Hall.

30. *The Great Hall of Clevedon Court*

31. A longhouse at Hacket Forge, in the Langdales, near Bowness, Cumbria

2.1 THE LONGHOUSE AND 'LAITHE' HOUSES

In the upland areas of England, which are suitable only for grazing, a type of house evolved which combined living accommodation at one end of a long thin house with a barn for cattle at the other *(Plate 31)*. A division was made at the cross passage which connected with the house but not with the barn. At first the living accommodation was merely a Hall, but by the late sixteenth century a loft was reached by ladder which could be used for storage and for sleeping. This usually had one fireplace, often built on later as a projection on the side of the wall nearest the public highway; being in the stone belt they were built of local rubble.

The longhouse probably derived from an early stone and thatch building and, as living standards improved and demand for space grew, new shelters were built for the animals and the family moved into the old barn. Although this type of building probably died out in the sixteenth century in Devon and Cornwall, it started as late as the middle of the seventeenth century in the north, increased in popularity in the eighteenth century when enclosures reduced land-holding, and was still being built in the first half of the nineteenth century before the agricultural depression of 1875 onwards made these smallholdings uneconomical.

The 'laithe', a combination of house and barn, was the cheapest arrangement that could be built for the hill farmer. There was no cross passage and the residential part might comprise dairy, kitchen and living accommodation, the latter with a fireplace sited more or less centrally. The 'laithe' house is a different type of structure from the longhouse and today the ruins of these small homesteads can still be seen in upland areas.

2.2 HOUSES WITH OUTSIDE CHIMNEYS

Common in castles and church houses from the middle of the fourteenth century, wall-mounted chimneys gradually spread to houses when the smoky central fireplace became less acceptable. Built into the side wall of the hall so that they could be more readily seen by travellers, outside chimneys seem to have been constructed by fairly rich people and were something of a status symbol.

The position in the side wall is a logical one, as it does not interfere with the dignity of the dais arrangement at the top of the Hall, or the lavish decoration of the screens passage at the bottom. There was plenty of room on the wall, so the owner could have a massive chimneypiece with a decorated over-mantle rising to the ceiling, if he wanted, giving great scope for opulence. Offset towards the dais end of the Hall or Great Chamber, the chimneypiece became part of the decoration of the room, enhancing the status of the owner, and this became more visible with the improvement of the air in the room.

2.3 SMALL MEDIEVAL STREET HOUSES

Even from the earliest times, building plots in towns were relatively expensive, so that more modest houses tended to be built end on to the street. Originally thatched, as the high pitch to the roofs suggests, they seem very often to nestle together. Two houses in Church Street, Presteigne, Powys, Nos. 2 and 3, illustrate this type of house. Framed in the archway of the house opposite, and dwarfed by the Georgian house to the right, these fourteenth century houses stand opposite the church and are bounded to the south by Ave Maria Lane. They were lodgings for priests in what was surely an important religious community, and

32. Hill House, High Street, Burford, Oxfordshire

they must originally have been thatched.

Hill House, on the west side of High Street, Burford, in Oxfordshire *(Plate 32)*, is a well-preserved Hall House of the fourteenth century which had a wing added to the back two hundred years later. At the same time floors were inserted in the Hall, but the arch-braced collar-beam roof still exists above the bedroom ceiling. The front doorway dates from the fifteenth century and to the left is the former Solar, the first floor at this end of the

house being half-timbered and jettied out. At the back of the Hall is a two-light window of about 1320.

Cerne Abbas, in Dorset, makes an interesting contrast with its use of timber-framing as opposed to the stone of the Cotswolds. In medieval times it was a town of some importance which had developed around its Abbey and a group of timber-framed houses of about 1450 with jettied upper floors can be seen opposite the church in Abbey Street. No. 5 The Pitchmarket and its neighbours have been stripped down to their timbers, and a charming decorated doorway revealed with quatrefoils forming an ogee-shaped lintel *(Plate 33)*. Even in a stone area builders often preferred timber fronts to street houses because of the flexibility they offered in providing windows.

33. Timber-framed houses in Abbey Street, Cerne Abbas, Dorset

34. *Old Soar, Plaxtol, Kent*

35. *Northborough Manor House, near Peterborough*

2.4 STONE MANOR HOUSES 1300-1400

Old Soar, at Plaxtol, in Kent, is a remarkable survival **(Plate 34)**. The two-storeyed structure is the Solar end of a stone manor house of about 1290. Today there is an eighteenth century red-brick house where once the medieval hall stood, and the Solar wing is built of ragstone blocks, the lower level being a tunnel-vaulted undercroft with a rectangular chapel running out from the east corner, and a smaller square projection from the north corner which must have been a garderobe. Both of these structures must have linked to the Solar at first-floor level, but there is a newel stair running from the undercroft up to the Solar. Also, the Solar has an original crown-post roof, that is with a vertical timber standing on a tie-beam and supporting a collar-purlin, but in this case the braces which run to the collar purlin are, unusually, straight. In the chapel there is a piscine made up of five lobes and also a foliage corbel, both of which suggest a date after 1300.

Also in Kent is Starkey Castle Farm. Built of ragstone, the building is rectangular and has two projections to the south-

west. The higher part of the building lies beyond what must have been a screens passage, with a late fourteenth century doorway to the west and a second doorway in line with it, and would, therefore, have been the service part of the house. A staircase links the two levels of this structure. The Hall is of two bays and the projection was a generously proportioned garderobe tower with a privy pit.

Northborough Manor House, in north Huntingdonshire, is a wonderful survival of a Hall and gatehouse of 1330-1340 **(Plate 35)**. Although there was much alteration in the seventeenth century, the earlier Hall can clearly be seen with its two twin-light windows with straight heads and blocked reticulated tracery. Beyond the screens passage you can still see the traditional three service doorways which must originally have led respectively to the buttery, kitchen and pantry. Particularly remarkable is the survival of the west gable of the Hall range with its decorative leaf carvings surmounted by a chimneystack.

2.5 THE STANDARD MANOR HOUSE 1300-1500

The traditional layout of the medieval manor house has already been described in the introduction to this chapter and it says much for the growing security of the fourteenth century that fortified houses rather than fortresses became so quickly the norm, even in frontier areas. Stokesay Castle, at Craven Arms, in Shropshire, is a case in point *(Plates 36 and 37)*. The Great Hall range was built in about 1280 and what is truly remarkable is that windows of such a size could be risked with only a moat for protection. To us today, of course, the wide valley of the river Onny and the gentle Shropshire hills seem the essence of tranquillity, but this was not always so.

The castle is approached through a Gatehouse, with the ground floor built of stone, but the upper parts of charming sixteenth century timber work. Even here the door is flanked with pilasters and figure brackets, and there is still more carving in the blank arches that support an oriel above the gateway. Opposite the Gatehouse is the Hall range, flanked by two towers, but only one of them is seriously defensive and that is of a slightly later date. Licence to crenellate was granted to Laurence de Ludlow, the son of a clothier, in 1291. To the right and integrated with the main building is a small tower which must have been the original Stokesay dating from the twelfth century, although, again, the upper parts are from the sixteenth

century. Its basement must have been used as a kitchen, and indeed it has a well, while the second floor has a living space with a fine fireplace of the early fourteenth century.

The Hall is entered from the north close to the north tower and its doorway has a single chamfer. The windows, both to the courtyard and over the moat, are high with transoms and with cusped heads to the lights, but with simple circles without foils above. Windows of the same pattern, but much shorter, stand above where the back door should be. The roof timbers seem to be of two dates and the early fourteenth century ones show that the Hall was originally divided into three by wooden posts supporting the roof with two aisles flanking a 'nave'. There are also blank arches, lozenges, an oriel and corbelling, but soon after the Hall was built a defensive, south tower was added. Had the lord underestimated the need for security?

The Chantry House, at Mere, in Wiltshire, was built in about 1340 as a summer palace for the Abbots of Glastonbury *(Plate 38)*. It is worth commenting that, in both the abbeys and bishops' palaces of the medieval period, and in more modest houses like the one at Mere, the same arrangements as have been described in the houses of secular lords applied to ecclesiastical ones. The same feudal notion of the quasi-divine role of the lord can

be seen, as can the idea of the semi-sanctity of his taking the great meal of the day surrounded by his tenants. There is the same careful decoration of the lord's surroundings to enhance his status, so that all was organised to suggest that the religious community was in the shape of a pyramid with the bishop or abbot at its apex.

The building at Mere is L-shaped, with the Great Hall at the east of the entrance and on the upper floor. Today we see three large pointed windows which have been blocked, but there may have been more originally. In the wing at the back there is a large first-floor room with a fine original fireplace with its projecting hood and canted front, quite a rarity at the time, as well as tall two-light windows, one of them with a transom.

The early medieval manor house was often moated, not only for defence, but also to make use of river water for milling. There are some 5,500 such sites in this country, with nearly 2,000 in Essex, Suffolk and Hertfordshire. One such was the manor of Wheathampsteadbury in the

37. Stokesay Great Hall with its timber staircase and cruck roof

38. The Chantry House, Mere, Wiltshire: south front

39. *The Old Farmhouse, Wheathampstead, Hertfordshire*

valley of the River Lea *(Plate 39)*. It has a long history, having been a Saxon farmstead of 10,000 acres (4,047 hectares), gifted in a Charter of Edward the Confessor to Westminster Abbey in 1060, and might well have been a Roman farm before this. After a period of being run by the monks 'in hand', Wheathampsteadbury was by 1410 tenanted and, remarkably, the property was leased in one form or another until 1945.

An estate map of the middle of the eighteenth century shows the manor house at the centre of a moated site and visitors would have had to pass through farm buildings and over a causeway to reach it. The plan of 1758 shows Bury Farm Cottages at the south-west corner of the moated area and we can conclude, therefore, that the two adjoining houses that stand today in Ashgrove, Wheathampstead, Hertfordshire, were probably built by the monks of Westminster Abbey early in the fifteenth century. The owners of one of the houses, David and Ann Godfrey-Evans, have researched the history of the

present building and of the Manor of Wheathampstead-bury, and I acknowledge their help in writing this entry.

At some point, most likely in the eighteenth century, Bury Farm Cottages took over from the Manor House as the main domestic structure. It was 77ft. (23.5m) long by 18ft.6in. (5.5m) wide and consisted of a Hall, chambers and gatehouse, jettied to the north and south and with close studding . Also in the eighteenth century the building was re-ordered, with a ceiling inserted at purlin height, the original windows and door on the north blocked and new windows and a doorway inserted on the south side.

The survival of Bury Farm Cottages is remarkable. Although not the original building of the Manor, it was upgraded to Manor House, only to lose this status again in the nineteenth century with the building of the Victorian farmhouse, now also gone. Studying the structure itself over the past decades has revealed how changes were made over four hundred years to satisfy the commercial and domestic requirements of the time.

40. 48-60 Stonegate, York

2.6 HIGHER HOUSES 1350-1450

Stonegate, in York, is one of the finest shopping streets anywhere in England. Unusually for the city it is generally straight, being on the line of one of the main roads of the Roman fortress, and the northern view is closed by the wonderful Minster Chancel rising beyond Minster Gates. Its buildings are of three or four storeys, some Georgian, others medieval buildings refaced in Georgian times, and others still visibly medieval, romantically oversailing or gabled, especially the group numbered 48 to 60 *(Plate 40)*.

The original pattern of shop space on the ground floor, with the traditional disposition of medieval living spaces on the upper floors, can be clearly seen. No. 58 has a fine

oriel, while in No. 50 there are the remains of a late Norman house with a round-headed upper window, the mullion of which has a colonnette, and the whole under an arch. On the opposite side No. 17, Mulberry House, with its three gables, was built in the fifteenth century and has five oriels on the first floor, with three smaller ones above.

In Chester and Ludlow the same higher houses are to be found as in York though, where there was direct access to a river in medieval times, as there was in Watergate Street, Chester, the ground floor or cellar area was used for storage, rather than as a shop giving on to the street as in Stonegate.

2.7 PELE TOWERS 1350-1650

The Pele Tower was a necessity in the border area during the unruly earlier part of the period when Scottish cattle raids were frequent. A relatively quiet later period and the need for more space resulted in the Pele Tower being integrated with the new building, which frequently dates from the late sixteenth or early seventeenth centuries. The most famous of these houses is Levens Hall, in Cumbria, with its world-famous topiary garden *(Plate 41)*, but there are other interesting examples.

As is so often the case, wool money, here at the trading end of the spectrum, provided the wealth to repair Borwick Hall, at Borwick, in Lancashire, a fourteenth century Pele Tower, and to link it to a large house *(Plate 42)*. The form is typically Elizabethan, with a series of tall but narrow bays which advance and retreat to give a

41. Levens Hall, Cumbria, from its topiary garden

42. Borwick Hall, Lancashire: a 14th century Pele Tower

deliberately varied façade. Each has a kneeler at the top where the masonry spreads wider than the building to give a better seat for the finials. There is a sense of symmetry in that there are roughly similar bays either side of the tower. Then, to the left, out of the picture, there is another projecting one which balances the entrance bay and, as it is larger than the others, it also helps to balance the Pele Tower. The small panes of the leaded windows held by mullions and some transoms, as well as horizontal projecting masonry, give a more homely balance between the horizontal and vertical axes than would otherwise have been the case.

Sitting snugly in a fold of the Westmorland hills, Killington Hall *(Plate 43)* is one of the most truly picturesque buildings that you can come across. A working farm, Killington has a wonderful atmosphere enhanced by the cawing of the rooks as they fly in and out of the ruined fifteenth century Pele Tower with stone round-headed cusped windows. The main house dates from 1640, which is quite late for this Elizabethan looking building, and illustrates how slowly fashions changed in the north. The ground floor was gothicised in about 1803, the entrance being given a two-centred pointed arch and the family crest. On the right there is an ogee gothic window surrounded by a heavy drip rail which looks rather clumsy and out of place, yet in this microcosm of untouched English architecture it would be churlish to carp. It shows how people saw early English architecture two hundred years ago, and how they felt it could be enhanced.

43. Killington Hall, Cumbria

44. George Inn, Norton St Philip, Somerset

2.8 THE MONASTIC INN 1400-1530

The guest quarters in a monastery were usually situated in the gatehouse, one of the most impressive of the community buildings. Where numbers of visitors were too great for this accommodation, a hotel was provided nearby. At the Dissolution some of these became secular inns and have remained so. Because of the three incompatible functions of an inn – the preparation and serving of food, bedrooms for guests and stabling – the best arrangement was found to be around a courtyard with outside stairs. The main reception and dining areas generally faced the street, with bedrooms above, and the two other service functions were in facing side wings. Access to the courtyard was through a tall arch from the road and this arrangement survived well into the nineteenth century. Where old inns of this kind have been converted to private occupation, the original purpose of the building is often signalled by the high arch and by the size of the building compared to those around it.

The George Inn, at Norton St Philip, in Somerset, is one of the most remarkable medieval inns in the country and is a good example of these monastic inns *(Plate 44)*. Built most probably by Hinton Priory, it was commonly used in the earliest times by merchants who came to buy the Priory's produce. At the front only the ground floor is of stone, but the back wall is all stone, and the entrance archway is four-centred and consequently broad, while to the left of the entrance there are two canted bays with two-light windows under an arch. Above the ground floor to the front two timber-framed storeys oversail, and on the first floor there are two charming oriel windows. It was in the George Inn that Judge Jeffreys held the so-called Bloody Assizes after the defeat of the Duke of Monmouth at the Battle of Sedgemoor in 1686.

Just as remarkable is the Angel Hotel, in Grantham, Lincolnshire *(Plate 45)*. Built most probably originally by the Knights Templar, and later the property of the Hospitallers, where travellers could receive accommodation, the inn's medieval status can be judged from the

45. Angel Hotel, Grantham, Lincolnshire

fact that Richard III signed the death warrant of the Duke of Buckingham in this building and sealed it with the Great Seal. The Angel Hotel is certainly one of the finest pre-Reformation inns with a rich late fifteenth century façade in stone. On either side of the archway there are first stepped buttresses, then narrow bays and then canted bay-windows. On the first floor the windows have armorials on corbels, while over the arch is an oriel, and the façade is also decorated with gargoyles and diamond-patterned panels. Inside, all the bay windows and oriels have panelled soffits and one has a pelican as its boss.

Equally sumptuous is the George and Pilgrim Hotel, in Glastonbury, Somerset *(Plate 46)*, originally the pilgrims' inn of the Abbey. Dating most probably from the 1470s, the inn has a stone façade of three storeys, which in itself is remarkable, and bears the arms of the Abbey and of Edward IV above. Also interestingly the first floor is taller than the other two, making it a kind of *piano nobile*, but to the left of the archway there is a canted bay with a window on each side, while to the right there are two windows. Overall the windows are set in vertical panelling with horizontal string courses, which gives an appearance of order to an asymmetrical arrangement. Inside the building there is a fine stone newel staircase and some original panelling.

46. George and Pilgrim Hotel, Glastonbury, Somerset

CHAPTER 3

1450-1530

3.0 INTRODUCTION

The second half of the fifteenth century saw the consolidation in importance of the Great Chamber over the Great Hall, the further development of the Parlour as a place where the family could eat privately without 'State' and, in the grander houses, the keeping of a suite of rooms for a visitor of higher rank than that enjoyed by the owner of the property. The move of the High Table from the Great Hall to the Great Chamber was pioneered by the King, and by 1450, when the *Booke of Nurture* was published, there was a distinct preference for the greater privacy of the Great Chamber, as can be seen in this couplet:

> Pope, emperor, king, cardinal, prince with
> golden royal rod, duke, archbishop in his pall
> All these for their dignity ought not to dine
> in the hall.

Although the same source recommended that other notables should eat in either place, the *Booke of Courtesy*, of about the same date, considered that, while the lord ate in his Chamber, his place on the dais of the Hall would be taken by his steward or other household officer, and this remained the usual practice until the seventeenth century.

Great Chambers were usually on the first, and rather more rarely on the second, floor, at the dais end of the Hall, and, as the Hall lost prestige and became smaller, so the Great Chamber gained in status, decoration and size. Originally a bedchamber, the bed often remained in the room even though no one slept in it and the main use of the Chamber was as a dining room. In 1500, however, the Great Chamber was changing. In smaller houses it was being used as the most important room in the lodging with the lord eating perhaps in the Parlour. In the grander houses the High Table had been moved into the Great Chamber from the Hall, but the bed would remain in the room for the use of a high-ranking guest. At the very highest social level the Chamber would be used only for eating.

As the chambers were usually high up in the house they often had open timber roofs of great elaboration, as can be seen, for instance, at Cothay Manor, Somerset, or at Haddon Hall, Derbyshire. Their chimneypieces and windows were decorated frequently with panelled stonework and tracery, while an oriel was often a feature. Such a niche added greatly to the status of a room, especially when it is remembered that glass was a very expensive item.

47. Haddon Hall: the Great Chamber

48. The Parlour of Haddon Hall

49. *Great Chalfield Manor, Wiltshire*

Parlours were originally found only in monasteries and were the only rooms in which visitors could speak, but by the fifteenth century they were being used as family eating rooms and were usually found at the dais end of the Hall below the Great Chamber. A clear contrast can be drawn between the Chamber and the Parlour at Haddon Hall *(Plates 47 and 48)*, where the latter has a flat ceiling with painted panels, carved wall panels and armorial window glass. It is an intimate room of great beauty and must have been infinitely more appealing, especially during the winter, than was the Great Chamber.

Great Chalfield Manor, near Melksham, in Wiltshire, is an excellent example of a medium-sized manor house in which the medieval hierarchy of the rooms can be clearly read from the outside of the building *(Plate 49)* and where the growing formality of society required that a suite of rooms suitable for a distinguished guest should be kept.

Thomas Tropnell, steward of the great Hungerford family and a Member of Parliament for Bedwyn, in 1429 acquired the manor and fought a series of lawsuits to establish his right to the property. Successful in 1470, he started building immediately and completed the house ten years later. The Great Hall can be clearly seen to the left of the porch and beyond the Hall alcove there is a Parlour on the ground floor and a Great Chamber above marked by a fine oriel. At the screens end of the Hall there is a dining room on the ground floor and a second oriel above. This room is also expressed externally and is slightly less grand than the one at the dais end of the Hall and, as the family's arms are placed on the screens end oriel, it seems likely that this was the family lodging with the other suite of rooms kept for a distinguished guest. The whole arrangement is appropriate for the officer of a great household and speaks clearly of generous hospitality.

50. The entrance front of Otley Hall, Suffolk

Otley Hall **(Plates 50 and 51)** is one of the most interesting late medieval houses in Suffolk and it illustrates both that houses of a relatively modest size were arranged in a similar manner to those much higher up the social scale and also that the motifs for re-building were often dynastic. There is evidence that there was a moated manor

51. Medieval screen in the Great Hall of Otley Hall

on the site of Otley Hall from the end of the fourteenth century and that John Gosnold II most probably altered the property in the 1490s. But the entrance arch to the house today is four-centred, suggesting a later Tudor dating, while the initials of Robert Gosnold confirm a rebuilding date of 1512 when he proved his father's will. The Great Hall screen also has two four-centred arches, but the re-construction of the rather traditional screens passage might have been a deliberate tribute to his father on Robert's part.

The moulded beams and joists of the Hall ceiling are other fine features and their decoration with the *fleur-de-lis* motif boldly asserts the Norman origins of the Gosnold family at a time when Cardinal Wolsey was sending English troops to fight against the French. Both family and national pride can be seen in this modest manor house, while eight-light windows grace both the Great Hall and the Parlour alongside. One of the other great joys of Otley is the early sixteenth century linenfold panelling in the Parlour. This is so finely carved that the hand of the King's craftsmen is suggested and its origin, Hampton Court. It has been dated to 1525-1530, when Robert Gosnold became a Justice of the Peace and when Wolsey himself acquired the King's lands at Otley. At this time it was quite usual for a departing owner to take panelling with him, as we might take curtains, and Wolsey left Hampton Court in 1528 and might have taken his closet's panelling with him and stored it at Otley prior to installing it at the Ipswich Grammar School he was intending to endow before his fall from favour.

3.1 BRICKS 1400-1600

The Romans had used thin bricks, but like so many of their sophistications the art was forgotten until the fifteenth century when bricks were used in major buildings in areas like the south-east where stone was not available. The art was re-imported from the Continent and for most of the fifteenth century the use of bricks was confined to prestigious buildings, but by the early sixteenth century bricks were being used functionally for chimneys and for impressive houses built by the wealthy.

Brick-making was carried out on site. Local clay was worked to make it soft and moulded in boxes before being turned out to dry and then stacked in an igloo-shaped kiln, which was then filled with wood and fired. The process was crude and the results varied widely. The bricks nearest the heat turned the darkest in colour and were selected to form patterns in the buildings (diapers); those furthest from the heat were lighter in colour. The mixture of shades, textures, shapes and irregularities that was produced gives old walls a satisfying appearance. The shape of the boxes could be adapted to produce curved or angle bricks to form complex mouldings. Until almost the end of the period the bricks were arranged in English bond, in which a course of bricks laid lengthwise (stretchers) alternates with a course laid end-on (headers). Variations are often met with, for example English garden wall bond, which has more rows of stretchers than headers. The mortar used was one part slaked lime to six or seven of sharp sand. This dries to a white colour and repairs carried out with even a small proportion of cement show a darker dull blue colour which detracts badly from the appearance of the remainder of the original work.

Terracotta, used mainly between 1510 and 1580, provides a superior form of building block. The difference from brick is that the clay used is of a finer texture, sieved so that small stones are excluded, and fired to a higher temperature. The result is smooth and hard. Almost certainly the terracotta blocks were made off site by specialists and often incorporated classical motifs like shells, figures and geometric patterns. The idea of removing stones entered the brick makers' vocabulary in the seventeenth century when 'rubbed and gauged work' became fashionable. The use of terracotta as decoration is dealt with in 3.91.

The buildings of Repton Priory were taken over by the school and on the river frontage is Prior Overton's Tower **(Plate 52)**. Made Prior in 1437, Overton had his study on the first floor of the brick tower. The structure has two

52. Prior Overton's Tower, Repton, Derbyshire

turrets corbelled out and unusual windows where one mullion and one transom are combined in tall two-light arches on two floors. The whole makes one of the most ornate pieces of early brickwork in the country, but the effect is more north German than English.

53. Brickwork of the entrance gate to Sissinghurst Castle, Kent

54. *Haddon Hall, Derbyshire, over the Derwent*

3.2 THE STONE COURTYARD HOUSE
1450-1600

Haddon Hall, near Bakewell, in Derbyshire, must rank as one of the most beautiful houses in Britain *(Plates 54 and 55)*. It is all that those who dream of the Middle Ages as a time of chivalry and valour, of noble sentiments and of poetic beauty could wish for. Set not on a fearsome crag, but in deep countryside with the river meandering below grey rambling walls and battlemented towers, Haddon evokes not the noise and grime of warfare, but the security and peace of well-ordered sophisticated life. The earliest defended part of Haddon is Peveril's Tower,

which was the original entrance in the late twelfth century, but it was during the late fifteenth and early sixteenth centuries that the lower courtyard assumed its present form and the castle of dreams was given coherence. The north-west gate tower and the Earl's apartments over the archway were built in about 1530, the chapel received its new chancel in 1430, and the Hall, which has been previously discussed, its porch, chimney and battlements in 1450.

Although Haddon is a fortified courtyard manor house,

55. *Entrance porch to the Great Hall of Haddon Hall*

56. Cothay Manor, Somerset

the Vernons observed the tradition of castle building in placing a Principal Lodging in the western range over the gateway and in the north-west tower. Approached by spiral stairs, the rooms speak today of the seventeenth century and incorporate what is known as the Duke's Bedroom and Inner Chamber, but they were occupied by the Earl in the 1530s.

This picture of relaxed informality is repeated at Cothay Manor, in Somerset *(Plate 56)*. Built of reddish brown stone, Cothay had belonged to the Bluet family from the middle of the fourteenth century, but was not inhabited by them until 1457. The house is approached through a gatehouse which has battlements and contains rooms on two levels reached by a spiral stair. Across the forecourt the east front of the house has cross gables at either end and attached to the left one is the smaller gable of the porch, The windows in the left gable are mullioned with a four-centred head to each light, typical of about 1500, while the two larger transom windows in the middle speak of the presence of the Hall behind. In the right gable and on the first floor, behind another transom, is the Solar, while the window below is Elizabethan.

Cotehele *(Plate 57)* is probably the most important Tudor house in Cornwall, set picturesquely in woods above the river Tamar. As we see it today, it is largely the

creation of Sir Richard Edgcumbe, who died in 1489, and of his grandson, Sir Piers. Again the main courtyard of the house is approached through the gatehouse, which has a granite tunnel-vault with transverse ribs, while to the left is the fifteenth century chapel and, opposite, the Hall. Unusually, the doorway leads directly into the Hall with no screens passage and the Hall itself has an early sixteenth century roof with arched principals, purlins and braces, which is a rather dated technique for the time.

Holcombe Court, at Holcombe Rogus, Devon, is another compact courtyard house *(Plate 58)*. Although the interiors were remodelled in the second half of the sixteenth century, the traditional fortified manor house was provided in the early sixteenth century with a splendid buttressed tower over the entrance to the house which was clearly intended for show rather than for defence. Above the archway is a bay window corbelled out with arched lights that extend over all three upper floors. The tower archway leads into the screens passage and unusually there are four stone archways, three giving access to the services and the fourth to a broad spiral stair which climbs to a suite of rooms over the arch and the services which must have been used by a principal household officer for the owner. This is work done for the Bluett family in the Tudor period.

57. *Entrance courtyard with the Great Hall of Cotehele, Cornwall*

58. *Holcombe Court, Holcombe Rogus, Devon*

3.3 THE TWO-FLOORED HOUSE 1480-1530

By the 1480s the church was building, possibly pioneering, a new form of small house, one which had a floored upper chamber built into the construction of the house. In fact the plan was very like the first-floor Hall House but without the massive stone construction and small defensive windows. The construction could be of stone or timber-framed according to the material available. The chimney might be inside or attached to the side of the house.

The shape was rectangular and the depth was dictated by the width of the timbers available for floor joists and rafters. To us this looks a very common shape, but towards the end of the fifteenth century, with the kitchens integral to the house, it must have looked new and box-like. By the end of the sixteenth century it was the standard pattern. Many Hall Houses were altered to provide upstairs accommodation, albeit with the upper space hindered by the great tie-beam.

Built probably as a chantry priest's house close to the church in the 1480s, the Chantry at Trent, in Dorset, is tall but small with rooms on the two storeys well lit by moulded windows both towards the road and the churchyard. These are of two lights with a transom beneath hood mouldings to stop water from dripping on to the glazed leaded windows. On the road side (**Plate 59**) the chimney projecting to the right of the door is of the same date and adds to the overall impression of worldly wealth and comfort.

The Guest House of Cerne Abbey, Dorset (**Plate 60**), will be discussed in more detail later in the book (4.3), but it is a small and simple house of the late fifteenth century and has, like the other examples, an upstairs integral to the building. Again, it is quite tall and the rooms are spacious and well heated by the integral chimney. There is also a small oriel to give light to what was perhaps the position of the board in the main guest chamber.

59. The Chantry, Trent, Dorset

60. Cerne Abbey Guest House, Dorset

61. Athelhampton, near Dorchester, Dorset

3.4 LATE-MEDIEVAL MANOR HOUSES

From the south Athelhampton, in Dorset, is the perfect example of a late Perpendicular manor house *(Plate 61)*. The porch, Great Hall oriel and Parlour wing are enriched without fussiness and the contrast between the limestone ashlars of the earlier work and the golden Ham Hill stone of the dressings is charming. The Great Hall of the house was built in 1485 for Sir William Martyn, Lord Mayor of London in 1493, while the Parlour wing was completed by about 1550. The Hall, oriel and porch are all battlemented and there are strong string courses crowning the plinth and below the battlements.

The porch has chamfered edges articulated with simple shafts, while the entrance arch itself is given a strongly moulded wave and hollow set under a hood moulding with head stops. The impression is given of conscious, sophisticated design rather than simple function, even though, in the manner of the time, there is little evidence of a co-ordinated design for the Great Hall façade as a whole. Both impressions are supported when the oriel window is examined. The oriel is four-sided and deliberately fails to rise to the full height of the wall to accommodate its own battlements. Each face of the oriel has a two-light window with two transoms, while simple tracery embellishes the heads and figures below the lower transom.

The Parlour range, probably completed by 1550, has several distinctly Tudor flourishes which speak of the imminent Renaissance in England. Three evenly spaced bays of four lights face east and above there are two gabled dormers placed with no concern for the windows below. In the south gable end a four-light window is placed at the top and the link between the east window line and that in the south gable, which has taller ground floor window lights, is achieved by making the string course do a decorative jump around the angle buttresses. These buttresses are Tudor in inspiration as they are octagonal with concave faces and terminate below the Martyn monkeys in a series of volutes, very much a sign of the coming Renaissance. As strong an indication are the lozenge panels below the gable windows.

Inside the Great Hall, the roof structure of collar-beams on arch braces is almost obscured by the astonishing cusps on the braces. Just as remarkably, the oriel is vaulted with cusped ribs and framed with three shafts surrounded by an even more prominent shafted entrance arch.

Ightham Mote *(Plate 62)* is one of the most complete medieval manor houses anywhere in England and its setting is the stuff of magic. As you descend through the woods you pass a lake and then, quite suddenly the square courtyard house is in front of you set within its moat. Really, you ought to approach Ightham Mote directly to the western bridge and the gatehouse tower, but the National Trust, which owns and opens the house, brings you from the car park and the ticket office to the north-east corner, enabling you to appreciate its half-timbered, stone and brick structure that many hands have worked on over six centuries. The nucleus of Ightham was built in the 1340s and consisted of the Great Hall and its associated solars, the chapel and the kitchen in a wholly conventional manner.

The tomb of Sir Thomas Cawne is in Ightham church and he must surely have been one of the earliest owners, though probably not the builder, and from him the property descended to Sir Nicholas Haut who fought in the campaign in France which was to end at Agincourt in 1415. It was his grandson, Richard, who owned the house between 1462 and 1487, and his great-grandson, Edward (1487-1519), who built the three remaining ranges that, at least in their original form, enclosed the courtyard. The photograph of Ightham Mote shows (on the left) the north front, which is more regular than its neighbours. Constructed in the 1480s, the half-timbering supported by the stone of the ground floor and basement contains the original Great Chamber which was converted in the sixteenth century into the New Chapel, while behind the stone gable at the end is the Drawing Room introduced by the Selby family in the eighteenth century. The Old Chapel is in the east range, with a crypt below it, which speaks clearly of the fourteenth century.

62. North range of Ightham Mote, Kent

Gainsborough Old Hall, in Lincolnshire, presents a number of dating and stylistic puzzles *(Plate 63)*. We know that the manor of Gainsborough was pulled down in 1470 during the Wars of the Roses, but that Sir Thomas Burgh was able to entertain Richard III there in 1483. It seems likely, therefore that the present building was erected between those two dates and was largely

63. Gainsborough Old Hall, Lincolnshire

completed by the 1490s. The Great Hall occupied the northern range of a three-sided courtyard building and is timber-framed and close studded, employing only a few diagonal members. The six bays of the Hall with their arch-braced roof-trusses create a magnificent space open to the roof and uninterrupted by cross tie-beams, which is an unusual feature. Just as striking is the stone bay window lighting the High Table. It consists of tall two-light windows with perpendicular tracery and, when the surrounding studding is examined, it would seem that this is a later feature and might have been brought in from elsewhere. As there is no chimney, the Hall must have been heated by a central hearth, with the smoke escaping through louvres.

If the mixture of stone and timber-framing is unusual, so is the use of brick. The tower at the north-eastern corner is of brick and is similar in style to that at Tattershall Castle, also in Lincolnshire (see Plate 7), and this and the retainers' western lodging, also of brick, were probably built in the 1480s or 1490s.

A more modest example of the late medieval manor house is Higher Abbotts Wootton Farm, at Whitechurch Canonicorum, in Dorset. This is a complete house of about 1500 built of rubble with quoin stones. The south doorway is especially fine, as is the window to the left of it. This has a deep hollow and ovolo moulding and a heavy hood with square labels typical of the first decades of the sixteenth century.

64. *The brick gatehouse of Oxburgh Hall, Norfolk*

3.5 EAST ANGLIAN BRICKWORK

The licence to crenellate Oxburgh Hall, in Norfolk, was granted by Edward IV to Sir Edmund Bedingfield in 1482. Even though Norfolk saw fairly troubled times during the fifteenth century, the work that was done at Oxburgh was largely symbolic, but it has created the finest and most picturesque brick gatehouse in England *(Plate 64)*. The two turrets which flank the entrance are polygonal and are surmounted by two-stepped battlements, the

wonderful brickwork being relieved by cusped friezes. Over the archway, the large mullioned windows to the main chambers, occupied by Henry VII and his queen when they stayed at Oxburgh in 1487, demonstrate that defence was only a secondary consideration. The passageway into the courtyard has a depressed brick tunnel vault divided into panels by thin moulded ribs. The staircase in the Gatehouse tower is also of brick, and the King's and

65. *St John's College, Cambridge, gatehouse*

Queen's rooms both have ribbed brick vaults.

The Gatehouse of St John's College, Cambridge, dates most probably from about 1515 and is also a large as well as a most beautiful structure *(Plate 65)*. Three storeys high, it has stone quoins to its angle turrets and two windows to each level facing towards the street, and one facing First Court. The ground floor is fan-vaulted, while there is a spectacular display of heraldry, now repainted. The animals displayed are yales, with goats' heads, antelopes' bodies and elephants' tails, and the background to the arms is dotted with daisies and borage. The figure of St John is seventeenth century and is by George Woodroffe.

In Hadleigh, Suffolk, the brick Deanery Tower *(Plate 66)* is all that remains of the palace built by Archdeacon Pykenham in 1495. Just as at Oxburgh, the polygonal turrets flanking the entrance are surmounted with

66. *The Deanery Tower, Hadleigh, Suffolk*

stepped battlements, but the scale of the whole gateway is not so ambitious as it was there. The middle element of the tower has three stages and on the first floor the two oriel windows are surmounted by a canopy on four arches, and this device is echoed in the vertical divisions of the turrets. Inside, the first-floor room was panelled in the eighteenth century. The brick chimneys date from 1830.

Horham Hall, near Thaxted, is one of the finest brick mansions of the early sixteenth century in Essex *(Plate 67)*. Built in about 1520 by Sir John Cutte, Treasurer to Henry VIII's household, this part of the house consists of one range facing east and a northern wing. The south wing, which contains parts of an earlier building, has brickwork that dates from the 1570s. The original frontage of the Hall itself, however, has brickwork with a variety of shades of colour, and is approached through a two-storeyed porch leading into the traditional screens passage. Most of the windows of the Hall range are high up, except for the magnificent canted bay window with three transoms and six lights in the front stretching up to

the parapet and battlements. Inside, the bay window has tracery reveals.

East Barsham Manor, near Fakenham, in Norfolk, built by Sir Henry Fermor between 1520 and 1530, is yet another fine example of an early Tudor brick house *(Plate 68)*. From the royal arms carved in brick *in situ* on the two-storeyed Gatehouse, it would appear that it was built shortly after the house in about 1527 and was always independent of it. The house has a long façade with battlements throughout its length and is punctuated by eight buttresses with finials that show no sign of Italianate influence as there is at Layer Marney in Essex. Roughly in the centre, the porch has a stone arch which looks as though it might date from before 1520, and the Great Hall runs to the left, with one recessed bay and a prominent one to give light to the dais end of the hall. This window has six lights and a transom, but the amazing group of ten chimneystacks, all with differing patterns of decoration, including fleurs-de-lis and diapers, represent a *coup de théâtre* and must date from 1525.

67. *Horham Hall, Thaxted, Essex*

68. *Entrance front of East Barsham Manor, Norfolk*

69. *Porch House, High Street, Potterne, Wiltshire*

3.6 LARGER TOWN HOUSES

Porch House, in the High Street of Potterne, Wiltshire, is one of the most spectacular timber-framed houses in the country. Built in about 1480, it is striking that the timbers are all vertical with no diagonals *(Plate 69)*. The building is a simple Hall House with a gabled section containing the services and another, larger one accommodating the Chamber and the Solar, both of these elements running flush with the street frontage. The third gable houses the porch which does project and also boasts an oriel above the entrance. Indeed, the windows are particularly fine, the Hall bay having a transom with tracery above and below, while both the Solar and the Chamber have oriels.

Inside, the Great Hall, which rises to the height of the two-storeyed cross section, has a hammer-beam roof and three pairs of wind-braces. The Solar is a full-height space and the roof structure consists of collar-beams on arched braces.

Paycocke's House, in West Street, Coggeshall, Essex, is an especially fine half-timbered town house *(Plate 70)*. Built by Thomas Paycocke, the main clothier of the town in the late fifteenth century, it has a façade which runs along the street for five bays and, while speaking clearly about the importance of its owner to the late medieval economy of Coggeshall, also combines a family house with the headquarters of a flourishing business.

At the left-hand end there is a carriageway, then a

doorway giving on to West Street and the first of the two ground-floor oriels. These have five lights and the window flush with the façade has three, all of them boasting transoms. The upper floor hangs over the street supported on a wonderfully carved bressumer and is punctuated with five oriels, while in the frieze are Paycocke's initials. Inside, the opulence of the exterior is maintained by the moulded and carved beams in several of the rooms and by the presence of original fireplaces. The importance of the family is underlined by the brasses to various members of the Paycocke family in their chapel in the parish church of St Peter-ad-Vincula.

Half way up High Street in the bracing North Wales town of Conwy is Plas Mawr *(Plate 71)*. Recently restored, this is one of the finest Elizabethan town houses in the British Isles and was built by Robert Wynn between 1576 and 1595 on a truly grand scale. Robert Wynn had a different career from Thomas Paycocke, having been a member of the household of Sir Philip Hoby, an ambassador representing both Henry VIII and Edward VI, who renewed and extended his grandfather's leases. But, being without manorial land, he chose to establish himself in the town of Conwy.

Plas Mawr was also built in a different way from Paycocke's. Robert Wynn originally bought an existing mansion house fronting on to what is today Crown Lane from Hugh Mershe in 1570, enlarged the property to the

70. *Paycocke's,
Coggeshall, Essex*

71. *Plas Mawr,
High Street,
Conwy, North
Wales*

north by 1576, but was only able to complete his new house after 1580 when he acquired a corner plot fronting on to High Street from Robert Laythwood, who no doubt stood out for a high price.

In comparison with other sixteenth century town houses, Plas Mawr has a number of unusual elements. Stone in this part of North Wales is not all that surprising, but the crow-stepped gables are and most probably were inspired by Robert Wynn's journeys to the Low Countries in the entourage of Sir Philip Hoby. The walls were of local rubble, but the carving stone for the mullions and transoms came from Deganwy, across the Conwy Estuary. The woodwork of the roofs and floors was probably carried out by one local craftsman, but the plasterwork, comprising highly-coloured overmantels in the Great Hall and Great Chamber, and heraldic devices with geometrical patterns in the ceilings of the main rooms, was no doubt undertaken by itinerant craftsmen guided in their designs by pattern books provided by Robert Wynn.

Although the frontage on to the High Street is fairly narrow, Robert Wynn's guests would pass through the Gatehouse and the first courtyard before climbing the steps into the Great Hall to be greeted by their host. By this time in Elizabeth's reign, the Hall was used to welcome visitors and only infrequently as a place for great feasts. After 1585 Robert Laythwood's timber-framed house facing on to High Street had been raised to a three-storeyed stone Gatehouse with a projecting porch. This façade is symmetrical and incorporates several

Renaissance devices such as pedimented windows and faceted finials, but still continues to employ the tower spiral stair, which is quite narrow and must have been quite inconvenient for the ceremonial that would have been associated with the Great Chamber on the first floor.

72. Walkey's Cottage, Clyst St Lawrence, Devon

73. The Old Rectory, Clyst St Lawrence, Devon

74. A Devon longhouse

3.7 COB HOUSES AFTER 1500

Cob is mud, earth or clay mixed with anything that will bind it together. It is formed between shutters like concrete, in which case the horizontal lines formed by slight leakage between the boards are sometimes visible, or it is made into lumps or 'batts' like oversized bricks and baked dry in the sun. To survive it is important that cob buildings are well-protected from rain, as they do not have the hardness of brick. This is achieved by broad overhanging eaves and by painting regularly with lime wash. The best place to see cob is in the Devon farm buildings where the inherent instability of the unprotected material can be appreciated by the primitive buttressing used to keep it standing.

There are two examples of this type of house in Clyst St Lawrence, Devon. Next to the church is Walkey's Cottage **(Plate 72)**, made of cob and thatched, and recently restored and painted white in a manner which seems highly appropriate. Opposite is the Old Rectory **(Plate 73)**, another cob house, but this one is also a longhouse accommodating, in the early days, both the family which owned it and their animals. So traditional is the form of this longhouse, that it is next to impossible to hazard a date just by looking at the façade, but it is interesting to see that the house was given a new wing in the eighteenth century, most probably for the Rector.

3.8 RENAISSANCE INFLUENCE

With Cardinal Wolsey's death in 1530, Henry VIII began to devote himself to monarchical pursuits, amongst them the acquisition of estates (some of them sequestrated) and the construction of buildings. At Hampton Court and Nonsuch he created the great architectural symbols of his reign, although in the addition of terracotta busts set in roundels in the Renaissance manner *(Plate 75)*, as he did in the Holbein Gate to Whitehall Palace, he was following the work of Italian craftsmen such as Giovanni da Maiano brought over by Wolsey to work at Hampton Court.

After Wolsey's fall, the Renaissance influence in England for the ensuing forty years was primarily French, as can be seen in the recreated capitals in Chelsea Old Church (originally carved in about 1528) and in the embellishment of Lord Marney's tomb (1523) at Layer Marney, Essex *(Plate 76)*, with pilasters and baluster shafts. Henry VIII began building Nonsuch, in Surrey, in 1538, largely out of funds from the Dissolution of the Monasteries, and it was in the south range of the Inner Court facing over the gardens that a deliberate attempt seems to have been made to emulate Chambord. Here the long range of building was constructed between two large octagonal towers, the upper parts of which were pavilions with many windows surmounted by cupolas and weather vanes *(Plate 77)*. For decoration Henry used foreigners and the style that was copied was that of François I at Fontainebleau. Frames and cartouches, antique columns on bases with entablatures above and round-headed doorways with ornamental keystones were used, the

75. *Roundel of the Emperor Augustus by Giovanni da Maiano, at Hampton Court, Surrey*

76. *Lord Marney's tomb in Layer Marney church, Essex*

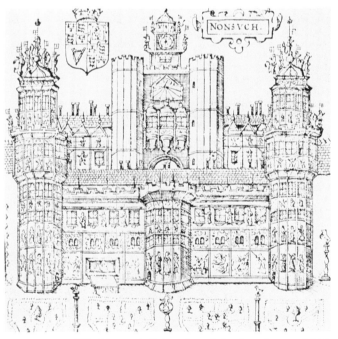

77. *Nonsuch Palace from John Speed's map 1611*

78. *Frontispiece of Hengrave Hall, Suffolk*

designs further adorned either with nude figures or herms in plaster telling the stories of classical antiquity.

Beyond the King's works, it was in the architectural work of members of the court that the Renaissance influences can be most clearly seen. Hengrave Hall, in Suffolk, was begun by a London merchant, Sir Thomas Kytson in 1525 but not finished until 1538. The triple oriel window over the gateway, recently restored, is an interesting example of court art brought into the provinces by a wealthy builder *(Plate 78)*. The bay windows themselves have an air of the contemporary gothic about them, but the armorial panels and the corbels below with classical reliefs, Roman lettering and a selection of putti speak of the new style with its English origins in Hampton Court and the tomb of Henry VII in Westminster Abbey.

This mixture of the Renaissance with the gothic terminations to the Gatehouse turrets makes Hengrave a special case, but the enigmatic but wonderfully evocative Kirby Hall, in Northamptonshire *(Plate 79)*, derives its classical style from a different source. Built most probably by Thomas Thorpe in 1570-1575 for Sir Humphrey Stafford, Kirby Hall follows the plan for a substantial house broadly unchanged since medieval times with a large forecourt terminated at the north by an enriched archway. Classically decorated giant pilasters create a loggia of seven arches on the ground floor and a series of windows on the first floor where triangular and segmental pediments alternate. If this design echoes Michelangelo's

Capitoline palaces in Rome, the porch of 1572 giving access to the Great Hall is even more remarkable *(Plate 80)*. The two lower levels have superimposed orders of a pattern which was to become common during Elizabethan times, but the upper level has seven miniature Corinthian columns with returned entablatures and a carved gable above. It seems likely that the designs we see at Kirby Hall derive from books published in England such as John Shute's *First and Chief Groundes of Architecture*, from the printing in the Low Countries of Italian books like Sebastiano Serlio's *Five Books of Architecture*, as well as perhaps foreign carvers following other pattern books.

79. Inner forecourt loggia of Kirby Hall, Northamptonshire

80. *Great Hall porch of Kirby Hall*

81. South front of Barrington Court, Somerset

3.9 THE GRAND E-SHAPED HOUSE

Barrington Court, in Somerset, was built by Lord Daubeney at the time of his marriage in 1514. Charmingly sited in deep countryside and constructed of warm, honey-coloured Ham stone, it has the triangular gables and finials that are associated with the Tudor period, but remarkably its south façade is symmetrical with a projecting porch in a manner that is more usually considered to be Elizabethan *(Plate 81)*. Barrington's E-shaped plan, the short stroke of the E being the four-storeyed porch, above which is a gable, is perhaps as much as fifty years ahead of its time. The projecting wings have two floors, with a third in the gables, and both the finials and the chimneystacks which punctuate the skyline are twisted.

This symmetry certainly heralds the Renaissance, but surprisingly there are none of the accompanying Italianate motifs mentioned in the previous section. There are also deviations from strict symmetry: to the right of the porch there is a small bay beyond two four-light windows which must once have been a staircase, whereas to the left there

is only one four-light window and a larger staircase bay. Both bays have windows facing the porch, however, and three-light windows facing south, so the symmetry of the design has been carefully considered. Also consistent with its date, Barrington's main windows are mullioned and transomed, and above the original ones there are hood mouldings and four-centred heads to the individual lights in the Tudor manner.

Although the north façade is today the entrance front, it is not especially symmetrical and, indeed, in the early sixteenth century the doorway would just have been the back exit from the screens passage. Inside there is panelling and furniture of the right period, but it is not original to Barrington. More than anything else, this splendid house illustrates the stuttering adoption of Renaissance principles in this country, the tenacity of the gothic, and, most probably, the lack of understanding of those principles both among owners and craftsmen the further you go from London.

82. *Denver Hall, Norfolk*

3.91 HOUSES WITH TERRACOTTA

83. *Gatehouse of Layer Marney, Essex*

Several mentions have already been made of terracotta as a decorative material employed widely in England by the Italian craftsmen led by Torrigiano who introduced it shortly before 1510. It is hard, unglazed pottery and was used to make decorative tiles, moulded roundels, architectural enrichment and urns. Denver Hall, near Downham Market, in Norfolk, has a fine east gable of about 1520 which is stepped in the East Anglian manner with rounded pinnacles and chimneystacks **(Plate 82)**. But underneath the steps there are terracotta panels with the letters IWE and WEN and ornamental motifs; the letters are considered to refer to the Willoughby family. The mullioned windows on the ground floor are under hood mouldings, while the upper floor windows have either hood mouldings or pediments.

Perhaps more excitingly it is to be seen on the Gatehouse tower of Layer Marney, Essex **(Plate 83)**. Dating from 1520-1523, the tower has the usual corbelled frieze at the top, but above this, instead of battlements, are little gables in the form of half shells with dolphins on them (very much an early-Renaissance motif) in buff-coloured terracotta. Also, the two large rooms above the archway seem at first blush to have conventional five-light perpendicular windows, but on closer inspection the mullions and transoms are seen to be in terracotta decorated with candelabras and topped by Renaissance scrolls in the same material.

84. Charlecote Gatehouse, Warwickshire

3.92 GATEHOUSES 1500-1570

Also at Denver Hall there is a small detached gatehouse which dates from 1570. The ground-floor archway has a passage only for pedestrians, but the upper floor, small as it is, might have been used as a summer banqueting room. With the growing security of the countryside during the Tudor period, garden pavilions of many different kinds were used to entertain guests to fruit, nuts and sweet wine during the interval between the completion of the meal and the beginning of the evening's entertainment when the servants cleared or 'voided' the table in the Great Chamber This course became known by the French equivalent of the word 'void', namely *dessert*, and the practice developed during summer evenings of the host leading his guests to a garden pavilion such as the upper room, or up on to the leads as was done at Longleat.

The only real Elizabethan feature at Charlecote, in Warwickshire, is indeed the Gatehouse *(Plate 84)*. Built of the most lovely brick, which after four centuries has mellowed to a rose pink, the Gatehouse was built at the same time as the original house, in 1558. On either side of the building closest to the park are two spiral stairs inside octagonal towers with ogee cupolas. The top of the building has a pierced balustrade employing a rosette motif which has been stretched horizontally, and the only oriel is on the exterior façade. The windows are mullioned and

transomed and the first-floor room, now used as a museum, must have been a charming setting for a summer evening's dessert. The arch is vaulted in stone with ribs ending in two large pendants which have strong gothic overtones, while the shell-headed niches have a Renaissance flavour.

By contrast to these recreational uses of the gatehouse, Layer Marney Gatehouse, in Essex, illustrated above in 3.91, was intended for family occupation. When Henry, 1st Lord Marney, built it between 1520 and 1523 he clearly intended to construct the main house on equally opulent lines. But he died in 1523 and it was never even started. Had the house been built, the Gatehouse would most probably have been occupied by the lord's principal household officer, who would be a knight or gentleman of importance in his own right and who would expect accommodation fitting his station. Flanking what was originally intended to be a passage for carriages beneath the tower and the two main rooms above are two towers each eight storeys high and two sub-turrets of seven storeys, both towers giving access to rooms at each level. Inside Layer Marney, one of the ceilings consists of polygonal panels of different sizes made into a pattern, and this must be one of the earliest such ceilings, comparable to Wolsey's room at Hampton Court. In another room there is a good early sixteenth century fireplace with pilasters and an ornamental frieze.

3.93 KENT LOBBY HOUSES

During the sixteenth century the medieval house plan tended to dominate the building tradition in Kent, but the demands for symmetry which heralded the Renaissance did have their effect. The first sign of change was the construction of a new chimneystack at the service end of the Hall, blocking the screens passage, but providing a hearth in the room beyond it. It also reduced the front of the passage to little more than a lobby, but it had the advantage of providing the main ground floor and first-floor rooms with heat. Characteristically, therefore, these houses had four centrally placed flues.

These lobby-entry plans probably had their origin in inns, such as the now-demolished Fleur-de-Lys in Canterbury, but Cobb's Hall, at Aldington in Kent, which adheres to this arrangement, was a new house rather than a conversion *(Plate 85)*. Built for Thomas Cobb, Steward of the Archbishop of Canterbury's estate, between 1509 and 1528 when he died, Cobb's Hall is an early building to dispense with the traditional Hall open to the rafters, and one reason for the novel construction is that it was intended to combine court house and lodging. The very nearly symmetrical façade is jettied throughout its length.

85. Cobb's Hall, Aldington, Kent

CHAPTER 4

1530-1570

4.0 INTRODUCTION

In his book *The Religious Orders of England*, David Knowles made this judgement on the Dissolution of the Monasteries: 'Nothing, perhaps, in the whole business of the Dissolution is more revealing and more sordid than the unanimity with which abbots and priors, abbesses and prioresses, of hundreds of houses, great and small, accepted rich prizes for the abandonment alike of the service of God which they had vowed and of the flock for whom they stood responsible at the last account to the great Shepherd of souls.'

The end of the Wars of the Roses led to a long period of stability and prosperity, often deriving from the wool trade, out of which emerged a hard, new materialistic middle class who traded cannily and married shrewdly. Education in theology and church law at the universities declined in favour of the study of Civil or the Common Law at the Inns of Court, and it has been estimated that, of the men who rose to power and position in the century from 1490 to 1590, no fewer than three out of every four were lawyers. With few intellectual interests, and governed by a consuming lust for

material gain, they bribed, plotted and ingratiated themselves with the monarch and the court in their progress towards wealth, land and rank. Yet, strangely, their paranoia and avarice left room for consideration for their fellow Englishmen. In all history, perhaps, no mass transfers of land have been achieved with such consideration towards the dispossessed, or with such indifference to political or religious justification. The Dissolution of the Monasteries had nothing to do with the Reformation!

In 1533, within months of the Pope's final condemnation of Henry VIII's marriage to Anne Boleyn, commissioners visited the most important of the 840 or so monasteries and friaries, and listed their lands, buildings, valuables and cash. The substitution of Henry for the Pope as Head of the Church gave legal title for the assets of the suppressed and surrendered monasteries to 'revert' to the King. Some were small and in decay; others supported only a few monks. It is interesting, for instance, to look today at the vast ruins of Bylands Abbey, in Yorkshire, and to realise that this huge building and a retinue of servants supported only twenty monks.

Such was the nervousness of the times that the continued presence of the old monastic buildings acted as a threat of the possible return of the monks, so instructions were given to pull the buildings down. The roof lead and bells were melted down; the walls were treated as quarries for new structures; vestments, holy pictures, doors, locks, paving stones, pulpits, furniture, carvings, in fact anything that could be turned into cash, was removed and sold. The rest was looted; missals were used to patch wagons; manuscripts were used as bird-scarers. As one devout churchman explained: 'I did see all would away, and therefore I did as others did'. However, demolition was expensive, so that sometimes, rather than pay for 'plokyng down' buildings, roofs were removed and the walls left to decay. Sometimes purchasers converted parts of churches or monasteries into houses, and a common conversion was into a gatehouse.

By 1540 all the monasteries were closed and their wealth passed to the Crown. The Abbots of Colchester, Reading and Glastonbury – all very rich establishments – resisted and were executed, but those who surrendered after only

86. Rievaulx Abbey ruins from the Rievaulx Terrace

87. *Sir Henry Unton dining in his Great Chamber (anon)*

88. *Frieze of musicians in the Great Chamber of Gilling Castle, Yorkshire*

minimal pressure were given pensions which, for the most part, were actually paid, less deductions, of course. Former abbots filled most of the bishoprics for the next decade and their subordinates appropriated lesser posts. This made good financial sense because salaries extinguished pensions. Other abbots and priors retired to one of their granges, accommodation which they negotiated for themselves. For instance, the Abbot of Bury St Edmunds negotiated a house for himself and a pension sixty times a workman's wages. Even the ordinary monks received subsistence pensions, unlike their French equivalents 250 years later, where pensions stopped after a couple of years. The dispossessed clergy seem to have adapted themselves to secular life quite well. In Lincolnshire, Norfolk and Suffolk about a third of nuns were married within five years.

Perhaps not surprisingly, the King's annual revenues improved by some forty per cent, but this amount was substantially less than the monasteries had yielded. The costs of war, the expenses of the Royal Household, and, of course, the normal Tudor 'slippage' of revenue all took their toll. By Henry VIII's death, the Crown was little better off than it had been at the start of his reign. But high inflation soon made the ten or twenty year purchase price very cheap. A new and powerful class of house-builders had been created.

But what of the style in which the new houses were built?

Households tended to be smaller than they had been in medieval times, but in other respects the new landowners were content to follow the social practices of long-established families. Accordingly life centred around the Great Chamber, but changing tastes and ambitions had their impact on the design of houses and how they were used. The qualities of the courtier and the lawyer understandably became more important in Elizabeth's reign than those of the soldier, and this was expressed in wit and repartee and given visual expression in the device. Courtiers began to adopt their own devices and to incorporate them in jewels, furniture and in their buildings as well.

But there was more to this than mere allegory. Of great importance was the relationship between the universe and man; between the Queen and her subjects; and between the lord of the house and his tenants. Hierarchy was based on a natural order and that order was expressed in the external symmetry of a building, and in the importance within it of the Great Chamber. Very often now referred to as the Great Dining Chamber, this beautifully decorated room was mainly used for the lord to dine in surrounded by his principal tenants, but this was not its only purpose. Great Chambers were also used for masques and plays, for music and dancing. A rare painting depicting the life of Sir Henry Unton, painted after his death in 1596 at the commission of his widow, looks back to a dinner and masque taking place in Sir Henry's Great Chamber (*Plate 87*).

Moreover the musical functions of these chambers were also occasionally commemorated in their decoration. The frieze in the Great Chamber of Gilling Castle in Yorkshire, now perhaps appropriately the Dining Room of the junior school of Ampleforth College, shows not only the family trees of the Yorkshire gentry entertained there, but six musicians, three men and three women, with their music and instruments (*Plate 88*). Orpheus was, of course, often depicted in Elizabethan Great Chambers, and one of the finest is to be seen today in the overmantel of the Withdrawing Chamber of Hardwick Hall, in Derbyshire. Sculpted in relief alabaster, it dates from about 1570 and is likely to be by an English craftsman.

89. *Broughton Castle, Oxfordshire: the entrance front*

4.1 BRINGING THE MEDIEVAL HOUSE UP TO DATE

Perhaps the most remarkable thing when you compare the mid-sixteenth century house with the medieval one is similarity rather than difference. A new world had dawned, politically, socially and economically, but when it came to the arrangement of houses it was the authority that comes from following traditional patterns rather than the novel that held sway. The accession of the Tudors ushered in a long period of comparative peace and growing wealth in the hands of a new social class, many of them lawyers, but when these new men altered the houses they had acquired or inherited, they readily adopted the shape of the old house and sought in the main to confine their works to increasing domestic comfort.

Broughton Castle, in Oxfordshire, is one of the loveliest houses in the county (*Plate 89*), but in spite of substantial changes made in the 1540s and later on in the century, it remains a largely complete medieval building. Built most probably soon after 1300 by John de Broughton, one of Edward I's knights who had fought

abroad and against the Scots, the house received its chapel thirty-one years later and was acquired by William of Wykeham, Bishop of Winchester, in 1377. After his death it passed to Sir Thomas Wykeham and, in 1451, when his grand-daughter Margaret married Sir William Fiennes, later the 2nd Lord Saye and Sele, it came into the hands of the family that still owns it today.

The fourteenth century house consisted of a Great Hall with, at the west end, the kitchens and other offices, while the living accommodation was at the east end on three levels with a Great Chamber and Chapel on the first floor. In the sixteenth century this arrangement was simply reversed, with little increase in size domestically and with many of the medieval details preserved. An effort at symmetry can be seen on the north (entrance) front, with two-storeyed bay windows being added and an extra window bay introduced at the west end to balance the chapel block. On the west side, the original kitchen wing, the building has been extended with mullioned and transomed windows and a central bay over two storeys.

The sixteenth century provided Broughton with opulent interiors and differences in style separate those which took place in the 1540s from the later Elizabethan ones. In the Star Chamber on the first floor there is a wonderful stucco overmantel, the centrepiece of which is an oval with figures in high relief depicting the winds and a grotesque head at the top, the whole being framed by a Roman soldier and a female figure between fluted Ionic columns. This is Renaissance design undertaken by French or Italian craftsmen and the subject matter recalls the work of Rosso Fiorentino in the Galerie François 1er at Fontainebleau. It seems likely that this remarkable work at Broughton (which is not necessarily still in the position for which it was prepared) relates directly to Henry VIII's now lost Palace of Nonsuch begun in 1538 which was inspired by Fontainebleau.

By contrast, the Renaissance style of the two grand rooms in the west wing seems to be inspired by Flemish pattern books. The ceiling of the White Room on the first floor has spectacular plasterwork pendants and cherubs *(Plate 90)* and the arms of Richard Fiennes and his wife and the date 1559. In the Drawing Room below, intended as a dining room, the plasterwork and the panelling is quite restrained, although the internal porch with its strapwork and obelisks throws caution to the winds *(Plate 91)*. Appropriately, some medieval wood carving has been preserved in the classical panelling of this room.

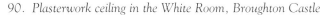

91. Drawing Room of Broughton Castle with its internal porch

90. Plasterwork ceiling in the White Room, Broughton Castle

92. *Thatchways, Thurlestone, Devon, with external chimneystacks and thatch*

93. *Manor House, Winterbourne Clenston, Dorset*

94. *Manor House, Sandford Orcas, Dorset*

4.2 HOUSES IN THE SOUTH-WEST

These houses are now often painted white, one suspects with waterproof paint to combat the damp from the high rainfall. The most common material in which they are built is rubble, and they are covered with a thatch roof. A charming example of this type is Thatchways, at Thurlestone, Devon, which was most probably built in the 1540s *(Plate 92)*. The plan is, however, basically medieval with a cross passage, while the huge side chimneystack was presumably added later and, besides providing warmth to the Hall, announced to the traveller the importance of the owner. Another chimneystack round the corner, and now apparently unused, would have underlined the prestige of the house, as would what appears to be the remains of an oriel on the upper floor.

The thatch makes an interesting comparison with similar work done in East Anglia. The top ridge has no extra layer and the thatch flows with the shape of the rafters and, like pastry on a dish, is pulled down around the corners and tucked up at the ends. The near gable end resembles a small upturned boat. By contrast, the East Anglian version has a stiffer, more even look with an extra layer on the ridge, often with the thatcher's individual signature in the carefully cut curves. Here the material is straw wire-netted to minimise bird damage.

A more sophisticated but equally elusive building is The Manor House, at Winterbourne Clenston, in Dorset. The main façade faces west and is a two-storeyed Tudor house built of flint banded with greensand, while the windows are made of warm-coloured Ham Hill stone. The porch is one of the most remarkable aspects of the design *(Plate 93)*. It is octagonal and the upper parts are corbelled out to support a gable, while the door itself is modestly placed on the side but none the less has the same moulding as the corbelling has. More surprisingly still, there are small windows running up the two-storeyed porch, clearly

revealing that a staircase is accommodated inside.

In plan The Manor House is T-shaped, the vertical element of the T being three-storeyed and lying towards the east. It must originally have housed the service wing and was probably reorganised in the early years of the seventeenth century. Each of the two floors of the main part of the house had two rooms, the upper ones being originally open to the rafters, and the two-light window, next to the bold chimneystack, helps to date the building as being 1530-1540 by its deep hollow-moulding surmounted by a hood-moulding with splendid head-stops.

Dorset is rich in houses of the mid-sixteenth century and one of the best is The Manor House at Sandford Orcas *(Plate 94)*. It is known that Edward Knoyle inherited the property in 1533 and the style of building would suggest a date of, perhaps, 1550. To the left of the east-facing porch is a splendid canted bay over two storeys, its windows arranged with two three-lights in the front and single ones on the side, and, when the equally fine windows on the south façade are taken into account, it seems likely that the Great Hall was a single-height room on the ground floor with the Great Chamber above. Further along the south front, however, there is no evidence of the Solar that might have been expected and Sandford Orcas was therefore built on the very cusp of the change in this area from the house planning of the medieval period to that of the early Renaissance. Yet the main east façade shows little sign of it. The gabled two-storeyed porch is not placed centrally; the windows to the right of it are not symmetrically above each other while the windows of the porch do not line up with the four-lighter to the right. On the other hand, the shafts framing the porch do seem to speak of a knowledge of classicism, which makes the date of the house that much more intriguing.

95. *Porch of the Abbot's Hall, Cerne Abbas, Dorset*

96. *Entrance front of the Bede House, Lyddington, Rutland*

4.3 THE CONVERSION OF MONASTIC REMAINS

The purchasers of the former monastic buildings available to the Crown in the late 1530s did not hesitate very long before converting the religious structures to domestic purposes. Many of the most famous of these buildings, such as Woburn Abbey and Lacock Abbey, were not only turned into grand houses, but altered subsequently over the centuries, until it is very difficult to spot the remains of medieval ecclesiastical architecture.

At Cerne Abbey, in Dorset, however, founded first in the late ninth century, there are some traces of the earlier buildings standing in the gardens of Abbey Farm. The main gabled projection of the farm must have been the principal gateway to the monastic buildings, especially as Abbey Street seems to be aligned on it. Here you can see the angled buttresses to the gate, while the springing of the entrance arch, with its fine double chamfer, is now embedded in the wall. There was a serious fire at Cerne in the eighteenth century and it would appear that much of the remaining stone of the gateway was used in the rebuilding; the central window of the gateway projection, consisting of four-lights, gives the date of the renewal.

The porch of the Abbot's Hall still survives and is a fairly grand affair *(Plate 95)*. The vault of the archway is a fan with bosses, while outside the oriel extends over two storeys and had rows of shields carved below the windows. Inside, the door giving access to the Hall has further shields in the spandrels and there are also shafts connected with the Hall. The Guest House of the monastery is a much simpler building (see Plate 60), but it does have both fifteenth and sixteenth century windows and an elaborate oriel made up of six lights in three pairs.

At Lyddington, in Rutland, there is a bede house constructed from monastic remains by Thomas, Lord Burghley in 1602 *(Plate 96)*. Originally, the house and park had belonged to the Bishop of Lincoln from the reign of King John, but the existing structure was probably only part of a range built by several bishops of the fifteenth and early sixteenth centuries. In 1547 the former ecclesiastical property was ceded by Henry VIII. The south front of Bede House has buttresses and large chimneystacks and on the upper floor, in the middle, is a square oriel. The north side may well have

97. *The Bishop's Presence Chamber at the Bede House*

faced a courtyard, but the ground floor, once perhaps an undercroft, was partitioned to create the rooms of the bedesmen. A staircase leads to two doors, one perhaps a gallery, and the other the Bishop's Great Chamber *(Plate 97)* with, beyond, a small room which was probably an oratory. Both rooms were probably given ceilings in the early sixteenth century and servants' rooms created above. It is fortunate that, in Bede House, relatively little change was needed in the early days to create an almshouse, enabling much of the original structure to last into relatively modern times.

Madeley Court, in Shropshire, was, before the Dissolution, a grange of the priors of Wenlock. It was bought from the Crown in 1553 by Sir Rupert Brooke, Speaker of the House of Commons, and probably converted into a dwelling house in about 1560. The Gatehouse *(Plate 98)* is complete, even though it is today two cottages, and is a fine structure of two towers with a round-headed gateway in the middle and a three-light window above with both mullions and transoms.

The porch of the house itself curiously does not line up with the gateway and is entered at the side. The house is L-shaped, with the main Hall range facing the Gatehouse and the wing projecting towards the Gatehouse standing just to the right of the porch. It is most likely the porch was added at the beginning of the seventeenth century, but the main windows of the building are Elizabethan and there is a large gable over what must once have been the parlour.

98. *Madeley Court Gatehouse, Shropshire*

99. *Seckford Hall, Woodbridge, Suffolk*

4.4 EAST ANGLIAN BRICKWORK

The reign of the Tudor monarchs was a time of great national self-confidence and of rivalry with France and Spain and it is not surprising that the use of brick for display reached a spectacular peak. Bricks continued to be made on site wherever possible and travelling brickmakers ensured that there was a wide variety of colours, and to some extent of size, in different parts of the country. Moulded bricks played a particularly important role at this time in their use in four-centred arches and in labels, while the firing process produced flared headers which were widely used for diaper patterning and for diamond and saltire cross designs, and even heart and key shapes. East Anglia used bricks widely, but the middle of the century also saw the beginnings of permanent kilns in London brickworks.

Seckford Hall, near Woodbridge, in Suffolk, was built by Thomas Seckford some time between 1553 and 1585 *(Plate 99)*. Constructed of red brick, it has a long symmetrical north front with large stepped gables to the left and right sides and four- or two-light transomed windows below. Towards the middle are two smaller gables and in the centre is a two-storeyed porch without a gable, the façade having good finials. It has been suggested that the house was originally E-shaped in plan, as the hall does not run right across the house but leaves space for small rooms beyond. On the south side two wings of differing lengths

project, one of them with Doric pilasters and a pediment, while in the middle another doorway correctly shows Doric on the ground floor with Ionic on the floor above.

Heydon Hall, in Norfolk, is a beautiful building, seen at the end of an avenue across the lawn *(Plate 100)*. The central five bays of the house are of 1581, built for Henry Dynne, one of the Auditors of the Exchequer, and the material is brick with dressings and the angle shafts have finials. There are two rectangular bay windows that have mullions and transoms and the porch in the middle also has angle shafts. The doorway has a typical four-centred arch and heraldry panels above, while the roofline is dominated by two rows of chimneys.

Melford Hall, at Long Melford, Suffolk, is one of the most impressive brick houses of East Anglia *(Plate 101)*. Built in about 1560 by Sir William Cordell, a lawyer who was successively Solicitor-General, Speaker of the House of Commons and Master of the Rolls, the house goes around three sides of a courtyard and the porch and projecting wings face the garden.

On this side, which turns its back on the Green, Melford Hall is of two storeys with mullioned and transomed windows. Undoubtedly the building's most important vertical accents are the porch with its superimposed Doric and Ionic pilasters and the shell motif above, as well as the turrets with their striking ogee tops.

100. Heydon Hall, Norfolk

101. West front of Melford Hall, Suffolk

4.5 EAST ANGLIAN TIMBER HOUSES

The use of jettied upper storeys was discontinued by about the 1550s. Like the earlier East Anglian houses, a steep pitch for the roof was necessary if thatch was to be used. A building in search of greater prestige might employ a crow-stepped gable, while the growing scarcity of timber was becoming apparent in the use of framing and internally in the wider-spaced floor joists. Most houses of this type have the typical upper-end chimneystack which heated the top end of the Hall (now less important than it once was and occupying proportionately less space) and the private family room beyond. The fenestration has not been greatly affected by changes taking place in the sixteenth century, and rebates in the wall plate indicate that sliding shutters were often used, possibly at first as an alternative to glass. Mullions are made square at this time and set diagonally.

In terms of the quality of the mid-sixteenth century house, a guide can be obtained when it is realised that the average width of the house varies between 14ft. (4.25m) and 19ft. (5.75m), whereas the average width of the fifteenth century house might be as much as 22ft. (6.75m).

Wolmers, East End Lane, Stonham Aspal, in Suffolk, is a good example of this type of timber house *(Plate 102)*. Tucked away down a lane and built in about 1570, Wolmers has a plain, rectangular wooden frame, with a chimneystack at the upper end of the original Hall and a high-pitched thatched roof. A later two-storeyed porch adds a touch of quality to the design. It is interesting that the Hall, which at this social and administrative level has neither a judicial nor a prestige function, is no larger in size than the room on the other side of the chimney.

102. Wolmers, Stonham Aspal, Suffolk

4.6 TIMBER HOUSES IN THE NORTH WEST

Houses of the mid-sixteenth century in the north-west of the country have decorative exteriors using quite different motifs from elsewhere. Churche's Mansion, in Pillory Street, Nantwich, Cheshire, is a good example of this. Built by Thomas Cleese in 1577, the house has a plan not dissimilar from Dorfold Hall, near to Nantwich, that is with two gabled wings with a central hall and porch together with a bay window *(Plate 103)*. The ground floor has close-framing, almost close-studding, while the first floor has the typical north-western decorative motifs that are a clever mixture of vertical and horizontal support, and indeed the work is all of the highest quality.

The ground-floor plan is a basic 'H' shape with the entrance to the cross-passage at the bottom of the hall. The pitch of the roof is low, which suggests that it was always tiled and not thatched. The chimney would have been original in a house of this date and quality, so it is a little surprising to find it on the back wall heating the Solar.

The first view you have of Rufford Old Hall, in Lancashire *(Plate 104)*, is of a timber-framed house of great importance, finely proportioned and richly decorated, and yet remarkably little is known of its origins. The Great Hall *(Plate 105)* is medieval in layout, with the entrance leading into a screens passage which gives access to a buttery, pantry and kitchen through arches on the left, while the Hall is entered at its lower end on the right. At the far end of the Hall the High Table would have stood, lit by the wonderful five-sided bay or 'compass' window, with access to the family quarters originally beyond. Elaborate carpentry work such as this is a feature of the first decades of the

103. Churche's Mansion, Pillory Street, Nantwich, Cheshire

104. *Rufford Old Hall, Lancashire*

105. *The Great Hall with the movable screen at Rufford Old Hall*

106. *Farmhouse in Yeaton, Shropshire*

sixteenth century rather than of the medieval period and a tentative date of 1530-1550 is also suggested by the stone fireplace in the south wall, offset in its length towards the High Table.

The decorative patterning of the exterior of the Great Hall is very much of a piece with other buildings in the area, including Samlesbury Upper Hall, but inside Rufford Old Hall the exuberance of the decoration is unmatched anywhere else in the country. Five hammer-beam trusses bear the structural load and are embellished with angel figures, arched braces ascend to collar-beams and three tiers of wind-braces form quatrefoils. Most striking of all, however, is the 'spere' arch, a fixed wooden structure serving as a screen at the lower end of the Hall. This has a wide, central opening between posts and short screen walls, with a large moveable screen in the opening to cut down the draughts. Today the only such screen to survive intact, it has finials on each side and in the middle made of single pieces of wood with horizontal rails mortised in and containing eight panels with tracery, and angels bearing shields supported on the top rail. Friezes of stylised vine leaves add to the Late Gothic ornament and the shields carry the arms of the medieval heiresses who had brought money to the Hesketh estates. In spite of this conservative decoration, however, it does seem likely that the screen dates from the 1540s when this spectacular Great Hall was built.

The village of Yeaton lies in a jumble of north Shropshire lanes east of the A5 between Shrewsbury and Oswestry. The farmhouse in the centre of the village (*Plate 106*) presents the decorated frame pattern which one associates with Shropshire and Cheshire, and thinks of as early seventeenth century. But it only takes a moment to realise that one is looking at effects which come from evolution rather than the calculated decoration of the rich houses like Churche's Mansion in Nantwich.

The first obvious change is the introduction of square sash windows which, as they are arranged symmetrically, supports the idea that they may have been put in during the middle or the last part of the eighteenth century. The space to the right of the window immediately above the front door suggests the original existence of a single mullioned two-pane window.

Next the eye moves to the roof. The aggressively new blue Welsh slates cover a roof of a pitch which is rather too low for the traditional arrangement and one sees that the timber of the last three feet (metre) is much smaller than that below. The suspicion of a later change is confirmed on the left, for here is the remains of a gable end with the two principal end rafters sawn off just after they spring from the studs which formed the walls of the gable ends. The shape of the previous house becomes clearer, but was there a house before that? Perhaps there was a gable-ended house sideways on to the street, or a house to the right built parallel to the street which had a cross-wing attached.

107. *Little Moreton Hall, Cheshire*

4.7 COURTYARD HOUSES

First views of Little Moreton Hall, in Cheshire, always provoke smiles *(Plate 107)*. This wonderful black-and-white house looks so disorderly with its Long Gallery perched precariously on the south range and leaning outwards in three directions, the whole structure controlled only by the water of the moat. And yet the point is that Little Moreton Hall is a courtyard house which proclaims the stages of its construction clearly on its numerous façades *(Plate 108)*. The Moretons had been powerful landlords since the thirteenth century, collecting taxes on the King's behalf, and they had doubled the size of their estates by buying up land which came on to the market as the result of the Dissolution of the Monasteries, the sale of church land and the Reformation in the first half of the sixteenth century.

The earliest part of the Hall is the east wing and most of the Great Hall, which dates from the 1450s, and this was completed by the first William Moreton in the 1480s with the addition of the west wing and the porch leading

into the screens passage. But it is the work that was done by a carpenter called Richard Dale for the second William Moreton and his son John between 1559 and 1570 that mainly concerns us. The precision of the date '1559' is due to the inscription placed by Dale on the two great courtyard bays, one of them undoubtedly replacing the old Hall's dais bay and the other adding a bay to the Withdrawing Room, the south wall of which most probably marked the limits of the fifteenth century house.

As part of the modernising of the house in 1559, William Moreton II inserted a first floor across the Great Hall, but this must have been removed before 1807 when the complete Hall interior was drawn by John Sell Cotman. The sawn-off floor beams can still be seen, and the Great Hall bay was built so that it could light both levels. Although the Parlour was from the earliest building period, it has crude panelling painted directly on to plaster and a series of biblical scenes depicting Susanna and the Elders painted on to paper and then

108. The courtyard of Little Moreton Hall

stuck on to the wall. This Protestant decorative scheme dates from about 1570 and its survival makes it a great rarity. The Chapel was built when the east wing was extended in the mid-sixteenth century and two of the walls are decorated with texts taken from the Tyndale translation of the Bible into English which was published in 1539. This translation was most probably also the source for the illustrations of Susanna and the Elders.

Beyond a doorway leads into the south wing built by John Moreton from 1570, and a newel stair leads past the Guests' Hall up to the Long Gallery, the jewel in Little Moreton Hall's crown *(Plate 109)*. Filled with light, panelled and with a roof structure of two tiers of cusped and concave wind-braces, it is a room which proclaims its original purpose, that of exercise and games, and indeed an early seventeenth century ball was found behind the panelling during restoration. At either end of the Gallery there are plaster depictions of 'Destiny' and 'Fortune', which are taken, rather garbled, from the 1556 edition of *The Castle of Knowledge* by the mathematician Robert Recorde. The book was a thesis on the sphere, but the quotations illustrating 'Destiny' and 'Fortune' were clearly intended to be a Protestant text exhorting self-reliance rather than a blind acceptance of fate. As such the plasterwork is a good example of the love that the Elizabethans had for devices and emblems.

109. Little Moreton Hall Long Gallery

110. Carrow Manor, Norwich

4.8 'DUTCH' GABLES 1550-1700

It is tempting to think of the Dutch gables to be found in East Anglia as peculiar to the area because of its proximity to Holland, but in a number of respects this needs qualification. Because of the distance of the eastern counties from the source of supplies of reliable stone, brick replaced both it and timber quite early on, and certainly by 1570. It became natural to use brick for decorative details as well as for construction, and two types of brick gable are seen in Norfolk from about that date. One is the double-curved gable *(Plate 110)* which made its appearance in the county at Carrow Manor, in Norwich, where the gables are dated 1578, and the other crow-stepped gable *(Plate 111)*, which appears in the early seventeenth century at, amongst other Norfolk houses, Kirstead Hall in

1614. Another type of building which has the double-curved gable in front of its hipped roof is the Shire Hall of Woodbridge, Suffolk, thought to have been built by Thomas Seckford in 1575, but considerably altered since then.

Although it is understandable how the brick buildings of East Anglia might be seen as the result of immigration from Flanders, in fact sixteenth century English brickwork throughout the country was influenced by Flemish craftsmen and these itinerant workers came to these shores not across the North Sea but from the south coast ports. Rather, the distinctive Low Countries characteristics lie in the material itself, the use of Flemish bond from the 1630s onwards and the design particularly

Opposite. 113. East front of Montacute, Somerset

111. Kirstead Hall, Norfolk

112. Trerice, Cornwall

of the gables of the buildings.

Trerice, near Newquay, in Cornwall, dates from the 1570s and is a house once owned by the Arundell family. Built mainly of elvan, it has a symmetrical entry front with a two-storeyed porch and wings that project a little from the façade *(Plate 112)*. But what is extraordinary is the variety of gables that decorate the upper levels. Those that terminate in scrolls alternate with what at first glance seem to be 'Dutch' gables, but then you notice that they are more rounded and, indeed, decorative. And, are the flourishes in stone on top of the scroll gables over the wings and porch classicising elements? The remoteness of the house's location in the sixteenth century makes these issues more intriguing.

There are many people, and I am one, for whom Montacute, in Somerset *(Plate 113)*, is the loveliest house in England. Partly, of course, this is due to the Ham Hill stone of which it is built, which varies in colour from

114. *Blickling Hall, Norfolk*

gold to a reddish tan, but it is also because of the impression of permanence that it gives, in which the 'Dutch' gables have an important part to play. Although Montacute was built between 1590 and 1598 by the stonemason William Arnold for Sir Edward Phelips, a successful lawyer and politician, it looks back in many respects to the gothic tradition, while adopting some of the classicising elements that were having a profound effect on Elizabethan architecture at this time.

The east front is symmetrical adopting an E-shaped plan, the three storeys are divided by classical entablatures, and there are shell niches, the upper ones filled with statues of the Nine Worthies. Above all, the glittering glass, so much a feature of Hardwick Hall, in Derbyshire, is restrained by the ornamental stonework at Montacute, and there is little feeling that the gables are classical in origin, except in so far as they might have come from Italy through the filter of the Low Countries and the pattern books published there by Vredeman de Vries. As we have already seen, this fashion for Flemish gables came into England after 1550, was essentially decorative, and at Montacute, also, I think, theatrical.

Similar patterns for the gables can be seen on the north front of Blickling Hall, in Norfolk (**Plate 114**). Built by the craftsman carpenter, Robert Lyminge, for Sir Henry

Hobart, also a lawyer and one who was intent on establishing a dynasty at Blickling, the use of these 'Dutch' gables in 1616 might be seen as a deliberately archaising device. Lyminge had previously worked at Hatfield House, making this connection with the Court a close one.

With Raynham Hall, Norfolk, begun in 1622 by Sir Roger Townshend, we encounter another aspect of the 'Dutch' gable story (**Plate 115**). Raynham is the most important house of its date in Norfolk and it seems likely that Sir Roger took his builder, William Edge, with him to Holland, and the influence of Dutch design on the two of them must have been considerable. What is immediately apparent, however, is that the gables of both the north and south fronts are much more classical in form. Here the gable is framed by simple volutes with a central circular window and is surmounted first by Ionic capitals and then by a pediment. The design is original and might derive from the work of Inigo Jones somewhat misinterpreted by Edge.

If the connoisseurs appreciated the classicism of Inigo Jones and provincial wealth still went into the gothic building of earlier times, there was a class of London merchant that built houses with gables in the form of pediments because they underlined their awareness of Renaissance devices. Kew Palace, or the Dutch House, in Kew Gardens, dates from 1631 and was built by Samuel

115. Raynham Hall, Norfolk

Fortrey, who was of Dutch descent, and is a magnificent example of virtuosity in brick-laying *(Plate 116)*. An early example of the use of Flemish bond, the roofline is broken by three gables, the two outer ones surmounted by triangular pediments and the middle by a segmental one.

Hemingstone Hall is a brick mansion of 1625 which sits securely below a wooded ridge deep in the Suffolk countryside *(Plate 117)*. Two projecting wings and a porch, which is almost but not quite in the centre of the façade, have gables. Those on the two sides are large and consist of both convex curves and the ogee part of the

device, while the one over the porch has a convex curve followed by a semicircle and is surmounted by a finial. The design has a charmingly naïve feel to it. Of the original mullioned and transomed windows relatively few now remain.

High House, Huntingfield, in Suffolk, well illustrates how long old-fashioned styles continued to be built in the provinces. Here is a house, dating from 1700, which has gables on a compact brick structure, two at the front and two at the back, as well as one larger one at each end of the building.

116. Kew Palace, London

117. Hemingstone Hall, Suffolk

118. *The Market House, Rothwell, Northamptonshire*

4.9 CURIOUS DEVICES

As was pointed out in the introduction, this book is really about different types of houses, so sadly there is no excuse for including one-offs and oddities no matter how interesting or amusing they might be. But the Elizabethans adored puzzles, novelties and the unusual. Something which at first sight was clear none the less turned out to have a double meaning; equally something complex that they could unravel amused them. They enjoyed a good pun or a well-phrased allusion and Shakespeare's sonnets clearly typify this interest. It also carried over into building houses and decorating them to the extent that these 'Curious Devices' justify inclusion.

Sir Thomas Tresham was certainly the most interesting Elizabethan builder to indulge in architectural symbolism, but even he was merely making a cult of what to his generation was an intellectual game. Tresham did not actually build a house for himself, but he altered two old

properties, built a market house and an extraordinary lodge. In 1578 he commissioned the builder William Grumbold (or Grumball) to build the Market House of Rothwell, Northamptonshire, ostensibly for the public good, but really to act as a heraldic monument. A two-storeyed, rectangular structure, the Market House is a crucifix in plan *(Plate 118)*. Then, in 1594, he built a large summer house called New Bield *(Plate 119)* some little way from the Old Bield, at Lyveden, on land owned by the Treshams, using as his designer Robert Stickells. Here the plan was that of a Greek Cross with five-bay windows on two floors added to each arm. The religious symbolism is obvious in the roundels containing instruments of the Passion and in the frieze above the ground floor which contains references to the Mater Dolorosa and to the IHS sign.

In the same year Sir Thomas Tresham began the Warrener's Lodge, usually known as the Triangular Lodge, at Rushton,

119. The New Bield, Lyveden, Northamptonshire

Northamptonshire **(Plate 120)**. Perhaps the most eccentric building of the age, the Lodge is a complex Trinitarian symbol on a triangular plan and with each side rising to a triangular gable, with a triangular chimneystack standing in the middle. Tresham was a convert to Catholicism and was persecuted for his beliefs, spending some part of his life in prison. Over the doorway, which is itself in the shape of a trefoil, he proclaimed the triune nature of his building with the words 'tres testimonium dant', and all the windows of this extraordinary structure are also trefoils.

Little is known about Sir Thomas Gorges who built Longford Castle, in Wiltshire, except that he was born in 1536, became a Gentleman Usher of the King's Chamber, and was knighted in 1584, dying in 1610, but nothing of what we do know would suggest that he was other than sympathetic to the Elizabethan Settlement. None the less, Longford Castle, which was completed in 1591, is built on a triangular plan, but although it was thought by contemporaries to be Trinitarian in inspiration, it is more likely that the theme came from Spenser's *The Faerie Queene*. Gorges was a 'fantastical' man in the meaning of the time, interested in the occult and in astrology, and the shape of Longford and its three large round towers, one pointing north and the other two to the south-west and south-east, help to give a magical air to the place.

Newhouse Farm, at Goodrich, Herefordshire, is dated 1636 and was built as a parsonage by the Revd Thomas Smith. Again a Trinitarian allusion, the building consists of three ranges built radially, with each range being three storeys high, each with a canted bay window.

120. Triangular Lodge, Rushton, Northamptonshire

CHAPTER 5

1570-1610

5.0 INTRODUCTION

The money from the Dissolution of the Monasteries and from foreign trade was passing to a new generation to whom the court of Elizabeth I was the great hope for success and fame. It was a paranoiac world of boredom, intrigue and dissimilation, of spies and treason and fear of Catholic invasion. To have a house that the Queen would visit was one route to success. Prodigy houses, that is showy properties of the end of the sixteenth and the beginning of the seventeenth centuries, combining Renaissance detailing with Gothic elements such as mullioned and transomed windows, were in fashion, and courtiers and more modest members of county families competed for the honour and the expense of accommodating the Queen and her court during her annual progresses from 1564. By the end of the century most of the nobility were in debt. The reign of the first two Stuarts was also one of prosperity, and a great deal of building and rebuilding took place then as well.

The main difference between a house built for family use and one in which the Queen and her Court would be entertained was the 'lodging'. This consisted of a group of perhaps three rooms reserved for the exclusive use of a person of quality, and in the first part of Queen Elizabeth's reign this meant continuing the courtyard house, with the two long sides of the courtyard being given over to accommodation of this kind, while, opposite the entrance, the Hall and the service wing would be located. As we shall see, house planners of the period used great ingenuity in providing the lodgings required for the members of an entourage, and a spectacular suite of rooms, often on the second floor and linked by a gallery running the full length of the building, for the Queen's use or that of the owner when he or she was 'keeping State', was provided, and this within a more compact plan than the old courtyard arrangement.

The builders and designers of the two generations at the end of the sixteenth century also initiated the real Classical challenge to traditional Gothic. To begin with Classical motifs were used just like any other type of decoration, without any thought for a possible set of rules: a pediment floated without supports here; a pilaster started halfway up a wall there; but the shadow in the Gothic sky soon became something more substantial. The new houses of the end of the century were symmetrical, at least so far as the façades were concerned, and Italianate features were introduced, such as loggias on the ground floor, repeated bays running the full height of the building projecting forward, shell-headed niches or roundels for statues or busts, though often left empty, and balustrades at roof level uniting the composition.

And yet there are a number of distinctively English features in these houses. The most striking one is the bold appearance of the entrance façades which makes a self-confident assertion not only of power and wealth, but of awareness of classical principles, combined with the use of large areas of glittering glass, which in the case of Hardwick, in Derbyshire, gave rise to the saying:

> Hardwick Hall,
> More glass than wall.

Glass was expensive, of course, so this was part of the self-promotion of the Elizabethan builder, but, perhaps more significantly, it was also the application to domestic structures of the glories of perpendicular glass windows seen in cathedrals, churches and college chapels. Glamour and comfort were more important now than defence as Elizabeth, with her introduction of lords lieutenant answerable to herself, had bypassed the landed magnates and made the countryside a much safer place. Placing the most important suite of rooms high up and giving fine views from oriel windows in the Long Gallery down to a formal garden began to unite the house with its immediate setting for the first time *(Plate 121)*.

The filtering of classicism through the pattern books of Flanders also had an important effect on decoration in these Elizabethan houses. Strapwork *(Plate 122)* probably came originally from Italian shields, scrolls and cartouches, but in the hands of the Flemish engravers it became architecture, cut, as it were, out of leather, and was taken up by English

Right. 122. Velvet cushion cover decorated with strapwork at Hardwick Hall, Derbyshire

Below. 121. The Long Gallery, Montacute, Somerset

designers to give a festive appearance to a building and its rooms. *Grottesche* also had great appeal, recalling as they did the decoration of classical Roman houses, theatres and tombs as seen through the work of Raphael in the Vatican *Loggie*. These grotesque heads were often presented in compartments and given articulation by the adoption from

Sebastiano Serlio's treatise on architecture of the more substantial Orders. But it was not only the adoption of these ideas that makes the last part of the great Queen's reign so important in the history of the English house, but also the emergence of the first individual who can, perhaps, be called a domestic architect in the modern sense, Robert Smythson.

123. Longleat, Wiltshire: the entrance front

5.1 PRODIGY HOUSES

The great houses of Elizabeth's reign were built by the courtiers and ministers who surrounded her, often to entertain her on her annual progresses. The Queen herself built nothing of real consequence and so to call the construction of Longleat, Wollaton, Hardwick or Burghley court architecture would not be correct, though they were inspired by the cult of sovereignty and were monuments to loyalty. It is well known that both Lord Burghley at Theobalds and Sir Christopher Hatton at Holdenby confessed that they virtually bankrupted themselves as a result of their building activities, and in the case of Holdenby the Queen never visited her Lord Chancellor at his great house and one can only conclude that, in this instance, the courtier's building mania was an example of conspicuous waste.

But the houses that do remain are perhaps the greatest demonstration of English domestic architecture. Longleat, in Wiltshire, is the first of these houses, and perhaps the greatest *(Plate 123)*. Sir John Thynne was a keen builder from the time of the Protectorate, but Longleat as we see it today was begun in 1568, after a serious fire, and not completed until after Sir John's death in 1580. It is a symmetrical, outward-looking house and

introduces for the first time the bay-window unit over three floors and a basement which avoids the corners, and therefore the French practice of employing corner pavilions. The vertical bay window design comes from Somerset House, in London, demolished to make way for Chambers' great classical building, and suggests that Thynne was his own designer, though the laying out of the façade design was in the hands of the freemason, Robert Smythson, for whom Longleat was as much a training ground as a job. More remarkable still is that the great façades were wrapped around the original courtyard house with its Great Hall and screens passage.

What Smythson learnt at Longleat stood him and his clients in good stead until his death in 1614. He settled at Wollaton, on the outskirts of Nottingham, and built Wollaton Hall for Sir Francis Willoughby between 1580 and 1588, and his epitaph records that he was 'Architecter and Survayour unto the most worthy house of Wollaton with divers others of great account'. The house *(Plate 124)* stands in a very prominent position and is, like Longleat, outward-looking. This time, however, there is no courtyard, but a central hall which, windowless in the lower parts, has clerestory light, and above again a Great Chamber with turrets at the corners.

During the building of Wollaton in the 1580s, Smythson was employed by the Earl of Shrewsbury to enlarge his hunting lodge at Worksop, also in Nottinghamshire. This modest but very influential house was alas burnt down in 1761, but there is a ground plan among Smythson's papers which shows that it measured 180ft. by 40ft. (55m by 12m). To accommodate a great nobleman's household the design had to rise to three, and in the towers to four, storeys, as a drawing by Robert Hall engraved in 1677 shows. The most remarkable characteristic of Worksop was the Long Gallery, which stretched the whole length of the second floor, and the glittering glass of the windows of this house not only made a clear statement of the owner's prestige in the area, but has elements that recall the houses that were built by the Earl's last wife, the famous Bess of Hardwick.

As well as prefiguring the building of Hardwick, the style of Worksop Manor inspired two other houses by Smythson that have survived – Barlborough Hall in

124. Wollaton, Nottingham

97

Derbyshire and Doddington Hall in Lincolnshire *(Plates 125 and 126)*. There are no direct references to Smythson over Barlborough, but the builder was Francis Rodes, a lawyer who owed his rise to prominence to the patronage of the Earl of Shrewsbury and whose arms he boldly displayed on the façade of his new house. Stylistically, too, there are similarities, as Barlborough stands over a high basement, as at Wollaton, the glitter of the windows is not upstaged by chimneys and the towers are kept away from the corners of the building as they are at Hardwick.

Barlborough, built in 1583, is a courtyard house and one of the more remarkable elements in its design is a corridor which runs around the courtyard in the manner of Hengrave Hall in Suffolk, built, as we have seen, a half

century before. But, in 1582, Charles Cavendish, Bess's third son, had married Margaret, the heiress of Sir Thomas Kytson, of Hengrave Hall, so, at the operative time, there was a close link between the Shrewsbury circle in which Francis Rodes moved and the Kytsons at Hengrave Hall. As Mark Girouard has shown in his book on Robert Smythson, this might well account for an unusual feature.

Doddington Hall was built in 1593 for Thomas Taylor, Recorder to the Bishop of Lincoln, and although, again, there are no documents connecting the house with Smythson, the design was clearly inspired by Worksop Manor. Standing in a lovely setting and built of mellow red brick, it is not a courtyard house, but has a Great Hall on the ground floor, a Great Chamber on the floor above

Above. 126. Doddington Hall, Lincolnshire

Left. 125. Barlborough Hall, Derbyshire

127. *Hardwick New Hall, Derbyshire*

and a Long Gallery above that again. The projecting wings and the three towers surmounted by cupolas make for a very strongly articulated façade, but it is, perhaps, surprising that Renaissance detailing seems to be confined to the entrance porch.

After 1588 nothing further of a specific nature is known about Smythson until we read his epitaph, but there are drawings which suggest that he worked for Bess of Hardwick on her New Hall, at Hardwick, Derbyshire, after her husband's death, between 1590 and 1597. Hardwick *(Plate 127)* is a house of great beauty, similar to the lost Worksop, while the concentration on the projecting towers gives it a castle air reminiscent of Wollaton. Apart from the openwork incorporating Bess's monogram, Hardwick is plainly carved in the Anglo-Flemish manner and we can be sure that there were no Italians employed on this house. The New Hall always assumed the continued existence of Hardwick Old Hall for the servants' occupation, and Smythson achieved Hardwick's compact plan by placing the Hall on the axis of the entrance through the loggia. This is the first

occasion in English architecture of a hall running through the depth of the house, and the first time also that a plan by Palladio (for the Villa Valmarana at Lisiera) was adopted. What is also striking is that the State Rooms on the second floor are not laid out as symmetrically as is the façade, because the windows of the High Great Chamber, the most important room in Hardwick, are in the right tower and the two to the left of it.

By comparison Burghley House, in Lincolnshire, is quite conservative *(Plate 128)*. Approached through a traditional gateway with turrets, the entrance frontispiece in the courtyard is an exciting design derived from the gateway to the Lord Protector's Somerset House in London. Inside there are few original features, with the exception of a vaulted stone stair on the pattern rather more familiar in France.

With the death of Queen Elizabeth in 1603 the provision of Royal lodgings became even more complicated, as a minister like Robert Cecil, later Earl of Salisbury, might have to accommodate both James I and his Queen. The south front of Hatfield House, Hertfordshire **(Plate 129)**, formerly the principal entrance, is in an U shape allowing the King's and the Queen's lodgings to be located on the first floor with Lord Salisbury's own suite of room on the ground floor below the King's. Again we know the architect of much of this great house to be a carpenter, Robert Lyminge, who was employed at Hatfield from 1607 until 1611. Lyminge does seem to have been personally responsible for the originally open loggia and the three-storeyed frontispiece on the south side, while, on the north, the entrance door opens on to the screens passage, with the Great Hall running along the façade in the traditional manner.

Right. 128. Entrance courtyard of Burghley House, Lincolnshire

Below. 129. South front of Hatfield House, Hertfordshire

130. Chastleton House, Oxfordshire

5.2 GABLED STONE HOUSES

Despite the impression of mellow age that these houses give, they often also exude an arrogant verticality and a restless sense of movement in the advance and retreat of the heavily fenestrated bays. There is drama too in the roof lines, where gables, crenellation and chimneys draw attention to themselves. As in the High Victorian era, one has a sense of undisguised flamboyance as new men spent new money to advertise themselves and to seek social advancement by ostentation.

In 1602 the Chastleton estate, in Oxfordshire, was purchased from the Catesby family, of Gunpowder Plot infamy, by Walter Jones, a lawyer, whose ancestors came from Wales to establish themselves as wool merchants in Witney. Very much a man of his time, Jones served as Town Clerk of Worcester and as a Member of Parliament, styled himself a gentleman and built this beautiful and romantic house between 1607 and 1611.

Although we do not know who designed Chastleton *(Plate 130)*, it is close in style to the houses by Robert Smythson that we have already noticed and is a very accomplished plan. It is outward looking and compact with a small internal courtyard not unlike that at Burton Agnes, in Yorkshire, and the Great Hall has two projecting bays, one for the dais and the other for the porch which is entered at the side. Although the porch is not visible from the entrance courtyard, it has presence and is decorated with pilasters and strapwork.

Inside the decoration is rich but not very sophisticated, encouraging the notion that Chastleton was indeed the house of *nouveaux riches*. The Hall is quite plain, but the Great Chamber on the first floor is opulent, decorated in the Flemish style with a pendant plaster ceiling and a carved and painted fireplace and overmantel displaying the arms of Walter Jones and Eleanor Pope. The spectacular Long Gallery *(Plate 131)* runs the length of the house at the back and has a fine tunnel-vaulted ceiling with delicate plasterwork which suggests that the

131. Chastleton: the Long Gallery

132. Wilderhope Manor, Longville, Much Wenlock, Shropshire

craftsmen who made it also worked in the Oxford colleges.

Situated high on Wenlock Edge, between Ludlow and Much Wenlock in Shropshire, sits the late sixteenth century Wilderhope Manor *(Plate 132)*. Although it is not much different in date from Chastleton it is clearly more primitive with the Great Hall always having been a single-storeyed space with the Great Chamber above. The front has four gables, with the left one set back, and the second housing the porch. The Hall window, in the third bay, has six lights and projects by three and has two transoms, while the right gable marks the Parlour. At the back a semicircular tower houses the staircase; it is massive and somewhat cold.

The Old Post Office, at Wickhambreux, in Kent, is a house that resists categorisation, but is so charming as to merit a place *(Plate 133)*. It must have been originally medieval, as there is a window of two arched lights to the left of the porch. The main structure is of squared blocks of stone and flint, but the brickwork of the upper parts of the crow-stepped gables and of the end elevations is of the Elizabethan period.

133. The Old Post Office, Wickhambreux, Kent

134. Astley Hall, Chorley, Lancashire

5.3 WINDOWS AND GLASS 1570-1650

The word 'window' comes from 'wind' and 'eye', eye being the direction from which the wind comes. Something which stops the wind blowing in obstructs the wind eye or window. At first these were wooden shutters and in East Anglia one can still see the rebates on which they ran at the sides of fifteenth and sixteenth century windows. Glass was expensive and therefore, like so many household improvements, started with the rich and made its way down the social scale as demand stimulated new means of production and the price dropped. Better houses were glazed by 1600 and by 1650 most houses had glass windows. At first glass was held in metal frames and diamond panes were still in use in the 1660s, and in the north for another thirty years. Rectangular panes start towards the middle of the seventeenth century and predominated as sash windows came into fashion in the last quarter.

Glass requires suitable sand, heat and an alkali (later soda or salt cake), and these materials were found on the Weald in Kent where glass had been made from Roman times. Window glass for palaces and churches, made by Dutch craftsmen, may date from the fourteenth century; certainly by the mid-seventeenth century all but the poor there had glazed windows. Experiments were made using

coal instead of wood for heating and by 1612 'green glass for windows' was available from Southwark, south of London Bridge. Anxiety to preserve forests for ship-building resulted in James I proscribing the use of wood for furnaces and granting a monopoly to the existing coal-using producers in 1615. The monopoly lasted until 1738, by which time the prospering industry was centred on the coalfields of Newcastle. By 1650 there were several manufacturers in the area who supplied most parts of England by sea. The hardest part to reach was the north-west where the industry was small and probably wood-fired. Production of glass using coal started there in the very late seventeenth century, reached Liverpool and expanded with the town from about 1700. By 1750 it was an important industry and by 1812 was exporting over half of its output to America. By the end of the eighteenth century the combination of fine sand and canal transport made the St Helens area of Lancashire the leading producer of glass.

The first type of window glass was made by blowing the molten material into a cylinder, slitting it along its length and then flattening it out on an even surface. This was very expensive because the side that touched the surface

135. St Winnow, High Street, Burford, Oxfordshire

had to be ground and polished. It was known as broad or green glass and was made through the eighteenth century, but by 1830 had virtually finished. Crown glass was made by rapidly turning molten glass fixed to a central iron bar or punty and twirling it so that the effect of centrifugal force produced a round plate which, as it touched no surface, retained a natural polish and had a lustrous finish. It could only make small square panes, as the maximum diameter was 50in. (127cm) from which the central punty mark had to be cut out. Production was introduced from Normandy during the 1560s, but it faded out; it took off again in London in the 1680s and spread to the provinces during the early part of the eighteenth century.

The method of producing cylinder glass was improved significantly in the 1770s, but it failed to impress the market. Apart from entrenched customer preference, tax at twice the prime cost of production was levied by weight, but the selling price was by size and quality. As crown glass was about a third thinner than this sheet glass (and during the Napoleonic period was made even thinner), it was more profitable for the manufacturers to continue using the old plant rather than investing in new equipment for a less profitable product.

Sheet glass started to be exported in 1832 because it enjoyed the same rebate on duty to allow for waste as the circular crown glass, but as it was produced in squares there was no waste. Consequently the bulk of sheet glass was exported until 1839, after which demand increased, but even by 1844 home sales of crown glass only accounted for a quarter of production. In 1839 Joseph Paxton was an early customer for sheet glass, which he used to glaze the conservatory at Chatsworth. In 1845 excise duty was withdrawn and sales of sheet glass increased. In 1847 a simple change of process enabled rolled plate glass to be produced, which was translucent rather than transparent, but was tough and cheap. It was used in the Crystal Palace for the Great Exhibition and this inevitably brought the product to the notice of many more potential users and sales dramatically increased.

Many houses could be used to illustrate this discussion on glazing, but few have the impact of the south front of Astley Hall, Chorley, in Lancashire *(Plate 134)*. The design seems to plead for symmetry, and with the deep bay windows either side of the entrance door almost achieves it, but a different pattern of glazing to the right of the right-hand bay disturbs the rhythm. The house itself is most probably a modest sixteenth century timber-framed structure of two storeys, owned by the Charnock family since the fifteenth century, and today it still exists behind the glazed stone mullioned and transomed façade built after 1653, most probably by

Richard Brooke who was married to the heiress of the last Charnock. It is surely a pretentious display of wealth.

A curious survival which shows, perhaps, how Gothic traditions lingered on during the sixteenth century, and how greatly valued window glass was, is St Winnow *(Plate 135)*, on the west side of the High Street, in Burford, Oxfordshire. Dating probably from 1580, the present doorway is an original window of three Gothic arches, the heads of which now make up the fanlight above the door. Further to the left on the ground floor is a another sixteenth century window of a single light with a hood-moulding and decorated stops.

5.4 LOBBIES

From the early seventeenth century a new plan for the smaller house emerged which was particularly favoured in the south and east, outside the stone belt. The cross passage and hall arrangement were no longer needed because, at this social level, there was no judicial function to be performed in the house, but there was a growing interest in privacy for the family, and perhaps an awareness of the desirability of symmetry. Wood had also become expensive, so a plaster front was used rather than a display of close-studded timber.

The lobby entrance plan placed the single stack behind the front door, leaving only a small lobby for the entrance. The brick chimney heated both downstairs rooms, but not those upstairs. One could be used for the family, while the other contained services. A small staircase could be accommodated around the chimneystack which could rise either from the lobby itself, or from the area behind it and the outside wall. This was a design used by the more prosperous peasantry; the

gentry would be much more likely to build in brick.

When expansion was needed, an extension, often for services, could be built at the back to form either an L plan, common outside East Anglia in the first part of the sixteenth century, or a T plan. A further design possibility was to build a lean-to along the entire length of the back of the house, but this was more common further north.

5.5 STONE HOUSES OF THE MIDLANDS AND NORTH

The shortage of timber caused more interest in building with stone all along the stone belt from Dorset to Lincolnshire and more widely still in the north. The cheapest method was to collect small pieces of stone and to set them into a limestone mortar at random, that is, making no attempt to keep to level courses. Bigger and more expensive stones might, perhaps, be used to form the corners of the building

136. Thorpe by Water, Lyddington, Rutland

and also to provide the lintels. Consequently, the use of timber could be restricted to the rafters and the floor joists.

Ablington Manor, Bibury, Gloucestershire was built by John Coxwell in 1590, and it displays a number of the ambiguities of the period that have already been noticed. The porch, which reveals the name of the builder and the date, has angled buttresses, a gable with a pinnacle and finial which is quite gothic, but, underneath the inscription 'Plead Thou my cause, O Lord', are five carved heads, one depicting Queen Elizabeth, set within triglyphs in a Renaissance frieze. Typically, the façade consists of three stone gables while the walls are of rubble set into mortar. It is interesting to note that there are traces of yellow ochre wash on the walls, applied perhaps as a shelter coat, but this practice was soon discontinued elsewhere.

This Cotswold type of house with multi-gables built as continuations of the front wall was also used in Northamptonshire, but further north a quite different type emerged. A long rectangular house was built with, at the top level, roughly squared-up stone, while further down the social scale rubble was used. Large end gables housed chimneys and sometimes in the Midlands windows. The internal plan followed the medieval cross-passage form, with the result that it is only the more fashionable houses that bowed to classical symmetry. There are mullioned windows in either stone or wood. The Hall was not heated and the family lived in the Parlour at the far end of the building where the little fire window can be seen. A good example of this type of house is at Thorpe by Water, near to Lyddington, in Rutland *(Plate 136)*.

Further north in Derbyshire and Yorkshire the rubble-built farmhouses tended to be squat single-storeys before 1700, but two-storeyed structures became increasingly popular as the eighteenth century progressed. Wolfscote Grange *(Plate 137)*, near Hartington, Derbyshire, is an example of such a northern house, with mullioned windows, the interior being laid out to an irregular plan. The prominent porch was added to this house in 1649.

137. Wolfscote Grange, near Hartington, Derbyshire

138. *The Grammar School, Chard, Somerset*

5.6 USING CLASSICAL MOTIFS

The Grammar School, in Chard, Somerset (**Plate 138**), was built as a private house in 1583 and only became a school in 1671. It illustrates that, at a modest provincial level, the need to introduce classical motifs into domestic building was by this time recognised. There is a consciousness of the need for symmetry in the design of this house, for there is the same number of lights in the corresponding windows each side of the imposing three-storeyed entrance. Frontispieces of this kind became very popular in the early seventeenth century, though not normally rising to more than two storeys high.

This up-to-date house left behind the medieval plan and money was spent on the most expensive form of flint decoration, that is squaring. Flint is difficult enough to cut accurately, but squaring up the faces of the flint is very time-consuming. Here they are carefully laid and

the limestone harmonises well. You only have to look at the crow's-foot effect on the dormers and the well-laid quoins to see that care has been taken with the appearance of the completed decoration. The pattern even continues around the side of the building where one might expect economies to be made.

Still more money has been spent on stringing lines which increase the horizontal emphasis already provided by the moulded window heads. It is surely curious that the money lavished on this building should not also have included the chimneys, but perhaps they have been replaced at a later date. The shaped irons seen in the porch are threaded on to rods which run through the building to discourage the porch from moving forward. It is surely sad that the best house in the town has to have road signs placed right outside the entrance door.

139. *The Little Castle, Bolsover, Derbyshire*

5.7 ROMANTIC CASTLES AND THE COURT

The cult of the Virgin Queen was celebrated in court pageants; romanticism mixed with nostalgia was fashionable. Before castles became totally obsolete for defensive purposes there was a revival of interest in them, perhaps for little more reason than to enhance the social standing of the builder. Tournaments were held every year on the date of the Queen's Accession and some very distinguished nobles, including the Earls of Essex and Pembroke, and Lord Arundel, took part bearing *impresa* on their shields and the Queen's or their lady's favour around their wrists.

There has been a castle at Bolsover, in Derbyshire, since the twelfth century, but by the time it was granted to the 6th Earl of Shrewsbury, Bess of Hardwick's last husband, in 1553, it had become ruinous. It was Bess's son, Charles Cavendish, who purchased Bolsover from his step-brother the 7th Earl, and he and his heir, William, later 1st Duke of Newcastle, destroyed the medieval structure and built a mansion, the Riding School and the

Little Castle **(Plate 139)**, beginning in 1608.

It is the romantic silhouette of the Little Castle, occupying the highest point of Bolsover, which conveys a theatrical spirit of the medieval past, and was worked on by Sir Charles Cavendish and his architect, Robert Smythson, between 1608 and 1613 and completed after his father's death in the following year by John Smythson. Modest in size, the Little Castle none the less has the rooms that would have been found in a medieval house, and its decoration seeks to underline this nostalgic air. The Great Hall and the Parlour called the Pillar Chamber are on the ground floor, while the Star Chamber, the Great Chamber of the Little Castle, is on the second floor and approached up a staircase from the dais end of the Hall, while the Marble Closet and the Heaven and Elysium Rooms protect access to Sir William's own residential suite. Even the names of the rooms contribute to the illusion of the medieval past.

140. West Woodhay House, Berkshire

5.8 THE 'H' PLAN HOUSE 1590-1650

Lord Burghley's son, Sir Thomas Cecil, built an H-plan house in London in about 1590, and Rushbrooke Hall, Suffolk, alas now demolished, followed a decade later. The same form arrived in the rather smaller house as a result of right-angled extensions to Hall Houses, the new wings jutting forward beyond the original building line. At both levels the H tended to be pronounced on one side, but flatter on the other, usually the back, so that, with the addition of a small central porch, they were more E than H.

From the early part of the seventeenth century, as the ideal of symmetry became stronger, so the old screens passage gave way to a centrally placed Hall entered from the side through a small porch or entrance hall. It was natural that the design should be used in the early years of the century when brick and a hipped roof came into fashion.

West Woodhay House, Berkshire *(Plate 140)*, is most probably dated 1635 (though there are aspects of its façade design that suggest a later date), which makes it fourteen years before the great Coleshill, which we shall come to later in this book. The porch is a much later addition and the original wooden mullions have been updated by sash windows. The decoration has been confined to quoins and a pattern of bricks to emphasise the symmetrical windows. Had there been a touch more decoration it might have been regarded as 'Restoration', that is post 1660 when Charles II's reign began, and is often credited to Sir Christopher Wren. West Woodhay, with its somewhat projecting wings and recessed centre, was built by a nobleman or politician who knew everybody in the small

cultured world of pre-Civil War London. It is hard to imagine that he escaped the long shadow of Inigo Jones, or at least someone directly influenced by him.

5.9 THE JACOBEAN 'E' PLAN

Arriving at the south and west fronts of Felbrigg *(Plate 141)*, in Norfolk, is likely to make the visitor suck in his breath with surprise. The stately, weather-beaten Jacobean façade on the south with the words 'Gloria Deo in Excelsis' in openwork over the three projecting bays could not present more of a contrast to the laid-back classical west front in brick built in the 1670s by William Samwell for William Wyndham I. But it is the symmetrical south façade in multi-coloured stone that concerns us at the moment. Built by Sir John Wyndham and his son Thomas between 1621 and 1624, the house was an adaptation of an early Tudor building with two projecting bays over two storeys with a central projecting entrance leading into a screens passage with the Great Hall running along the façade to the west, and what is today the Morning Room beyond a lobby to the east.

That the new house at Felbrigg was intended to accommodate a dynasty is clear as the arms of both Sir John and his son and their respective wives are carved in stone above the door. Also, Sir Henry Hobart, Chief Justice of the Common Pleas, had gathered a group of fine craftsmen at Blickling, only eight miles away, with the same intention, and details of the work at both houses leave little doubt that

141. The Jacobean front of Felbrigg Hall, Norfolk

the same craftsmen, led by Robert Lyminge, moved over to Felbrigg in 1621. The Wyndhams' new house is typical of its period, combining the traditional late medieval plan with the symmetry of the façade and the chimneys breaking the skyline.

Barningham Hall *(Plate 142)*, in Norfolk, was built in 1612 for Sir Edward Paston, as the carved stone on the porch reveals. A red-brick structure with stone dressings, the west side of Barningham is the most remarkable and the two bays rise through two storeys to incorporate

double-height dormers, while the central porch is even more vertical with tall double dormers and three projections terminating with finials. Although there is little decoration around the porch, the windows are mullioned, transomed and pedimented, while the chimneys are also splendid, being polygonal in shape with star tops.

142. Barningham Hall, Norfolk

143. *Godinton House, near Ashford, Kent*

Just to the north of Ashford, in Kent, is Godinton House **(Plate 143)**. The park provides a wonderful setting and the formal garden close to the house is by Reginald Blomfield and dates from 1902. But the house itself was built for Capt. Nicholas Toke and the rainheads reveal a date of 1628. On the east, entrance, front, gables shaped in semi-circles, novel at the time, stand above two shallow projecting wings and also the two window-bays flanking the porch. The original window pattern was of three-light mullions, although the window bays (perhaps of the 1630s) follow a different pattern.

What we have seen so far is Jacobean, but the east façade conceals that Godinton was originally timber-framed and was a Hall House of the fourteenth century, with a courtyard. When Capt. Toke rebuilt the house in 1628 he added a grand staircase with heraldic animals on the newel posts, in the manner of Knole, in the courtyard to the south of the Hall. The outstanding room in Godinton, the Great Chamber, lies at the top of the staircase and occupies the middle part of the east range. The chimneypiece is a particularly fine example of the vigour of Jacobean carving which was just beginning to lose popularity when this was made in the early 1630s.

Condover Hall **(Plate 144)** is surely the grandest late Elizabethan house in Shropshire. Still unfinished when the owner, Thomas Owen, a Justice of the Common

Pleas, died in 1598, Condover was probably designed by the architect-mason Walter Hancock. The gabled house is built of pink rather than red sandstone to an E-shaped plan with the shallow projecting wings on the east side having canted bays of seven lights, those on the ground floor with two transoms, while the first-floor ones have only one. There is also a continuous frieze at first storey height The doorway is graced with a classical pediment, while there are gables over the wings and, at the top of the porch, two obelisks and strapwork.

Interestingly, the centre of the west side of the house has a loggia of nine bays which must once have been open as they were at Burghley and at Hatfield, and, as Hancock's career would seem to have been confined to Shropshire, this and the other innovations are likely to have been introduced by Thomas Owen himself, perhaps with pattern books reinforcing what he had observed being done by the contemporary leaders of fashion in building. Inside, few original features remain, as changes were made in both the nineteenth and twentieth centuries, but there is a fine stone fireplace in the Great Hall with paired Ionic columns below and arches above framing two surprisingly naïve standing figures. For a considerable period Condover Hall was run by the Royal National Institute for the Blind as an educational institution and is now to continue as a school run by Priory Educational Services Ltd.

144. Condover Hall, Shropshire

145. Audley End, Essex

In the context of great Jacobean mansions mention should be made of Audley End, in Essex **(Plate 145)**, although it is a house which has been greatly reduced from the palace constructed for Thomas Howard, Earl of Suffolk and Lord Treasurer, by Bernart Janssen, from 1603. The west façade, as it appears today, is largely unchanged, but in front of it was a substantial courtyard made on two sides by projecting wings and on the third by a one-storeyed gatehouse. To the east of the Great Hall there was originally another inner courtyard and beyond two projecting wings similar to those that now run to the east. So in effect one whole courtyard has vanished and so has nearly half of the main building.

The west side of Audley End has a pleasing symmetry with two porches and a Great Hall window bay placed in the middle of the Hall rather than at the dais end, while turrets mark the projecting wings and a balustrade decorated with strapwork conceals the roofs. Inside, the Great Hall is a splendid space, with at the north, screens passage, end a wooden screen decorated in the Jacobean manner with large, somewhat coarse figures. At the other end of the Hall is a stone screen giving access to the staircase, which was, most probably, built by Sir John Vanbrugh in the 1720s deliberately to recall Jacobean work.

146.
Sparrowe's
House,
Buttermarket,
Ipswich

5.91 PARGETING 1600-1670

Pargeting is plasterwork on the exterior of buildings from the late Tudor period onwards, decorated with patterns made either by moulding or by incising. This form of decoration is to be found all over the country, but is particularly conspicuous in the eastern counties. One of the most spectacular houses in Ipswich, Suffolk, is Sparrowe's House, also called the Ancient House *(Plate 146)*. Indeed, the structure is much older than the casual glance might suggest, as it has a fifteenth century hammer-beam roof of what must have been a Solar.

The pargeting of the façade on to Buttermarket dates from 1670 and consists of reliefs between coupled pilasters depicting a vase, the coat of arms of Charles II, Neptune and a pelican, while round the corner are a shepherd and shepherdess. The oriel windows are also decorated in stucco below their sills with symbols of Europe, Asia, Africa and America. It is a very fine display.

By contrast, No. 78 Bank Street, Maidstone, in Kent, is a timber-framed house of 1611, four storeys high with two overhangs *(Plate 147)*. The upper jetty is supported on Ionic and Corinthian columns with pargeting behind depicting the Royal Arms and the Prince of Wales's feathers, and repainted recently in not very appropriate pastel colours.

Essex is a county rich in pargeting, no town more so than Saffron Walden. There, at the corner of Market Hill and Church Street, is a group of timber-framed houses of the fourteenth and fifteenth centuries with lively plasterwork decoration of about 1670 featuring geometrical patterns, birds in foliage and human figures *(Plate 148)*. In Stansted Mountfitchet, Essex, Crown House at Bridge End also has a splendid display of pargeting featuring not only natural motifs, but also classicising swags and a crown *(Plate 149)*.

147. *78 Bank Street, Maidstone, Kent*

148. *Pargeting on the corner of Church Street,*
Saffron Walden, Essex

149. *Crown House, Bridge End, Stansted Mountfitchet, Essex*

150. *Sissinghurst Tower from the garden, Kent*

5.92 DECORATED GATEHOUSES 1570-1630

The gatehouse tower of Sissinghurst *(Plate 150)*, which soars over the wooded hills of the Kentish Weald, is all that remains of an Elizabethan courtyard house built by Sir Richard Baker. The date of the great brick tower, now indelibly associated with Vita Sackville-West and her husband, Sir Harold Nicolson, is unknown but must have been between the date that Baker inherited in 1558 and 1573 when he entertained Queen Elizabeth there. The four-storeyed tower is built of red brick with quoins and has a wonderfully romantic air that must have been redolent of the medieval past even in Elizabeth's reign. On plan the tower is a rectangle with octagonal turrets attached to the short sides and taken up to a greater height than the main structure and originally finished with cupolas. Above the central archway, four-light windows with transoms but no arched heads give light to the accommodation used by Vita as book and writing rooms.

Shute, in Devon, also boasts a late sixteenth century decorated gatehouse *(Plate 151)* which possesses a similar medieval romance, but accompanied by the clash of the Barons' Wars rather than the tranquillity of a monastic cloister. Built probably by William Pole in the late 1570s, there are two storeys of mullioned and transomed windows over the arch and battlements over the whole structure. In the left gatehouse turret a staircase leads to the upper room and, although the two pavilions date from the same constructional period, they have probably been altered since.

The timber-framed gatehouse of Stokesay, in Shropshire, is everyone's dream of a late-medieval castle entrance *(Plate 152)*. Bearing a stylistic similarity to the Council House Gatehouse in Shrewsbury which can be securely dated to 1630, Stokesay must surely have accommodated a household officer of distinctly higher rank than that of a porter, as the oriel and the one original brick chimney bear witness. Perhaps even more persuasive is the riot of regional timber-framing that decorates the exterior. The ground floor is close-studded; the jettied first floor has square panels with lozenge patterns and arches below the windows, while the gables have quarter-circle braces. As a provincial gesture to the Renaissance, which was gathering strength even in this remote location, the gate and the oriel are flanked by posts carved as pilasters. In a more medieval manner the outside of the gatehouse is decorated with carved figures of Adam and Eve on either side of the Tree of Knowledge in the Garden of Eden.

151. The Gatehouse,
Shute Barton, Devon

152. Stokesay Castle
Gatehouse, Shropshire

117

153. *Frontispiece of the Old Schools, Oxford*

Although not strictly a domestic building today, the gatehouse to the Schools' Quadrangle *(Plate 153)*, giving access to the Bodleian Library in Oxford, is too remarkable to leave out and probably was used as a residence in the early days. When its date of 1613-1624 is considered, this building is both formidable and unique. Most probably the conception is that of Sir Thomas Bodley himself rather than his master-masons, John Ackroyd and John Bentley. The archway, which has a panelled door, is surmounted by five tiers, higher than any other in this country, and in inspiration it is Italo-French, having been introduced to England by the Lord Protector at Somerset House in the 1550s. Bodley correctly uses the Orders: coupled Tuscan columns followed by Roman Doric ones; then Ionic columns with decorated plinths; and above that Corinthian framing a

niche with a seated statue of James I attended by Fame and the kneeling University. Above that again are three statuettes leading to Composite columns with strapwork plinths and another six-light window, with, at the top, spires framing pierced strapwork and the Royal arms. This frontispiece is pure display.

The gatehouse to Stanway House, Gloucestershire, is also a remarkable building *(Plate 154)*. Built most probably by a local master-mason, Timothy Strong, in 1630, it is in the form of three decorative gables surmounted by the scallop shell, the device adopted by the Tracey family, and either side of the archway there are lodges with bay windows over three storeys. On either side of the archway are fluted columns standing on plinths, and over the centre is a broken pediment, all of them very much the typical classical devices of the Jacobean period.

154. Stanway House gatehouse, Gloucestershire

155. *Woolbridge Manor, Dorset*

5.93 THE FIRST-FLOOR PORCH

Woolbridge Manor, at Wool, survives remarkably complete in tranquil Dorset countryside *(Plate 155)*. The most striking contrast lies between the stone end walls and gable and the brick north front together with its projecting porch, and inevitably poses the question as to whether both elements can be part of the same building project. The stone gable end is three storeys high with the main windows having transoms, while the smaller two-light window is mullioned. This suggests a date of about 1630, while the motifs on the brick entrance front might suggest a later date in the seventeenth century.

Also apparent are the brick relieving arches over what must have been the original windows in the front façade, and the mullioned stone windows in that elevation must,

therefore, have been later additions. The archway itself has a pendulous keystone carved with brackets and on either side narrow niches are set into the brickwork. This pattern is followed also on the first floor and it seems likely that this two-storeyed porch is the work of craftsmen employed in bringing up to date a stone house with a slightly fussy brick design in the 1630s. Certainly, the notion of bringing light into a low-ceilinged room or passage on the first floor is inspired, perhaps, by the practice adopted at larger houses such as Montacute, in Somerset. Here, on the east side the porch rises to three storeys with mullioned and transomed windows, while the two-storeyed porch of Clifton Maybank, a house near Yeovil built in about 1570, was incorporated in the west façade of Montacute in the mid-eighteenth century.

156. Otley Hall, Suffolk: the Playhouse wing

5.94 BUILDING A PLAYHOUSE

Robert Gosnold III built a fourth wing to Otley Hall in 1588 **(Plate 156)** and various details of its construction suggest that at least one purpose of the building was theatrical. The influence was Edward de Vere, Earl of Oxford, a kinsman of the Gosnolds, and a nobleman who, it is thought, received covert backing from Queen Elizabeth to support the performance of Shakespeare's plays. Four Italianate columns on the ground floor were painted red and originally formed an arcade behind which were two retiring rooms, and the orientation of the new wing meant that the open-air stage was in the sun all the afternoon. The Elizabethan courtyard has been discovered beneath the present rose garden.

Perhaps understandably the wing had to serve several purposes so that on the first floor there was a Banqueting Room, which might have been used as a vantage point from which distinguished guests could privately watch the plays taking place below, or as a more conventional Great Chamber where plays or masques might be performed after dinner. Certainly, the use of this new wing for hospitality and entertainment is emphasised by the grapevine pargeting on the outside of the Playhouse. It is interesting that the Gosnolds were linked not only to the Earl of Oxford, but must also have known the Earl of Southampton, another important figure in the Elizabethan theatrical world.

CHAPTER 6

1610-1650

6.0 INTRODUCTION

During the first half of the seventeenth century in English architecture one name stands out above all other: that of Inigo Jones. Born in London in 1573, Jones belongs to that group of artists, designers and builders who matured just when the Elizabethan age reached the crest of the wave, when Shakespeare began to produce his greatest plays, when Hatfield and Audley End were being built, and when Rubens reached his peak of creativity. It is appropriate to mention the artist Rubens in this context because, to understand Jones' role fully, he has to be seen more as a designer than as an architect and in a European rather than just an English context. What he was able to do was to transplant the full panoply of classical design, a Mediterranean phenomenon, to the still gothic north, challenging the traditions of English building in both planning and in style.

The son of a Smithfield clothmaker, Jones was probably apprenticed to a joiner and, although virtually nothing is known about his early years, it does seem likely that he

157. Scene 5, Coelum Britannicum (Inigo Jones): A garden and a Princely villa

visited Italy for the first time perhaps in the entourage of the Earl of Rutland in 1596, before accompanying the Earl on an embassy to Denmark in 1603. The first visit to Italy was important for Jones, as this was the time that he learnt to draw. Previously English draughtsmen had produced neat 'platts' and 'uprights', but they had no concept of the free drawing which for more than a century had been the usual means of expression of Italian painters, sculptors and architects. This new skill of Jones can be seen most clearly in the designs that he did for Court Masques and was soon extended beyond costumes to embrace landscape settings and the buildings of necessity found in them (**Plate 157**).

In this, not only was Inigo Jones an innovator, but so were James I and his Queen. Elizabeth had been no builder, relying on her courtiers to accommodate and entertain her, but the new King was a generous host and needed the appropriate setting in which to hold court. In 1611 Jones was appointed Surveyor to Henry Prince of Wales which brought him into contact with Thomas Howard, Earl of Arundel, one of the most influential figures in the development of English art. After the death from typhoid of the Prince of Wales in the following year, Jones joined the Earl's entourage escorting King James' daughter, Elizabeth, newly married to the Prince Palatine, to Heidelberg. It was after this that Jones paid his second visit to Italy, again with Arundel, visiting

158. South front of the Queen's House, Greenwich

159. *The Banqueting House, Whitehall*

Rome and studying classical buildings and annotating his copy of Palladio's *Four Books of Architecture*, probably the first time an Englishman had made this kind of study.

Back in England Inigo Jones became Surveyor of the King's Works on the death of Simon Basil in 1615 and one of his first tasks was the design of the Queen's House at Greenwich *(Plate 158)*. Although changes were made to the upper part of the house in 1629-1635 and again in 1661, the building was designed to all intents and purposes between 1616 and 1618. Following the plan of the Medici Villa Poggio a Caiano, the Queen's House is a rectangle with the three central bays brought forward on the north side to form a two-storeyed 40ft. (12m) cube Great Hall and a loggia on the upper floor of the south side. The lower half of the building is rusticated and the roof surrounded by a continuous balustrade. It is the very epitome of restrained Palladian design.

The other seminal building is the Banqueting House in Whitehall *(Plate 159)*. Built between 1619 and 1622, it was intended not only for State banquets, but also for the reception of ambassadors and for masques, and is again based on a design by Palladio for a palace in Venice. Three central

windows on the two floors break forward, their four engaged columns standing on plinths and contrasting with the more modest pilasters on either side that are coupled at each end. Constructed on a rusticated basement, the Hall's ground-floor windows are surmounted alternately with triangular and segmental pediments, while there is a bold frieze below the balustrade. More than anything else there is a sense of harmony in the design which comes in large measure not only from symmetry but from the relationship between the windows and the wall in which they are set. This building is totally unlike any other seen in England before the 1620s and was to have an important long-term influence.

Later on in this chapter Inigo Jones' contribution to the development of the great London squares and terraces will also be discussed. However, as much of his building work was confined to the Royal residences, Jones had only limited effect on the work of his contemporaries and it was to be through his pupils and followers, especially John Webb and the generation of Palladian architects led by Lord Burlington at the beginning of the next century, that his true genius was to be recognised.

160. Harecastle Farm, Talke, Staffordshire

6.1 MIDLANDS MANOR HOUSE

Harecastle Farm, at Talke, Staffordshire, is a remarkable house built in stone in the 1630s *(Plate 160)*. Today a public house, its façade is, as one would expect, symmetrical, with two gabled wings and a recessed centre where the Hall was. The door, however, is pushed to the left, as is the Hall dais window. Surprisingly, however, the upper window returns to a central position. In most cases the windows are of five lights and they have mullions and transoms.

Harecastle Farm was, clearly, a building of some pretension, whereas Woolsthorpe Manor, in Lincolnshire, is much more modest *(Plate 161)*, even though it was the birthplace of Sir Isaac Newton. Built in the 1620s, it has the characteristics of its period, being on a T-shaped plan, while its three-light windows have neat, straight hoods to keep the weather away from the glass. At the western end the land is built up to give the house a semi-basement.

161. Woolsthorpe Manor, Lincolnshire

162. Abbot's Fireside, Elham, Kent

6.2 CONTINUING HALF-TIMBERING IN KENT

The difficulty of using hard and fast dates in provincial architecture is well illustrated by the Abbot's Fireside, in Elham, Kent *(Plate 162)*. The timber-framed exterior with the jettied upper storey would persuade the casual observer that this house belongs firmly to the sixteenth century, but more careful inspection of the style of the grotesque caryatids in wood on brackets that support the upper level of the building might give one pause. In fact the building dates from 1614 and, above the carved bressumer, the close-studding is made into rather hesitant patterns, while there is a fine piece of seventeenth century brickwork at the south end. Although much altered, the projecting bay windows on the ground floor might well have been oriels, but it is noticeable that the windows above are flush with the close-studding and might have run right along the façade in the manner of the previous century. Inside there is one splendid fireplace with an overmantel dated 1624 and below figures depicting the Five Senses.

125

163. Anderson Manor, Dorset

6.3 BRICKS, THE DOUBLE-PILE PLAN AND THE INFLUENCE OF HOLLAND

Bricks had been used since the thirteenth century and two million of them were used to build Eton College in the 1450s. The few houses built entirely in brick before 1620 were mainly in the eastern counties close to Holland from where the idea of building in brick was imported. In areas where there was no stone, but suitable clay deposits existed, increasing shortage of timber encouraged building in brick. The style chosen was classical, but interpreted in the Franco-Dutch manner, rather than the Italianate upon which Inigo Jones based his designs.

As we have already seen, the Dutch gable was a favourite motif and supplanted the plain triangular gable. It was first recorded in 1619 by John Smythson on a visit to London. Jacobean delight in an impressive roofscape and the use of brick have both also been noted above (in

4.8) in relation to Kew Palace, in Surrey, for Samuel Fortrey, a London merchant whose ancestors came from Holland. But this house has another distinction, in that it is the first 'double-pile' house in England. Dated 1631, the Dutch House at Kew is in plan two rectangular buildings placed alongside each other and divided along their length by a corridor. Of course Inigo Jones' design of the Queen's House, in Greenwich, in two parts, one on each side of the Deptford to Woolwich road, implied a similar pattern, but this was not introduced as a formal design until the Dutch House and, as we shall see in the next chapter, only given definitive shape in Sir Roger Pratt's design of Coleshill, Berkshire.

An example of local affinities, in both the use of brick and the double-pile arrangement, can be seen in

Anderson Manor, Dorset *(Plate 163)*. Built for John Tregonwell in 1622, the house is a lovely rich red colour set off by the white stone dressings, and it is the unusual bond which is striking. Here there are two rows of stretchers and one of headers, which creates a strong band, very much a popular device of the time in Dorset. Anderson Manor was also among the earliest houses in the county to be constructed on the double-pile principle, but the porch leads into the lower part of the Hall in the old manner. The Hall runs to the right along the façade and into the right-hand wing, forming an L shape.

Jacobean designers also relished the ease with which brick could be used to form pilasters, to mould horizontal stringing lines across the face of buildings, to create arches, to establish patterns around windows, make quoins, and mark variations of the roofline at relatively little extra cost compared with wood and carved stone. Chimneys, which had in any case always been made of brick, continued during this period to be as tall and as impressive as possible. There can be few more dramatic displays of seventeenth century cut and moulded brickwork than Broome Park, near Barham, in Kent *(Plate 164)*. Built in red English-bonded brick in 1635-1638 for Sir Basil Dixwell, this is a grandiloquent house which looks back not to Jones' Queen's House or his Banqueting House, nor to the brick Prince's Lodging he built at Newmarket, but to the great Jacobean houses such as Blickling. And yet the classical vocabulary is present: giant pilasters, a bold entablature and a deep cornice at the level of the eaves. In plan the house is H shaped and symmetrical, but one could say that the classicism is perversely Mannerist, with the pilasters, for instance, standing on pedestals but having no capitals, just as Raphael did in his Villa Madama. This is daring work which looks beyond England for its inspiration to the Low Countries and to France.

164. Broome Park, near Barham, Kent

165. Bridge Place, Bridge, Kent

Close to Bridge, in Kent, is Bridge Place **(Plate 165)** which is, in spite of its formal appearance, only part of a major seventeenth century house. Now we see a north front of five bays and an east of four, whereas in a drawing by Willem Schellinks in the National Library in Vienna dated 1661 it is shown as being of nine bays by seven and probably built around a small courtyard. The house was constructed for Sir Arnold Braems between 1638 and 1643 and consists of two storeys above a basement and a hipped roof supported by very stylish brackets. Brick pilasters stand on pediments and have Tuscan capitals

and there is a full entablature at first-floor level, while the chimneys are, again, bold and distinctly English.

Swakeleys House **(Plate 166)**, at Ickenham, in the Borough of Hillingdon, was built in 1638 for Sir Edward Wright, Lord Mayor of London in 1640-1641, and it illustrates how different were the tastes of the Court and the City. In plan the brick house was traditional, with the Hall entered asymmetrically through the doorway giving access to a screens passage, while the projecting wings are still treated in the Jacobean manner. The flamboyant gables following Smythson's drawing of a house in

166. *Swakeleys, Ickenham, London*

Holborn of 1619 borrow from Netherlandish classicism, while the central range of the house is double-pile and the Great Chamber, which occupies the whole of the central part of the first floor, has a plaster ceiling divided into fifteen compartments in the Jonesian manner.

The other house that ought to be mentioned in this context has also been commented on before in relation to gables (see 4.8), and that is Raynham Hall, in Norfolk. Although Sir Roger Townshend seems to have begun building the house on its present site in 1622, it was not finished until 1638. An H plan was adopted and the main rooms are disposed in accordance with Palladio's designs, with the Hall on the east side of the house, though, curiously, it was entered at both ends through screens passages. The house is rectangular and is made of brick and stone, the brick being English bonded on the upper floor but in the Flemish way below. In the centre of the east front the narrow pavilion running through the house is given an applied Ionic portico which looks very like the style of Inigo Jones. Even if the Surveyor himself was not responsible, it would seem likely to be someone familiar with the Prince's Lodging, at Newmarket.

129

167. *Wood Lane Hall, Sowerby, Yorkshire*

6.4 WEST YORKSHIRE H-PLAN HOUSES

Writing in A *Tour through the Whole Island of Great Britain* in 1720, Daniel Defoe had this to say about the Calder Valley: 'Hardly a house standing out of speaking distance from another, and the day clearing up and the sun shining, we could see that at almost every house there was a tenter, and on almost every tenter a piece of cloth…from which the sun glancing, and, as I may say, shining (the white reflecting its rays to us), I thought it the most agreeable sight I ever saw…we could see through the glades almost every way round us, yet look which way we would, high to the tops and low to the bottoms it was all the same; innumerable houses and tenters, and a white piece on every tenter'.

Still tucked away down a leafy glade on the steep banks of the Calder Valley, Wood Lane Hall, Sowerby, is a fine example of such houses, with a low pitched roof and ashlar blocks of black millstone grit highlighted by the lime cement **(Plate 167)**. Built in 1649, the house has a circular porch window decorated with six gothic mouchettes; the suggestion of castellation and the jolly use of Jacobean finials are old-fashioned. The columns have an entablature, but are decorative rather than

correct. The well-lit central Hall is open to the ceiling with a balcony giving access to all the bedrooms. Symmetry has, clearly, not yet arrived in the area.

At the other end of the scale, **Plate 168** is typical of the smaller seventeenth century houses of the Calder Valley. Built in the same stone, and with the same roof-pitch as Wood Lane Hall, the blocks are smaller and less well worked. The central section has quoins and is built of smaller blocks, suggesting that a small unheated house has been added to on both sides. The barn is of a typical shape and has a Venetian window. Like Wood Lane Hall, the wealth that built this house came from wool. Behind the house there is the chimney of an abandoned Victorian factory which attests to the importance of the sheep over many centuries.

A rather grander house of the same pattern and dated about 1620 is today the Fleece Inn, in Westgate, Elland, West Yorkshire **(Plate 169)**. Here the Hall is set back beyond the two gables, with the doorway giving access to the screens passage offset to the left. Again, the substantial dormer probably gave light to a Great Chamber, and throughout the building the windows are mullioned.

168. *Smaller 17th century house in the Calder Valley, Cumbria*

169. *The Fleece Inn, Westgate, near Elland, Yorkshire*

170. Castle Ashby, Northamptonshire

6.5 COURTYARD SCREENING

Castle Ashby, in Northamptonshire, presents us with another intriguing question of attribution. The mansion is approached along a three and a half mile avenue and when first seen is symmetrical and self-confident, as we expect Elizabethan and Jacobean houses to be. There has been a castle on the site since the eleventh century, but a courtyard house was built by the first Lord Compton beginning in 1574, with more work being done in about 1600. On the south side the most important element is the white ashlar screen rising only to two storeys **(Plate 170)**, the upper level being the Long Gallery.

In his *Vitruvius Britannicus* (1725), Colen Campbell attributes the design to Inigo Jones, but scholars are not convinced. The screen is nine bays wide and the central arch is topped by a triangular pediment and projects forward, as do the two end bays. Pilasters and columns articulate the façade, Tuscan on the ground floor and Ionic above, and there is some rustication, but the most interesting feature is the Venetian window above the entrance arch. Jones had introduced the Venetian window to England when he used it at the Queen's Chapel, in London, in 1623, and it seems likely that the screen was the work of the 2nd Earl of Northampton in the early 1630s. There are some elements of the design that are not purely classical and, although this should not automatically eliminate the attribution to Jones, for, as we have seen, he could occasionally be less than purist in his use of classical motifs, it is the lack of harmony between window and wall that suggests that another hand is responsible for the screen.

6.6 LAKELAND HOUSES

Townend, at Troutbeck, Cumbria, is a remarkable survival *(Plate 171)*. Built in 1626 by a wealthy yeoman farmer called Browne, it stayed in the same family until 1943 and is now in the hands of the National Trust. Although modest in size, it follows the same pattern as rather larger houses with the Hall in the centre and the entrance to the screens passage at the junction of the two blocks at right angles to each other. Some of the original mullioned windows still survive and the chimneystacks are characteristic of the area. Inside the house there is also some particularly interesting carved woodwork.

Another house on much the same pattern is Hodge

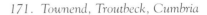

171. Townend, Troutbeck, Cumbria

172.
*Hodge Hill,
Cumbria*

173.
*Swarthmoor
Hall, near
Ulverstone,
Cumbria*

174. Killington Hall, Cumbria

Hill, at Cartmel, in Cumbria *(Plate 172)*. Dating from about the 1630s, the plan is again an L with the entrance to the original screens passage set into the intersection of the two wings, but, in this case, there is a good dormer, while the other Hall windows have clearly been altered. The chimneystacks follow the local pattern.

A rather grander building is Swarthmoor Hall, near Ulverstone, also in Cumbria *(Plate 173)*. In this case there is much more concern for symmetry and there are good mullioned windows with dripstones above them in

the three-storeyed building. The likely date of this structure is 1650.

Killington Hall, in Cumbria, is a fine house repeatedly altered. Part of it dates from the fifteenth century, but the two gables projecting forward from the roof-space with their stepped three-light windows proclaim a date of about 1640 *(Plate 174)*. On the ground floor the Gothic doorway is most likely to be of the early nineteenth century, and this is confirmed by an inscription to that effect.

175. The Newe House, Pakenham, Suffolk

6.7 MODEST GABLED HOUSES

Houses such as Chastleton, in Oxfordshire, at the top of the social scale, made use of a series of gables to provide an impressive roofline, and this practice has already been commented on. Within a few years, however, the device was being used in the Cotswolds and in Northamptonshire on small rectangular-plan stone houses at a lower level of society. The gables were a continuation of the front wall and usually contained a mullioned window. The fact that they were intended to impress is clear from their size, which is often bigger than that needed to provide light for the attic bedroom behind, and there are also insets for pigeons. Equally, towards the end of the period stone finials were set on the top and at the point where the gables met the eaves. At first the windows in

176. Hinton House, St Nicholas Hurst, Berkshire

177. The Old Vicarage, High Street, Burford, Oxfordshire

the gables had a simple straight drip moulding, but later the moulding bent round the window, a form always used in the revival houses of the nineteenth century.

The type continued into the eighteenth century, by which time the classical Georgian house took over for the upper part of the market and the simple unadorned cottage had to do duty for those not so well placed. Local variations include the late use of classical features, such as a pediment over a window. Symmetry depended largely on the number of bays in a façade, but more important than that was the effect produced on the observer.

The Newe House, at Pakenham, Suffolk, is a fine Jacobean brick house of 1622 *(Plate 175)*. Although not a big house, it has a very sophisticated exterior with exceptionally charming Dutch gables and was probably built as a dower house. The Hall is entered through a door in the centre of the façade and, although the interior has been somewhat altered, it originally consisted of three rooms arranged in a line – Parlour, Hall and Kitchen – with subsidiary services being in a wing projecting at the rear. The windows are of three or four lights, both mullioned and transomed, while the chimneystacks are placed at the ends of the building and the chimneys set diagonally.

Hinton House, St Nicholas Hurst, Berkshire *(Plate 176)*, is not a large house, but it has an air of quiet assertion. Built of diapered brick most probably between 1615 and 1620 by William Hide, the house has a symmetrical façade with a central entrance, but both the Hall and Parlour on the ground floor are of equal size and are entered through the Hall on the left side of the door. Immediately behind the front range of Hall and Parlour is the main stair, and perhaps originally a service stair as well, while the rear range consisted of services including the kitchen. The Great Chamber was above the Parlour and access to the other chambers was provided by the staircases in the manner which was to become familiar with Coleshill. On the top floor the position of the staircase was altered to permit a small gallery to be introduced. Hinton House is in reality a triple-pile house.

On the west side of High Street, Burford, in Oxfordshire, the Old Vicarage *(Plate 177)* is another house of the period the façade of which is quietly assertive. It is dated 1672 and has a particularly stylish frontage embellished with three Dutch gables. Interestingly, this is perhaps a slightly old-fashioned house, as the design of the gable is more reminiscent of the 1630s than of the 1670s.

179. 17th century cottages in Biddenden, Kent

6.8 COTTAGES

Small, simple one- or two-cell houses are usually to be found in a village or in an urban terrace with others. The open field system would have made it possible to live in a village and work the fields during the day and, of course, other key members of the agricultural community, such as the smith, would also live and work in the village. This is the logical follow-on from the one-storey house discussed earlier. But, small as they seem to us today, they were a far cry from temporary hovels, and these dwellings were often built of stone or brick and had all the characteristics of the small house.

In School Street, Sidford, Devon, there is a long row of early seventeenth century cottages *(Plate 178)*. They

have undoubtedly been altered from their original condition, but their detailing is of a high order underlining the fact that they were important dwellings when they were built. Particularly impressive are the chimneystacks built of local ashlar and flint projecting into the street. One such stack is even patterned in the manner of East Devon.

There is also a fine row of timber-framed cottages in the village street of Biddenden, Kent *(Plate 179)*. The upper floor close-studding deliberately forms a pattern and there are oriels too at this level. These are, therefore, properties of some sophistication. Certainly of the seventeenth century, they date probably from the 1620s or 1630s.

Opposite: 178. Cottages in Sidford, Devon

180. Lindsey House, Lincoln's Inn Fields, London

6.9 LONDON'S FIRST FORMAL SQUARE?

Random development of already crowded areas of London was causing official concern in the early seventeenth century and a Commission on Buildings was set up in 1618 to establish some measure of regulation. The Surveyor of the King's Buildings, Inigo Jones, was a member. Perhaps the first layout of a formal square was in Lincoln's Inn Fields, of which only Lindsey House (1640) on the west side still remains *(Plate 180)*, and with this project Jones seems to have had no involvement.

Jones was, however, involved in the planned development of Covent Garden, at that time on London's fringe. The 4th Earl of Bedford owned land and houses to the north of The Strand, and he obtained a licence from the King and Council to demolish the old properties; a condition of that licence seems to have been that the new structures should have a special architectural quality. In the 1630s, therefore, Jones on behalf of the Earl created the first formal square in England,

181. Engraving of the Place des Vosges or the Place Royale, Paris

lining it on the north and east sides with uniform, classical houses of two storeys and a dormer raised above arcades. On the west he built St Paul's church, while the south was kept open, as this adjoined the Earl's private garden.

The inspiration for this influential piece of town

182. Lazenby Hall, Danby Wiske, Yorkshire

planning was most probably the Place des Vosges *(Plate 181)*, in Paris, known at that time as the Place Royale as it contained the Royal houses of its builder, Henri IV and his Queen. Dating as it did from 1607-1612, it was a very recent precedent, but it can hardly be said that the presence of the King's house has anything like the dominance that the portico of St Paul's enjoys in Covent Garden. For this Jones turned to a design by Sebastiano Serlio, published in Book 4 of his *Four Books of Architecture*. This scheme of Inigo Jones was to become a classic, leading to the squares, terraces, crescents and circuses of London and Bath and many other places as well.

6.91 PATTERN BOOK DETAILS

Classical details had been used by provincial builders from the earliest times and they were applied without regard to their correct use or, indeed, their relationship to other details. Like a lavatory chain and handle worn around the neck of a primitive tribesman, they were purely ornaments designed to impress, a source of amusement for travelling cognoscenti, and a source of enjoyment for the rest of us. They present one facet of the restless search for self-assertion that makes the English house such a rewarding study.

Lazenby Hall, Danby Wiske, in the North Riding of Yorkshire *(Plate 182)*, dates from about 1650 and is a case in point. Well-constructed pilasters are arranged with little regard for their correctness, although in the recessed centre it has to be confessed that the short pilasters of the two storeys have, correctly, the Doric capital on the lower level and the Ionic on the higher. Above the porch, however, the

cluster columns have bases which are out of proportion to their size, while the shafts between the windows are grouped three in a row, the first slender in form, the second stronger, and the third back to the slender again. They have weak Ionic capitals, but no suggestion of a base.

The publication of pattern books in English showing classical details started to appear from 1560. Perhaps the greatest influence on English architecture was Sebastiano Serlio, who produced altogether seven books, but the most influential publication on work here was the Venetian quarto of 1566 which contained Books 1 to 6. Serlio also came into this country in the work of others, notably that of John Shute, whose *The First and Chief Groundes of Architecture* appeared in 1563. It was a thin work, dedicated to the Queen and illustrated with copper-plate engravings, and it relied to a great extent on Serlio's work and also used Philander's *Commentary* on Vitruvius, the first century Roman military writer. Shute's book was essentially an English publication and it was re-issued in 1579, 1584 and 1587, so it certainly had an effect.

But books imported, particularly from Flanders, were also influential. Hans Blum's *Quinque Columnarum* was in use in England by 1570, while J. Vredeman de Vries' *Architectura* must have been available here from the same date. Among the French works, one of the most important was du Cerceau's *Architectura*, published in 1559, and we know that Lord Burghley sent to Paris for a copy of Philibert de l'Orme's *Nouvelles Inventions* when he was involved in the final stages of building Burghley House. But, for all these authors, Serlio was the most widely recognised authority and the aspiring patron could use published illustrations to demonstrate his requirements to his mason.

183. *Coleshill House, Berkshire: the entrance front*

CHAPTER 7

1650-1715

7.0 INTRODUCTION: COLESHILL AND AFTER

It is ironic that arguably the most influential house of the seventeenth century, Coleshill, in Berkshire, was burnt down in 1952 and is known to us principally through the black and white photographs taken of it by *Country Life* magazine *(Plate 183)*. Built after 1650 by a gentleman architect, Sir Roger Pratt, for his cousin, Sir George Pratt, it heralded a much more careful use of classical motifs in the Dutch or French manner after the showy gothic of the Jacobeans. Advised to use the classicism of Palladio by Inigo Jones, Sir Roger had preferred an equality of visual importance between the two main storeys and the arrangement of dormers, hipped roof and bold chimneys, more suitable, perhaps to the English climate. It was a style which was to be pivotal to the development of the English house for the next century.

Coleshill also contained other new features. First, the new double-pile plan, whereby two parallel ranges of the old rectangular building were built close to each other allowing

184. *Staircase of Coleshill*

both to be covered by one roof, enabled a corridor with subordinate staircases at either end to be introduced where the two rectangles joined. Second, the windows of Coleshill were tall and narrow, echoing the towering chimneys, and

185. *The garden front of Kingston Lacy, Dorset*

this form suited the new sash windows which came into general use at the end of the century, having first been used at Ham House, Surrey, in 1672. The windows at Coleshill must, therefore, have been a replacement for mullions. Third, the introduction of a rusticated half-basement for service rooms was an innovation, while the layout of the stair, with its double flight and uniting gallery *(Plate 184)*, speaks of the Baroque to come. Fourth, the spacing of the windows in the symmetrical façade allows greater space to be given to the Hall and Great Parlour on the ground floor and the Great Dining Chamber above, and the three windows grouped more closely signal the presence of a guest lodging consisting of a Chamber, a bedchamber and space for a servant.

In the 1660s Sir Roger Pratt applied the remarkable innovations of Coleshill to Kingston Lacy *(Plate 185)*, in Dorset (alas much altered in the nineteenth century), and to Clarendon House, in Piccadilly, for the Lord Chancellor, Edward Hyde. This house only survived for sixteen years, but, as we shall see, it was closely copied in Belton House, Lincolnshire. As a contrast to the restraint

of this design, however, flamboyance continued in the Baroque style arising from the Roman Catholic Church's renewal of self-confidence as it counter-attacked against the damage inflicted by Protestantism.

In the Baroque, the language of classicism was better understood, but altered by the need for a feeling of movement. Architects such as Thomas Archer, who had actually been to Rome, and geniuses like Vanbrugh, who had not, produced buildings of which Blenheim Palace is the supreme example which well suited the national mood after victory brought to an end nearly thirty years of war against Louis XIV's France. Like other styles before it, the Baroque worked its way down the social scale from grand country houses to smaller ones and then, towards the end of the period, into provincial towns and villages.

At the other end of the classical scale came houses from Sir Christopher Wren and his followers. They were in cool red brick using the vocabulary of Palladio, quiet, smaller houses between the excitement and theatricality of a Blenheim and the restraint of a Coleshill.

7.1 CORNER TOWERS AND CUPOLAS

The south (garden) front of Wilton House, Wiltshire, is a long, low block of State Rooms given emphasis by the central Venetian window with its shield and figures and, strikingly, by the pedimented towers at either end *(Plate 186)*. It is likely that Charles I suggested the new wing to the Earl of Pembroke in the 1630s and Inigo Jones was consulted, but, being heavily involved with the Royal works, suggested Isaac de Caus as designer both of the State Rooms and the gardens associated with them. None the less, even a casual glance at the fenestration and the corner towers shows how much the work of Jones influenced the design. It does seem that the towers, one of which screened part of the old house, were making their first appearance in England, where they were to have an important effect early in the next century, and were an Italianate design deriving from Palladio. The Civil War delayed work on the wing and after a serious fire in 1648 the work of reconstruction was undertaken by Jones' assistant, John Webb, early in the 1650s, the wonderful decoration of the State Rooms being in the French manner and having the distinctive stamp of Jones.

One type of house which appeared in the seventeenth century and which disappeared before the eighteenth arrived was the tall heavily decorated house in what Sir John Summerson has called the 'Artisan Mannerist' style of which the Cupola House, Bury St Edmunds, Suffolk, is a late but good example *(Plate 187)*. Built for a wealthy apothecary, Thomas Macro, in 1693, the classical references are there, with quoins and pediments over the bold dormers, but they are subsidiary to the work done by the carpenters and bricklayers who used every device to proclaim height, bulk, and therefore wealth.

When Celia Fiennes visited only five years after it was completed, she sat in the gazebo-like Cupola and praised 'the pleasing prospect' to be had from it over the surrounding streets. The use of great height may have come from the desire to make the most of an expensive city site and when this design appeared in the countryside it often looked out of place. It is also odd that such an ostentatious design should have its roots in a period of Puritan domination.

186. South front of Wilton House, Wiltshire

187. Cupola House, Bury St Edmunds, Suffolk

Ashdown Park, now in Oxfordshire, shows the same towering style and when originally constructed high up on the Downs surrounded by forest rides leading to the house it must have been an impressive sight. Built for the Earl of Craven, probably about 1660, it is a perfect, tall dolls' house, standing three storeys high above a basement, five bays square, of chalk with brown dressings. The roof is hipped with a balustrade surmounting it and a cupola, as had been done at Coleshill only a decade before. The style is Dutch and there is the same massive eaves cornice as there is at the Cupola House. Restraint is, again, the overall theme, but its height makes one think of a tower house.

145

188. 14 Essex Street, Temple, London

189. 39-43 Old Town, Clapham, London

7.2 EARLY LONDON TERRACES

As with so many other types of seventeenth century building, the urban terrace can be traced back to Inigo Jones' work at Covent Garden, in London. Not surprisingly, however, the matter was much more complicated than simply the introduction of a style and economics; building practices and the law all played a part. In 1636 William Newton, a builder from Bedfordshire, had obtained a licence to build fourteen large houses on the south side of Great Queen's Street, and informed opinion in the eighteenth century considered these houses to be the first uniform London street. As we have seen, uniformity was first imposed by the King by Order in Council, but after the Restoration there was no evidence of this administrative process being adopted and it was the development plans of the great landowners that achieved the distinctive harmony. Essex Street, between The Strand and the river, was built by Nicholas Barbon between 1675 and 1682 on the site of the demolished Essex House **(Plate 188)**.

The usual arrangement was for the head lessee, rather than the great noble who was most likely the ground landlord, to impose uniformity of elevation when granting the building leases, and if it was not done at this stage there was very little uniformity that could be achieved later in the process. This group of three houses **(Plate 189)** in the Old Town, Clapham, built in about 1705, shows a concern with classical symmetry, but not an obsession, as the two houses on the left have a larger gap between the windows to emphasise the change and the joint doors on the right are not entirely comfortable in design. Tuscan columns, triglyphs and dentil mouldings speak the classical language, but the boldly pitched roof is English.

The bold wooden cornice and the wide wooden window casings standing flush with the walls became illegal towards the end of the first decade of the new century, but, although that only applied to the Cities of London and Westminster, the parapet which replaced it became fashionable. The soffits of the top windows are cut with a serpentine pattern which is typical of 1700-1730.

190. *Thorney Abbey House, near Peterborough*

7.3 THE IMMEDIATE EFFECTS OF COLESHILL

Thorney Abbey, in the county of Peterborough, is a house which consists of two parts (*Plate 190*). The first was built in the sixteenth century with gables and mullioned windows, but the other, of 1660, is connected with the older part by a short range and is a scaled-down version of Coleshill. A contract between the Duke of Bedford and John Lovin, of Peterborough, exists, and this later house is a square, stone-built, two-storeyed structure with a hipped roof and dormer windows. It lacks a cupola and the half-basement of Coleshill, but the careful fenestration and the bold string course between the levels of windows gives a strong horizontal emphasis to the overall design.

There are characteristics about this house which have caused it to be attributed to Peter Mills, a bricklayer of the City of London and an architect of considerable competence. He was the designer of Thorpe Hall (*Plate 191*), also in the county of Peterborough, made in 1653-1656 for Chief Justice St. John. One of those designers referred to by Sir John Summerson as 'Artisan Mannerist', Peter Mills created a four-square house at Thorpe, its north and south façades being of seven bays and the height of the structure two storeys and a half-basement, with dormer windows set into a hipped roof. This style of house was to run parallel to both classical

and Baroque ones during the remainder of the century.

Mothecombe, in Devon, is a charming house (*Plate 192*) which stands behind a white-painted fence at the end of the village street. Although it was built in about 1710 for John Pollexfen, it is very much of the classic post-Restoration type: a five-bay frontage of two storeys over a basement and with a hipped roof from which dormers project. The stone of which it is constructed is quite roughly coursed, with simple pilasters and a central window picked out with quoins. The plan is simple but sophisticated, and the authorship, if it was not that of the owner himself, is intriguing. It has been suggested that Vanbrugh's work at the Royal Dockyard in Plymouth might have created a team of designer-masons who spread the master's manner more widely in Devon than he would have been able to do by himself.

Although not appropriate at this point, it is worth mentioning that Sir Edwin Lutyens was called in at Mothecombe in 1922-1925 to replace Victorian additions at the back of the house with a characteristically sympathetic dining room wing projecting from the south front. Its low, hipped roof respects the dimensions of the Queen Anne façade, while Lutyens also created a terrace overlooking the eighteenth century walled garden.

191. *Garden front of Thorpe Hall, Peterborough*

192. *Mothecombe, Devon*

193. Tintinhull, near Yeovil, Somerset

Tintinhull House, in Somerset *(Plate 193)*, is another example of the same quiet style, although the house itself is of the early seventeenth century to which a new façade was added in 1700. Five bays wide, the frontage has rusticated quoins and giant pilasters together with a pediment to lay emphasis on the three middle bays. There is also a circular window in the pediment.

Another building in the same tranquil and unassertive style, but this time in brick, is Lucton School, at Lucton, in Herefordshire *(Plate 194)*. Built by John Pierrepont in 1708, it none the less looks back twenty years or so and responds to the design innovations of Coleshill in its hipped roof and bellcote, though perhaps to the influence of Holland in the three-bay centrepiece surmounted by a triangular pediment. Above the door is a lively statue of the founder in white-painted wood.

The influence of Coleshill in a town setting presented

different problems to the builder. No. 16 Cobthorne, Oundle, Northamptonshire *(Plate 195)*, was built at the early date of 1658 and illustrates the transition from the classicism of Coleshill to a new style which was to develop into the Georgian gable-end house with dormers. The careful symmetry of the façade makes its origins clear, as does the cornice to the broad-eaved roof and the confident dormers. But when one follows the cornice round to the side of the up-to-date double-pile plan, it looks distinctly uncomfortable plastered on to the gable end with nothing above or below to give it meaning. It is then apparent that the designer took his ideas from a house which had a hipped roof, but that he did not like the idea of covering the great depth of this house with such a device. Instead, he stuck to what he knew – the gable end; but to be sure he was up with the fashion he added the side adornment which in fact forms the banding.

*194. Lucton School,
Lucton,
Herefordshire*

*195. 16 Cobthorne,
Oundle,
Northamptonshire*

196. *Groombridge Place, Kent*

7.4 BRICK COURTYARD HOUSES

Groombridge Place, in Kent, long owned by the Wallers, was rebuilt by Philip Packer some time between the two visits that John Evelyn paid to the house in 1652 and 1674. Unlike many an owner intending to reconstruct an old house, Packer built within the courtyard of the older property, and therefore also within the moat, and he created one of the loveliest and most mellow of English houses in the southern counties. Since the second half of the seventeenth century little, apart from the sashing of the windows, has changed.

Made of brick, Groombridge *(Plate 196)* has a hipped roof, and the two-storeyed building over a basement is constructed on an H plan, with the central bar of the H accommodating only the Hall with a chamber above, the door leading into a lobby which must be one of the last traces of the screens passage. The fenestration is only regular on the entrance side and the chimneybreasts project, both of which elements suggest an early date for Groombridge, perhaps the mid-1660s. The sandstone loggia and the pediment are classical features.

152

7.5 DUTCH STONE HOUSES

When Charles II was proclaimed King in Westminster Hall in 1660 Dutch influence on the architecture of this country immediately started to grow. The new King had assimilated many recent developments in Holland during his exile. He had seen Pieter Post build De Saal van Oranje, near The Hague, while Jacob van Campen had built the Mauritshuis, also in The Hague, in 1633-1635 and the Town Hall in Amsterdam in 1645-1651, all three buildings in a chaste classical style. The King had also acquired many obligations while in exile, among them one to Hugh May, who had been to Holland during the Commonwealth period in exile in the entourage of the Duke of Buckingham.

May was appointed Paymaster to the Office of Works and built, among houses, Eltham Lodge *(Plate 197)* in 1664 for Sir John Shaw, a banker, in a style which displayed a restrained elegance underpinned by an acceptance of classical forms. The house is a rectangular block of two storeys with a basement made of brick with stone dressings. The entrance front has seven bays, the middle three being articulated by slim Ionic pilasters and a stone pediment, while a dentil cornice runs around the house at eaves level with a hipped roof and dormers above. The door leads into the Hall and it becomes apparent that the plan is that of a triple-pile.

The Dutch connection established during the Commonwealth can also be seen in the design of Belton House, Lincolnshire, today owned by the National Trust

197. Eltham Lodge, near Woolwich, London

(Plate 198). It was built for 'Young' Sir John Brownlow in 1684, most probably by Capt. William Winde who had fought with English forces at Bergen-op-Zoom, in Holland, and, on his return to England in 1660, also against the Duke of Monmouth's forces at Sedgemoor. A gentleman architect, he probably provided little more than a rough drawing for Belton and the detailed work of building was undertaken by William Stanton.

Undoubtedly Belton looks back to Pratt's Clarendon House, in Piccadilly, of 1664, and consists again of a double-pile house in the form of an H plan with two equally proportioned storeys and a basement, a hipped roof with dormers, a balustrade and a cupola. Inside the house, the Marble Hall and the Saloon are on the main north-south axis and the rooms were originally arranged in a series of lodgings in the manner of Coleshill, but the restraint of the exterior is not pursued inside where the carving of Grinling Gibbons, the joinery of Edmund Carpenter and the plasterwork by Edward Goudge are spectacular.

As is so often the case, such influences can be seen in more modest locations. Discussed previously in relation to gables (see 6.7), The Old Vicarage stands on the west side at the bottom of the High Street, in Burford, Oxfordshire. Dated 1672, the three gables, with blank stone medallions rather than dormers, are surmounted alternately with triangular and segmental pediments. The first floor of the house is treated as a *piano nobile* with deep mullioned and transomed windows in the classical manner.

In contrast to the influence of the restored monarch,

198. Belton House, Lincolnshire

199. *William of Orange House, Strand, Topsham, Devon*

trade also introduced the Dutch style, especially in the ports that had commercial links with the Continent. This sophisticated classical house of the early eighteenth century **(Plate 199)** was built most probably by a merchant or by a prosperous shipowner on The Strand, Topsham, Devon. He was certainly familiar with contemporary Dutch style and, indeed, the name of the property today is William of Orange House.

155

200. Boughton House, Northamptonshire: the north front

7.6 FRENCH INFLUENCE

French influence on English building in the last decades of the seventeenth century was limited for understandable reasons, given the continuing wars, and where a French style can be discerned, positive links across the Channel can generally be discovered. Three houses show this stylistic tendency and the link is the Montagu family. The first house was Montagu House, built by Robert Hooke between 1674 and 1680 for Ralph Montagu, later the 1st Duke of Montagu, on the site of what is today the British Museum. The inspiration was Vaux le Vicomte, of the 1650s, by Le Vau, and Montagu House was constructed like a French hotel around a court with a gateway in the street wall, and opposite this a *corps de logis* with a domed centre. Six years after completion the house was burnt and rebuilt 'in the French manner', as *Vitruvius Britannicus* says, by the otherwise unknown designer, M. Puget, or Bouget, though whether the

design of the rebuilt house is based on a plate in the *Petit Marot*, and whether there is a link to the French Huguenot designer who came over to England with William III in 1689, Daniel Marot, remains an open question.

The French link is not surprising, as Ralph Montagu had been ambassador extraordinary to Louis XIV in 1669 and again in 1676. Shortly after the reconstruction of Montagu House, Ralph Montagu started to rebuild Boughton House, in Northamptonshire. Today the view of the north front of Boughton **(Plate 200)** is like seeing a serene Ile de France château set down in the English shires. Actually, the long open arcade on the ground floor with State Rooms for the Sovereign over and very French pavilions at either end were intended to screen the earlier house and consequently did not have a central feature as was so apparent at Montagu House.

Ralph Montagu's stepdaughter, Elizabeth, married the

201. The west front of Petworth, Sussex

202. Winslow Hall, Sheep Street, Winslow, Buckinghamshire

Duke of Somerset, who rebuilt Petworth between 1688 and 1696. Here again the west front of the house *(Plate 201)*, that is facing the park, which was once the main entrance front, is strikingly French in its style, and the square dome designed to stand over the main entrance but never built would have enhanced this impression and again recalled the design of Montagu House. Certainly, the entrance hall was designed and decorated by Daniel Marot, and it does seem likely that he had a hand in the design of the west façade as well, judging from the ornaments that were incorporated on it.

7.7 'WRENAISSANCE' HOUSES

Sir Howard Colvin has written: 'With the possible exception of Inigo Jones no English architect has been the victim of more reckless and ill-informed attributions than Wren'. As he makes clear there are practically no houses known to have been designed by Wren himself, his time being spent in Royal service and in the design of churches to replace those lost in the Fire of London.

With one house, however, he was connected; it was built for a Royal servant, and most of the work was carried out by craftsmen with Royal positions. Winslow Hall, Sheep Street, Winslow, Buckinghamshire *(Plate 202)*, was started in 1700 for William Lowndes, Secretary to the Treasury, and its three storeys, fine pediment and the generous use of quoins and dentil cornice suggest an architect who accepted Palladian thinking. The grouping of the chimneys to constitute the third of a three-pile plan, the segmental door-hood, a round window in the tympanum, and long thin sash windows, all come together to produce a very restrained and elegant design. Even the use of traditional black headers and red stretchers give texture.

157

204. *Calke Abbey, Derbyshire*

7.8 THE USE OF GIANT ORDERS

Cound Hall, Shropshire, will be discussed more fully in relation to Provincial Baroque (see Plate 222) , but it is perhaps also appropriate to mention it for the way it uses giant orders. Built in 1704 for Edward Cressett by John Prince, of Shrewsbury, the materials used were red brick with stone dressings, but what is really dramatic about the elevation is the giant Corinthian pilasters that frame both storeys of the three-bay centre and are also at the angles. The pilasters stand on rusticated bases, and there is decoration between the flutes in the lower part of the façade, while the capitals are large and richly carved, and

above again there are decorated slabs and part of the entablature. In the true sense of the word this is dramatic design and heralds the Baroque.

It seems likely that this use of the giant orders derives ultimately from Michelangelo's use of them in the design of the Palazzo del Museo Capitolino and in the Palazzo dei Conservatori, on opposite sides of the Piazza del Campidoglio, in Rome. A similar use of giant pilasters was made by Dean Henry Aldrich in his design of Peckwater Quad, in Christ Church, Oxford. Dating from 1705 to 1714, this building **(Plate 203)** is impeccably classical and makes up three sides of a quadrangle. Each block has fifteen bays, is two and a half storeys in height with smooth rustication on the ground floor and giant Ionic pilasters above. But, even more remarkably given the date, the central five bays of each range have giant attached columns with a pediment over, taking us one stage further towards the unified temple-front design which was going to be introduced in London squares such as Grosvenor later in the eighteenth century.

It was between 1701 and 1704 that Sir John Harpur employed William Johnson to execute the rebuilding of his house, Calke Abbey *(Plate 204)*. The south front consists of thirteen bays of three storeys, the middle seven being recessed, and the two flanking pavilions marked by giant, fluted Ionic pilasters on high pedestals. There are two further Ionic pilasters framing the portico and pediment, which was added to the façade in 1806.

203. Peckwater Quad, Christ Church, Oxford

205. Classical house in Yetminster, Dorset

7.9 STONE VILLAGE HOUSES

In contrast to the theatrical use of the giant columns and pilasters of the country houses of the period, the style of village houses in the early eighteenth century was more sedate. This symmetrical façade of a house in Yetminster, Dorset *(Plate 205)*, speaks of the assimilation of the classical vocabulary without emphasis. Four-light windows on the ground floor give way to three above, while a two-light window is centrally placed over the door. All the mullioned windows are set in simple classical surrounds and the mullions are square in section. With the classical doorcase, there is a symmetry about the frontage of which few village houses could have boasted in the seventeenth century.

A comparison between this house and the three-storeyed stone house in Borwick, Lancashire *(Plate 206)*, which dates from the seventeenth century, shows how significant had been the assimilation of classical principles even at a modest domestic level by the time the new century had dawned. The same can be said of Moresby Hall, in Cumbria *(Plate 207)*. It has a distinguished façade of seven bays, the windows well spaced, with those on the *piano nobile* surmounted alternately by triangular and segmental pediments. The doorcase is framed with pilasters crossed with rusticated bands and has a broken segmental pediment above it. It is all very grand with the classical motifs applied in 1690-1700 by a reasonably assured hand

Barnsley, in Gloucestershire, is one of those villages

*206. Small village
house of the
17th century in
Borwick, Lancashire*

*207. Moresby Hall,
near Whitehaven,
Cumbria*

209. Pentecostal Church, Bury St Edmunds, Suffolk

where foreign influences have been resisted and where even metropolitan practices are kept firmly in their place. Barnsley House *(Plate 208)* is the very epitome of a village house of the end of the seventeenth century – a two-storeyed building in Cotswold stone, five bays wide, with mullioned and transomed windows and three neat dormers projecting from additional rooms in the roof-space. The garden front has a date stone of 1697 and the initials B.B. for Brereton Bourchier. For many years it was the home of David and Rosemary Verey; they introduced a Tuscan Doric temple of the end of the eighteenth century which came originally from Fairford Park, and Rosemary Verey created the influential garden there which made the house famous, and to many visitors archetypically English.

7.91 CHAPEL MEETING HOUSES

The Presbyterian Chapel, now the Pentecostal Church, in Churchgate Street, Bury St Edmunds, is one of the stateliest buildings of its kind in Suffolk *(Plate 209)*. Built in about 1711 of red brick with brick trimmings, the three-bay façade has big arched windows. The doorway is flanked with pilasters and has a segmental pediment and the top parapet is raised over the centre. Again, it is a restrained and proportioned structure. Although the Chapel is not strictly a domestic building today, there is evidence that it was used as a residence by the minister in the eighteenth century and its street elevation harmonises today with its more domestic neighbours.

Opposite. 208. Barnsley House, Gloucestershire

210. Goose-pie House, Whitehall, by and for Vanbrugh

7.92 VANBRUGH: BAROQUE ON THE GRAND SCALE

Soldier, wit, man-about-town, theatre-owner and playwright, Sir John Vanbrugh used his social connections to obtain his first commission – Castle Howard, in Yorkshire – at the age of thirty-five. During his architectural career, which lasted from 1699 until his death in 1726, Vanbrugh worked with the lesser known Nicholas Hawksmoor to design some of the great Baroque houses of England, and the professional relationship between the two men is one of the most fascinating partnerships of the time. Vanbrugh was born in London, the son of a wealthy cloth merchant turned sugar baker, and as a gentleman was not apprenticed to a trade, but became a soldier. Arrested as a possible spy in Calais in 1690, he spent two years in French prisons and while he was incarcerated in the Bastille began to write a superb comedy of manners still occasionally produced today, *The Relapse*. Leaving the army in 1696, Vanbrugh turned to the theatre writing altogether ten plays, including another modern favourite, *The Provok'd Wife*.

Vanbrugh's literary facility made him some enemies, including Jonathan Swift who wrote some critical verses on Vanbrugh and on the house that he built for himself in Whitehall called by his critics 'Goose-pie House' (**Plate 210**), using the couplet:

Van's genius, without thought or lecture
Is hugely turned to architecture.

Patronage helped Vanbrugh socially and professionally because the Earl of Carlisle, for whom he was building Castle Howard, was Lord Treasurer and arranged for Vanbrugh to be made Comptroller of the Office of Works, and also touched as a Herald. At a stroke Vanbrugh was on an architectural pinnacle equal to Wren, whereas Hawksmoor, who had no such advantages, was much more of a journeyman designer. Born in Nottinghamshire, he came to London at the age of eighteen and, probably with the patronage of the great plasterer, Edward Goudge, entered Wren's office as his 'domestic clerk', but within a short time was assisting with Wren's work on Chelsea Hospital. As well as being the Clerk of Works on a number of official projects, Hawksmoor worked on his own account and, from 1699, on all four of Vanbrugh's greatest houses.

It is not possible to decide, at this remove, which of the two men did what design work, and it is better to regard their association as a true partnership, though it is probable that what we today would call working drawings were prepared by Hawksmoor. What the two men achieved was the reversing of the emphasis which since the time of Inigo Jones had been laid on the interplay of the elements of classical design in favour of the intrinsic qualities of mass, rhythm and proportion in a building. Even Wren believed that architecture was a language which should be employed with the correct use of grammar, and it was only in St Paul's Cathedral that mass and its opposite, void, were given equal importance. His two successors had a sense of theatre where mass advanced and recessed, heightened and foreshortened, to give an impression of movement, which was, after all, what the Baroque set out to achieve. They avoided fussy detail and used strong shapes and, in fact, adopted two devices to assist this, the first being to continue the cornices of the pavilions across the façade of the main block, and the second to add broad vertical pilasters to each angle of the middle range. Both devices are apparent in the designs that were prepared for the new Palace of Whitehall after the grave fire of 1698, which were never carried out, while a glance at the series of great churches for East London and at the screen and entrance gate of All Souls College, Oxford, designed by Hawksmoor, makes clear how unfair to him it would be to regard Vanbrugh as the sole design genius of the partnership.

Castle Howard, Yorkshire **(Plate 211)**, was built between 1699 and 1712 and, although not completed fully in accordance with Vanbrugh's designs, is one of his greatest houses. Facing the gardens is a long range of building surmounted by the dome, while, on the north side, curved arcades join the principal apartments to pavilions housing the chapel and the kitchens. Both the devices mentioned earlier can be seen clearly on both fronts of Castle Howard, while the drama is maintained where the pendentives of the dome meet the supporting fluted columns in the entrance hall.

While Castle Howard was rising, Vanbrugh was selected by the Duke of Marlborough to design the house which Queen Anne conferred on the Captain-General of

211. South front of Castle Howard, Yorkshire

212. Blenheim Palace: the north front

her victorious armies in tribute to the battle of Blenheim. Blenheim Palace *(Plates 212 and 213)*, begun in 1705 and eventually finished by Hawksmoor in 1724, was both Vanbrugh's supreme achievement and the root of all his troubles. He met his nemesis in the inflexible will of Sarah, Duchess of Marlborough and, after the Duke himself was removed from his command by the Tories in 1711, Vanbrugh's relationship with the Duchess went from bad to worse and he was finally excluded from his masterpiece altogether. From the north side the central block with its great Corinthian portico is a separate

entity, though Doric colonnades sweep round to larger pavilions, which, together with arched attics and grouped chimneystacks, break the skyline in a characteristic way. On the garden front, pilasters and columns focus attention on the Saloon where the Duke was intended to take his great meal of the day.

When it came to his own houses, Vanbrugh could be just as original. 'Goose-pie House' has already been mentioned, but Vanbrugh's Castle (1717), overlooking Greenwich Hill, evokes an imaginary medieval past in its round towers and pointed roofs *(Plate 214)*, while his

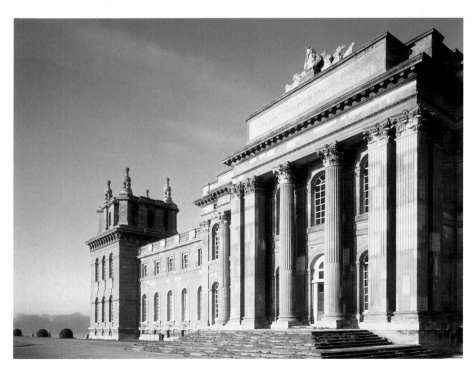

213. The south front of Blenheim

214. Vanbrugh's Castle, Greenwich Hill, London

country house at Esher had an Elizabethan plan (1711). Vanbrugh sold the property in the same year to Thomas Pelham-Holles, later Duke of Newcastle, and four years later built for the new owner the Belvedere in the grounds which has many of the same qualities that have already been noticed.

Also in 1711, Vanbrugh built King's Weston House, near Bristol, for Sir Edward Southwell *(Plate 215)*. Again the middle three bays of the main, south-west front project and have giant Corinthian pilasters, while the six large chimneystacks are connected by heavy arches, making a remarkable skyline eye-catcher. Seaton Delaval Hall, near Newcastle upon Tyne, for Admiral Delaval, is one of Vanbrugh's last houses, designed after 1718, it is said without Hawksmoor's involvement *(Plate 216)*. Today the central block has been partly restored after two serious fires and the building being left derelict for a long period. Certainly, it is the paintings by Claude Lorrain and the Picturesque that come to mind when seeing this remarkable building for the first time, rather than architecture.

215. King's Weston House, near Bristol

216. North façade of Seaton Delaval, Northumberland

217. The Cascade House, at Chatsworth, Derbyshire

7.93 THOMAS ARCHER:
ITALY AT FIRST HAND

The remarkable thing about the work of Thomas Archer is that he is the first and only English architect of his time to have studied the work of Bernini and Borromini in Italy. Born of a good Warwickshire family, he attended Oxford University and after four years of travel returned to England in 1693. Twelve years later he secured the lucrative office of Groom Porter and was at this time working for the 1st Duke of Devonshire at Chatsworth, building the domed Cascade House at the top of Grillet's Cascade in 1702 *(Plate 217)*. He was also probably responsible in 1705 for the curving north façade designed to link up the east and west wings of the house which differed in their projection to the north by about nine feet (three metres). The curving façade is five bays wide and has giant pilasters above the ground floor.

Archer also built Heythrop House, Oxfordshire *(Plate 218)*, for the 12th Earl and 1st Duke of Shrewsbury at much the same time as he was working at Chatsworth. Although much altered after a fire in 1831, especially in respect of the wings, Heythrop also displays its Italian origins, though this time the precedent is Bernini. The entrance front is eleven bays wide and certainly on a grand scale, with giant orders and a portico in the centre with Corinthian columns, while inside is a doorway curved in the manner of Borromini. The windows that flank the entrance are articulated by pilasters, while the two bays at the ends of the façade are defined by half columns at the angles. The whole looks very like an Italian palazzo

The 1st Duke died childless and, although the 13th and 14th Earls of Shrewsbury lived at Heythrop, their

218. Heythrop House, Oxfordshire

descendants lost interest in the house and settled themselves at Alton Towers, in Staffordshire. Heythrop was let, most famously to the Duke of Beaufort who brought his hounds over from Badminton and established the Heythrop Hunt. After being owned by Thomas Brassey in the nineteenth century, Heythrop was acquired by the Jesuits in 1922 and was in their hands for about forty years. It is now a country house hotel.

Between 1709 and 1712 Archer built two important garden buildings for the 1st Duke of Kent at Wrest Park, Bedfordshire, one of which, the domed Banqueting House *(Plate 219)*, still survives. Here the plan adopted is that of Borromini's S. Ivo della Sapienza, in Rome, which gives a hexagonal shape with round and square projections on alternate sides. The entrance is quite open with Ionic pilasters surmounted by a heavy pediment. The room inside the Banqueting House is quite large with a cupola bringing light flooding down.

Chettle House, Dorset *(Plate 220)*, is a house of Thomas Archer's maturity and it is without doubt an outstanding example of the English Baroque. Built for George Chafin, who held the post of Ranger of Cranborne Chase between 1710 and 1715, Chettle is of brick with Chilmark stone dressings and places weight again on a curved plan. The façade is seven bays wide to

219. The Banqueting House, Wrest Park, Bedfordshire

which must be added round-cornered end bays, two storeys high, but set on a high vaulted basement. In the centre the tall storey height rises even more dramatically through a further attic storey. There is a deep cornice and a balustrade above, while both facades are articulated by brick pilasters. Inside the greatest excitement is the two-storeyed entrance hall on the eastern side with a staircase in it.

220. Chettle House, Dorset

221. *Hales Hall, Cheadle, Staffordshire*

7.94 PROVINCIAL BAROQUE

Commonly met with in areas outside the stone belt, brick houses in the Baroque style made use of classical motifs with a complete assurance unrelated to Palladio, but with an understanding of the importance of symmetry. These houses were built by prosperous men who were not afraid to show their wealth, and they abound in detail with an emphasis on the centre. The sash windows with glazing bars thicker than those made towards the end of the century are tall and thin and occupy a large proportion of the wall area. The hipped roofs with dormers indicate the debt that they owe to Coleshill.

Hales Hall, Staffordshire *(Plate 221)*, was built in brick in 1712 in a rectangle on a basement with two storeys

above, the stone decoration around the door taking the form of restrained pillars surmounted by the owner's coat of arms supported by a curved pediment. Stone continues to the next floor breaking into floral decoration and scrolls. Elsewhere stone is used for window surrounds and keystones, a stringing line to divide the floors and, most curiously, the quoins which have been trimmed to ensure their recognition as pillars, acknowledged by the shaping of the eaves above them as a reference to capitals. The roof, with a heavy dentil cornice, is carefully symmetrical with a tidy group of four chimneys and the three dormers with well-pronounced curves. Even the rainwater down pipes with their dated heads are carefully balanced.

172

222. Cound Hall, Shropshire

Attention has already been drawn to the massive pilasters on the fronts of Cound Hall, near Shrewsbury. This rectangular house **(Plate 222)** has west and east façades that are almost identical, though the east has keystones and a small pediment. The windows, tall in relation to their width, are typical, as is the bold treatment of almost every feature except the main entrance which by comparison with everything else seems rather puny.

There is also something strange about the roof. Either the top storey has been added and there was originally a termination above the parapet, or some extra building has been demolished. The determination of the architect to produce something important is illustrated by the fact that

all the bricks are rubbed. Normally these were used only when a moulded design was to be incised into the brick, for instance, decoration around a door. The glazing bars on the left are original, the thinner ones to the right being late Georgian or perhaps Victorian. There is indeed a feeling of controlled opulence about this fine building reminiscent of the quality Queen Anne walnut with which it would originally have been furnished. At present Cound Hall is being most carefully restored for family occupation by the Renaissance Group, of London, and the most striking interior feature is the staircase, which must have been skilfully introduced into the entrance hall to preserve the wonderful space later on in the eighteenth century.

Finchcocks, near Goudhurst, Kent *(Plate 223)*, was built for Edward Bathurst between 1718 when he came into his inheritance and 1725, the date which appears on the rainwater heads. It is the most notable Baroque house in Kent and illustrates the time when the grand designs of Vanbrugh, Hawksmoor and Archer were being interpreted by provincial builders. Made of brick with more vigorously red dressings and darker chimneys and parapet, the house faces east and has a three-storeyed main block seven bays wide, with two-storeyed wings. The first view of the façade as the drive curves round is of a noble, tall front, which is further enhanced by the three central bays which break forward and are surmounted by a pediment filled with martial trophies. It is the pilasters that unite the façade, while the plain doorcase is Tuscan on half columns. The west front basically echoes the east, though without the pediment and the pilasters.

223. Finchcocks, Goudhurst, Kent

224. Encombe House, Dorset

Encombe House, near Corfe Castle, in Dorset **(Plate 224)**, shows what can be done by a follower of Vanbrugh who truly understands the principles of the Baroque. The architect of the house is unknown, although John Pitt succeeded to the estate in 1734 and had the reputation of being an amateur architect. The building is in a wonderful Purbeck ashlar and the south front, originally the entrance front, gives the impression of a spreading two-storeyed building set below sweeping high hills. The prominent cornice line and the string-courses emphasise the horizontal, which is broken only for the pedimented dormer in the centre. The architect has been able to control the spread of building by uniting the whole conception with the Tuscan Order which frames the central doorcases and those of the wings.

CHAPTER 8

1715-1760

8.0 INTRODUCTION

Dr Johnson said: 'A man who has not been to Italy is always conscious of an inferiority', and this could easily be the guiding philosophy in architecture and interior design in the first half of the eighteenth century. Since Elizabethan times English scholars and ambassadors had travelled abroad, but the Civil War in the middle of the seventeenth century had interrupted this flow of visitors to France and Italy and, by the time that the wealthy and the informed were again ready to travel, the wars with Louis XIV's France had placed a further impediment in their way. But with the British victories in the War of Spanish Succession, beginning with Blenheim in 1704, and the signing of the Treaty of Utrecht in 1715, the urge to travel returned. This time, however, in addition to those who travelled for their business or for their scholarly pursuits, the Grand Tour, as it became known, was seen as the acknowledged completion of an upper-class education and as a way of qualifying as a gentleman.

Typically lasting for about a year, though Thomas Coke, of Holkham, in Norfolk, was away for four and a half years from the age of fifteen, the journey would take in Paris, the south of France, Venice, Turin, Florence, Rome and Naples, and the traveller would probably return through Switzerland, perhaps visiting Berlin as James Boswell did, and then back to England through the Low Countries. The Grand Tourist would study architecture, especially among the classical remains in Rome, pictures and sculpture in the greatest Continental collections, often relieved by drinking and whoring. An English gentleman of the period spoke Latin with some degree of facility and was familiar with the Roman authors and their mythology, so it was inevitable that Italian architecture should excite the interest of the more discriminating. In any event a reaction away from the decorative excesses of Stuart architecture was inevitable and the restrained language of classicism provided a natural alternative.

But at the beginning of the eighteenth century the preferred style was not all that restrained. As we have seen, the Baroque version of classicism that produced Castle Howard and Blenheim Palace appealed to the late seventeenth century mind, but the latter years of Queen

Anne's reign and the accession of the German George I brought about political changes which created a new group of patrons. Power moved away from the Court, George I spoke no English and had little interest in the domestic politics of his new country, and power and the consequent wealth fell into the hands of the second generation of Whig landowners whose fathers had, thirty years before, supported the 1689 Protestant Settlement. They now dominated Parliament and their need was for peace in which trade could flourish and its fruits could be placed in the ownership and embellishment of landed estates. These Whigs were educated in the more restrained philosophy of writers like Addison and Steele in their essays in *The Spectator* and *The Tatler*, which were the best-sellers of the period.

The rich Englishman's heart was in his country estate, but the need to maintain political influence and to take care of the futures of his unmarried daughters meant that he should spend time in London, living for part of the year in classically decorated houses grouped in squares, terraces and crescents that began to be built in the 1720s and 1730s following the example set by Inigo Jones in Covent Garden. Further down the social scale the economical terraced houses, whether in squares or along main roads, became very popular in the building boom of the period between 1715 and 1730. This continued in a slightly less exuberant fashion in the 1730s and 1740s, but by then life was overshadowed by further war with France and by the realised nightmare of the Scottish Jacobite invasion.

The designs of the Venetian architect, Andrea Palladio (1508-1580), interpreting the wisdom of the Roman author, Vitruvius, in his *Four Books of Architecture* **(Plate 225)** were published for the first time in English in 1715, and from the early 1720s the strict rules of Palladianism took over at the top social level from the more ebullient Baroque as the acceptable form of classicism. Richard Boyle, 3rd Earl of Burlington **(Plate 226)**, was not only one of the wealthiest Whigs, he was singularly well placed in society, a Privy Councillor, Lord Treasurer of Ireland, Lord Lieutenant of both the East and West Ridings, and from 1730 he also held the Garter.

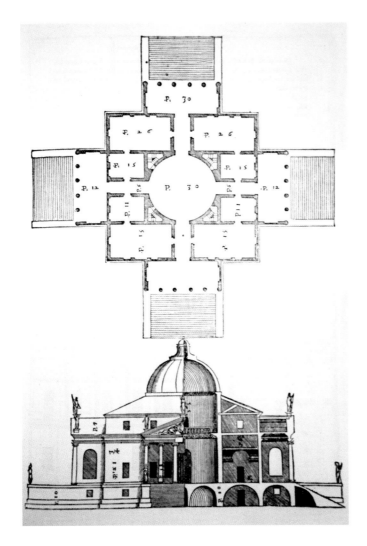

226. Lord Burlington and his bagnio by Jonathan Richardson

225. Drawing from Palladio's Four Books of Architecture *of the Villa Rotonda, Vicenza*

He and his group of friends, including William Kent, promoted Palladianism, a type of rather unadventurous Roman classicism, and from the 1720s to the late 1740s they took the role of arbiters of taste in the interpretation of the strict rules of proportion and decorative detail. By mid-century, however, research in southern Italy and the sponsorship of travel by connoisseurs from England by the Society of Dilettante had established that Roman classicism was merely a copy of the Greek, and that other and more relaxed standards of beauty existed. The effects of this neo-classicism and the work particularly of the Adam brothers will be discussed more fully in the next chapter.

But the victory of Palladianism over the Baroque only really occurred at the top level of society. The prosperous middle classes in the provinces had long accepted the need for symmetry, but were generally unimpressed by the need for the *piano nobile*, for which, of course, they had little use, though the small window in the pediment on the third floor seemed a good idea.

Consequently a typically English compromise emerged between the elegance of Coleshill and the unadventurous, almost sterile Palladianism. This was publicised by 'Do-it-Yourself' books published in the 1720s, of which James

Gibbs' *A Book of Architecture* of 1728 is perhaps the best known. He provides the client with simple methods of establishing a straightforward, functional classical design. The outcome to these happy eighteenth century relationships between client and master-mason are to be seen all over provincial England. In many ways they are the ideal English house and continue to be greatly admired today.

As we have seen, classical details had been used since the fifteenth century, but as individual elements of decoration and not as a comprehensive system. Only gradually did the idea of a coherent system take hold. John Evelyn, the mid-seventeenth century diarist, tells how his cousin took the advice of a friend about the building of an archway in his garden and got the classical details that he was striving for completely wrong. In the end he had either to knock the arch down or have it altered to avoid being teased by his friends. In the 1720s help came to hand to avoid situations like this with the publication of pattern books such as that by James Gibbs. Beautifully drawn plates with the correct ratios clearly shown helped generations of country gentlemen to build those apparently simple and gracious houses which are one of the glories of the English countryside.

177

227. *Biddesden House, Ludgershall, Wiltshire*

8.1 BAROQUE SURVIVALS

The progress of English architecture has been anything but steady and ordered, and this is strikingly apparent during the development of Palladianism. At the very moment when Vanbrugh's Blenheim was in the course of construction, the great churches of Queen Anne's reign were being designed by Hawksmoor and Wren's St Paul's was being finished, although the architect himself was by then very old, a group of philosophers and, in the main, amateur architects well connected socially were instituting a Rule of Taste which was to allow Palladian classicism to dominate English building for the following forty years. And yet it is worth remembering that there were political and social undertones to Palladianism, discussed earlier, which were not necessarily accepted by the generality of builders during the period, and their work shows how varied was the patchwork of structural styles that could be seen in the country between 1710 and 1720.

Biddesden House, near Ludgershall, in Wiltshire, was built in 1711-1712 by an unknown architect for General Webb **(Plate 227)**. That its designer must have been aware of the work of Vanbrugh, Hawksmoor and Archer is clear, but the brick house patterned in red and blue has its own distinct character. Symmetrically designed of seven bays by seven, it has a bold projection of three central bays on the south front. The house is of two storeys, with a half storey above the cornice, and there are three circular windows with keystones at each corner matched by three keystones on the round arch-headed windows on the first two floors. The central element of the south façade is a high entrance hall with a large segmental pediment above it. Unsurprisingly,

228. Brizlincote Hall, Derbyshire

bearing in mind the military career of the owner, there are trophies of arms in stone, but, more unexpectedly, there is also a round tower with castellations at the north-eastern corner which breaks the symmetry. This was built, so it is said, to accommodate a bell brought back by the general from Lille. Vanbrugh's Castle, on Greenwich Hill, comes to mind seeing Biddesden, but so does the much earlier castellated work by Hugh May at Windsor Castle.

Orgreave Hall, near Alrewas, Staffordshire, is a country version of an updated seventeenth century house. Probably built in 1668, Orgreave was a small building on an L plan enlarged in about 1720; of its contrasting north and south fronts, the latter is probably the earlier. The north front is quite naïve Baroque, of three storeys with a parapet that sweeps down in curves that brings it too close to the end windows, which are consequently dummies. The light-coloured quoins are only skin deep and may have been added in Victorian times to match the keystones over the windows. Contrasting with the rest of the façade, the doorcase has splendid Corinthian pilasters and an elegant pediment.

Brizlincote Hall, in south Derbyshire **(Plate 228)**, was built in about 1707 for the 2nd Earl of Chesterfield, although it is inscribed 1714. A brick house of two storeys over five bays, it also has a hipped roof and a pedimented doorway. What is remarkable, however, is the segmental pediment which traverses the entire front and is large enough to accommodate five windows, the outer ones being small and circular. The side elevations also have pediments, though not as large as that on the main front.

229. *14 Tooks Court, off Chancery Lane, London*

8.2 EARLY GEORGIAN TERRACES

The first wave of speculative building in London got under way in the economic stability which existed between 1715 and 1730 following the cessation of the French wars and as a result of the dominance of the Whig government. An example of this can be seen in Tooks Court *(Plate 229)*, north of Cursitor Lane, and close to Chancery Lane, in the City of London. Both No. 15 (Dickens' House) and No. 14 are early eighteenth century, each house consisting of three storeys and three bays with segmental window-heads of rubbed brick. The individual houses are framed with giant Ionic pilasters, also of rubbed brick, and are applied for decorative effect without regard to convention in a manner that is typical of the Baroque of the 1720s. Indeed the pilaster on the right has no base, the middle one no entablature, while the one on the left ends in mid-air. Although the discipline of strict classicism has been ignored, the pilasters have entasis (a swelling about a third of the way up to counteract visual distortion of the vertical), and the first-floor windows have the height

which suggests that the idea of the *piano nobile* is known. There is also rustication in the doorcase, all of which suggests that Palladio is in the offing.

It is also fair to say that the building work is high. The Ionic capitals and the cornice are made from specially moulded brick and are of a high quality, while the pilasters and voussoirs are of rubbed brick laid with fine joints. There is a fine sense of verticality both for effect and to make full use of a narrow prestige site, while the Building Acts of 1707 and 1709, which forbade the use of timber cornices and required that window casings be recessed, have been heeded.

8.3 THE PARAPET

The solid square fronts unrelieved by an indication of roof, with large symmetrically placed windows, are without the sense of movement required for the truly Baroque house. The large projecting cornice echoes the hard line of the parapet to add to the solid Englishness of the design. Relief comes from such details as quoins, keystones over the windows, a suggestion of pilasters and often a slight projecting forward of the centre section with some decoration around the doorcase.

No. 68 The Close, Salisbury, Wiltshire, is perhaps the most stately town house in the Close *(Plate 230)*. Built in 1718, it is ashlar faced, though it relapses into brick at the sides and the back. The front is of seven bays, with three breaking forward, and the structure consists of a basement, two storeys articulated by giant pilasters, an attic above a huge cornice and with a parapet on the attic. The decoration over the doorway is a segmental pediment supported by Corinthian columns.

Rainham Hall, Rainham, in Essex, is a splendid house with a parapet of about 1729, less ponderous, perhaps, than No 68 The Close, partly because of the segmental window-heads, and also because the cornice, though heavy, sits above the attic storey. The painted quoins also help the feeling of lightness, while the broken-segmental pediment is supported by pillars with Corinthian capitals.

Westbury House, Bradford-on-Avon, Wiltshire, is a fine house in this wonderful stone town *(Plate 231)*. Built perhaps in the early 1730s, the house has pilaster strips articulating the façade, broken by two string courses, segmental-headed windows on the ground floor and a balustrade at the top. It seems that the doorway was once replaced by one of a series of plate-glass windows, somewhat spoiling the look of this elegant house, but this has been restored. There is a general air of restraint, and it is noticeable that the windows in the middle storey are the largest. The influence of Palladianism is not far away.

230. 68 The Close, Salisbury, Wiltshire

231. Westbury House, Bradford-on-Avon, Wiltshire

8.4 PALLADIAN COUNTRY HOUSES

Writing of Colen Campbell's Wanstead House, the key building of its age, Sir John Summerson summed up the effect that Palladianism had on contemporary patrons: 'To us it may seem pompous and artificial, but to the Whig mind of the 1720s, it was a good expression of that moderation, that resistance to "fancy" and "enthusiasm", that balanced combination of the useful and the beautiful, of prosperity and good breeding, which was its ideal'. An ambitious Scots lawyer, Colen Campbell published *Vitruvius Britannicus* in parts, starting in 1715, as a vehicle to popularise, among the rich, the designs by Palladio and also himself as apostle of the work of Inigo Jones.

For the wealthy Whig landowners of the time, the book came just at the right moment and its tone was well judged in that it offered a respectful conspectus of English country houses which were considered as architecture.

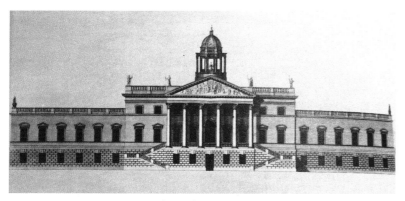

232. Drawing by Colen Campbell of his design for Wanstead House II, Essex

233. Engraving of Wanstead House, Essex

Moreover, Volume I gave considerable space to the work of Vanbrugh and also covered Talman's Chatsworth and other Office of Works' designers such as Hawksmoor and Archer. After this introduction, Campbell subtly introduced his own Wanstead **(Plates 232 and 233)**, then approaching completion for Sir Richard Child, and conveniently sited for visiting, on Wanstead Flats, to the east of London. It is ironic that this most influential house was demolished in 1822.

Wanstead, as built, looked back to Castle Howard, but there were three designs for the house, the first of which was a double-pile house with hall and saloon on the main axis and six inter-connecting rooms on either side. The second version, which was closest to the house as built, was nearer to Castle Howard than this with a more distinct central pavilion and a cupola over the hall, though this was never built. In the third design, Campbell added towers, which again were never built, but which brought its elevation close to that of Castle Howard, but here there was to be no cupola.

Wanstead was much admired in its day, and all three versions inspired buildings throughout the following thirty-five years. The first in 1733 was Wentworth Woodhouse, in Yorkshire, for Thomas Watson-Wentworth, later Lord Malton, and in the enormously long façade of 606ft. (185m) the central hospitality block is a close imitation of Wanstead II. Begun at almost the same time, Nostell Priory, also in Yorkshire, for Sir Rowland Winn, was inspired by Wanstead I, but the central pavilion was curtailed in size and kitchen, library, laundry and brewhouse were originally intended to be in separate pavilions joined to the central block by quadrant corridors. The main reason for the building of Prior Park, above Bath **(Plate 234)**, by John Wood the Elder in 1735, was to enable the owner, Ralph Allen, to demonstrate the superiority of his Bath stone over Portland, but, again, the inspiration for the design was Wanstead I.

As if the inspiration that Wanstead offered to others was not enough, Campbell also designed Houghton Hall, in Norfolk **(Plate 235)**, for Sir Robert Walpole from 1722. In Volume II of *Vitruvius Britannicus* a design was dedicated to Sir Robert in which the designer sought 'to introduce the Temple Beauties in a private Building', underlining the quasi-sacred nature of the portico in Palladian design in England. For Houghton, Campbell took seventeenth century models, corner towers instead of wings as at Belton, and linked them to Inigo Jones'

234. Prior Park, Bath, Somerset

towers at Wilton, including the pediments above the attic. The elevation of Houghton can be seen as a smaller version of Wanstead, and the towers are also a version of Wanstead III, but the design is worked out in Jonesian terms, with the Stone Hall being a 40ft. (12m) cube, the same dimension as the Queen's House at Greenwich, but 10ft. (3m) more than at Wanstead. Palladio's Palazzo Thiene, in Vicenza, also inspired the rustication to the Venetian windows at Houghton, a device which was to be very popular in the middle of the century

Houghton was not built fully to the designs that Colen Campbell devised for it, the most obvious difference being the substitution by James Gibbs after Campbell's death of the domes for the high attics. Internally, the arrangement of the main hospitality floor has the Saloon on an axis with the Hall, while the corner towers were used as the centres of four apartments, where the main rooms were the Parlour, two Drawing Rooms and a Dining Room. Houghton became the standard type of house in the 1740s and 1750s, one of the notable followers being Hagley Hall, in Worcestershire, by Sanderson Miller for Lord Lyttelton (1751).

235. West front of Houghton Hall, Norfolk

236. Mereworth Castle, Kent

shade from the harsh sun, reduce the wall space for windows, so much a feature of villas in this country, while chimneys, which have no place in the warmth of Italy, are in the case of Mereworth hidden between the inner and the outer skins of the dome. The consequential lack of glass in the dome gives a severe appearance to the design which is further compromised by the dominance of the Ionic porticoes. The overall impression is given of an academic exercise in design.

Stourhead was built for Henry Hoare, second son of the banker and interestingly brother-in-law of William Benson, who was instrumental in promoting the Inigo Jones revival. Having bought the manor of Stourton in 1720, Henry Hoare immediately purchased Colen Campbell's books and both the 1721 façade and the internal layout follow these designs. The most striking feature of the façade as designed is its compactness. This is achieved by the rustication at ground level and the balustrade at the main roof-line, together with the portico's four columns rather than the six at Mereworth. Inside, Campbell's plan had a Chapel on an axis with the Entrance Hall, the whole being within an 80ft. (24m) cube. Several changes were made to the east front of Stourhead after it was built by Nathaniel Ireson: an attic was built above the portico while, in 1792, Colt Hoare tripled the length of the façade by adding a Library and a Picture Gallery on either side of the main block in a restrained neo-classical style. Then, in 1902, a serious fire destroyed the central part of the house and, although rebuilt largely in replica, the house was lengthened to the

But neither Houghton nor Hagley can be called Palladian villas in the same sense as Mereworth, in Kent (1723), or Stourhead, in Wiltshire (1726). In the case of the first *(Plate 236)*, Palladio's Villa Rotonda, above Vicenza (see Plate 225), was the precedent for the design for Col. Fane, while the second *(Plate 237)* derives from the villa Palladio designed for Leonardo Emo at Fanzolo. Col. Fane's use of Mereworth was always intended to be occasional and, while noble, the design illustrates several problems inherent in translating Italian forms to the English countryside. The porticos, which in Italy offer

237. Stourhead, Wiltshire

238. *Entrance façade of Chiswick House, London*

west to accommodate an enlarged Saloon in the position of the original Chapel.

Between 1715 and 1724 Colen Campbell established the style on which English Palladianism was based. But the work of two of his successors – Lord Burlington, and his protégé, William Kent – was to enrich Campbell's style and create a distinctively English version of Palladianism. At the age of twenty-one Burlington took on heavy political responsibilities, but they did not prevent him from undertaking a first Grand Tour from 1714 to 1715, during which time he was fired with an enthusiasm for the practice of architecture. After engaging Campbell to continue the remodelling of Burlington House, his London residence, Burlington left on a second Grand Tour in 1719 with the express intention of studying the work of Palladio.

During the 1720s Burlington undertook a number of building projects, including, from 1725, a villa at Chiswick *(Plate 238)*, which consisted of a series of State Rooms for hospitality and display, attached by a lower link building to the Jacobean family home, now demolished. Although the inspiration for this villa is clearly Palladio's Villa Rotonda, on the outskirts of Vicenza, it is smaller, and just as clearly Burlington's own aesthetic statement in building. Fashioned as a jewel box for displaying his Grand Tour purchases, with sculpture and paintings on the *piano nobile* and books and architectural plans below in the rustic, Chiswick House has a number of external features which set it apart both from its Italian prototype and from the work of Colen Campbell in this country. There is only one portico, and

the rusticated stone is confined to the area immediately below the columns and their balustrade, while the drum and dome rise directly from the sloping roof and have unusual, divided semicircular windows.

On the garden front, the fenestration is remarkable, consisting as it does of three Venetian-style windows with solid relieving arches that describe the same semi-circles as the recessed openings that surround them *(Plate 239)*. The design comes directly from Palladio's own *Four Books of Architecture* which Burlington had bought in Italy, and both he and William Kent were to use the device in later projects. Internally, Burlington has set a series of inter-

239. *Chiswick House: the garden front*

240. *Marble Hill House, Twickenham, London*

connecting rooms around a central Octagon, but behind the central window on the garden side is the Gallery, the form of which was to be just as influential. At each end the doorways are set in apses with coffered half-domes decorated with geometrical patterns, while statues in niches frame the entries to the circular rooms at either end of the Gallery. The effect is both rich and harmonious, as much in the manner of Inigo Jones as of Palladio.

Making a contrast with Chiswick House is the exquisite Marble Hill House *(Plate 240)*, at Twickenham, in London, built between 1724 and 1729 for Henrietta Howard, later Countess of Suffolk, and mistress of George II. The designer was Roger Morris, the style distinctively Palladian. Indeed, several members of the group surrounding Lord Burlington were probably involved with Marble Hill, including Lord Herbert, later the 9th Earl of Pembroke, and Colen Campbell, as a drawing attributed to him, now at Wilton House, shows Marble Hill with low pavilions omitted when building was undertaken. There is also a drawing of the house in *Vitruvius Britannicus*, which shows a fine double staircase, also omitted during construction.

The resulting villa is very chaste and depends for its effect on the harmony between the unadorned stucco with stone dressings of the exterior and the window openings. A three-bay centre projects forward on both north and south sides, with a pediment and cartouche, and further emphasis is given to the north by giant Ionic pilasters over a rusticated basement. Other than that the exterior decoration is confined to the simplest of mouldings and plain horizontal stone bands. The inspiration for Marble Hill is, of course, Inigo Jones' Queen's House, at Greenwich, but the design was to be influential on the villas built in the 1750s and after. Inside the house there is a low entrance hall on one side, typical of Palladian design, and staircases on the other leading up to the Great Room on the *piano nobile*, which is a 24ft. (7.3m) cube extending up into the attic level. This lovely white and gold room looks back to the Single Cube Room at Wilton House for its inspiration. The walls are divided into three with central pedimented doorcases and chimneypiece, flanked by picture frames which originally had copies of Van Dyck paintings in the Wilton manner, and above a decorated architrave and a plain coved ceiling.

During the late 1720s, doubtless under the influence of Lord Burlington, William Kent became the complete architect. He had started as a painter, but, at his patron's

241. *The garden front of Holkham Hall, Norfolk*

request, had undertaken the editing of the *Designs of Inigo Jones* and many of his subsequent interior designs owe much to Jones' work. Kent's most personal architectural work is undoubtedly Holkham Hall, in Norfolk **(Plate 241)**, but even here the references to earlier work are apparent. The plan with a central suite of hospitality rooms joined to four pavilions by straight passages is derived from Palladio's unbuilt Villa Mocenigo, while the main block is based on Campbell's Houghton Hall and the Venetian windows come from Chiswick.

The entrance hall to Holkham **(Plate 242)** is one of the great monuments of English eighteenth century architecture. Inspired by a Roman basilica, the Hall is flanked by fluted alabaster columns and, at the entry to the Saloon, the visitor mounts a flight of stairs and passes through an apse richly surmounted by a coffered half-dome. The effect is that of dramatic display, but perhaps this is appropriate as Holkham contains Thomas Coke's collection of Roman antiquities, which even today is the most important remaining in private hands.

242. *Holkham Hall: the entrance hall*

While not as grand as the Palladian houses discussed so far, Thornhill House *(Plate 243)* is the work of an artist who was very much aware of the latest trends in design. Although William Hogarth continually bemoaned the lowly status of the artist in early Georgian times, his father-in-law, Sir James Thornhill, who built the house, was no ordinary journeyman, as he became Sergeant Painter to the King, was given a knighthood and made a fortune large enough to enable him to buy back his ancestral estates in Dorset in 1725 and to build himself a substantial country house. The north entrance front acknowledges its debt to Palladianism with a three-bay centre brought forward, framed by a bay on each side and surmounted by a triangular pediment. This is reinforced with stone quoins set into rendered walls, a hipped roof and dormers, and a version of a Venetian window. The overall effect of the villa is charming, but shows how even the best informed observer could create an idiosyncratic building by following a style which was being evolved by a small group of like-minded men.

Hatch Court, at Hatch Beauchamp, Somerset, is also a lesser known country house built in the mid-century in the Palladian style *(Plate 244)*. It was designed by Thomas Prowse, of Axbridge, a friend of the amateur architect Sanderson Miller, and it is not surprising, therefore, to see the four square pavilions at the corners, as they recall the latter's Hagley Hall, in Worcestershire. There are canted bays on the east and west fronts, but the south front has an arcade of five arches and the whole design is topped by a balustrade.

243. Thornhill House, Thornhill, Dorset

244. Hatch Court, Hatch Beauchamp, Somerset

245. Glenthorne, High Street, Burford, Oxfordshire

8.5 PALLADIAN TOWN HOUSES

The proportions of the Palladian style make particularly satisfactory town houses. The High Street in Burford, Oxfordshire, boasts a number of such buildings and the effect is both elegant and grand. Glenthorne *(Plate 245)*, on the west side of the steep street leading down to the Windrush, has a front which consists of five bays and was most probably built by Christopher Kempster in about 1700. Quoins and a balustrade articulate the shape of the house, the central window on the first floor is blocked and on each side of the main door the windows are grouped in pairs. Englefield *(Plate 246)* is also formally Georgian, with a façade of three bays and three storeys. The doorway has an especially lovely fanlight and a hood with brackets. Lower down the High Street, where the shops take over from the purely residential buildings, is No. 115, a sixteenth century house refronted in about 1720 for a mercer named Richard Whitehall. Here the top of the façade has a straight parapet with a

247. *The Old Rectory, Priory Lane, Burford, Oxfordshire*

moulded cornice, while below the *piano nobile* has five tall windows, and on the ground floor two bay windows date from the end of the Georgian period. Another pleasing feature of the time is the long window giving light to the staircase.

The Old Bull Hotel dates originally from the sixteenth century, but was most probably refaced in brick in about 1715 by the innkeeper of the time, William Tash. Some of the details are quite Baroque, which should not surprise us as Burford is a long way to the west, but there are also keystone windows, brick quoins, stone pilasters and a panelled parapet. At the bottom of the High Street Priory Lane leads off to the west and on the north side is the Old Rectory *(Plate 247)* of about 1700. This is one of the most sophisticated stone houses of its date in Oxfordshire and must surely have been by one of Wren's masons, most probably Christopher Kempster. The ashlar façade is of five simple bays with chamfered quoins and a hipped roof and the windows are grouped so as to emphasise the pedimented doorway at the centre. Today it is the Guest House of the nearby convent.

246. *Englefield House, High Street, Burford, Oxfordshire*

248. *The Great House, Witney Street, Burford, Oxfordshire*

By contrast to most of Burford's early Georgian façades, the Great House *(Plate 248)*, in Witney Street, a continuation of Church Lane, is like a grand Italian palazzo. The date is about 1700, the overall impression classical, but there are eccentricities. Formerly an inn, the Great House was altered and enlarged by John Castle, a physician. The front is of seven bays with chamfered quoins and pedimented doorway. Above, the *piano nobile* windows have alternatively triangular and segmental pediments, and round and octagonal windows in rectangular frames, while, curiously, the parapet is castellated and so are the chimney-pots, perhaps, as Sir Nikolaus Pevsner has suggested, a reference to the name of the builder.

Chipping Campden, in Gloucestershire, possesses a similar harmony in its High Street buildings. The two-storeyed Seymour House *(Plate 249)* dates from the early eighteenth century; its façade consists of seven bays and the doorway is flanked by fluted Tuscan columns. Clifton House, which has an inscribed date of 1717, is embellished by Ionic pilasters and a modillion eaves cornice. Dover's House *(Plate 250)* is a house of great elegance and sophistication. Two storeys high and consisting of five bays on to High Street, it also has a cornice and parapet, with alternate quoins of different lengths, while the garden elevations have attractive Venetian windows.

249. Seymour House, Chipping Campden, Gloucestershire

250. Dover's House, Chipping Campden, Gloucestershire

251. The Courts, Holt, Wiltshire

Situated in the centre of the small village of Holt, in Wiltshire, is The Courts *(Plate 251)*, the beautiful gardens of which are opened by the National Trust. The early eighteenth century façade of this house is of five bays, with, on the ground floor, open triangular pediments, followed by a more sinuous one, a niche and the doorway pediment; then the same elements are repeated in reverse. This remarkable sequence is repeated on the first floor, the overall impression of this design being to employ as many elements of early Georgian design as possible.

To the west of Bradford-on-Avon, Wiltshire, on the Winsley Road, stands Belcombe Court *(Plate 252)*. Really this is a house that ought to be found in or near Bath, in Somerset, as this part of the house was designed by John Wood the Elder in 1734 in a severe Palladian style. The wing that John Wood added to an older house for Francis Yerbury, a clothier of the town, has plain pilasters topped by Ionic capitals carrying a large pediment, while the ground-floor windows also have pediments and are framed with narrow pilasters.

On the outskirts of Market Drayton, in Shropshire, is Buntingsdale *(Plate 253)*, a fine classical house of 1720-1730. There are similarities in its design both to Kinlet and Mawley Hall, also in Shropshire, and on this basis it seems likely that Buntingsdale is by Francis Smith of Warwick. The structure is of brick with extensive stone dressings, and the two main façades – west and east – are similar but not identical. The original house was of nine bays, although extended northwards in 1860, and comprised a basement, two main floors and an attic storey above an architrave. The most striking elements of the early eighteenth century design are the giant pilasters with beautifully carved capitals. On the entrance (eastern) side of the house the pilasters are fluted where they articulate the edges of the building, that is bays one and nine, and the three-bay centre. The other pilasters are plain, however. The main windows, including those on either side of the door, have segmental tops, and smaller fluted pilasters framing the door lead up to a broken segmental pediment. The heavy cornice above the upper main floor is broken to allow the central three bays to go up to a triangular pediment which breaks the roof-level balustrade.

The entrance hall was clearly intended to offer a space large enough to entertain the tenantry and it runs through the two main storeys with a gallery on the west with a wooden balustrade which curves up charmingly at the centre, a feature of Smith's style. On the garden (western) side the three-bay centre projects forward. Requisitioned during the Second World War, the house returned to the family in a poor state, but since that time has been carefully and lovingly restored.

194

252. Belcombe Court, Bradford-on-Avon, Wiltshire

253. Buntingsdale, Market Drayton, Shropshire

8.6 DECORATED SMALLER HOUSES

It is in the provincial areas far from the influence of London and the Court that the distinction between the Baroque and Palladianism, so beloved of art historians, becomes most blurred. Both are classical, the Baroque deriving from late Renaissance Mannerism, while the Palladian comes specifically from the work of the sixteenth century Italian designer, Andrea Palladio, considered by its English exponents to be purer than the Baroque, but ironically rather later in the Renaissance than Mannerism. But, in this country, it is the density of decoration on a façade and the subtlety of cultural differences between owners and their designers that most clearly distinguish the two styles. We say that the Baroque is more theatrical and exuberant, and indeed it often is, but this tends to restrict the influence of the style, when the reality of the development of Palladianism was that it sprang from every aspect of cultural and social life, but of a very limited number of people closely associated with the Court.

In the more rural areas the Baroque lived on well into the middle of the eighteenth century and beyond. The two houses described in this section are, perhaps the more extreme examples of Baroque decoration of the smaller house, and it is interesting to see how often the roof-line is the dominant feature. Many houses will have just one or two touches of what is seen here in profusion, a density of decoration which can seem to be too much and which goes some way towards explaining the success of Palladian restraint.

Sherman's **(Plate 254)** stands in the High Street of Dedham, in Essex, and was built in about 1730, most likely by the same masons who built the Grammar School. But here in a very restricted space are pilasters, pediments, a niche, segmental window-heads, corbels, decorated capitals of no recognisable pattern, a heavy cornice stepped forward and with dentil moulding, inset brick panels and keystones. It is all very lively but restless.

Swanton Street Farm, near to Bredgar, Kent, was built in 1719 for a retired London silversmith, Edward Holliday, and it is an exuberant display of the bricklayer's craft on the front of a building that was at the time little more than a cottage. The strong line of the heavily curved cornice that sweeps up to gain an extra storey in the centre is a strong Baroque element, while the labels below the windows and the exaggerated key blocks above confirm the pedigree of the design. Everything is emphasised, but there is none the less a subtlety about the brickwork which carries off the design and leaves one enthusing.

254. Sherman's, High Street, Dedham, Essex

8.7 USING THE CLASSICAL ORDERS

It was important in classical building to get the proportions right, and Palladio's *The Four Books of Architecture* spelled out the formulae. The elements that made up columnar or trabeated architecture included a column, usually but not always with a base, a capital and an entablature, decorated post-and-lintel construction, in fact. Before the development of neoclassical architecture in the second half of the eighteenth century, the canonical five Roman Orders – Tuscan, Doric, Ionic, Corinthian and Composite – were accepted and these were described by Palladio in his *Four Books* (**Plate 255**). But it was not acceptable to 'mix and match' a column with any capital and entablature and the ratios, shapes and sizes for every Order, and even the spaces between columns, were laid down, the aim being to produce a building of beauty.

Beauty derived from mathematical proportions and this was accepted as uncritically as late twentieth century tabloid newspapers defined female desirability. Moreover, to Palladio and also to his followers in the seventeenth and eighteenth centuries in England, 'harmonic proportions' was more than just a turn of phrase. It was thought to be Pythagoras who first pointed out that if two strings are plucked the difference in pitch will be an octave if one is half the length of the other, a fifth if one is two-thirds the length of the other, and a fourth if the relationship is 3:4. From this flowed the notion that both structures and the spaces they contained were visually harmonious, if they followed the ratios 1:2, 2:3, or 3:4. Even during the Middle Ages such a sense of proportion was acknowledged and Palladio himself wrote: 'Such harmonies usually please very much without anyone knowing why, apart from those who study their causes'. It is also clear from a study of *The Four Books* that Palladio even favoured subtler relationships, as he marked measurements for his villas to be major and minor thirds, 5:6 and 4:5. It is also worth pointing out that to the sixteenth century mind the laws of harmony related aspects of life on earth to a heavenly ideal and references can be found to this effect in Shakespeare's plays.

There was, therefore, great scope for mistakes in designing classical buildings, and consequent ridicule, hence the willingness to involve one's contemporaries in architectural discussions and to obtain the advice of one's superiors. That said, even some of the purest Palladian buildings show touches of the Baroque in the overall design. Comments to this effect have already been made about Chiswick House, while the dome of Mereworth Castle, in Kent (see Plate 236), when seen in isolation, looks Baroque, and is not as flat as its model in *The Four Books*.

255. A Composite Capital: drawing by Palladio from his Four Books of Architecture

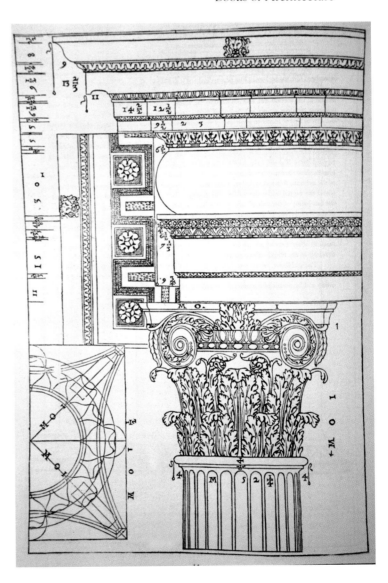

256. Huthwaite Hall, Thurgoland, Yorkshire

8.8 GABLE-END HOUSES

There are hundreds of these symmetrical, sash-windowed houses to be seen all over the country, though the bulk are to be found in the Midlands and in southern England. They are universally known as Georgian and have a quiet dignity and good planning that makes them almost the ideal for modern living. Built most usually by local masons in the stone or brick of the area, the construction of these buildings was watched over by educated owners who had read Gibbs or one of his contemporaries who appreciated the principles of symmetry and how to achieve it with a compass and pencil. They retained the traditional rectangular plan, though where a large house was needed they were happy to use the double-pile plan of two parallel rectangles side by side (see page 142). Also traditional was the retention of the gable ends rather than the hipped roof. Chimneys usually went into the gables to leave room for a substantial entrance hall that offered a grand reception area out of which an elegant staircase would lead to the first floor. These houses represent the middle-class English synthesis of the classical and the vernacular, which had its roots in the gothic.

Two contrasting examples might be given. Huthwaite Hall, at Thurgoland, in south Yorkshire (**Plate 256**), was most probably designed by John Carr of York and dates from 1748. Its façade is of five bays and of two storeys and a basement, and it has a pedimented doorway with a window above. The overall appearance is elegant and simple. Eagle House, in Blandford Forum, Dorset (**Plate 257**), also stands free but is in the town centre. Dating from the 1730s, it also has a façade of five bays but is made of blue brick with stone dressings and alternate bays have angled pilasters.

257. Eagle House, Blandford Forum, Dorset

8.9 TEMPLE-FRONT TERRACES

It has already been noted that the development of terraces and squares in London had its origin in Covent Garden and in Lincoln's Inn Fields, but it seems unlikely that architectural uniformity was achieved at least on one side of a square until the east range of Grosvenor Square was developed between 1725 and 1735 by a single speculator, John Simmonds. Now demolished, this consisted of seven houses, the central one of which was larger, given some rustication and columns, and crowned by a triangular pediment, while the two end houses were similar to the rest but given some extra prominence.

An even more daring scheme for the north side of the square was undertaken by Edward Shepherd and, although several owners refused to fall in with his plan, and what was built was not even symmetrical, the whole block was intended to have the appearance of a Palladian country house such as Wanstead. As the engraving of a drawing by Thomas Malton shows **(Plate 258)**, Shepherd rusticated the ground floor and set on it at the centre a portico of six engaged Corinthian columns to create the appearance of a temple front, following the precedent that had been set by Dean Aldrich in Peckwater Quad at Christ Church, Oxford, dating from 1707-1714. A major step forward had been taken in the growth of street architecture.

Two houses in Bloomsbury Way, in London, alas now demolished, showed how the Palladian influence of the 1740s could be interpreted in an urban terrace. If the sizes of the windows are smaller than in previous styles, one must remember that space was left for the 'implied pilasters'. These would rise from the stringing course above the first floor to the stone cornice. Considered in this light, the wider gaps between the windows and the pilaster size seem to achieve a better balance. As one would expect, the

259. 154-158 Kennington Road, Lambeth, London

long windows on the first floor imply the *piano nobile* and the square windows of the chamber floor below the parapet are all in keeping with the Palladian rules intended originally for substantial country houses.

The slightly projecting three-bay centre is also strongly Palladian. The modest door, with its Doric columns and pediment, side windows with blocked voussoirs, is also typical. Above, there is a form of Venetian window (which, incidentally, is divided by more than 18in. (45.7cm) and therefore counted as three windows for Window Tax purposes) and also a half-circle window which is a pattern taken from the Diocletian Temple of the Winds, the whole design being surmounted by a dentil cornice with *sima recta* moulding.

Above the cornice and parapet we do not find the small windows which would have made up the full Palladian dress, but pedimented dormers rising from a mansard roof. Perhaps these were added later. The building has now been demolished, unfortunately, to make way for some new offices, but we have included a description of it here to give an idea of one of the best examples of a Palladian terrace development.

There are many examples of town houses built in identical blocks during a slightly later period and their differences are largely determined by the means available to prospective purchasers. One typical development much admired today is Davidge Terrace, 154-158 Kennington Road, Lambeth, in London, which dates from about 1775 **(Plate 259)**. Each house is three bays wide and consists of three main storeys over half-basements. The development, as might be expected in this location, is of brick, and the basements are stuccoed, the doorcases classically simple and effective, while the window heads are of stone. The lack of a balustrade at the roof-line is, perhaps, especially striking, but the whole development is elegant and flexible.

258. *Engraving of Grosvenor Square, London, by Thomas Malton*

262. Houses in The Circus, Bath

8.91 CRESCENTS AND CIRCUSES

After about 1730 when Shepherd's development in Grosvenor Square was largely completed, the focus of the story moves to Bath and to the work of John Wood the Elder. The small wool town of Bath underwent great growth in the eighteenth century when the Court and the haut-monde associated with it moved to the Somerset town during the summer to take its famous waters. Building in the Palladian style had already started in the Abbey Churchyard in the 1720s, and one of the earliest houses still survives – General Wade's house **(Plate 260)**. By 1725 the building pressures had increased; the social attractions of the Assembly Rooms under the Master of Ceremonies, 'Beau' Nash, were growing, and the entrepreneur Ralph Allen was seeking to promote the qualities of the local stone from his quarries.

John Wood the Elder came to Bath to live and work in 1727 through the agency of Lord Bingley, of Bramham Hall, in Yorkshire, and Lord Chandos, for whom he did some work both in Cavendish Square, London, and subsequently in Bath. While still in Yorkshire, however, Wood made proposals to two owners of land near to the centre of Bath and one of them, Robert Gay, engaged him as his agent. Consequently, John Wood found himself not only the architect of what is today Queen Square in Bath, but also the main leaseholder of the houses he built as well. With his experience in London it is, perhaps, not surprising that the north side of Queen Square (1729 onwards) displays many of the characteristics of Grosvenor and Cavendish Squares **(Plate 261)**. The ground floors of the houses are rusticated, the *piano nobile* windows have alternately triangular and segmental heads, there is a strong upper cornice line broken by the central five bays which project forward, have engaged columns standing on the rustication, and are surmounted by a triangular pediment. This is surely the fulfilment of Edward Shepherd's conception in Grosvenor Square.

But this was only the beginning of John Wood's achievements. He had read widely and, knowing of Bath's Roman history even if not of the Roman Baths, conceived the plan for a series of Roman monuments, including a Circus, a Forum, only part of which was ever built at South Parade, and even an Imperial Gymnasium. The Circus **(Plate 262)**, which Wood soon altered to become three blocks of identical town houses treated in a unified way rather than a circular space for 'the exhibition of sports', was a great success, although not without its eighteenth century critics. Its design origins have produced many

260. *General Wade's House, Abbey Churchyard, Bath*

261. *North side of Queen Square, Bath*

263. House on the west side of Gay Street, Bath

theories, some of them rather outlandish, but the façades of the houses obey to a large extent the Palladian rules, while the rond-point of the Circus is approached up the first planned road of the estate – Gay Street *(Plate 263)* – and short extensions lead to the Assembly Rooms on the east and along Brock Street to the Royal Crescent on the west.

Both the Assembly Rooms and the Royal Crescent *(Plate 264)* were built by John Wood's son and namesake, John Wood the Younger, between 1767 and 1775. This great sweep of thirty houses, built on an elliptical pattern following, more or less, the plan of half of the Colosseum in Rome, was to have a profound effect on urban design in this country well into the nineteenth century. The façades are simpler and grander than his

father's work in the Circus. Giant Ionic engaged columns are raised on a high base, while above a heavy cornice line is surmounted by a balustrade behind which an attic storey lurks. With its splendid elevated views over Bath and the valley of the Avon, it is surely one of the pinnacles of eighteenth century town planning.

Although the Circus has not been much copied, the Crescent has had an influential career. Its most immediate progeny was The Crescent at Buxton *(Plate 265)*, in Derbyshire, by John Carr of York, in 1779, though Carr introduced an arcade at ground level which was reminiscent of Inigo Jones at Covent Garden. The Crescent also reached the seaside with the Royal Crescent in Brighton, in 1798.

264. The Royal Crescent, Bath

265. St Anne's Terrace, The Crescent, Buxton, Derbyshire

266. Sudbrook Park, Petersham, Surrey

8.92 GIBBS' COMPROMISE

'As outwardly every man carries himself gravely in public places, yet inwardly has imagination and fire…so the outward ornament is to be solid, proportionable according to the rule, masculine and unaffected'. James Gibbs designed for the prosperous Tory countryman who wanted neither the strict and restrained Palladianism of Burlington and the Whigs, nor the dramatic theatre of Vanbrugh; rather what was wanted was a touch of new style, perhaps, but leavened with traditions in which he could feel comfortable.

The most important thing about Gibbs was that he was a Catholic and, as a Scot who could readily be accused of Jacobitism, for understandable reasons he remained a covert one. Born in 1682, Gibbs was older than most of the architects of the early eighteenth century, even William Kent, and in 1703 he went to Holland and, following a Grand Tour route, visited France, Switzerland and Germany before arriving in Rome. He soon decided against the priesthood and a career as a painter, and entered the studio of Carlo Fontana, studying architecture with this distinguished and elderly man until 1709, the date when Kent was only just setting out on his Grand Tour.

Although initially on his return to London he made an Italian mannerist contribution to the architectural scene with St Mary-le-Strand, the accession of George I and the beginning of the Whig ascendancy made it an inopportune time to flaunt his Roman tendencies. But neither did Gibbs become a wholehearted Whig, preferring the personal style of Wren as it had been expressed in the Library of Trinity College, Cambridge. The traditionalist in Gibbs can be seen in the round-headed windows and those with architraves and keystones, which came from Inigo Jones, and corner and central elements in a façade breaking forward, a device which, as we have seen, was employed by Sir Roger Pratt at Coleshill, Berkshire, and at Kingston Lacy, in Dorset.

Although he was a Tory, whose Surveyorship to the Church-building Commission was rescinded by the Whigs, James Gibbs did not design exclusively for Tory landowners and his client at Sudbrook Park, Petersham, Surrey, was the Duke of Argyll and Greenwich. Built in 1726, the house *(Plate 266)* is of nine bays and made of brick with stone dressings. Consisting of a *piano nobile* and upper floor, the building sits on a half-basement and all three sets of windows have round-heads and aprons below, while there are brick quoins and a parapet. Dominating both the entrance and the garden façade are giant porticoes of Corinthian columns surmounted by friezes and balustrades. Today Sudbrook Park is the club house of the Richmond Golf Club.

At Ditchley Park, Oxfordshire, the Gibbsian manner can be seen at its most mature *(Plates 267 and 268)*. It was built between 1720 and 1722 for the 2nd Earl of

267. Ditchley Park, Oxfordshire

Litchfield, and although the two pavilions with their cupolas on the entrance front joined to the main hospitality block by quadrant corridors are at first blush Palladian, there are a number of differences. The doorway and the quoins are all rusticated, all the windows have architraves and keystones, while the rooms do not obey the proportional rules that Palladio laid down in his *Four Books of Architecture*. Perhaps the design of the quadrant corridors looks back to William Winde's Buckingham House rather than to Palladio, while the example that Gibbs turned to in allowing the pavilions at either corner of the façade to project further forward than the three-bay centre is surely Clarendon House, in Piccadilly, again the work of Sir Roger Pratt.

The Palladian characteristics continue inside the house in the main hospitality rooms, although, typically of William Kent, they are touched with his Baroque flourishes. The written records reveal only that he was paid for the two paintings from mythology which flank the entry to the Saloon in the Great Hall, but the design of the doorcases, chimneypiece and the furnishings all have his stamp, and it seems likely that his was the creative mind behind the decoration. Further, the form of the principal doorway recalls that of Houghton Hall, in Norfolk, where Kent worked from 1727 immediately after he left Ditchley, and also looks back to the work of

268. The Great Hall of Ditchley Park

269. The Fellows' Building, King's College, Cambridge

Inigo Jones, whose designs Kent was at the time publishing for Lord Burlington.

Gibbs does not seem to have been involved in decorating Ditchley, but he must have recommended the team who had been responsible for Canons, at Edgware, and the Italian stuccatori, Vassali, Artari and Serena, achieved wonders both in the Great Hall and in the Saloon, where they were given much more freedom of expression, and the result is truly poetic and quite

Rococo. Ditchley Park played a significant political and social role in the twentieth century when it was the home of Ronald Tree and his wife, Nancy, who undertook its restoration, and today it is owned and operated by a trust which promotes Anglo-American understanding and co-operation.

In comparison with his masterwork, St Martin-in-the-Fields, James Gibbs' domestic work may seem quite restrained, but the Fellows' Building at King's College,

270. Normanton Prebend, Southwell, Nottinghamshire

Cambridge (1724-1730), is both simple in its conception and monumental in its execution *(Plate 269)*. With its rusticated ground floor and roof-line balustrade, this rectangular block seems conventional enough, but it is no exaggeration to say that one's breath is taken away by the manner in which the central passage is framed by a Doric arch while, above, a great semicircular window has two stone mullions, the whole being set below a triangular pediment where the central element of the façade breaks forward. It is, indeed, a bold piece of design.

In spite of his conservatism, James Gibbs' influence has been considerable and this is undoubtedly due to his publication in 1728 of *A Book of Architecture*, which included most of his buildings up to that date and a notable series of designs which have their origins in French and Italian, as well as English, sources. The book acted, of course, as an advertisement for Gibbs as well as providing the six hundred gentlemen subscribers, and one carpenter who also subscribed, with elegant patterns which could be constructed by any competent mason, and also showed how, with a simple compass, one could arrive at the correct Palladian proportions, assuming that you wanted to do so!

It might well be that Gibbs' book acted as an exemplar for the designer who constructed the Normanton Prebend, at Southwell, Nottinghamshire *(Plate 270)*. The house stands serenely on Church Street, in the surroundings of the Minster, five bays wide and three storeys high with keystones over the windows. The date is about 1765 and the entrance door has a well-proportioned porch with flanking Doric columns.

207

271. Somerset House, Rawson Street, Halifax, Yorkshire

8.93 MERCHANTS' HOUSES WITH WAREHOUSES

Like other prosperous houses, merchant properties were often set back from the street building line and had their best accommodation on the first floor. They were flanked by two lower ranges or symmetrical wings placed at right angles to the main block. These could be connected or separate, but the architectural unity of the whole group was emphasised by the use of common features, such as quoins or cornices. One wing might be provided with fireplaces and used as offices or perhaps as additional domestic quarters.

As the eighteenth century progressed, the prosperous merchant, or his family, became anxious to move up the social scale, so he often built a fashionable house on the outskirts of a town, leaving his old home to be used for offices or to be split up to provide a number of dwellings in what had become, by this time, a socially declining neighbourhood. An example of this development is Somerset House, in George Street, Halifax *(Plate 271)*. At the time of writing subject to restoration proposals, Somerset House was built in the 1760s by John Carr of York for John Royds. Originally larger than it is today, it occupies a site between George Street and Rawson Street and what remains is a three-bay frontage with projecting wings on to Rawson Street, on the original garden side. The present façade to George Street is a rebuild in the neo-Georgian

272. 44/45 Irish Street, Whitehaven, Cumbria

273. Broadoak, Leek, Staffordshire

manner, but the colonnade linking the house and the wings is original, even if the columns themselves are not. A similar arrangement can be seen at 44/45 Irish Street, Whitehaven, in Cumbria *(Plate 272)*. The house was built in 1725, but the wings were raised in the nineteenth century when an additional window and a door were added to the left wing in the places of the original coal hole. The end of the right-hand wing was blank in 1900.

8.94 MIDLANDS' BRICK

Brick has some currency as a fashion statement, as has been suggested already. At Broadoak, near Leek, in Staffordshire, is a roadside house dated 1742 *(Plate 273)*. The owner has chosen to have a brick front which he has heavily trimmed with stone. The quoins and the windows on the first floor

are made of large blocks of limestone carefully dressed to give a clean 'ashlar' surface. He seems also to have felt the need for symmetry, but to have wanted a second door. Away from the road he has reverted to the local stone, which you can see on the side of his house and on the structure next door, either an ironstone or a white granite.

So far as the bricks are concerned, he either ordered two few or had to purchase a second lot. The first delivery contained a large number of well-fired 'bottom of the kiln' bricks and the builder made these last up to the bottom of the top-floor windows. The second lot included a few black ones, so for the last dozen courses or so there is a strong, unmodulated red appearance. Sometimes this change indicates the addition of a storey, but in this case it does appear that the building was completed as part of one campaign.

274. 114-116 High Street, Tenterden, Kent

275. Weatherboarded cottage in Chapel Street, Steeple Bumpstead, Essex

8.95 WEATHERBOARDING

From the 1730s, particularly in Kent and Essex, weather-boarding came into use as a cheaper building material in lieu of a brick or render facing. Smallish buildings with sash windows come to mind and these often are allied to industrial uses or where money needed to be saved. In Kent there are numerous examples, but the High Street of Tenterden is especially rich in examples of weatherboarding *(Plate 274)*, as is Steeple Bumpstead, in Essex *(Plate 275)*. Among the weatherboarded mills, Moulsham Mill, at Chelmsford, in Essex, and the Tide Mill, at Woodbridge, in Suffolk, are particularly striking.

276. Sham Castle on Bathwick Hill, Bath

277. The Tattingstone Wonder, near Holbrook, Suffolk

278. *Speedwell Castle, Market Place, Brewood, Staffordshire*

8.96 EYE-CATCHERS

The idea of having a pleasant view naturally influenced the choice of building site from an early date. Classical architecture in this country produced the idea of introducing something interesting for the eye to settle on, perhaps a small temple, a monument, or even a purpose-built ruined building, and the choice of structure was given greater significance by the literary and historical associations that it carried for the well-educated landowner of the eighteenth century. There are so many such buildings in Picturesque landscapes like Stowe, in Buckinghamshire, Rousham, in Oxfordshire, or Castle Howard, in Yorkshire, that a visit to these parks in earlier times must have taken on the air of a tutorial. At Painshill Park, in Surrey, both a ruined abbey and mausoleum were constructed by the owner, the Hon. Charles Hamilton, to stimulate in the minds of his visitors the appropriate feelings of medieval religious fervour and melancholy respectively.

But, among the pure eye-catchers, the Sham Castle on Bathwick Hill, above Bath *(Plate 276)*, designed by Sanderson Miller in 1755 and built for Ralph Allen seven years later by his Clerk of Works, Richard Jones, was intended to enhance the view from Allen's town house in Old Lilliput Alley. Just as remarkable is the Tattingstone Wonder *(Plate 277)*, built in about 1790 to give a focus to the view from Tattingstone Place, in Suffolk. Two older cottages were given a flint front with Gothic church windows and a third was added in the form of a flint church tower. One of the motivating factors in these eye-catchers was to foster the notion of borrowing a view, implying that the land on which the Temple of the Mill, near to Rousham, in Oxfordshire, stands belongs to the owner of Rousham Park, even if this were not the case.

Perhaps not so much an eye-catcher as a folly, Speedwell Castle *(Plate 278)*, in the Market Place of Brewood, Staffordshire, was built out of winnings on 'Speedwell', the Duke of Bolton's horse, in 1750. Truly a 'Gothick' structure, Speedwell Castle is made of brick, with two canted bay windows on three floors, the windows having round-headed and ogee tops to them and an ogee doorcase. Inside the building there is a fine plaster ceiling and a staircase in the Chinese-Chippendale style.

279. Mansard roof in Bocking, Essex

280. Mansard House, Bardwell, Suffolk

281. Gambrel roof near Hawkhurst, Kent

8.97 GEORGIAN MANSARDS

The mansard roof has two pitches instead of the conventional single one. It runs the length of the building, the upper pitch being less steep than the lower one. It was invented by François Mansart, a French seventeenth century architect, and one can see all over metropolitan France just how well the idea caught on. It enables accommodation on the top of a house to be achieved at a lower cost than would have been incurred by continuing the walls upward to produce more or less the same space. Almost invariably the mansard roof incorporates dormer windows.

There is also a distinction to be made between mansard and gambrel roofs. Gambrel comes from an old French dialect term and means a crooked stick on which an animal carcass is hung – a reference to the shape seen from a gable end. The mansard has a lower pitch on the upper slope than the gambrel and is too shallow for tiles or thatch, and

therefore has to be slated, with a lead flashing where the two slopes meet in order to make the connection waterproof. The higher, upper slope of the gambrel allows tiles or thatch to overshoot the join, thus making for cheaper waterproofing.

The mansard roof is found in towns and on more sophisticated houses, while the gambrel roof, a favourite in the United States of America, is seen on more humble houses in the south and the east of England, dating mostly from the eighteenth and early nineteenth centuries. The obvious distinction is that mansard windows appear down the side, while gambrel windows are usually only in the gable end. Interesting examples of these roof types can be seen in Bocking, in Essex *(Plate 279)*, and in Mansard House, at Bardwell, in Suffolk *(Plate 280)*, for the mansard roof, and, for the gambrel roof, this early nineteenth century example is near to Hawkhurst, in Kent *(Plate 281)*.

215

282. Tom Tower and the gateway of Christ Church, Oxford

8.98 DOMESTIC GOTHIC

Writing of the use of the Gothic style in mid-eighteenth century houses, Osbert Lancaster said: 'Out of this innocuous and rather charming chrysalis would one day come blundering the humourless moth of Victorian revivalism'. The origins of the style are more complex than this judgement might imply, but it is, perhaps, domestic Gothic's roots in decoration rather than in structure that account for the term 'Jolly Gothic' that is often applied to the style. To find the beginnings of a style that reached its apogee in Horace Walpole's

Strawberry Hill, at Twickenham, in Middlesex, in the mid-eighteenth century and which certainly took itself seriously at the time, you have to go back to the work of Sir Christopher Wren at Tom Quad, Christ Church, Oxford, and to 1681-1682. Wren approached the task of building the upper part of Tom Tower gateway *(Plate 282)* objectively and scientifically, saying that 'he resolved that it ought to be in the Gothick style to agree with the Founder's [that is Wolsey's] work', and he converted the gateway's square plan into an octagon

216

283. Chapel, screen and gateway of All Souls College, Oxford

filling the splayed corners with features derived from Tudor buttresses and surmounting the whole design with an ogival dome.

Nicholas Hawksmoor continued and refined this intellectual approach to neo-Gothic in the west gateway and cupola to All Souls College, Oxford (Plate 283), in 1734 while, as we have seen earlier (7.92), Sir John Vanbrugh had twenty years before used the Gothic in a theatrical and medieval way in Vanbrugh's Castle, on the slopes of Greenwich Hill.

It is ironic that it was to be a man with little feeling for the historical origins of the Gothic, William Kent, who was to be most influential in the development of the rather flimsy, decorative style that can be seen at Strawberry Hill. One of his first contributions to the style was to be the rebuilding of Clock Court and its gateway at Hampton Court, in 1732. Here he inserted a plaster vault in the gateway and a window divided into three in imitation of the Tudor style but strangely grouped under a single arch. At Rousham also, in the Temple of the Mill, already referred to, we can see his use of the quatrefoil, but it was in the screens that he built at the south end of Westminster Hall in 1738-1739 to separate the Courts of Chancery and King's Bench, which occupied part of that great space until the early nineteenth century, and in Gloucester Cathedral in 1742 (Plate 284), both of them now removed, of course, that the early traces of 'decorator's Gothic' can be seen.

Here, Kent's approach to the style is that he took features such as the depressed ogival arch and used them not only in architecture but also in the lax scrolls of his furniture design; the corbel-table that he used in the Westminster screen had pendants that might have been French lambrequin tassels; while, more influentially, he used Gothic features in a classical manner, articulating architraves, friezes, cornices and superimposed orders in a way that made them acceptable to clients brought up on Palladianism. The end of this phase of the Gothic came in the 1750s with the design, perhaps by William Kent, of Shobdon Church, in Herefordshire, for Lord Bateman, and an octagonal church by Henry Keene at Hartwell, Buckinghamshire, for Sir Henry Lee, in 1753, which

284. Engraving of the Choir Screen, Gloucester Cathedral by William Kent

heralds a greater concern for archaeological accuracy in dealing with the Gothic than had been seen before.

The same year, 1753, saw the design of a new Hall in the Gothic style at Lacock Abbey, in Wiltshire **(Plate 285)**, by one of the two amateur designers who were to be so influential in domestic Gothic – Sanderson Miller. His client was Sir John Ivory Talbot and the immediate reaction on seeing the façade of the Hall is that it is a work of Kent, but with a pierced parapet and a rose window, both of which were innovative.

If Miller was an amateur architect, Horace Walpole certainly was not. The fourth son of Sir Robert Walpole, he was the main cultural commentator of the age; he called himself 'a dancing Senator'. He had a fine taste in architecture, as in the other arts, but no special aptitude for it, and his contribution to the development of domestic Gothic is the story of his house. He was aged thirty when he bought the remainder of a lease on a small house overlooking the Thames at Twickenham, and from

1748, using the services of an executive architect, William Robinson, he began to enlarge and alter the house to reflect his historical studies and those of a group of friends who constituted the Strawberry Hill Committee.

The earlier, eastern parts of the house do not display anything more radical than would have been done by Kent, but from 1753 the changes grew more adventurous. Richard Bentley designed the north entrance and façade, the staircase with its traceried panels, and the screen and fireplace in the Holbein Room. This last feature demonstrates Walpole's growing interest in archaeological accuracy, as its design was based on Archbishop Warham's tomb in Canterbury Cathedral. John Chute, of the Vyne, in Hampshire, a second member of the Committee, designed the interiors of the Great Parlour and the Library in 1754, again guided by antiquarian books, while Thomas Pitt, later Lord Camelford, created the spectacular Gallery between 1759

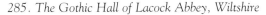

285. The Gothic Hall of Lacock Abbey, Wiltshire

286. *North façade of Strawberry Hill, Twickenham*

287. *The Long Gallery of Strawberry Hill, looking west*

and 1762, which has canopied niches filled with mirrors and a ceiling based on that of Henry VII's Chapel in Westminster Abbey **(Plate 287)**.

These changes have something of Rococo prettiness about them, but it should always be remembered that the received taste of the mid-eighteenth century was still to see the Gothic as debased. The house was still regular, but by building a circular tower at the south-west corner in 1759 **(Plate 286)** Walpole adopted a deliberately asymmetrical plan, while the tower itself was given a battlemented parapet and a corbel-course of pointed arches. In 1763 a Tribune with a Cabinet, the design of which was based on the York Minster Chapter House, was constructed, incidentally using a young Robert Adam as architect, and finally the Beauclerk Tower was inserted between this and the Round Tower in 1777.

The influence of Strawberry Hill was undoubtedly great and indeed Walpole had to restrict the numbers of people applying to see it, but it was in its asymmetry rather than in its Gothic detailing that its longest lasting contribution was to lie. Few Georgian Gothic houses of the 1760s and 1770s respond to its Gothicism, but the Vicarage at Stoke Poges, Buckinghamshire, of 1802, shows how much the architects of succeeding generations, such as James Wyatt who built Lee Priory, Kent, in 1785, owed to this pioneering house.

CHAPTER 9

1760-1790

9.0 INTRODUCTION

On his Grand Tour in Rome in 1755 Robert Adam wrote: 'If I am known in Rome to be an architect, if I am seen drawing or with a pencil in my hand, I cannot enter in genteel company...shall I lose hope and my introduction to the great, or shall I lose...my taste for the grand [that is Classical ruins]?' In fact he managed to do both, but he had travelled from the previous year in the entourage of Charles Hope, Lord Hopetoun's brother, and his rank meant that most doors were opened to Adam as well as to Hope. For Charles Hope the journey was undertaken for pleasure, but for Adam it was rather more. In Rome he employed Charles-Louis Clerisseau as architectural draughtsman, tutor and guide, and together they collected drawings and materials for one of the great books of the age, *The Ruins of the Palace of the Emperor Diocletian at Spalato in Dalmatia* **(Plate 288)**, which was published in 1764 and presented to George III. From the time of his visit to Florence, Robert Adam kept several draughtsmen, including Piranesi, busy recording buildings, ruins and their details, and when he returned to London to set up a

fashionable practice he brought with him bundles of drawings with which to impress potential patrons.

In Adam, the student, the explorer, the architect and the Grand Tourist came together, but among the English of the time he was not alone. William Chambers had left Rome just at the time that Adam arrived in Italy, while Robert Mylne, son of a Scottish architect as well known as Robert Adam's father, William, was making as great an impact in Rome as his more illustrious countryman. To these names could be added Nathaniel and the younger George Dance, Robert Taylor, James Wyatt and John Soane.

The 1750s was also a time when the more remote sites of the Ancient World began to be explored by intrepid English travellers. Robert Wood, private gentleman and politician, made an important contribution to scholarship in the second half of the century by the publication of *The Ruins of Palmyra* in 1753, followed four years later by *The Ruins of Baalbec*. While on his expedition, Wood met James Stuart and Nicholas Revett who were studying Grecian remains and, although they announced the publication of their book in 1751, volume 1 of *The Antiquities of Athens* did not appear until 1762.

The emphasis was moving away from Italy to Greece, heralding the development of Neo-classicism which was to be promoted with such success in England, particularly by Robert Adam and his brothers. The change was cultural rather than simply architectural, and Europe-wide. The dominance that Italy had enjoyed during the first half of the century lessened and leadership passed to France, with the first clearly Neo-classical building being J.G. Soufflot's great church of Ste-Geneviève of 1755-1756, today the Panthéon. The pre-eminent theorist of Neo-classicism was also French. The Abbé Laugier's *Essai sur l'architecture*, published in Paris in 1753, emphasised the importance of the post-and-lintel construction of the primitive cabin, and considered that the perfect building should have columns in the round rising from the pavement. It was not his view, however, that every building should necessarily have an Order and he recommended that a designer should always work from

288. *Atrium of Diocletian's Palace, from Adam's book on the*
Ruins of the Palace

289. *Casino at Marino, Clontarf, Dublin*

first principles, saying that 'architecture...owes all that is precious and solid to the Greeks alone'.

This Greek-centred classicism coincided with a cultural acceptance of the historical nature of antiquity. The view gained ground throughout Europe that different styles held sway at different times; that it was no longer possible to see European culture as developing in a continuous manner, interrupted only by the barbarism of the Dark and Middle Ages; and that antiquity should be viewed only through the perspective of the Renaissance. In this archaeology had a part to play, and it is not surprising, therefore, that the excavations at Pompeii and Herculaneum in mid-century had a great influence on thought and design.

9.1 NEO-CLASSICAL HOUSES

The last forty years of the eighteenth century were dominated architecturally by two Scots – William Chambers and Robert Adam. Born within five years of each other of prosperous middle-class families, they covered the whole range of building in Britain, Chambers predominantly the official architect and Adam with a long list of illustrious private clients. It might seem perverse with Somerset House, in London, among Chambers' greatest works to suggest that he was at his best with small buildings, but the Casino he built for Lord Charlemont at Marino, Clontarf, Dublin, from 1759, is one of the most perfect small structures *(Plate 289)*. Although now

221

290. *The courtyard of Somerset House, London, looking south*

surrounded by housing estates, the Casino was intended to be a garden building set in sweeping parkland, but, inside, it is a residential summer house and belvedere on three floors, four if the flat roof is included, as it offered even more extensive views over Lord Charlemont's demesne.

In plan a Greek cross, the Casino has plain, free-standing columns that mark each of the four projecting arms and four more at the corners of the central block. The stone walls are channelled, and doorcases and windows are given triangular pediments, the latter with consoles. The frieze is carved with ox-skulls and shields interrupted with triglyphs, while above a balustrade contains the attic storey which is embellished by garlands on the faces of the stone panels. In its appearance this small building has all the attributes of a Greek temple.

By contrast, Somerset House **(Plate 290)**, set between the Strand and the Embankment in London, is seemingly a vast building, though today we see two flanking wings on the river elevation that were only completed in the nineteenth century. Chambers had been architect to the King and Commissioner of the Board of Works since 1760 and became Comptroller nine years later. By the

time that he was in full charge of the project to unite many government offices that had been spread throughout London, the old Royal palace of Somerset House had been demolished, including, alas, the work of Inigo Jones on the Strand frontage. In 1775, therefore, Chambers had the opportunity to design the largest public building since Greenwich Palace in the previous century, and his solution was to break the large area down into four elements and build as if each was a substantial town house.

The façade on to the Strand housed the newly-formed Royal Academy as well as the Royal Society and the Society of Antiquaries. The building is three-storeyed with a Corinthian Order on the *piano nobile,* and high attic breaking the balustrade, and a three-arched entrance to the courtyard of Somerset House, which is inspired surely by the Louvre designed by Le Vau in the preceding century. Coupled columns linked to cross-vaults are set inside the round-headed arches and entrances to this block are set into the lateral walls of the archways. Once inside the courtyard, the main building that faces you, forming the river frontage, has a modest pediment and dome, but is otherwise as unassertive as the two flanking buildings, which recall the town houses with their central columned entrances that we have already seen in Grosvenor Square. On the riverside the design is the very antithesis of monumental, and the long façade is divided into three not only by the porticoes, but by the Palladian bridges below that remind one of the water-gates to the great palaces along the Thames of which the only one to remain is the York Watergate. Of course the river used to flow into the lower arches before the Victoria Embankment was created.

It is, perhaps, ironic that the 'Adam style', which has been so widely known since the eighteenth century, should be such a complex arrangement of influences. Adam enjoyed the variety of silhouettes and the consequential shadows that the splitting up of Palladian façades and the diversity of their window openings created, while, from the Paris hotels, he took the succession of rooms of different sizes and shapes. The archaeology came from Dalmatia, Syria and Greece as well as Italy, especially Etruria, and the Renaissance masters that he most admired included Michelangelo and Raphael, of course, but also Giulio Romano, Pirro Ligorio, Giovanni da Udine and Algardi. This accounts for the emphasis on decorative work, with *grottesche* in both plaster and paint. Indeed, Adam's painterly eye caused him to adapt the classical details that he had brought back from his Grand Tour to provide fine, light and infinitely subtle decoration based quite loosely on the Classical. Architecturally, what to Burlington had been a set of rules was to Adam merely inspiration for his imagination, tempered, of course, by what his client wanted, for he was always careful to subordinate his views to the requirements of the person paying the bills.

Within two years of launching his London practice in 1758, Robert Adam had a string of eminent clients and much domestic work, though it is interesting that, for a decade, he hardly built a house from scratch, either taking on projects begun by others or remodelling old buildings within their existing shells. The latter was what was done from 1762 at Syon House, Middlesex, for Sir Hugh Smithson, later 1st Duke of Northumberland of the new creation. Syon was Jacobean built around a courtyard, which, innovatively, Adam intended to fill with a great Rotunda connected to the progression of differently-shaped rooms on all four sides. Alas, the Rotunda was never built, though Adam did build a more modest version at Luton Hoo in 1766-1770.

Syon's entrance hall is shaped like a basilica with two apsidal ends, one leading to an oval ante-room (**Plate 291**) and the other to a rectangular space which was reduced to a square by freestanding columns. The dining room is a rectangle with apses at either end, on the chords of which are columns *in antis*, rather like the Library at Kenwood, in London. The skill of the designer can also be seen in the way he was able to reduce visually the immense length of the Long Gallery by dividing it into bays and then subdividing it again by using differing widths of pilasters.

At Kedleston Hall, in Derbyshire, Adam took over the partly built plan of another architect, James Paine.

291. Ante-room of Syon House, Isleworth, London

Although the plan was, like Holkham Hall, based on Palladio's unbuilt Villa Mocenigo, only the two northern pavilions were constructed at Kedleston, today housing the private accommodation on the east and the kitchen on the west. Adam first came to Kedleston to build the Fishing Room and the Bridge and Cascade in the park, and by this time the north front with its rather ponderous portico was in train, but the south front **(Plate 292)** is Adam at his most inventive, even if there is something clinical about it. The theme of the façade was the triumphal arch expressing the domed Saloon, the most important room in the house, behind it. Giant Corinthian columns stand proud of the façade with statues placed above the entablature recalling the design of the Ante Room interior at Syon. They divide the frontispiece into three, while carved panels display classical ornaments and a flowery dedication to the owner of the estate, Sir Nathaniel Curzon, later the 1st Lord Scarsdale. The inspiration for the design was the Arch of Constantine in Rome and the central recess and the flanking niches convey the openings of the original structure.

292. South front of Kedleston, Derbyshire

293. *The Marble Hall of Kedleston*

Behind the northern portico and on an axis with the Saloon is the Marble Hall *(Plate 293)*. Intended to provide the grandest of settings for the owner's hospitality, this magnificent room, with its flanking alabaster columns, statuary in niches and painted plaster ceiling, was inspired by the atrium of a classical house that would have led to the vestibulum. Adam had seen such an arrangement in the Palace of Diocletian and had illustrated it in his great book (see Plate 288).

In the 1770s Robert Adam was involved in the development of three London town houses, of which two – 20 St James's Square and 20 Portman Square – still

225

294. Adam staircase at Home House, Portman Square, London

exist as a tribute to his ingenuity in planning and Neo-classical decorative style. 20 Portman Square was built in 1775-1777 for the Countess of Home and is today a private members' clubhouse. Behind a conventional terraced façade, Adam has inserted a fine top-lit staircase **(Plate 294)**, while the sequence of hospitality rooms familiar in country houses – Music Room, Drawing Room, Library, Saloon, State Bedroom and Dining Room – are provided. The decoration of the Music Room in Home House is both restrained and coherent, while its plaster ceiling incorporates a series of painted roundels by Antonio Zucci and is especially harmonious.

Attingham Park **(Plate 295)**, on the outskirts of Shrewsbury, in Shropshire, is also a remarkable house of this period. Built between 1783 and 1785 by George Steuart for Noel Hill, later 1st Lord Berwick, the house has a monumental Ionic portico which led originally into a splendidly proportioned Entrance Hall with the staircase situated beyond a screen of coupled columns. This was altered, however, in 1805 by John Nash when he created a separate Picture Gallery behind the

Entrance Hall by the simple expedient of filling in the spaces between the scagliola columns and moving back the staircase. It would appear that Steuart's Neo-classicism in this front part of the house derives from the early work of the French architect Claude-Nicolas Ledoux, while the unusual capitals of the original screen, which can still be seen today, come from J.D. Le Roy's *Les Ruines des plus beaux monuments de la Grèce*.

Stoke Park, at Stoke Poges, Buckinghamshire, is one of the most interesting, late-Georgian houses in Britain **(Plate 296)**. Begun by Robert Naismith, an assistant to Robert Adam, in 1789 for John Penn, Stoke Park was soon taken over by James Wyatt and he worked on it for five years from 1793. The central seven bays must be by Naismith, but it was Wyatt's genius that added the four single-storeyed pavilions that end in bow windows, linked them together across the frontages with a Greek Doric colonnade, surmounting the whole with a dominating dome. Alas, the profile of the present dome is rather different from Wyatt's original, but, inside, the oval entrance hall is as the designer intended, though the details are, perhaps, different.

295. *Attingham Park, Shropshire*

296. *Stoke Park, Stoke Poges, Buckinghamshire*

297. *Harleyford Manor, Marlow, Buckinghamshire*

9.2 SECOND GENERATION PALLADIANISM

Colen Campbell designed two types of Palladian houses in the 1720s, the great houses of parade, such as Houghton Hall, in Norfolk, and the villa, of which Stourhead, in Wiltshire is an example. In the following thirty years or so, the English country house underwent a change. For both social and economic reasons the large properties no longer seemed appropriate and, prompted by Lord Burlington's Chiswick House and Roger Morris' Marble Hill House, the smaller villa design came much more into prominence. In the 1750s and 1760s Sir Robert Taylor built three such villas on the outskirts of London and, for city merchants, Harleyford Manor, at Marlow, in Buckinghamshire, Danson Hill, in Kent and Asgill House, Richmond.

At Harleyford *(Plate 297)* Taylor's client was Sir William Clayton, and the style in which he designed was a much freer version of Palladianism than had been considered acceptable in the earlier period and, indeed, incorporated both the Rococo and early Neo-classical elements. Built in brick, Harleyford is of five bays by five and comprises a half-basement, a main storey and a half storey for the upper level. What is most striking about the house are the bay windows – a fine three-bay bow towards the Thames and a canted bay to the east accommodating respectively the Drawing Room and the Library on the main floor. Such an arrangement makes clear that, although villas of this type were markedly smaller than the

great houses of the 1720s, providing fine settings for entertainment was still considered to be essential. Exterior decoration is restrained, even severe, while, inside, a vaulted passage leads to a domed inner hall with the staircase set into a square well behind it. Hospitality would have been dispensed on the *piano nobile* with the main rooms running enfilade around the central staircase offering suitable settings for dancing, supper and cards. Although this was a villa for entertainment, there was no space in the main house for kitchens and today you can still see at half-basement level the end of the tunnel which ran for one hundred yards (ninety metres) northwards to the kitchens, no longer standing, through which the food was brought to the guests. The setting of Harleyford, in grounds landscaped by 'Capability' Brown just above a beautiful stretch of the Thames, is idyllic and it is surely appropriate that the modern purpose of the Harleyford estate is leisure, with a golf course, marina and walled garden cottages, the Manor House itself being let as offices.

Taylor also designed Heveningham Hall, by far the grandest house in Suffolk *(Plate 298)*. Again his client was a wealthy London merchant of Dutch descent, Sir Gerard Vanneck, or Van Neck, who had bought the estate in 1752, but Taylor's design for the structure of the house was not undertaken until 1778 and James Wyatt's spectacular interior decoration was completed six years later. Heveningham has an immensely long façade of

298. Heveningham Hall, Suffolk

twenty-five bays in stuccoed brick with three-bay angled pavilions and attached columns, while the central seven bays break forward in the approved Palladian manner and have separate giant Corinthian columns. But, whereas the pavilions have pediments, as might be expected, the centre has a heavy attic embellished with garlands, two figures, a coat of arms, urns and lions. This conception is far from the Palladian tradition and takes its inspiration directly from Classical examples, but from the west across the lake and smooth lawns provided by Capability Brown, it has a serenity and beauty all its own.

James Wyatt's Entrance Hall is spectacular but refined. The general colour is green, screens of columns separate off the ends in the manner of Robert Adam, while pilasters separate panels which had niches for statues. The decorated plaster ceiling is basically a tunnel-vault on the upper sides of which are semicircles of plaster flanked by fans. This and the Dining Room, which is decorated with painted reliefs by Biagio Rebecca, one of Adam's assistants, are in Wyatt's early Neo-classical taste and of the highest quality.

A third house which should be mentioned is Wardour Castle, in Wiltshire. Designed by James Paine for the 8th Lord Arundell, Wardour was begun in 1770 and finished six years later. Constructed of ashlar, the house consists of a central block of nine bays with quadrant corridors leading to three-bay pavilions. The ground floor is rusticated and above this, on the garden (south) side, the central three bays break forward and are articulated by giant Corinthian columns. The two columns in the middle are single, but those at the two sides are coupled, the whole conception suggesting a rather free interpretation of the principles of Palladianism.

Immediately behind the Entrance Hall is the wonderful Staircase Hall *(Plate 299)*. Some 60ft. (18m) high with a diameter of 47ft. (14.3m), the divided, cantilevered stair rises to the *piano nobile* which consists of a gallery flanked by fluted Corinthian columns that terminate in a coffered dome and a glazed lantern. This is one of the most exciting internal spaces in Wiltshire and it is interesting that it must have been built shortly before Adam's stair at Culzean Castle, on the Ayrshire coast. In a sense the Wardour stair forms a link between the Palladian and the Neo-classical, back to William Kent and forward to Adam.

299. Staircase of Wardour Castle, Wiltshire

300. Artisan cottages at Combe Down, Bath

301. Lock-keeper's cottage at the top lock, Caen Flight, Devizes, Wiltshire

9.3 CANAL AND TURNPIKE COTTAGES

It is rare that the building of modest cottages is recorded for posterity, but the exception to this is where these small houses are part of a large commercial development. This is the case with the group of charming artisan cottages on Combe Down, above Prior Park, at Bath, Somerset *(Plate 300)*. Ralph Allen has been mentioned before and he had made a fortune by organising the Cross-post system whereby country letters could be routed direct to other provincial destinations without having to go through London, but the construction of his Palladian house of Prior Park, designed for him by John Wood the Elder, was intended to demonstrate the merits of Bath stone from his quarries over those of Portland.

In the 1720s a cartel of stonemasons kept stone prices high and quality often poor, but Allen broke their monopoly by importing 'scab' labour from Yorkshire and providing them with cottages built above the quarries at Bath by John Wood himself. These cottages can still be seen today, somewhat altered, of course, but still constituting a model village of stonemasons' accommodation. In a sense the small houses on the slopes of Combe Down are also canal cottages, as Ralph Allen constructed an inclined plane to enable the stone to be brought down from the quarries to the Kennet and Avon Canal, so that it could be transported to other parts of the country by water.

At Devizes, in Wiltshire, there are buildings which illustrate both canal and toll buildings. Standing at the top of the Caen Hill flight of 29 locks on the Kennet and Avon Canal is the small Canal House *(Plate 301)* with its distinctively canted front, which was where tolls for the use of the canal were paid, and where the lockmaster and his family lived. Quite close by is Shane's Castle *(Plate 302)*, at the junction of the roads to Chippenham and Bath. This is a building which is heavily castellated, with hood-mouldings over the windows. Dating from the early nineteenth century it was surely once a toll house.

302. Shane's Castle, Devizes, Wiltshire

303. 35-45 Camberwell Grove, London

9.4 TERRACED HOUSES

A comparison between terraces in London and in some provincial cities illustrates that the capital was usually twenty years ahead of architectural styles elsewhere. In Camberwell Grove, for instance there is a group of brick terraced houses in this densely planted, straight avenue, and Nos. 33-45 at the north end *(Plate 303)* were built in an understated style in the 1770s. Camberwell Grove itself had been started as a private street behind the

mansion house of the Cock family, but when that property was demolished and the land sold in 1776 a comprehensive development of terraces was undertaken.

At Hotwells, in Bristol, however, Albemarle Row was built in 1762-1763, probably by Thomas Paty, but the style of these spacious, brick houses is that of, perhaps, the 1740s *(Plate 304)*. The windows have square heads, which gives a rather stern appearance, and over each

304. *Albemarle Row, Hotwells, Bristol*

Below: 305. *5 and 6 Windsor Terrace, Clifton, Bristol*

opening there are the characteristic Bristol voussoirs. The whole composition is, indeed, classical, but compared with the work of the John Woods in Bath (always influenced by London rather than the locality), the principles are interpreted with casual freedom. Albemarle Row is built on quite a steep hill which means that the pediment of the central house is at the level of the parapet of the house above it; and, indeed, the central house is not quite in the centre. Although there are three houses below the grander one in the middle, each is made up of five bays, while two of the upper houses are of only three bays. And yet these Hotwells properties were for people just as fashionable as those who lived in the great terraced houses of Bath.

High above Hotwells is Windsor Terrace, in Clifton. Designed probably by John Eveleigh in 1790, only Nos. 5 and 6 **(Plate 305)** were built to his plan with a stone frontispiece of giant fluted Corinthian columns on a rusticated ground floor; this was due to the heavy expenditure involved in supporting the western end of the terrace where it terminated at the Avon Gorge. The project was only finished in 1810 in a variety of styles, but, even allowing for this, it is clear that the design of Windsor Terrace was some twenty years out of date in 1790. It is equally true to say that even the troubled history of the Terrace is forgotten in the magnificence of the setting.

306. *Sherwood (right) and Lydia Houses, Dartmouth Grove, Blackheath, London*

9.5 NEO-CLASSICAL SEMI-DETACHED HOUSES

There are two houses in Condover, Shropshire, which date from 1777 and are built in the Neo-classical style. The neat symmetrical arrangement provides two houses with the decorative dignity of one larger one. Emphasis is placed on the cement, while the voussoirs have been fanned out to suggest their construction in brick. There is also a rather weak pediment which is merely a continuation of the wall and is pitched to match that of the necessarily wide one over the two front doors.

Money has clearly been spent on the entrance woodwork, with the doors sitting behind well-panelled returns. It was, perhaps, a mistake to lug the top of the doors; the outside projections look fine, but of necessity the inside ones meet and the effect is not entirely a success, as the point of providing the lug is to make it stand out like an ear.

In a rather more urban situation and perhaps more successfully, Sherwood and Lydia Houses *(Plate 306)* are a grand pair of houses in Dartmouth Grove, Lewisham, facing Blackheath, and built in 1776. Most probably the houses were designed by Thomas Gayfere Senior, the master-mason at Westminster Abbey when the west end towers were constructed, and they are stuccoed with canted bays on the ground floor and a central pediment with an oval window. At the rear side there is also a Diocletian window and half-pediments over the lower wings. The style is Palladian in origin, but has some of the eccentricities that we have also noted in the work of Sir Robert Taylor. Probably this pair of houses is an early example of a design which became very popular for semi-detached villas, especially in Blackheath.

9.6 ADAM AND HIS FOLLOWERS IN THE PROVINCES

It is tempting to think that the Adam brothers only built either great houses or town houses. In fact their practice was more broadly based than this and a modest villa, such as Brasted Place, in Kent, was given as refined detailing as any of the grander properties. Built for Dr Turton in 1784-1785, Brasted Place is made of beautiful grey and brown sandstone ashlar from Tunbridge Wells and the entrance front is of five bays, the central three of which are under a pediment. The porch on this side has coupled

Tuscan columns, and the detailing is Etruscan. On the garden front the house is only three bays wide, but the stonework is richly detailed, with twin Ionic pilasters articulating the wall, while a deep portico is given two pairs of tall Ionic columns that rise from a low plinth.

At the corner of Sileby Road, in Mountsorrel, Leicestershire, there is a very finely detailed house in the provincial Neo-classical style with arches over the windows and with decoration *(Plate 307)*. Built as a

307. Late 18th century villa in Sileby Road, Mountsorrel, Leicestershire

private house by a cleric, it has the date of 1782 on the rear gable. The brick façade is of five bays, the three in the centre having a pediment, and there are other Neo-classical details such as urns, thin glazing bars and recessed and balustraded sills on the first floor.

No architect is known for this house, nor for the Old Rectory at Church Langton, Leicestershire *(Plate 308)*. Begun in about 1783 by the son of the Revd William Hanbury, gardener and architectural expert, it was finished three years later. It is a villa construction, with a brick façade of five bays two and a half storeys high. The central three bays break forward under a pediment and the first-floor windows have sills with balustrades within blank arches. The Neo-classical details of urns and garlands have, at some stage, been removed, but the whole conception is elegant and symmetrical.

308. Old Rectory, Church Langton, Leicestershire

309. Home Farm, Sandon Park, Staffordshire

9.7 THE MODEL FARM

A report issued by the Board of Agriculture in 1814 codified earlier practice and described a standardised plan for model farms. It laid down that 'A main barn should have a tangent wing at each end for stables, cow ties, open sheds, etc., the yard opening to the milder points, the south or the south-east'. An interesting and fine example of such a planned farm is Home Farm, at Sandon, Staffordshire, which runs with Sandon Park, the home of the Earls of Harrowby. Dated 1777-1780, it was built by Samuel Wyatt in a restrained Neo-classical style. The house and the farm building are arranged axially, and are built in fine ashlar with low, pitched roofs. The house and dairy *(Plates 309 and 310)* share many of the polite design characteristics whether their purpose is to accommodate people or animals.

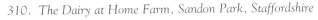

310. The Dairy at Home Farm, Sandon Park, Staffordshire

9.8 THE PICTURESQUE IN ARCHITECTURE

We have already seen how the Picturesque transformed the formal elements of garden design into naturalised parkland at estates such as Stowe and Stourhead, seeking to create a series of views that might recall the paintings of Claude, Poussin and Rubens. William Kent had dotted the smooth lawns with classical buildings to satisfy the cultural predilections of the owners and their friends, while other designers had added pavilions in the Chinese style and even constructed ruins to enhance the view. Later in the century Lancelot 'Capability' Brown had designed even more 'natural' landscapes by earth-moving to create hills and lakes, and extensive tree-planting to serve as eye-catchers and to tempt those who ventured into the countryside to go further and see what views were offered beyond the next belt of planting.

Doubtless the owner of the estate could look with pleasure and pride on both kinds of view from his house and walk into the park with pleasure too. But when he headed for home the dream was shattered. What had seemed entirely appropriate to the landowner in the 1750s, when he saw the classical portico of his house, within twenty or thirty years would appear to be a cold and symmetrical stone box with the end of a heathen temple tacked on to the entrance. It did not look to him as if it belonged in the natural surroundings and, indeed, with the steps up to the plinth on which the portico stood, there was no connection between the house, the formal garden and the parkland.

So, by the last decade of the century, Picturesque theory had dethroned the classical house just as it had the formal garden. Sir Uvedale Price, who wrote *An Essay on the Picturesque* in 1794, considered that it was 'the two opposite qualities of roughness, and of sudden variation, joined to that of irregularity…' that served to define the Picturesque. It was, of course, also the absence of roughness, variation and irregularity which Price found so lamentable in the work of 'Capability' Brown. Within a few months of Price publishing his essay, Richard Payne Knight, a wealthy landowner from Herefordshire, published a rejoinder entitled *The Landscape: A Didactic Poem in Three Books*, emphasising that, for him, the Picturesque was a way of looking and was not a characteristic enjoyed by certain objects, as Price considered it was.

In *The Landscape*, Knight used two illustration by Thomas Hearn to show that a really quite substantial house could be presented as an integral part of the countryside and he encouraged architects to let their buildings 'be a mere component part of what you see'.

311. Ickworth, Suffolk

Knight also practised what he preached, as his own house, Downton Castle, inspired by the fortified buildings in the background of paintings by Claude, is deliberately asymmetrical and stands immediately above the wild valley of the River Teme. Built between 1773 and 1778, it is one of the earliest mansions to be castellated in the medieval manner and its Gothic jumble of shapes on the skyline contrasts with its serene Classical interiors. At Downton Castle the coming of Romanticism is clear, as is the historicism of the Victorian period.

9.9 CIRCULAR HOUSES

It seems likely that the inspiration for the circular houses of the late eighteenth century was the Pantheon, in Rome, seen by so many English visitors on their Grand Tours. The best known example is Ickworth, in Suffolk *(Plate 311)*, started by Frederick Hervey, Bishop of Derry and 4th Earl of Bristol, in 1795, but not finished by his death in 1803. The Earl-Bishop was much travelled and he had previously started a house for himself at Ballyscullion, in Ireland, which had a circular centre and quadrant wings.

The design of Ickworth was by Francis Sandys, but the idea of an oval *corps de logis* must have been taken over from Ballyscullion by Hervey himself. Single-storeyed wings join the centre of the house to nine-bay pavilions which are two storeys high. Ickworth is 700ft. (213m) long and 100ft. (30.5m) high and was intended as a

temple to display the Earl-Bishop's Grand Tour collections in the two pavilions, while the owner himself occupied the Rotunda. Alas, the collections were confiscated by the French in 1798 and it is ironic that today the Rotunda is open to the public, while the two pavilions are devoted to other purposes. The walls have attached columns throughout, Ionic below and Corinthian above, and the entrance portico has four columns with a pediment.

Belle Isle, on an island in Windermere, in Cumbria, was built in 1774-1775 for Thomas English by John Plaw. The circular plan was also inspired by the Pantheon, in Rome, used earlier in the century for garden buildings, and its siting is just as deliberately Picturesque. The house has a dome with a lantern and a portico with four slender Ionic columns.

312. Barlaston Hall, Barlaston, Staffordshire

9.91 TALL GEORGIAN HOUSES

Tall houses are found throughout the country, often but not exclusively on the edges of towns. Sometimes they go up to four floors and if they are on the edge of a provincial town they can swamp the surrounding houses. On the eastern side of England they tend to have pantiles, although stone voussoirs with their keystones can be seen anywhere; indeed, in the west they might be pronounced, while the pitch of the roof tends to be quite steep. Top-floor windows are often small, but this might derive rather more from the lack of consideration for the servants than any respect for Palladio. These elegant, commodious houses with their simple plan of a central staircase and chimneys placed at

the end of the building successfully accommodated the large families of a professional man. Their successors now live elsewhere and use the buildings as offices.

Barlaston Hall, in Staffordshire, is such a house (**Plate 312**). Built for the Wedgwood family by Sir Robert Taylor in 1756, it is unsurprisingly of brick and is tall for its size, consisting as it does of five bays and two and a half storeys. The three central bays project and are surmounted by a pediment, but the windows have lozenge-shaped panes. The entrance door is framed by Tuscan columns, and the garden front has a fine central bow window; on the other two sides there are canted bays.

313-318

9.92 GEORGIAN DOORCASES

This period was a particularly good time for front doors and many modest houses with plain façades, as well as the grander ones, were improved by the simple addition of a doorcase surrounding the door. Good examples can be found around England, especially in London, Bath and Liverpool. Fanlights, used within Palladian doorcase designs from around 1720, became more simple in style as the century progressed. Generally the door would have had a central knob positioned at waist height. Letter plates were used for the first time in 1840 so are not original to the period.

CHAPTER 10

1790-1815

10.0 INTRODUCTION

In the closing years of the eighteenth century Romanticism effected the most radical changes in the arts of Europe since the Renaissance. Wordsworth's observation of nature made Alexander Pope's

319. *The Dome in Sir John Soane's house in Lincoln's Inn Fields, London*

obsession with the figures of classical mythology old-fashioned; Chopin and Liszt did the same even for Beethoven; while Constable charged his landscapes with an emotion which Thomas Gainsborough had never been able to achieve. One aspect of Romanticism was an interest in the primitive, with Queen Marie-Antoinette and her ladies playing at being humble milkmaids with Sèvres buckets, while some architects considered the primitive hut to be the start of design and advocated a return to first principles.

Neo-classical architecture as the forebear of the Roman held a natural appeal for this thinking and a second generation of English architects working in this style took over from Robert Adam, including James Wyatt, George Dance the Younger, Thomas Harrison and Sir John Soane. Another aspect of this interest in the primitive was historicism, the study not only of historical styles, but also of the collection and examination of early objects. The contents of the Soane Museum, in Lincoln's Inn Fields, as opposed to the settings in which they are displayed, suggest a sterility of approach on the part of the collector which was in sharp contrast to the vigour of the interest in the vernacular later in the nineteenth century *(Plate 319)*.

And what could be more Romantic than a small country like Greece fighting for its independence from a cruel tyrant such as Turkey? Lord Byron, surely one of the great Romantic figures of the century, identified himself with the struggle, and died there, but not before he had played a part in the controversy which is still with us today. In 1803, the British Ambassador to Constantinople, Lord Elgin, anxious to save some of the greatest treasures of the Ancient World from the depredations of the rulers of Athens, had the sculptures shipped home to England under the noses of the French who were themselves thinking of acquiring them. Not everyone, and certainly not Lord Byron, accepted the maxim that 'antiquity is a garden which belongs by natural right to those who cultivate it', and the argument over the Elgin Marbles was heated and prolonged, and continues today.

The period of the Napoleonic Wars from the mid-1790s until the Battle of Waterloo in 1815 saw a slump in the building trade in England. Few clients had the available resources to build grand 'parade' houses and those who did construct houses thought it more appropriate to do so on a more modest scale. There was also a shortage of materials; much timber came from Scandinavia which, in common with most parts of Continental Europe, was not accessible to English merchants.

The development of the Picturesque in architecture has already been commented on, but, in addition to the books by Sir Uvedale Price and Richard Payne Knight, the publication by Humphry Repton in 1795 of *Sketches and Hints on Landscape Gardening* drew attention to the latent characteristics that every estate possessed and which it was the aim of 'improvement' to draw out and emphasise *(Plate 320)*. Relating the house to its landscape setting became more important, and introducing French windows and verandahs improved the links between the inside of the house and its garden. Just as significant was the abandonment of the *piano nobile* with its circuit of State Rooms, the introduction of living rooms on a true ground floor and the transfer of bedrooms to the upper floor. All these changes meant a further retreat from formality and domestic arrangements more akin to those with which we are familiar today. Style tended to be eclectic, but Italian and Gothic villas were much in vogue, as was the cottage, and the plans of the houses were usually asymmetrical.

320. Sheringham, Norfolk: from Repton's Red Book

321. Cronkhill House, Shropshire

10.1 NASH AND THE PICTURESQUE

The son of a millwright from Lambeth, John Nash had a rather patchy early career, but as a youth he seems to have worked in the office of Sir Robert Taylor. At twenty-five he tried to develop an estate in Bloomsbury, but in 1783 the speculation failed and he was declared bankrupt, although some of the houses he built in Bloomsbury Square and Great Russell Street, finished with a stucco patented by the Adam brothers, survive. Nash spent the next decade in Wales building local prisons on the pattern of Newgate and also houses for the local landowners, but in 1795 he returned to London and joined Humphry Repton. The partnership lasted for only seven years, but it was productive and while Repton 'improved' the estates of his clients, Nash built Picturesque houses on them, as well as service buildings like lodges and dairies.

In style these houses were inspired by Downton Castle and by the writings of Richard Payne Knight, its owner. Indeed, Luscombe Castle, in Devon, designed by Nash

for the banker Charles Hoare, seems to be Downton in miniature, with its irregularity of plan, Gothic detailing, verandah and French windows opening directly on to the grass of the lovely valley which stands above the sea. The date was 1799 and there is a Red Book produced by Repton for the estate. The whole composition is surely the epitome of the Picturesque movement in both landscape and architectural design.

The idea that the Italianate house was essentially Picturesque might well have come from Payne Knight, though the appearance of a circular tower with a low conical roof in the background of Claude's painting of the *Pastoral Landscape with the Ponte Molle*, collected by a Grand Tourist and now in the Birmingham Museum and Art Gallery, is as likely to be the inspiration. Certainly, that tower has a striking similarity to that of the stuccoed villa of Cronkhill House, in Shropshire **(Plate 321)**. Built in 1802 by Nash for the Steward to the 2nd Lord

322. *Blaise Hamlet, Henbury, Bristol*

Berwick, of Attingham Park, the house is certainly in the vernacular of northern Italy and is distinctly Picturesque, that is pictorial in conception, as the tower is decorative rather than functional and does not contain a circular room as the exterior might lead one to expect.

Longner Hall is also nearby in Salop. Here the original house on the site was taken down in 1803 and John Nash built a new one in the Tudor style, placing the various elements of the structure together in a free manner. The porch on the entrance façade is large and has a tall window which lights the staircase with, beyond, the stables which have a high clock tower. Also, rather similar to Cronkhill House, Longner Hall has a colonnade with arches that run round the corner joining on to the main living rooms which face south and west, but it is glazed. Again, Humphry Repton landscaped the grounds in 1804.

This period also saw the development of the cottage. To begin with this humble building formed part of the Picturesque landscape, in a manner that can be seen in Gainsborough's paintings, but it soon took on an architectural significance of its own. Books of designs for admittedly rather more substantial cottages appeared regularly in the twenty years after 1790 and Nash himself became adept at using a variety of materials – brick, half-timbering and thatch – and incorporating Picturesque elements such as hips, dormers and gables. A group of what we might consider middle-class cottages designed by Nash and Humphry Repton's son, George, can be seen today at Blaise Hamlet, Henbury, on the outskirts of Bristol (**Plate 322**). The cottages, set informally around a notional village green with its own water pump/sun dial, were built by John Scandrett Harford, the owner of Blaise Castle, to accommodate his ageing servants in conditions of peace. Even today, though the tenants of the National Trust are perhaps rather different from those who originally occupied the cottages, the tranquillity of the setting lives on.

323. Ashridge, Little Gaddesden, Hertfordshire

324. Garden front of Eastnor Castle, Herefordshire

10.2 THE 'MODERN' CASTLE

'What absurdities, what anomalies, what utter contradictions do not the builders of modern castles perpetrate! How many portcullises which will not lower down and drawbridges which will not draw up…on one side of the house machicolated parapets, embrasures, bastions and all the show of strong defence, and round the corner of the building a conservatory leading to the principal rooms, through which a whole company of horsemen might penetrate at one smash into the very heart of the mansion – for who would hammer against nailed portals when he could kick his way through the greenhouse.'

The anomaly which Augustus Welby Northmore Pugin drew attention to in 1840 is that a castle had to be comfortable as well as imposing. He knew that, if you had made money and wanted to achieve acceptance and move up the social scale, the thing to do was to move to the country and set up as a squire; and if you had enough money, or felt that your existing country home did not do you justice, you could get James Wyatt or John Nash to build you a modern castle or, perhaps, alter your old one; but whether the resulting building had regard for authenticity was another question altogether. These large

246

325. *Cholmondley Castle, Cheshire*

estates were usually surrounded by a variety of lodges in old styles, for what is the sense of having a castle if one is faced at every turn by the squalid hovels of one's tenantry?

Caerhays Castle, at St Michael Caerhays, Cornwall, is the best preserved of Nash's castles. Built in 1808 for John Trevanion, a cousin of Lord Byron, it stands in a superb position overlooking a bay with its gardens running right up to the edge of the cliff. The plan is typical of the designer, pivoting on a long, two-storey balconied gallery, with a vaulted staircase at one end and closet, library and circular drawing-room at the other. Externally, the silhouette has square and round turrets, the roof-line being castellated. It is a truly romantic design, evoking the past, but with the conveniences of the early nineteenth century.

Ashridge, at Little Gaddesden, Hertfordshire, is today a Management College, set in extensive parkland owned by the National Trust *(Plate 323)*. Originally an English College of Bonshommes, founded in the thirteenth century by Edmund Earl of Cornwall, it came into the hands of Sir Thomas Egerton in the early seventeenth century and remained in the same family when the then Earl commissioned James Wyatt to build a romantic Gothic castle soon after 1803. The most striking feature about the asymmetrical building is the entrance hall and staircase tower behind, begun in 1808 by Wyatt, but finished by his nephew, Jeffry Wyatt (later Sir Jeffry Wyatville) after Wyatt's death in 1813. He also built the north porch, the east wing and the stables.

Eastnor Castle, in Herefordshire *(Plate 324)*, was built by

Sir Robert Smirke for the 1st Lord Somers. Begun in 1812, it is an early essay in the neo-Norman style, quite symmetrical with large angle towers and a raised centre. The castle is approached by a low gatehouse, but the illusion of a medieval past is dispelled by the main *porte-cochère* and the canted bay window in the centre of the main façades. The main room is a 60ft. (18m) long Great Hall, but the decoration of this and other of the principal rooms will be described when A.W.N. Pugin's work is discussed.

Cholmondley Castle, in Cheshire *(Plate 325)*, was designed in about 1801 by the 1st Marquess himself and the first part of the castle was built between 1801 and 1804, but extensions were made after 1817 when Sir Robert Smirke was called in, doubtless as a result of his work at Eastnor. One could hardly call the Cholmondleys *arrivistes*, as they had owned the site since the twelfth century, but what they built was, indeed, a new structure and a good example of its type. The large number of Gothicised windows makes it clear that it is a 'social' castle rather than one built for defence. It has small towers, castellation and machicolations, but these are cosmetic, fancy dress, perhaps, for a grand house of the late Georgian period. There is asymmetry, but none of the moral energy of Pugin or the wild romanticism of the skylines of later Gothic, nor does it hark back to the Gothic of Strawberry Hill. It is essentially a dignified expression of wealth and social standing, overlooking its thousands of acres and surrounded by large pleasure gardens, an ideal venue for lavish entertainment.

10.3 LONDON TERRACES

Dating from the first decade of the nineteenth century, this row of 'first rate' houses in Montague Street, Bloomsbury, London WC1, is still strongly Palladian even though these ideas had been fashionable since the mid-1760s *(Plate 326)*. The stucco covering the brickwork on the ground floor, which had been in use in this level of house for more than thirty years, enhances the notion of the implied temple arrangement by suggesting a solid 'stone' basement with differently shaped doors.

As usual, there is space for the pillars to rise between the windows, their bases resting on the balconies and their capitals meeting the top stringing line. The chamber windows are as usual square and above the pillars and, as one would expect, the tall *piano nobile* windows are present, here emphasised by the balconies which manage to ignore the naturalised patterns. The effect is minimal and restrained, but just a little boring, and one can sympathise with the Victorians for wanting something more interesting.

While strict Palladian minimalist terraces were built well into the nineteenth century, some less fashionable houses were built at a more human scale. Perhaps something of the Picturesque ideal had percolated down to this speculative level. Whatever the reason, this terrace in Sekforde Street, Clerkenwell, London EC1 *(Plate 327)*, the clock centre of the Victorian City, looks cheerfully provincial and homely by comparison with its grand Palladian contemporary. It was built in about 1830, the work of C.R. Cockerell and his office.

The window and door groupings, with their independent details, give each house an individuality, yet the collective design of the terrace as a whole is maintained by the use of stringing lines and crude triglyphs on the low parapet. A relaxed atmosphere derives from undisguised changes both of ground level and of chimney-grouping, where such alterations are necessary. Also, the appearance of the façade is softened by the use of half-circles, the recessed arch being typical of the period, while the round-headed doors and ground-floor windows, not always immediately below the upper windows, give additional informality. The use of the stringing line as an impost for the first-floor recessed arch is a good touch.

326. *21-29 Montague Street, Bloomsbury, London*
327. *Houses in Sekforde Street, Clerkenwell, London*

329. *Book Room of Wimpole Hall*

328. *Yellow Drawing Room, Wimpole Hall, Cambridgeshire*

10.4 SIR JOHN SOANE

Nash and Soane, the two great figures in this period of English architecture, were almost exact contemporaries, but there the similarity ends. As we have seen, Nash moved easily in society, while Soane was awkward. They were occasionally rivals for building work and whereas Nash designed in any style which took his or his client's fancy, Sir John Soane laboured hard and in private to arrive at a personal style from which he rarely departed thereafter. It is no accident, but rather a question of temperament, that we think of Nash as a designer of exteriors, like the great terraces of Regent's Park, and Soane of interiors. Perhaps both architects were conscious in their designs of the Picturesque, Soane especially towards the end of his career, but even here there were differences, as Nash was part of the group that included Payne Knight, Price and Repton, while Soane's knowledge came from their books and his meticulous studies when he became Professor of Architecture at the Royal Academy.

Soane first met Philip Yorke, heir presumptive to the Earldom of Hardwicke, in Italy in 1779. It was to prove fruitful for both young men and for Wimpole Hall, the great house in Cambridgeshire which Yorke inherited in 1790. Within a few years the house was to be transformed, with the most striking alteration by Soane being the design of the Yellow Drawing Room *(Plate 328)*. Several rooms in the old part of the house were knocked together and a keyhole-shaped space inserted consisting of two squares, one with a barrel-vaulted ceiling and the other given two apsidal ends and a circular top-lit centre which rises the full height of the house to a

dome. This too was a highly innovative design which must have been inspired by Soane's Italian visits, perhaps to Raphael's Villa Madama and to the side chapels of St John Lateran, both in Rome. It is also easy to see that the same concept was used in the Dulwich Mausoleum a decade later.

Quite as striking is the extension that Soane made in 1806 to the Ante-Library or Book Room *(Plate 329)*. The space was doubled by incorporating two bays of the Orangery, but it is the elliptical arches, decorated with *paterae* in plaster, springing from the bookcases and supporting a barrel-vaulted ceiling that is so distinctively from Soane's hand.

In a discussion of domestic architecture it might be thought that the Dulwich College Art Gallery has little relevance, and yet this wonderful building does incorporate the Mausoleum of the benefactor of the main gallery, Sir Francis Bourgeois, and is essentially domestic in scale *(Plate 330)*. Built in 1811-14, the Gallery's use of brick and round-headed archways and recessed windows gives it a simple appearance, which is belied by the complex breaking of internal spaces. This is truly innovative, even though the inspiration of the building lies surely with Vanbrugh and, in the Mausoleum itself, Adam.

Within a largely conventional house at No. 13 Lincoln's Inn Fields, Soane created a series of remarkable interiors for himself from 1812 and eventually gave the house and its contents to become the Soane Museum. Here the Picturesque element is strong, with Gothic style hanging arches separating the ceiling from the walls in the ground-floor Library, while in the Dining Room a large window

330. *The Mausoleum at Dulwich Picture Gallery, London*

331. Breakfast Parlour, Sir John Soane's house, Lincoln's Inn Fields, London

opens on to Monument Court, establishing a receding space just as was done in the Library. In the small Breakfast Parlour *(Plate 331)*, the centre of the room has an elegant dome, but concealed top-lighting on two sides allows sunshine to make the walls brighter than the sitting area.

In 1801 Soane bought Pitzhanger Manor, at Ealing, as a country estate for himself. Originally intending to clear the site, he kept the south wing which had been designed by his master, George Dance the Younger, in 1770 containing a ground-floor Dining Room with a Billiards Room above.

Soane created a Drawing Room, a Library, and an entrance hall and staircase well, all of generous dimensions, in the centre of the house and, using many of the devices that have already been described at Wimpole and Lincoln's Inn Fields, made a modest villa seem much bigger than it really was.

The front elevation of Pitzhanger *(Plate 332)* was grand, as befitted the designer of the Bank of England. Constructed of yellow London stock brick, the entrance front has four giant Ionic columns in Portland stone with a strongly projecting entablature over each column in the manner of Adam's south front at Kedleston. Terracotta statues stand on the top of the entablature against a windowless attic, but the centre rises further and the whole conception is topped by a balustrade. Today it is opened as a museum.

332. Pitzhanger Manor, Ealing, London

10.5 THE PICTURESQUE WITH RELIGIOUS OVERTONES

The ruined church or abbey was a powerful romantic image and at the beginning of the nineteenth century there were plenty of these left standing nearly three hundred years after the Dissolution of the Monasteries. Newstead Abbey, Nottinghamshire (**Plate 333**), was founded in the twelfth century by Henry II not as an abbey at all, but as a priory of Augustinian canons. Sold to Sir John Byron at the Dissolution, the residential part of the building was made into a new house for himself and he also plundered the church for the necessary building materials. Given the Strawberry Hill treatment in the mid-eighteenth century by the 5th Lord Byron, and provided with a fort as an 'eye-catcher' in the

1770s, Newstead was in a state of 'Picturesque decay' by the time the poet inherited and he could make only a few rooms fit for use. Even today it retains something of the melancholy which so appealed to the early Victorians.

Fonthill Abbey, at Fonthill Gifford, Wiltshire, was in marked contrast to Newstead (**Plate 334**). It was an abbey built from scratch by William Beckford, the prodigiously wealthy son of Alderman Beckford, from 1793 as a home for his collection of medieval art. He began building the Abbey about half a mile to the northwest of his father's Palladian mansion, Fonthill Splendens, which he eventually demolished in 1807, but

333. Newstead Abbey, Nottinghamshire

the tower of his remarkable Gothic structure, negligently built, collapsed in 1825. Today all that remains of Fonthill Abbey is a small building at its northern end consisting of the polygonal Oratory and the walls of the once vaulted Sanctuary surrounded by the pine woods that Beckford had planted, providing the dark mood essential for this version of the Picturesque.

Designed by James Wyatt, Fonthill at its peak was an enormous cruciform building with a tower 275ft. (84m) high above a tall Octagon at the junction of four ranges. The west wing held the entrance hall with a wide staircase leading straight up to the Octagon. To the north, King Edward's Gallery, 68ft. (20.7m) long, gave access to the Sanctuary and the Oratory; while on the south, the 112ft. (34m) long St Michael's Gallery had domestic offices leading off it to the west, with further accommodation to the east of the Octagon.

Fonthill Abbey was a hastily got up piece of theatre, and indeed a three-day party was held there in 1800 in honour of Nelson and his victory at the Battle of the Nile. After 1807, when he finally moved in, Beckford could enjoy a gigantic stage where one lonely man, cut off from conventional social life by his sexual orientation, could live out a Gothic fantasy.

334. Fonthill Abbey, Wiltshire, by Francis Danby

10.6 THE COTTAGE ORNÉ

One way of constructing a Picturesque scene was to feature a beautiful cottage. It would not be a real cottage, of course, but an idealised or Romantic interpretation of one. During the period some forty books appeared, mostly written by hopeful young architects with their versions of the ideal cottage. Naturally, many served as lodges at the ends of drives where the owner could enjoy them as he swept by and strangers passing the gateway could be impressed by the taste of the estate-owner.

Sir Jeffry Wyatville, as he styled himself, had received his architectural training from his uncles, Samuel and James Wyatt, and amongst his earliest works was Endsleigh, Devon (**Plate 335**). In 1809 the 6th Duke of Bedford, owner of this spectacular part of the Tamar Valley, commissioned Humphry Repton to produce a report and proposals for the site, which he expressed in the form of a plan and three watercolour perspectives, and he concluded that the most appropriate style of house would be 'an irregular farm-house, little better than a cottage'. As it turned out, Endsleigh was built by Wyatville who brilliantly interpreted Repton's vision by creating a substantial country house which deferred to the magnificence of its setting, presenting it as a thatched *cottage orné*. Built originally to a zig-zag plan resembling a group of farm buildings, Endsleigh established a pattern that was to be adopted by Devey, Shaw and Lutyens during the following century.

In 1814, while the house was building, Repton was finally commissioned to report on the garden setting and he prepared a Red Book for one of the most spectacular landscapes that it is possible to imagine. His ideas were expressed in a series of charming watercolours by John Cook Bourne dated 1841. Although not all Repton's recommendations were accepted, the Picturesque qualities of the landscape were maintained by the Dukes of Bedford, and by the Endsleigh Fishing Club, which ran the property as a hotel from 1962. The house is now in new ownership, but with a similar purpose, and is called Hotel Endsleigh.

The theme at Endsleigh was for the Duke and Duchess of Bedford to pretend for a moment that they were poor and this rural make-believe was also popular at the time in Ireland. One of the finest cottages ornés is The Swiss Cottage, at Cahir, built in about 1817 by John Nash for the Earl of Glengall, and this not insubstantial structure has verandahs on two levels as well as trellises and thatch.

The Grove, at Penshurst, in Kent, is also a cottage orné (**Plate 336**). Charmingly decorated with elaborately carved and painted fretted bargeboards, this stone house by Decimus Burton also has small leaded window panes and is a particularly good example of its kind, dating from about 1820.

Even more eccentric was the Picturesque village laid out by Lord Ongley at Old Warden, Bedfordshire, from 1830, where even the cottagers had to wear red cloaks and tall hats to harmonise with the red doors and windows of their thatched cottages. Some of the cottages remain today (**Plate 337**), but the theatrical requirements of the landowner are no longer enforced!

336. *The Grove, Penshurst, Kent*

337. *Cottages ornés at Old Warden, Bedfordshire*

338. 55-58 Regency Square, Brighton, Sussex

339. Greyfriars, also called Regency House, South Green, Southwold, Suffolk

340. *Regency bow window in the High Street, Woburn, Bedfordshire*

10.7 REGENCY BOW WINDOWS

The Regency bow brings to mind the squares of Brighton **(Plate 338)** where rows of houses angle away from the sea retaining their sea views from shallow bows. Strictly, we ought not to speak about the Regency until 1811, but the bow with its delicate ironwork is to be seen in the last decade of the eighteenth century, and seen also to grace many inland houses as well as the Brighton seaside made popular by the Prince Regent. Bows had, of course, been around since Elizabethan days, but, curiously in an age given to bold ornamentation, the shallow bow is particularly Regency. A particularly gracious house which combines both sea views and shallow bows is Greyfriars, also today called Regency House, on South Green, Southwold, in Suffolk **(Plate 339)**. Built of a lovely yellow brick, the building is actually a pair of houses with entrances at the sides, and it seems likely, therefore, that it dates from the end of the 1820s, but the top floor dormer bow was most likely added later.

Moving inland, this example of a shallow bow **(Plate 340)** is from the High Street, in Woburn, Bedfordshire, and shows how the bow can be used in conjunction with the typical metal support and gracious classical ironwork.

The house probably dates from the 1790s with the wonderful range of colours that comes from roughly made local bricks, and there are stone quoins marking what one takes as the original form of the building. But there is a problem. Why do the bricks on the right side of the quoins look the same as the main body of the building, if they are a later alteration? As so often happens with houses in important positions in a prosperous town, we are looking at a much earlier timber building which has been refaced. The first effort was probably early Georgian, evidenced by the voussoirs over the tiny window on the top floor on the left, the later fire resulting in a more extensive rebuilding in which the entire house was refaced and the bows added.

There is also a charming small house at Sittingbourne, Kent. No. 49 High Street is, perhaps, the most striking house in the road, and its stuccoed front painted white speaks of the early years of the nineteenth century. Although the façade is only of three bays, the two outer ones have Regency bows on each floor, while, over the windows, there are fan-shaped tympana; the porch is supported by Doric columns and that too has an ironwork balcony above.

10.8 PICTURESQUE THATCH

In medieval society the cottager had occupied a distinct rung in society. He had a small house, enough land to grow food, and rights on the common and in the woods. By 1800, however, the enclosures had reduced his position, so that he was an employee of a landowner, if he could get work at all. Since the beginning of the agrarian revolution there had been spasmodic unrest in the countryside throughout Europe, but, while there was actual famine on the Continent in 1795, in Britain food prices doubled. Workers lived in real squalor, with the average worker's cottage consisting of one room with a sleeping loft over. The mid-nineteenth century rosy view of a self-sustained peasantry that had continued since medieval times, enhanced by paintings which showed the best aspects of rural life, was hardly true of the last decades of the previous century.

A distinction is to be drawn, therefore, between the worker's cottage thatched to keep out as much rain as possible at minimum cost (at least at the time) and the thatched cottage built with the specific intention of creating a picturesque view. There is the charming Seaforth Cottage at Wool, in Dorset (**Plate 341**), that surely fits into the first category, but those built to enhance the view usually cannot conceal the formality of the purpose, the building symmetrical with a pediment and a hipped roof. The windows too have a typically intricate but repetitive pattern that one associates with the metal windows of the Carron factory.

There is also a fine group of vernacular cottages at Great and Little Pagehurst, near Staplehurst, in Kent. But whether they were built to enhance the view or to accommodate estate workers must remain an open question.

341. Seaforth Cottage, Wool, Dorset

10.9 INDIAN PICTURESQUE

One interesting variation on the 'Make money, and then become a Country Gentleman' theme was the Indian connection. A servant of the East India Company who made money, Sir Charles Cockerell had no compunction about using an Indian style in his own house, Sezincote, near Moreton-in-Marsh, Gloucestershire, and ensuring that it was reasonably realistic by employing Thomas Daniell, the respected topographer of India, to advise on the design *(Plate 342)*.

Remodelling a pre-existing house in 1805, Samuel Pepys Cockerell, Sir Charles' brother, had built the nearby Daylesford for Warren Hastings and topped it

342. Sezincote, Moreton-in-Marsh, Gloucestershire

343. *The Royal Pavilion, Brighton, Sussex*

with a Moslem dome. Now at Sezincote he constructed the eleven bays of the main house and added to it a long, curving greenhouse wing to the south, while to the north a further extension ends in a pavilion which was to house Sir Charles' own bedroom – an elaborate tent.

It was probably due to the scholarship of Thomas Daniell that the Indian detailing is so convincing. Mughal rather than Hindu, the ornament shows an understanding of the importance of linear patterns, and the most striking features of the design are the onion-shaped copper dome on top of the main house and the deep *chattris*, or cornice, that runs around it at eaves level. Even the stone is said to have been dyed to produce an authentic Indian saffron colour, while the asymmetry of the plan had, by this time, become obligatory in a building with pretensions to the Picturesque.

The Prince of Wales had leased a farmhouse facing the Steine, in Brighton, in 1786 and, using Henry Holland as architect, he had begun to build a Marine Pavilion. The plan involved the construction of a second farmhouse

joined to the first by a rotunda with two apsidal extensions. Outside, the rotunda had a modest dome pushed forward and a detached colonnade, and each wing had a pair of shallow bows, the forerunners of many such in Brighton, as we have already seen.

In 1804-1808 the Riding House and Stables were added by William Porden, a pupil of S.P. Cockerell, and this design incorporated a much more prominent dome. The Prince of Wales immediately wanted to give the rather chaste Pavilion itself a more exotic appearance and Humphry Repton produced designs in an Indian style in 1805. The Prince visited Sezincote two years later, but nothing was done to Brighton Pavilion until 1815, and the architect used by the then Prince Regent was John Nash. Nash was no scholar, but the domes, pinnacles and columns are Indian, while the basic classical form of the building was preserved and Gothic friezes added **(Plate 343)**. When it is remembered that, from 1802 onwards, many of the interiors were re-done in the *chinoiserie* manner, the building is a riot of colours and styles.

10.91 MIDLANDS ESTATE COTTAGES

At Budby, in Nottinghamshire, a group of two-storeyed cottages was built between 1807 and 1812 by the 1st Earl Manvers, of Thoresby Hall, for his estate workers (**Plate 344**). Although simple, these houses were substantial by the standards of the day and consisted of three bays, stuccoed walls and porches. The patterns of the casements look rather Gothic, but for the rest the overall appearance of the group is Neo-classical. It has been suggested by scholars that the style in which these cottages were built conformed to the requirements of Lord Manvers, as similar developments can be found at Holme Pierrepont and at Radcliffe-on-Trent, both also part of the Manvers estate.

344. Estate house at Budby, Nottinghamshire

345. Sutton Hall, Sutton-on-the-Hill, Derbyshire

CHAPTER 11

1815-1850

11.0 INTRODUCTION

The 'thin red line' of guardsmen who gave Wellington victory over Napoleon Bonaparte at Waterloo in 1815 heralded a hundred years of security from foreign interference, but more changes than England had ever experienced previously. The most obvious change was the move from the land to the town and the industrialisation which by 1851 resulted in half the population being urban dwellers. Bolstered by the Irish, who flooded into the industrial areas of the Midlands and the North West, the population more than doubled, even though large numbers emigrated to America and to the Colonies of Canada, Australia and New Zealand.

Social divisions widened. The high price of food which stimulated enclosures of common land led to rural poverty for the labourers, who also faced transportation for taking game from land they had previously relied on for sustenance. Cheap manufactured goods were easily transported by the new canal system; the roads were improved and the stagecoach flourished; and the new railways brought villages, which hitherto had been self-sufficient, within travelling distance of the towns, leading

to further loss of jobs and a decline in the social structure.

By contrast, the landowners and small farmers prospered, and in this world, obsessed by money and social advancement, the dangerous implications of the word 'idleness' were all too readily recognised by those who had not been able to achieve it. As the century progressed the illusion of leisure without responsibility proved damaging both to industry and the social structure. Houses had to be improved or built again, and there was no shortage of advice from the growing ranks of aspiring architects as to which of the many varieties of Classical or Gothic styles might best suit their newly rich clients. By contrast the Quakers maintained the balance between commercial acumen and social responsibility and produced some of the best social housing, largely in the second half of the century, without any loss of personal wealth.

The towns experienced the same widening social divisions. The poor either packed into the eighteenth century houses deserted by the better-off who had moved to new villas in the suburbs, or into crowded estates of poorly built houses lacking sanitation or privacy, categorised by Osbert Lancaster

346. Ilam Hall, Staffordshire

as 'Salubrious Dwellings for the Industrious Artisan'. Such was the condition of the industrial slums that the national death rate, which had steadily dropped in the previous century, remained static during this period.

The single greatest invention of the period was the railway. The first busy period was 1835-1837 when 1,600 miles were sanctioned. This fizzled out in the next two or three years, so that in 1840 no mileage was authorised. 1844-1847 saw the second railway boom and in 1846 4,500 miles were permitted, representing almost a doubling of the existing length of track. Again slump followed and railway shares, which had soared, lost half their value in two years. There was more frenzied activity in the decades that followed and by 1870, apart from the south-west and the far north, virtually nowhere was more than thirty miles from a railway station. In fact, one can say that the railway map of 1840 looked very like the current motorway map, while that of 1870 looked like a map of the trunk roads today. Industry was, of course, the great beneficiary, particularly in the building trade, and more standard components, such as metal windows, became common.

After the restrictions imposed by the Napoleonic Wars, the remaining twenty-five years of the period saw a revival of building. To begin with designs were naturally influenced by the Neo-classical, by the Greek movement, and then by the Gothic. Terraces were often given central or end features to produce a palace effect and every opportunity was taken to use curving features to create crescents. In the country houses grew substantially in size, due in part to the burgeoning wealth of the middle classes who aspired to join the ranks of the hereditary land-owners, and to a new source of wealth for the aristocracy – coal under their land to fuel the Industrial Revolution. Houses became larger to accommodate growing families and to re-awaken the medieval notion of an old-style English gentleman dispensing hospitality in his Great Hall. And, of course, a small army of servants was needed to attend to all their material needs.

The period after Waterloo was also marked by a cultural change expressed in the growing popularity of the Gothic (**Plates 345 and 346**) and in the construction of a growing number of country house chapels. After the debauchery of the Regency, the beginnings of the Victorian period saw a return to morality and, under the guidance of Pugin's and Ruskin's writings, the growing dominance of the Gothic, thought to be the Christian style.

263

347. *Cumberland Terrace, Regent's Park, London*

11.1 LONDON'S PALATIAL TERRACES

Augustus at Rome was for building renown'd
And of marble he left what of brick he had found
But is not our Nash, too, a very great master?
He finds us all brick and leaves us all plaster.

The work of John Nash has been discussed on several occasions during the decades at the end of the eighteenth and the beginning of the nineteenth centuries and each time it has been in regard to the Picturesque. Now the story concerns the way Nash brought the pictorial qualities of the grandest terraces to London. In 1811 Marylebone Park reverted to the Crown and, although the development of the farms and gardens that comprised the property had been under discussion for many years, nothing was done immediately. Two schemes were commissioned, one from Thomas Leverton and the other from Nash, who had been since 1806 Architect to the Office of Woods and Forests. His proposals were innovative, but also much in line with his previous work with Repton in the Picturesque manner. On the highest land of what we today call Regent's Park, a great double circus was to be built linked to a series of grand terraces, squares and crescents and more than fifty villas, all set in Reptonian parkland.

As if this was not enough, the *coup de théâtre* was to be the road, Regent Street, linking the Park in the north, through Adam's Portland Place, brilliantly changing direction at the ball-joint of All Souls, Langham Place, and sweeping down Regent Street and through the Quadrant to meet Pall Mall in the south on the axis of Carlton House. As Sir John Summerson has said, Nash was 'happiest in control of some big piece of contriving; planning, organising, and letting details look after themselves', but in the case of this piece of inspired urban planning London and its citizens are undoubtedly the winners. The two plans were accepted in 1812 and 1813 with Nash appointed as architectural and town planning consultant, as well as letting agent. Perhaps even more remarkably, the gigantic scheme was largely carried out by the time Nash died in 1835 and by that time Pall Mall had begun to be extended eastward to link to Trafalgar Square, and westward to take in St James's Park, and the new Buckingham Palace.

The first of the terraces was Park Crescent, begun in 1812, which is a chaste but striking design incorporating a colonnade of coupled Ionic columns. Subsequent terraces were grander, but perhaps not so successful, especially in their detailing. Chester Terrace, on the east side of the Park, however, introduced the triumphal arch (1825), while Cumberland Terrace (1827) consists of three linked blocks and was clearly inspired by Chambers' Somerset House (*Plate 347*).

During development changes to Regent's Park were made with the northern terraces removed from the plan

348. *Sussex Place, Regent's Park, London*

and few of the planned villas constructed in the Park itself. On the western side Ulster Terrace (1824) has coupled bow windows at the ends and an Ionic colonnade running between them on the ground floor. Cornwall Terrace (1820-1821) was the first terrace to be designed by the young Decimus Burton under the guidance of John Nash, and this is Corinthian with a central pavilion with six giant columns supporting a portico and two end pavilions echoing this design. Clarence Terrace (1823) is also by Burton and is Corinthian, while in the seventy-seven bays of Sussex Place (1822) Nash sets very unclassical steep octagonal domes above the bay windows *(Plate 348)*.

When most of the terraces around the Park were complete, John Nash created one of the most interesting suburban extensions to the main design in Park Village East and West. Laid out in 1824, they follow the Picturesque principles in which Nash was so expert and contrasted in an innovative way the modest villas of the Villages with the larger villas for the rich inside the Park itself. We have already seen how Nash created the Picturesque village at Blaise Hamlet, near Bristol, but the application of the village idea to the suburb was entirely new and was to have numerous progeny during the Victorian period. No. 12 Park Village West has an octagonal tower *(Plate 349)*, while No. 17 is in the Gothic style and others Italianate, the stuccoed houses fronting on to a curving street in a charming way.

349. *12 Park Village West, Regent's Park, London*

265

350. *226 Camberwell New Road, London*

11.2 SMALL FORMAL HOUSES

Once you get interested in houses it is surprising how often the eye picks out the fascinating small examples of great character. This example *(Plate 350)* in Camberwell New Road, London SE5, dating from 1833, is enhanced by its position between two standard late Georgian houses, for it underlines the changes that were taking place. The first thing that strikes one is the bold four-square arrangement with a strong accent on the horizontal which comes not just from the proportions of the building, but from the use of stringing lines without mouldings, which is neo-classical.

One of the best houses in Cockermouth, Cumbria, was known as the Grecian Villa and is now a hotel *(Plate 351)*. Dating from about 1830, it proclaims the Neo-classical solidly, but it has individuality. Inside a frame of plain frieze and giant pilasters kept just inside the corners, the central of the three bays consists of a loggia on both floors, articulated by Ionic unfluted columns, square on the first floor and round below. Stone divides the windows into three parts. It is a self-confident design.

Kingsland House, in Modbury, Devon *(Plate 352)*,

351. *Manor House Hotel, Cockermouth, Cumbria*

266

started life as a Scientific and Literary Institute, which most probably explains the classical formality of the structure. Founded in 1840 by Richard King, a native of Modbury who eventually settled in New York, the building has a provincial heaviness of the Greek about the façade. The pediment works well and the Ionic columns are well spaced and proportioned, even if a trifle short. The rusticated temple base looks too heavy in proportion to the top and the Tuscan pillars are excessively rustic. The design might be provincial, but it is charming none the less.

Also in Devon, though this time in Newton Abbot, is a development of the 1840s which brings together the classical and a version of the rustic villa advocated by J.C. Loudon. Devon Square *(Plate 353)* was designed by a local architect, J.W. Rowell, and his work fits the site like a glove and conveys the impression of a charming Devon town very clearly. At the top of the square the building is of three storeys linked together by a palace front, while, on the sides, villas climb the slope and a less formal arrangement completes the design.

352. Kingsland House, Modbury, Devon

Below. 353. Villas in Devon Square, Newton Abbot, Devon

354. *Paired villas in Wharton Street, Islington, London*

11.3 SEMI-DETACHED HOUSES

These precursors of the modern semi-detached houses arrived in England in different forms, but more or less at the same time. Of course, building houses in pairs provides a significant reduction in construction costs, and so examples of the practice stretch back at least to the seventeenth century; a typical example would be a pair of estate cottages. But their use in towns dates from the turn into the nineteenth century and at this time the purpose was not only to save money but also to achieve symmetry in design.

The terraces in Wharton Street and Lloyd Baker Street *(Plates 354 and 355)*, on the Lloyd Baker Estate, in Islington, London N1 are particularly good examples. Planned in 1818, but not begun until the 1830s, most probably to designs by W.J. Booth, this pair of villas in Wharton Street, two-storeyed and in stock brick, provides a classically acceptable gable-end dwelling entered from a low, flat-roofed section joining the two properties. The two entrances stand side by side, a practice avoided by

355. *Villas in Lloyd Baker Street, Islington, London*

356. *3-5 Porchester Terrace, Bayswater, London*

357. Back-to-back housing: Court 15, Hurst Street and Inge Street, Birmingham

most landlords on country estates as it might be considered socially unsatisfactory. The arrangement did provide an impressive façade for the whole building, however, and this was clearly the more important factor in early Victorian London. The houses in Lloyd Baker Street have their windows framed by great arches.

Nos. 3-5 Porchester Terrace, Bayswater, London **(Plate 356)**, was built by J.C. Loudon for himself and his mother in 1823-1825 and accordingly was one of the earliest pairs of villas to be built in the capital's suburbs. Featured in Loudon's *Suburban Gardener and Villa Companion* of 1838, the houses were entered from the sides, while the central domed conservatory concealed the junction of the two properties, making it appear as one. Loudon described the design as 'having some pretensions to architectural design', while the surrounding verandahs were intended to be especially convenient for invalids. What one sees is a four-square double-pile late-Georgian building with the kitchens in the basement. It takes little imagination to see how the idea could be developed by a speculative builder.

11.4 CHEAP HOUSES FOR THE URBAN POOR

As the introduction to this chapter suggested, the early decades of the nineteenth century saw a great migration from the countryside to the towns and cities. The Industrial Revolution had provoked a hunger for labour, so that by the middle of the century more than half the population lived in urban communities, the first time in the nation's history that this had been the case. To meet the demand for accommodation back-to-back houses were built in rows, and cheap these properties certainly were as each street of houses shared a single spine wall

with those in the next street and each row had just one façade. Houses such as these were built all over the country, but particularly in the Midlands and the North, from the 1780s onwards and, after a vociferous campaign by Victorian social reformers, new back-to-backs were banned by legislation in the 1880s.

Birmingham saw many back-to-backs built as its population expanded at an alarming rate, from 70,000 in 1801 to more than half a million by the century's end. So assiduous have modern urban planners been that few back-to-backs have survived in the city, but Court 15, at the corner of Hurst Street and Inge Street, has been restored by the National Trust, in conjunction with the Birmingham Conservation Trust, and four houses there are now open to the public **(Plate 357)**. Court 15 was built between 1802 and 1831 and was made up of eleven small houses with a room on each floor, constructed around a paved courtyard with shared wash house and lavatories.

It is, perhaps, surprising that the National Trust, with its reputation for opening upper-middle class and aristocratic houses, should have become involved in such a scheme of restoration, but its motives are those of a social rather than an architectural historian. The four houses that are opened feature the lives of those who lived in the back-to-backs at different periods in their history – in the 1840s, the 1870s, the 1930s and the 1970s – and it is interesting to observe that the early occupants were skilled artisans who were the backbone of an Industrial Revolution which had provided them with a degree of modest prosperity. Such properties undoubtedly became slums, but they were built originally as respectable dwellings and their deterioration says as much about poverty and building condition as it does about the type of house constructed in cities in the early years of the nineteenth century.

11.5 THE TASTE FOR NEO-NORMAN

Even today the first sight of Penrhyn Castle, in Gwynedd, with its backdrop of Snowdonia, causes the visitor to take a sudden breath in amazement. It is true that the west front of this enormous castle is now softened with creeper *(Plate 358)*, but the gaunt Keep with its round-headed openings for windows immediately evokes thoughts of Castle Hedingham, in Essex. The castellated style chosen for his residence by George Hay Dawkins Pennant in 1820 is appropriate to an area which boasts the royal castles of Caernarfon and Conwy, and to the elevated position that was chosen overlooking the entry to the Menai Straits where there had been a fortified house since the fourteenth century.

Penrhyn Castle, now owned and opened by the National Trust, must be one of the largest residences in the country and it took Thomas Hopper seventeen years to build in Anglesey limestone. His client had succeeded to the vast estates of his cousin, the 1st Baron Penrhyn, and a combination of slate quarrying and Jamaican sugar provided the money for a house which is 200 yards (183 metres) long and spreads over an acre (0.4 hectares).

The style of Neo-Norman was fairly short-lived, but, however scholarly Hopper was in his Norman detailing, it is probable that he thought of his design as being Castle Gothic as opposed to Church Gothic or House Gothic, for it was not until 1836 that a distinction was drawn between building

358. Penrhyn Castle, Gwynedd

359. *Benington Lordship, Hertfordshire*

before and after the Conquest. The collaboration between architect and client was close at Penrhyn, for the distribution of defensive towers, 124ft. (38m) high Keep and castellated State Rooms creates a medieval impression which is strongly Picturesque and the round-headed windows and doorways with their zig-zag decoration and engaged colonnettes at the sides, while not for a moment deceiving a medieval scholar, are redolent of Romanesque architecture. Inside, the narrow cloister leads into the great space of the Grand Hall with its decorated round-headed arches and stained glass by Thomas Willement, while the three flattened arches which separate

the Library from the Drawing Room recall that of the Norman chancel arch at Tickencote church, Rutland.

Benington Lordship, Hertfordshire, was a Georgian house remodelled in 1832 in the Neo-Norman style to recall the Keep of Benington Castle which was largely demolished in 1212 *(Plate 359)*. Pulham, the designer, was a landscape gardener rather than an architect and he also added a Gatehouse in the same style between the house and what remains of the Keep. This is very much in accordance with the principles of the Picturesque, as has been observed in relation to Penrhyn.

360. Abbotsford, Melrose, Roxburghshire

11.6 SCOTTISH NEO-BARONIAL

'The road to ruin is…to have an improvable estate with a taste for building'. So wrote Sir Walter Scott in 1825 and in his life and at Abbotsford, the house he built near to Melrose, Roxburghshire *(Plate 360)*, he put this principle into practice. Best known as one of the most successful authors of the period, Scott was steeped in Scottish history and in Borders' folklore from his birth in 1771 and poured out romances about Scotland's history between 1802 and 1830. He made a fortune and lost it, sinking vast sums into landowning, lavish house-building and in entertaining in an attempt to become a landed gentleman. He immersed himself in the romantic times he wrote about, met Burns, discovered the lost Scottish Royal Regalia, was given a baronetcy in 1818 and was bankrupted in 1826. He died in 1832 a national hero.

In 1811 Scott bought a 'small farm' on the banks of the Tweed about three miles from Melrose with the intention of 'bigging myself a tower after my own fashion'. What we see today at Abbotsford is a huge and sprawling pile which betrays its origins as the work of a man of impulse and emotions. To one side there is a pastiche of an early seventeenth century tower house with the inevitable corner turrets dressed up with conical roofs, crow-stepped gables projecting forward of the building line, and towering chimneys. But the accentuated quoins, sash and bow windows and retaining arches are more of the nineteenth century than the medieval period. The house was expanded to the other side, and this tails off into a jumble of the same motifs repeated in a minor key. Overall Abbotsford fails to convince that it has grown over the generations, which was clearly the impression that Scott had hoped to create.

361. Warleigh Manor, Bathford, Somerset

11.7 TUDOR REVIVAL

As we have seen, the Gothic Revival of the early nineteenth century took many forms. The movement away from Neo-classicism towards the Gothic was essentially a change from a style which was largely concerned with surfaces to one which was preoccupied with internal spaces. But the move took time and designers had first to learn about old tracery patterns, mouldings and vaulting before they were able to put them together. For this reason, amongst others, we find architects experimenting with the characteristics of a plethora of 'ancient' styles, among them the Tudor, or more specifically the style of Henry VIII's reign as can be seen most comprehensively at Hampton Court.

Warleigh Manor **(Plate 361)**, just to the south of Bathford, in Somerset, was built in 1815 by Neale Webb, an architect from Staffordshire. In outline it is a Picturesque Tudor villa with towers and turrets, while the elements most redolent of Tudor design are the flat four-centred arch, elaborate brick chimneys and square-headed mullioned windows with hood mouldings and label stops. The setting on the side of the valley of the Avon is idyllic and recently the house and outbuildings have been restored with care and the latter converted to provide ten separate residences. If Warleigh Manor was early in the revival of the Tudor, the more likely period for this style is mid-century, and this can be seen at Heron Court, at Rugeley, Staffordshire. Once St Anthony's Convent, Heron Court is now the St Thomas Priory Golf Club, and this characteristic brick building is Picturesque, and its designer seems keen to recreate a corner of Hampton Court with the low-pitched arch and plenty of castellation. The finials, though a necessary part of Tudor design, seem, however, to have been created by someone

who has Brighton Pavilion as the back of his mind.

Chalmington **(Plate 362)** stands about a mile from Cattistock, in Dorset, and the immediate impression is of a gabled house with overtones of neo-Tudor design, dating from, perhaps, 1830. Rendered, it has square dripstones above some of the windows and a rather modest chimney is corbelled out from the wall. There is also a lodge and stables and the whole creates a characteristic group of this type of historical design early in the century.

362. Chalmington, near Cattistock, Dorset

363. Highclere Castle, Hampshire, from the south-west

11.8 ELIZABETHAN GRANDEUR

Highclere Castle *(Plate 363)* is the grandest mansion in Hampshire. It stands in a 'Capability' Brown landscape which surrounded a square classical house, but in 1839-1842 this building was entirely remodelled by Sir Charles Barry for the 3rd Earl of Carnarvon. The style that was chosen was Elizabethan, but with a dash of the Italianate, and although this might be surprising it should be remembered that, in the competition for the rebuilding of the Houses of Parliament four years earlier, Elizabethan was specifically permitted as an alternative to the Gothic. The inspiration was most probably Wollaton, the house by Robert Smythson on the outskirts of Nottingham, but even here, with the exception of the tall central tower, the allusions are imprecise.

The house is faced with stone and rises to three storeys, except on the entrance (north) side where there is an additional level in the three-bay centre of the eleven-bay façade. There are corner turrets and the windows are of mullion-and-transom type. The façades are flatter than Elizabethan ones would have been, there is remarkably little decoration, and the fenestration as a whole is even, as the windows in a Georgian house would be. Inside the house the style is in the main Gothic, but the interiors are of 1860 and by Thomas Allom, not by Barry.

11.9 THE JACOBETHAN REVIVAL

An early nostalgic attempt to recreate an 'Old English' style, 'without dispute the unimproved product of the soil', got under way in the 1830s. Essentially it was opposed to classicism, either of the Roman or Greek variety, and the comfortable symmetry of the late Elizabethan and Jacobean manor house appealed to contemporary taste. The two styles have been joined by modern scholars to become 'Jacobethan', but often examples belong clearly to one style or the other. The tall chimneys and windows, the stone surround and the black-patterned 'diapers' are pricked out on the walls. As Robert Kerr commented in *The Gentleman's House* (1864), echoing Alexander Pope, 'these lifeless replications…wing nodding to wing, each chimney having its brother, and half the surface helplessly reflecting the other, were replaced by a more flamboyant – and less accurate interpretation – with asymmetry a virtue and decoration obligatory'. By the time this was written the cultural climate had changed, and interest had moved forward to favour the calm architecture of the early eighteenth century, that is, the Queen Anne Revival.

Whittington Hall, at Whittington, in Lancashire *(Plate 364)*, was built in about 1831 by George Webster for Thomas Green. This is a 'Jacobethan' house with the symmetry carefully observed in the main front, but with a touch of the Picturesque supplied by the tower. This gives the impression that the house was once a Pele Tower and that this feature has been incorporated in the design. The

364. *Whittington Hall, Whittington, Lancashire*

main entrance under the house is an individual peculiarity.

Clyffe House *(Plate 365)*, just outside Tincleton, in Dorset, was built for Charles Porcher by Benjamin Ferrey in what has been called the 'Manorial Gothic' style. To the mind brought up to Italian symmetry, the late Elizabethan or Jacobean manor house was an easy step to take in the flight from Palladio. Moreover, it was thoroughly English, and therefore the ideal house for a newly enriched English gentleman to live in. The materials are a brown brick in English bond and Portland

365. *Clyffe House, Tincleton, Dorset*

366. *Stansted Hall, Essex*

ashlar sharply cut. The entrance front, on the north side, has dormers with and without gables, and the E-shaped plan is clear to see, while the mullioned and transomed windows are exceptionally large.

After about 1870 the Elizabethan and the Jacobean was to replace the Gothic as the preferred style. This can be seen in Stansted Hall, Essex, built by Robert Armstrong in 1871 *(Plate 366)*. Brick with stone dressings, the house has clear antecedents, with the ornamental gables crowning both the projecting wings and the dormers, while a balustrade alternates with openwork, and decorated brick chimneys are grouped in a coherent fashion.

276

367. A cottage: plate 30 from The Gentleman's House *by Robert Kerr, 1864*

11.91 OVERGROWN COTTAGES

This type covers two distinct developments. The first was seen as failing to 'take an artistic position', that is failing to follow one of the established styles, and so was dismissed as an inferior product with cheapness as a sole redeeming feature. This was a typical 'Battle of the Styles' attitude. The second development was in the tradition of the Picturesque and showed an interest in the old houses of the south-east of England. This developed into the 'Vernacular Revival' and Richard Norman Shaw's 'Olde English' style.

The first approach is typified by this textbook example **(Plate 367)** from Robert Kerr's *The English Gentleman's House* (1864). It has plain window surrounds and a large hanging soffit, that is the visible underside of the low-pitched roof, supported by brackets and 'probably best described as an inferior sort of rural Italian'. Kerr included it because it was much built, presumably by clients anxious to avoid the tyranny of the 'Battle of the Styles'. Here it is shown as symmetrical, but 'any amount of symmetrical arrangement or freedom therefrom is equally suitable'. The young architect anxious to get his hands on a client was not going to be dogmatic; once he did so the story might well change.

Although Bentham Hill, near Southborough, in Kent, is a substantial mansion **(Plate 368)**, it is fashioned as if it is an overgrown *cottage orné* constructed in sandstone. Built by Decimus Burton in 1832-1833, it has bargeboard gables, mullioned and transomed windows, the lower of which have hood-mouldings, and Tudor chimneystacks. The plan is interesting, as the house is in an L shape with a canted bay projecting southward from the inner angle of the L. Together with the three arches of the stone porch, this is a real Picturesque arrangement.

368. Bentham Hill, near Southborough, Kent

Betteshanger House, near Deal, in Kent, is an even more substantial 'overgrown cottage' *(Plate 369)* which was added to until the 1890s. It started life in 1829 as a small square house by Robert Lugar, but it was the enlargements by George Devey for Lord Northbourne from 1856 that took it into the category that we are presently discussing. Betteshanger was Devey's first major job and he created an L-shaped entrance front facing south-west, engulfing Lugar's house with window bays, Dutch gables and an entrance porch with an oriel to the right, balanced by a battlemented tower at the other end. Although Devey used the Dutch gables a decade before Richard Norman Shaw, at Betteshanger they were employed because they underlined the historical continuity of the house in this area.

Named after the invention of the steam hammer which provided the funds to build it, Hammerfield *(Plate 370)*, near Penshurst, might also be called an overgrown cottage. Dating originally from the early part of the century, the house was enlarged by George Devey for James Nasmyth, the inventor, in 1858-1859 with mock-Tudor diapers. It is made up of a number of timber-framed and gabled units complete with decorative bargeboards. Its jumbled roof-line was intended to suggest that, like many of the manor houses of the sixteenth century, it was added to over a long period. Indeed, there is a hint of the Tudor ogee, roofed tower in the background. This house is in the tradition of the Picturesque strongly influenced by the vernacular or old English which was to evolve into

370. Hammerfield, Penshurst, Kent

371. Lodge at Ashour Farm, Penshurst, Kent

372. Chafford Arms, Fordcombe, Kent

Shaw's 'Olde English' style. Nearby, at the entrance to Ashour Farm, is a truly modest cottage **(Plate 371)** which must be by George Devey. Dated 1861, it is very much in his style, with half-timbering above a stone ground floor and a chimney which shows the influence of Richard Norman Shaw.

An equally charming building, which must also be by Devey, is today the Chafford Arms, at Fordcombe, Kent **(Plate 372)**. Decorated bargeboards give emphasis to the roof-lines, while tile-hanging, those dominating chimneys and a characteristic asymmetry certainly look forward to the 'Olde English' style.

373. Watercolour of St Marie's Grange, near Salisbury, by A.W.N. Pugin

11.92 PUGIN AND THE GOTHIC

'Let every man build to God according to his means, but not practice showy deceptions; better is it to do a little substantially and consistent with truth, than to produce a great but fictitious effect'. These words by Augustus Welby Northmore Pugin in 1841 underline the religious foundations on which his secular as well as his sacred buildings rested. Equally, they are principles which John Nash, who employed Pugin's French father as an architectural draftsman, studiously avoided. A.W.N. Pugin (1812-1852) converted to Roman Catholicism when he was twenty-one and his religious zeal and romantic fervour for the Middle Ages led him to advocate 'Pointed or Christian' architecture with an infectious clarity of argument which makes his books readable, but which, in the atmosphere of suspicion towards Rome then prevailing (the Catholic Emancipation Act having been passed only in 1828), limited his share of patronage. His loathing of the 'wooden' classical architecture derived not only from its surplus embellishment, but also from its origins in heathen temples, an anomaly which had not troubled the eighteenth century or indeed the builders of nonconformist chapels. Pugin's preferred period of the Gothic was that prior to the development of the four-centred arch. The pointed, or two-centred, arch gave the feeling of height, which was symbolic of the Resurrection of Christ.

Pugin's philosophy was developed from two rules that he published in 1841: 1, that there should be no features about a building which are not necessary for convenience, construction or propriety; and 2, that all ornament should consist of enrichments of the essential construction of the building. It follows that the smallest detail should have a meaning or serve a purpose, and even the construction should vary with the material employed. Reiterated by Ruskin (with, of course, reservations and distinctions), and reverenced by the Arts and Crafts architects, these principles echoed down the decades of the nineteenth century, although they were ignored by the builders of resplendently decorated town halls and Gothic abattoirs whom Pugin attacked in his book *Contrasts*.

'Truth' in construction meant that the plan of the house should dictate the elevation rather than the classical idea that the accommodation should be subservient to the need for a symmetrical front. The 'decoration of utility' meant, for example, that mouldings were to be decorated so that rainwater fell away from joints to prevent frost damage, and that plasterwork was only good for coating walls, not for creating ornament. The sensitive use of materials required smaller stones rather than large ashlar blocks, for which the regular jointing would detract from the design. Kentish rag was a favourite stone which gave a rugged, rustic surface with the appearance of age.

A teetotaller and a keen yachtsman, habitually dressed as a pilot, Pugin's contribution to the design of the Houses of Parliament was undoubtedly greater than the credit he received. He lived up to his comment that 'There is nothing worth living for but Christian Pointed Architecture and a boat' and died from overwork at forty having achieved more in his short lifespan than most architects can hope to produce

374. *South front of Scarisbrick Hall, Lancashire*

in two lifetimes. His succinctly expressed and well-illustrated writings are a delight to read and were very influential.

Pugin built St Marie's Grange, Alderbury, Wiltshire (1835) for himself on his marriage at twenty-three years of age **(Plate 373)**. Here he demonstrated how he believed Christian Gothic should be used domestically. The towers and high-pitched and complicated roof-line give the feel of medieval France, while the two-storeyed chapel with its stained-glass windows add the religious flavour. Pugin's obsession with the medieval resulted in a bridge to the house and a garderobe in the tower off his bedroom. The house was, however, picturesquely sited facing south-west and overlooking the water meadows towards Salisbury Cathedral.

Scarisbrick Hall, in Lancashire, was Pugin's first major commission for a house. It came in 1836 from the Catholic Charles Scarisbrick, whose family had lived on the site since the thirteenth century. The extensive remodelling and Gothicising of the existing house lasted for a decade and included the building of a Great Hall and the western rooms associated with it. The very striking south front **(Plate 374)** is by Pugin and he also built an east wing, including an octagonal kitchen modelled on the Abbot's Kitchen at Glastonbury, and a modest clock tower which seems to have been the model for Big Ben. Charles Scarisbrick died in 1860 to be succeeded by his elderly sister, Lady Anne Hunloke, who adopted the surname of Scarisbrick and employed Pugin's son, Edward, to make considerable changes to the east wing, including the erection of the immensely tall clock tower and a chapel. After a number of vicissitudes, Scarisbrick is now an educational establishment.

*375. The Grange,
Ramsgate, Kent*

The Grange, at Ramsgate, Kent, which Pugin built for himself in 1843-1844, has none of the romance of St Marie's Grange. Associated with St Augustine's Roman Catholic church, not only by Pugin, but also containing the family's burial vault, the Grange *(Plate 375)* is of yellow brick with stone facings and its outstanding feature is a battlemented tower on the south-east side, from the top of which Pugin kept watch for vessels in difficulties.

In his last few years, A.W.N. Pugin also designed two houses for clerics, both of them quiet, restrained works. The Roman Catholic church of St Giles at Cheadle,

376. Gothic Rectory, Chapel Street, Cheadle, Staffordshire

Staffordshire, was built for a very wealthy man, the Earl of Shrewsbury, who spared no expense on the church, and it seems unlikely that he would have limited Pugin when he came to build the Presbytery *(Plate 376)*. The former Presbytery, in Chapel Street, is not Gothic, nor is it decorated. Rather it is a simple brick-and-stone asymmetrical house with a touch of the Elizabethan about it, towering over the modern house on its left and even over the tall late Georgian structure on the right. Only the finial cross on the gable and the castellated chimneypots give us a hint that Pugin was involved in a substantial and appropriate building without 'showy deceptions'.

Rampisham Rectory (now Pugin Hall), Dorset, was built by Pugin in 1845. Without being told the name of the architect, one might assume that the Rectory *(Plate 377)* was the work of a sensitive Arts and Crafts designer of the last quarter of the century working somewhere in the Cotswolds. Certainly it does not look fifteen years earlier than the heavily hipped Red House at Bexleyheath, Kent, which has received so much acclaim as pointing the direction in which domestic architecture would develop. The use of small stones of irregular size, rather than large clean-cut blocks, follows Pugin's dictum that they were stronger than modern walls, endowing picturesqueness with 'constructional truth', thus providing a moral dimension. Pugin was among the first to feel deeply about the quality of masonry, wall textures and surfaces.

Pugin finished the decoration of the House of Lords Chamber in 1847 and in the Drawing Room of Eastnor Castle, Herefordshire, we can see the full panoply of what the designer called his 'House of Lords style' *(Plate 378)*. At this time he was so much in demand that Pugin turned his association with the firm of J.G. Crace into a business that could utilise the designs he had previously prepared for the House of Lords to be executed by Crace himself, the metal-

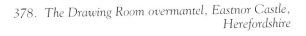

377. The Rectory,
now Pugin Hall, Rampisham, Dorset

working and glass-making firm of Hardman and Co., and the tile-maker, Herbert Minton. The work at Eastnor was carried out by Crace, and Pugin's design incorporated Francis Bernasconi's plaster Gothic vault, of 1813, but he covered it with polychromy, as well as creating the great chimneypiece with the family tree of Earl Somers above, the tables, desk and bookcase. Recently restored, this room is the most complete Pugin interior outside the Houses of Parliament.

But, even more than this, one gets the impression from these examples of his work that Pugin understood and respected vernacular Gothic which fitted happily into his philosophy of building. In his designs we can see the direction in which domestic building was going in the following generations and it is possible to consider Pugin as a Victorian Inigo Jones, for both their shadows stretch long over the centuries in which they lived and worked.

378. The Drawing Room overmantel, Eastnor Castle,
Herefordshire

283

379. Osborne, Isle of Wight, Hampshire

11.93 ITALIANATE VILLAS

When Queen Victoria married Prince Albert in 1840 the couple had three palaces in which to live – Windsor Castle, Buckingham Palace and the Royal Pavilion in Brighton – but none of these offered the facilities in which a family could be brought up privately away from the searchlight which even at that time played on the Monarchy. The Queen knew the Isle of Wight from youthful visits with her mother and liked what she knew, and the young married couple bought the Osborne House estate in 1844 from their personal resources and, further to avoid bureaucratic interference, Prince Albert was his own architect for the new house **(Plate 379)**; the builder was Thomas Cubitt.

The chosen style was Italianate, first introduced into this country in the 1830s by Sir Charles Barry at Trentham Park, Staffordshire, but there are also traces of the style in Cubitt's earlier London terraces. As has been commented on earlier, however, perhaps the real origins of the style can be found in the paintings of Claude Lorrain brought back into England by returning Grand Tourists in the eighteenth century. Certainly the Italianate suited the site on the edge of the Solent and the position is supposed to have reminded the Prince of the Gulf of Naples. Cubitt acted as executive designer, providing the working drawings and insisting on a high level of fire-prevention by constructing floors on brick arches running between iron girders. Indeed, the structure was of brick covered with 'Roman cement' to imitate Bath stone, which doubtless appealed to Albert's concern for economy, and the Royal Pavilion wing, with its State Rooms on the ground floor and the private apartments above, was finished in 1846. The Household wing followed in 1851 and the design was even at that time asymmetrical because the Durbar wing was not built until the 1890s. The bright colours of the interiors, which so recall the Italian Renaissance, were not in fact introduced until the late 1850s.

There can be little doubt that Osborne House was the inspiration for many of the Italianate villas built in this country from the middle of the century onwards. Even in *The English House*, published in 1904, Hermann Muthesius could write: 'The house is still in the cold grip of classicism, especially the ordinary small house. It was built to an axial and symmetrical plan like a box, in a form known as the "Italian Villa", and was plastered and painted with oil paint. The form had [been] introduced by John Nash…Rectangular rooms unthinkingly planned on the axis of the windows…St John's Wood, in north London, is a good example of this style of building as practised in the 1850s'. The plaster was called stucco and this imitation of stonework was exactly the sort of deceit that infuriated Pugin and Ruskin, although by the time of the Arts and Crafts Movement bricks were again being painted white, but this time directly on to the brickwork without deceit.

Two generations on Muthesius saw other disadvantages in what had been considered small, elegant villas. Soulless placing of small doors, fireplaces and windows was deprecated, as was 'the kitchen placed in a dark basement buried up to half its height in the ground'. Today we would have to accept that small inexpensive houses would probably have box-like rooms and there would be little option for the placing of doors, windows and fireplaces. Faced with these problems, the daintily tricked out villas so much criticised by Muthesius have considerable charm.

380. Villas in Calverley Park, Tunbridge Wells, Kent

The Calverley estate in Tunbridge Wells, Kent, designed by Decimus Burton, was begun in 1824. Built on land owned by John Ward, the scheme was for a suburb of villas *(Plate 380)*, complete with Holy Trinity Church. Beginning with Crescent Road, the layout was established by 1828 and Calverley Park Crescent *(Plate 381)* was constructed two years later. The style of the villas was quite simple: three-storeyed, the centre being of five bays with one at each end given prominence by an extra cornice and windows in three sections. The villas were of sandstone but each building had its own individuality. All were set in an extensive parkland, creating a layout which was very much a suburban *beau idée*.

381. Calverley Park Crescent, Tunbridge Wells, Kent

382. Cottages forming a square in front of the church at Penshurst, Kent

11.94 KENTISH COTTAGES

The French Revolution and the subsequent Napoleonic Wars closed Europe as a holiday destination or Grand Tour route between 1794 and 1815. This meant that the growing interest in the Picturesque was focused on Wordsworth's Lake District, Sir Walter Scott's pseudo-Tudor Scotland, and Wales. These locations were visited by nearly all the Romantic painters of the period, headed by Turner and Constable. Those who needed to be near the great marketplace of London moved to the rural and most picturesque parts of the Home Counties. After the railway boom of the 1840s, daily commuting to the capital became an increasingly desirable possibility and the atmosphere of the metropolis became ever more polluted, while the death of the Prince Consort from typhoid fever in 1861 drew attention to the social impartiality of disease.

One group of artists chose Penshurst, in Kent, with its romantic Tudor associations with the Boleyns, as it was within walking distance of historic Hever Castle, and the charming Ightham Mote. The area was mildly Picturesque partly through the patronage of a wealthy art collector who had moved there in 1810, built a house and created romantic gardens. In 1850 the architect George Devey, a man with good social connections, the son of an artist and himself talented with a pencil, designed three cottages in Penshurst village in the form of an open square leading to the church **(Plate 382)**, the central one of the three raised up to form a kind of lych-gate. Instead of building cottages ornés, however, he copied the design of existing building, using ragstone with jettied upper floors and rendering, so that today, 150 years later, the buildings have mellowed to a charming and Picturesque group.

11.95 BUILDING AN INDUSTRIAL COMMUNITY: NEW LANARK

A few miles upstream from the Royal Burgh of Lanark, in lowland Scotland, the River Clyde, which had been flowing quietly, suddenly plunges into a deep gorge at Bonnington Linn, over the Falls of Corra Linn and down to Dundaff. It was this natural phenomenon which persuaded David Dale to embark on an ambitious scheme to establish cotton mills there powered by the force of the river. The first mill was built in 1785, although the twists in the line of the Clyde required the construction of a weir upstream and a 1,000ft. (305m) tunnel cut through solid rock to bring the water to the site. Spinning began in 1786 and by 1793 there were four mills turning more than 10,000 spindles.

But the most remarkable thing about New Lanark was that, of the 1,200 people employed, 800 of them were children. To begin with Dale recruited in the nearby parishes and, although employing such large numbers of children might seem harsh to us today, it was commonplace in the late eighteenth century and contemporaries commented on how well the children were accommodated and treated.

It was the romance of his courtship of David Dale's daughter, Caroline, that brought the reforming socialist Robert Owen to New Lanark. His name is first mentioned in the records in 1798, but Owen and his two Manchester partners purchased New Lanark from his father-in-law and took over management of the mills on the first day of the new century. To begin with the employees were not enthusiastic about Robert Owen and it was only in 1806 that they began to regard him more favourably. It was his proposal to build a school at New Lanark which caused a breach with his partners, but the Glasgow businessmen who replaced them were no keener on the social aspects of the village that New Lanark had become than the Manchester partners had been.

Owen engineered a financial coup with the help of the London Quakers, William Allen and John Walker, and the economist Jeremy Bentham, and 1814, the date when he took virtually unfettered control, is the most significant one in New Lanark's history. His social theories were by this time matured and he realised that the remarkable technical advances of the previous half century had to be matched by the welfare of the workers – good housing, education for the children, and well-organised and benevolent working conditions – if this remote and largely self-sufficient community was to work contentedly and, just as importantly to Owen and his backers, remuneratively as well.

From the earliest times of Owen's administration, labour also came from Highlands emigration, with preference

383. Caithness Row, New Lanark, Lanarkshire

being given to families with at least three children fit for work, and, although at the start accommodation was provided largely in the dormitories of Mill No. 4, more housing was soon required. The first residential buildings were constructed near to Mill No. 1 and when the Highlanders began to arrive the elegant Caithness Row (**Plate 383**) was built to accommodate them. The school, first established under David Dale, was situated just to the east of the village centre, with the Institute and the shop behind, near to Dale's and Owen's houses.

Less appealing from a design point of view were the houses of Long Row, Double Row and Braxfield Row, but, when housing conditions elsewhere in Britain are compared, the quite striking advances made by both Dale and Owen can be seen. Robert Owen severed his association with New Lanark in 1825, but by then the seeds of planned public housing had been sown which was to lead to New Earswick and Bournville, to the Garden Cities of the end of the century and to the New Towns of the twentieth century. Out of the public gaze for more than a century, New Lanark continued largely to follow the principles of its founding fathers, but the decline of the cotton trade eventually brought diversification and when this too failed the mills fell silent in 1967. Under the threat of bulldozers, the long process of restoration began in 1974 with the formation of the New Lanark Conservation Trust, and today the benefits of the job creation schemes, Housing Association involvement, and the repair of the fine stone buildings is there for us all to see and admire.

CHAPTER 12

1850-1870

12.0 INTRODUCTION

Writing about the opening of the Great Exhibition in 1851, *The Times* said: 'The first morning since the creation of the world that all peoples have assembled from all parts of the world and done a common act'.

Flowery writing this might be, buoyed up by an unacceptable arrogance, yet never in British history was it more excusable. The nation owned half of the world's cargo-carrying capacity; the Royal Navy was invincible; and overseas trade expanded three times during the two decades to 1870. There was virtually no competition. The States were anything but united and it took some time for them to recover from the Civil War of 1861-1865. Germany was growing in might, but it was not until the Franco-Prussian War of 1870 that England began to sense the rise of another great power, albeit without the benefit of an empire. The railway boom itself generated huge profits by making it economic for good products to find new markets. Even agriculture prospered, as amalgamations of farms enabled new machinery to improve the efficiency of large holdings.

And the people too were changing. The God-fearing, hard-working generation which had withstood Napoleon and preserved social order in hard times was dying and their children often inherited assets sufficient to enable them to look beyond just earning a living. Darwin's suggestion that those organisms prepared to adapt themselves to their environment succeeded over those that did not rang true to a generation whose parents had

done just that. The poor needed education, therefore, and the stimulation of their intellectual curiosity, that is 'light', rather than handouts. The virtues of personal improvement were expounded relentlessly, with *Self Help* by Samuel Smiles selling 100,000 copies during the period.

God gradually lost his predominant position, as the reality of evolution began to sink in. The artistic rich threw their inherited money and energies into the enjoyment of art and beauty, that is 'sweetness', and made efforts to include the working classes. In his book on the so-called 'Queen Anne Movement', *Sweetness and Light*, Mark Girouard makes the point tellingly when he says: 'It was typical of the difference between generations that parents of the 1850s looked for books that would make their children good, and parents of the 1870s for ones that would make them artistic'. But it was a period of strict hierarchies and the newly rich middle-class man who wanted to could best climb socially by sending his son to one of the new public schools which taught 'muscular' Christianity. Thackeray's concept of the gentleman, as expounded in books such as *Vanity Fair*, involved giving up trade and buying a country estate where he could hunt, shoot and fish, and attempt to integrate his family socially perhaps by marrying his well-funded daughters into the old landed gentry. By contrast, those who did not make the change successfully were pilloried amusingly by authors such as Surtees in *Mr Sponge's Sporting Characters*.

384. The Crystal Palace, Hyde Park, from Dickinson's Comprehensive Pictures

385. Awaiting the Royal Procession at the Great Exhibition, 1851

Small wonder, therefore, that more country houses (as opposed to houses in the country) were built in this period than in any other, and that nationalism and the neo-medievalism of Sir Walter Scott should ensure the eventual victory of the native product over civilised but heathen classicism which had dominated the previous century. But it was inevitable that this heady, developing brew produced some over-decorated experiments as well as some downright ugly houses.

But the evolution of a new approach to architecture was a gradual process. While the glaring red brick, double-bay villa with a roof made of slate brought in by railway from Wales was being built, George Devey was designing timeless gabled houses for his rich friends and Richard Norman Shaw was sketching medieval houses in Kent. And, also at the same time, Ruskin was expanding the ideas of Pugin and Thackeray was looking back with affection to the mellow, red-brick Georgian houses. All these seminal activities had this in common: they looked back to the past with respect rather than with eyes made hazy by romanticism, and with an objective curiosity which led to development rather than sterile copying. The mindless replication of Classical and Gothic motifs was no longer considered to be enough. Gothic was making an attempt to develop a more acceptable domestic style and two main strands of design were emerging – Shaw's Old English style, which developed the native medieval building used mainly in the country, and the Queen Anne Revival, also promoted by Shaw, but here mainly in the towns, which used the eighteenth century house as its base. At this time the Arts and Crafts Movement was also in its infancy.

All this was progressive thinking, while in the north Gothic Revival public buildings and Classical abattoirs were still being built. In the suburbs buildings were being constructed that were free versions of both, and these owed more to enthusiasm and money than to an understanding of architecture or to taste.

This discussion of the architecture of the period has been in the main aesthetic, but the efficiency of a building should also be remembered. With the wider use of iron, to begin with cast iron and later wrought iron, its strength and flexibility improved as a result of an invention of 1785 and, with the addition of steel after the introduction of the Bressumer process in 1856, much larger structures became possible. In the 1840s the manufacture of plate glass became possible and the lifting of the duty on it made greater use of the material economic. Although it was originally confined to hospitals, prisons and other institutions, steam central heating began to be used in houses in the first half of the nineteenth century, while there were also great improvements in cold and hot water supply and in sanitation arrangements. By the 1880s electricity was available to those who were wealthy enough to generate and install it in their houses.

One building more than any other displayed many of these changes and was to have the most profound influence on architectural design not only in this country but throughout the world. Joseph Paxton's Crystal Palace in Hyde Park **(Plates 384 and 385)**, which housed the Great Exhibition of 1851, had about it many of the portents for the future. It was prefabricated, provided a wonderfully bright interior which contrasted with the foliage of the Park, and was made of iron and glass. Some 1,800ft. (550m) long and 140ft. (43m) high, with a volume of 33 million cu.ft. (933,900 cu.m), it had been erected in less than eight months. The wares of 15,000 exhibitors arranged in four categories – raw materials, machinery, manufactures and sculpture and the fine arts – certainly underlined the nation's industrial strength. But the Great Exhibition also attracted six million visitors and many must have come to see this remarkable greenhouse as well as the exhibits. What must have been clear to them is that it was built in such a way that it was infinitely extendable and could also be taken down again, as it was in the following year when it was re-erected at Sydenham, where it remained until being destroyed by fire in 1936. So much of what will be discussed in the following chapters can be traced back to the Crystal Palace.

386. *The Old Rectory, Coalpit Heath, Gloucestershire*

12.1 DOMESTIC GOTHIC

William Butterfield was one of the earliest architects to use heavily hipped gables and dormers and his work can be seen to great advantage at the house built as the Rectory of St Saviour's church, Coalpit Heath, Gloucestershire *(Plate 386)*. Dating from 1845, this building shows the first emergence of functionalism, anticipating Webb's Red House, at Bexleyheath, by fifteen years. The characteristics that immediately catch the eye are the large gabled roof, the chimneys, the medieval porch, but overall the way the elevation is dictated by the rooms inside the house and their purposes. Here Gothic is attempting to devise an architecture for the smaller house which would be acceptable to those not anxious to have an overtly church look.

Although he was trained in the Gothic Revival, Butterfield developed his own distinct style by the mid-1850s, which was perhaps halfway between the Gothic and the Queen Anne Revival. The key change was his cheerful use of small panes of glass secured by white-painted glazing bars, a clear reference back to the early eighteenth century. But it is the dormer window with the hipped roof which immediately calls Butterfield to mind when one sees it used, particularly alongside the pointed retaining arch. He favoured the use of windows in pairs and his travels in the south-east of England sketching old houses left him with a preference for hanging tiles which go well in that area, but which can seem out of place elsewhere.

Milton Ernest Hall, at Milton Ernest, Bedfordshire, has the feel of an overgrown rectory *(Plate 387)* and this is perhaps not surprising as the designer was a religious and self-disciplined bachelor who spent much of his time designing churches and the buildings that went with them, and the client a man who followed the practice of devout early Victorians by attending to the needs of the village church before seeing to his own comfort. Built in 1856 in buff stone and red brick, it is deliberately asymmetrical, and the dormers and windows, even the bays, have a thin-lipped, almost mean appearance. Sanctimonious is too strong a word, but the cusping, the pointed arches, the steep pitch of the roof and the buttressing give the structure a dull, church-like feel relieved only by Butterfield's use of the sash window. He favoured a simple and high line for the main roof, with a steep Gothic pitch, which towered up into a forest of gables and huge chimneys to sweep the eye and the mind heavenwards, rather like a Gothic church interior. In this slightly surprising way the Picturesque lived on.

George Edmund Street was one of the great forces behind the Gothic Revival, but in the Rectory at Upton Magna, Shropshire **(Plate 388)**, now privately owned, he shows great sensitivity towards the vernacular. In this charming brick house of 1864, the pitch of the roof is not excessive; there are Gothic retaining arches, but these are warmly filled with brick; there is half-timbering; and the chimneys feel no need to remind us that God is in Heaven. There are individual touches of interest, such as the strengthening of one corner, the curious height of the plinth which echoes the arch, and the windows. The house fits snugly into its surroundings, and there is the good balance one often sees in old houses between the horizontal and the vertical. This house illustrates well the range that an able architect can span, because a few years later Street was designing the Royal Courts of Justice, in the Strand, London.

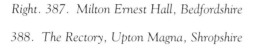

Right. 387. Milton Ernest Hall, Bedfordshire

388. The Rectory, Upton Magna, Shropshire

389. *Entrance front of The Red House, Bexleyheath, Kent*

Philip Webb was Street's pupil and the Red House, Red House Lane, Bexleyheath, in London **(Plate 389)**, was designed in 1859, just after he had left Street's office, for William Morris and his bride, Jane Burden. Dante Gabriel Rossetti said that it was 'More a poem than a house…but an admirable place to live in too', and it enjoyed professional acclaim in the 1860s, partly because Morris and his friends were popular, the house represented the Ruskinian idea of changefulness in design and detailing in its employment of hand-crafted materials, and finally because of Webb's rejection of style. It has been eulogised repeatedly and its iconic status has recently been confirmed by its purchase by the National Trust.

The influence of Butterfield and of Street is obvious, and all the motifs have been used before, including the English bond for the brickwork, which is, of course, the appropriate material for this part of the country. The debt to Pugin is seen in the honest construction by which roofs and windows indicate the character of the rooms within, but this had also been done before, as we have seen. The three narrow Butterfield sash windows crowded under a hipped roof with surprised looking arches do seem a bit mannered, while the single window below suggests a dark room.

Today the Red House is surrounded by suburbia and it takes an effort of will to remember that when Morris and his friends arrived from London at Abbey Wood station they still had a journey of three miles through the North Kent countryside before arriving at the house which Morris considered to be 'in the style of the 13th century'. Once inside the gate they, and we, see a house made of deep-red brick with red tiles on steep roofs. Some of the gables and dormers are half-hipped, and the chimneystacks are tall and placed according to need. The house is two-storeyed

and L-shaped, and the entrance is on the north side under a tall porch at the outside junction of the two arms of building while, uncharacteristically, the two major rooms lie on the upper floor of the northern arm, the Drawing Room at the west end and Morris' study at the east end. Between the two arms on the south side a courtyard is dominated by a charming well-head with a conical roof, making a really Picturesque approach.

It had originally been intended that the Red House should be a romantic community of artists and craftsmen, though it would appear that no one took this idea at all seriously with the exception of Morris himself. However, as designed, the Drawing Room on the first floor was open to the roof with floral designs covering the ceiling, and Burne-Jones began painting the walls with scenes from a medieval romance, and some of these remain on the south wall. The tall brick chimney with its hood still has the motto 'Ars longa vita brevis' and other pieces of furniture were decorated by Rossetti and Burne-Jones. Perhaps Webb's greatest achievement at the Red House was to build a simple Gothic house for a gentleman without the style intruding itself, and without having it decorated to establish the social position of the owner. Morris and his bride only lived in the Red House for five years before moving to London to live in a Georgian riverside house.

Tyntesfield, near Wraxall, in north Somerset **(Plate 390)**, is an object lesson in High Gothic, both in its adoption of the basic principles of the style and in the individual vision with which the architect put these principles into practice. The owner of the estate was William Gibbs, a businessman whose firm established a virtual monopoly in the import of guano from Peru as an agricultural fertiliser. It seems likely that the joys of a country estate in which to bring up his

large family, and his association with Brunel and the building of the Great Western Railway line, made the Bristol area an attractive location, in addition to the presence of relatives in north Somerset. Tyntesfield was bought in 1843 and there was at the time a symmetrical country house with Gothic detailing on the site.

Twenty years were to elapse before William and his wife Blanche were to undertake major rebuilding of the house. Their chosen architect was John Norton, who had practices in Bristol and London and whose Gothic was both muscular and knowledgeable. A pupil of Benjamin Ferrey, who was himself not only a pupil but an early biographer of A.W.N. Pugin, Norton has left a number of Bristol churches and was later to build the truly grand country house of Elveden Hall, Suffolk. At Tyntesfield he was to construct an asymmetrical house with a vigorous Picturesque form which, in the years after it was completed in 1864, was strikingly French, although some of these characteristics have now vanished. The south, garden, front shows how balance can be retained even though it is within an asymmetrical footprint, as the two great rooms, the Drawing Room and the Library, are on the same axis and are both 40ft. (12m) long; while the roofs are at different heights, the lower one ending in a pinnacle and the higher in a corbelled turret.

Today Tyntesfield is owned by the National Trust, the Trust having bought the property from the estate of Lord Wraxall with a substantial grant from the National Heritage Memorial Fund. One of the qualities that commended the house to the Trust was that they were also able to purchase the contents, and the Library, approached from the Forecourt

through a cloister, is one of the most beautiful rooms of its period in the country. This is the book room of a High Victorian gentleman and the splendidly bound books on the carefully labelled shelves are intended for use and not just display. William Gibbs was a devout man and there are many Bibles and prayer books, as well as the texts of the Oxford Movement, which coincided with the Gothic Revival, but also the works of Pugin, the classics, poetry and science. The deep-buttoned sofa and two round-backed chairs date from 1855 and are covered with upholstery by J.G. Crace and Son, one of the century's most distinguished firms of decorators. They also provided the carpet, as well as the lower part of the oak sideboard and the side tables in the Dining Room, the design of these pieces of furniture being strikingly in the manner of Pugin.

William Gibbs' devotion to High Church Anglicanism took the form of building churches in London, Bristol and Exeter, and he, his wife and their sons built and endowed Keble College, Oxford. At Tyntesfield his ecclesiastical patronage took the form of commissioning the chapel from Arthur Blomfield, and this fine building was constructed between 1873 and 1875, the year of Gibbs' death. Again, the feeling is French, the inspiration being the Sainte Chapelle, in Paris, and the arrangement of that medieval building was skilfully followed by Blomfield as the Gibbs family entered their chapel at first floor level across a covered bridge, enabling the building to be fitted in between the house and the steep hill and to occupy in consequence an appropriately dominating position reflecting the role that religion played in the daily life of Victorian Tyntesfield.

293

12.2 RUSKIN ON ARCHITECTURE

'No man's work contains more valuable information than Mr Ruskin's, but it is strong meat, and requires to be taken by one who has made up his mind…To such a man *The Stones of Venice* is an architectural romance full of information and instruction, but to one in search of a style and just beginning his architectural life it is almost destruction.' William Burges' judgement on the influence of Ruskin might seem to us surprising today on several grounds: that a critic's views could be so important to architects might surprise us, but even in matters of architectural style Ruskin saw both the social and the moral implications; the very eloquence with which he expressed his views, which we perhaps distrust, was appreciated by the Victorians who loved a good sermon; and he was also a draughtsman and a painter of great sensitivity, who was able to recognise the structure of a Gothic window, the physical and the aesthetic make-up of a Turner painting (he did more than anyone else at the time to champion him), and the abstract qualities of a piece of sculpture, rather than just its plasticity, while never losing his delight in the whole composition.

Coming from a wealthy but relatively joyless background, Ruskin was to a considerable extent self-taught. He did not go to school, but attended lectures at King's College, London, learned drawing from Copley Fielding and James Duffield Harding and, when he went up to Christ Church, Oxford, as a gentleman-commoner, he spent the time drawing architecture and writing poetry and left the university without taking a degree, though he did win the prestigious Newdigate Prize. At the age of thirty he published *The Seven Lamps of Architecture* and *The Stones of Venice* two years later in 1851, both of them hugely successful and reaching a wider audience than any other previous books on architecture (**Plate 391**). These two works enunciated Ruskin's fundamental belief that the essence of architecture is the ability to decorate, writing in the preface to *The Seven Lamps* that 'the architect who is not a sculptor or a painter, is nothing better than a frame-maker on a large scale…What we call architecture is only the association of these [two fine arts] in noble masses, or the placing of them in fit places. All architecture other than this is, in fact, mere building'.

He was influenced by the Picturesque, which typically he redefined. Until late in life low on self-criticism, Ruskin's enthusiasm for zesty polemics made his relationship with architects an uneasy one. Like the Bible, you can usually find a quote in Ruskin to support your own view, and it is largely his own fault that a gap existed between Ruskin the man and his current opinions, and Ruskinian views, the interpretation of which were what people thought he had said or would have liked him to have said. He was a talented communicator who lectured widely not only to professionals but to the masses in an age when aesthetics, 'truth to nature', moral values and 'the will of God' were meaningful and emotive concepts, and it was possible to see art, science and nature as part of a grand, unified plan organised by the Deity, a concept that began to disintegrate in 1859 when Charles Darwin published his *On the Origin of the Species by Natural Selection*.

Ruskin was prepared to make differentiations, to dogmatise, and to alter his teaching to suit the prevailing views, though many of his 'proofs' were based on emotion, religion and parallels in nature, rather than on the application of hard logic. He played an important part in the search for a new form of architecture fit for the rich and confident new middle classes. His view that only moral men can build good buildings probably provided the excuse for much civic and industrial opulence.

Of course, emotion and the romantic appeal of a redefined Picturesque were at odds with the cold ratios of classical Vitruvian architecture, which had dominated the field for nearly a century and a half. One critic was forced to agree that 'the doctrine of some, Vitruvius included, would go to convert our art [that is architecture] into a sort of barrel-organ, upon which all can grind music alike'. And yet influential buildings like the Oxford Museum, of 1855, and Trinity College Museum, Dublin, of 1858, erected by those sympathetic to his views, are almost symmetrical in form, at least on one of their fronts. It is clear that form was not something that greatly worried him.

Many of Ruskin's ideas had been previously put forward by others, but he was more in touch with middle-class prejudices than they had been. Pugin, for example, had defined 'Truth in materials', but he had been fervently Catholic in a country that was still deeply suspicious of Rome's ambitions and which had seen, in 1851, anti-Papal riots. Ruskin was equally passionate in his Protestantism and managed to disentangle the Gothic Revival from its Roman Catholic associations. But what emerged was a particularly Victorian form of the Gothic, something which many hoped would develop into a new style fit for a new age. This provoked a good deal of argument in the 1850s, particularly in view of the Great Exhibition and the revolutionary Crystal Palace built of new materials – iron and large panes of glass.

391. Study of the façade of the Casa Loredan, Venice, by John Ruskin

Ruskin's core thinking centred around his love of sculpture and colour, rich coloured surface textures with time's imprint, and enhanced by glowing sunlight. He stressed the importance of planning for light and shade on a new building, understandable concerns for a painter. Again, quoting from *The Seven Lamps*, Ruskin writes: 'I do not believe that ever any building was truly great, unless it had mighty masses, vigorous and deep, of shadow mingled with its surface. And among the first habits that a young architect should learn, is that of thinking in shadow…conceiving [the building] as it will be when the dawn lights it, and the dusk leaves it…; let him cut out the shadows, as men dig wells in unwatered plains'.

Although it is clear from this that Ruskin considered mass and shadow as tangible elements, it is the comfortable feeling of security and permanence that volume gives which was more important, as well as providing a canvas on which light can play. It follows also that a large object such as a buttress should be left in solid and undecorated form. Similarly, the Gothic style declined once windows were decorated, which broke up the contrasting masses of light and shadow. We find, therefore, Ruskin preferring the early Gothic to the Perpendicular. Also, by having rows of arches, classical architecture weakened the sense of mass, as did railway architecture, while for him the Crystal Palace was like a huge cucumber frame without the usual compensating mass.

Ruskin's attitude to mass was also fundamentally different from that of the eighteenth century. Then the notion of massiveness conveyed awe and dread in Picturesque theory, but now it was a virtue. The Picturesque too was the function of the distant view, and to Ruskin a building should be seen to be massive and compact from a distance, revealing its details only when one comes closer. However, the decoration must be in the correct proportion, so that the observer can appreciate its details and quality.

392. *Natural History Museum, Oxford*

12.3 RUSKIN ON DECORATION AND COLOUR

'All art in decoration should be informative, conveying fruitful statements about natural facts, if it is to convey any statement.' These words were written by Ruskin in 1855 and it was his view that all architectural decoration should be executed by the men who had designed it. This followed from his understanding of how the original Gothic decoration was inspired. When a friend became architect for the Oxford Museum, Ruskin was able to influence the external design and he was delighted to find the O'Sheas, a family of skilled Irish carvers, to whom he could entrust the decoration, having, presumably, given general instructions on the importance of following nature, particularly in a museum devoted to natural history *(Plate 392)*.

The result was a riot of meticulously executed naturalistic carving. Unfortunately, in *The Stones of Venice* he had laid down that the decorative function of a capital was to express the sense of support given by the pillar to the load it was bearing. Plants such as ferns unfolding as they climbed the capitals were fine, but when a corbel, which is in effect a capital using the wall for support rather than the pillar, was decorated with vapid bunches of flowers, the relationship between load and support was lost.

Reasonably, Ruskin attempted to point out the mistake, and to distance himself from the error, which arose, of course, from his romantic view of the intelligence of the workman, but it was impossible. Naturalistic carving proliferated without regard to its function or meaning. This

is typical of the way Ruskin's ideas could turn out unsatisfactorily in practice, but were nevertheless swallowed whole by the public, leading to the gap previously mentioned between Ruskin and what people thought was Ruskinian. Typically also in this period of heated discussion was the way in which Ruskin's pursuit of naturalism was countered by demands for stiff formalism in depicting nature from those, like Owen Jones, who disagreed with him.

From childhood, Ruskin had placed great emphasis on the exhaustive study of small areas of decoration and he considered that, if the artist could get minute and often naturalistic details aesthetically correct, then he would have no problem in getting such mundane matters as construction right. This was both an illogical and a dangerous argument; it focused attention on decoration and led to the crowded and fussy adornment of High Victorian buildings and detracted from the proper consideration of architectural form and balance.

By contrast to decoration, his ideas on walls, like so much else, came from his study of nature. On hillsides, horizontal bands of strong rock hold together less stable material and there is the added advantage that light reacts differently on each type of stone. In *The Seven Lamps of Architecture* he writes: 'If breadth is to be beautiful, its substance must in some sort be beautiful; and we must not hastily condemn the exclusive resting of the northern architects in divided lines, until at least we have remembered the difference between a blank surface of Caen stone, and one mixed from Genoa and Carrara...so that the surface be wide, bold and unbroken, whether it be of brick or of jasper; the light of Heaven upon it, and the weight of earth in it, are all we need.' Contrasting textures and sizes and shapes of stone are also important, as is colour. As a lover of the Picturesque it is not surprising that Ruskin preferred the warm stones of Italy, and in particular Venice and Lucca, with their jumble of styles and relative simplicity of construction, to the sophisticated intricacies of the cold northern Gothic, though typically he later moved his affections to French Gothic.

From the mid-1850s enthusiasm for Ruskin's ideas grew. It increased in the 1860s, but by the end of this decade the revival of interest in English vernacular architecture had begun. Even Ruskin himself was dissatisfied by much that had been achieved in his name. Although polychromed public buildings continued to be built, domestic style increasingly looked backwards. The effects of Ruskin's thinking and writing have been long lasting and, despite his often purple prose, he did teach people to think about architecture in a new way and in more depth. He rather than William Morris originated the sympathetic restoration of old buildings and his views on colour, light, decoration and mass are influential even today.

12.4 GOTHIC VILLAS

Sending cards and having a Christmas tree in the house came in with Queen Victoria and her German husband, Albert. Their cult of the importance of the family struck an echo in the aspirations of the increasingly prosperous middle classes. The Englishman's home might be his castle, but it could also be his romantic villa, even if he tended to forget the rules of the Picturesque and go for respectable symmetry, as well as preferring contrived prettiness to natural primitiveness.

On the road out of Burton upon Trent to Ashby de la Zouch is this double-pile house **(Plate 393)** which admirably illustrates this type of building. With two high-pitched gables and the entrance between, the decorative treatment of this villa lies in the bargeboards. Not only is the porch tricked out in the same wonderfully worked three-dimensional fretted boards complete with crockets, but the landing window above is given the same treatment in miniature. Just look at the inventive finials. The skyline lacks painfully the flamboyant ridge tiles that are on the central mini gable over the front door, but in the original black and white the house has great character.

So, is it possible to date the building? It is probably related to the *cottage orné*, though the style is not followed very closely. Careful inspection of the photograph shows hesitant lavatorial bands of yellow and black brick making their way at intervals across the façade, and there is also plate tracery above the windows. Not visible in the photograph are bold corbels with deep naturalistic carving which support the porch. In these elements we can see the influence of Ruskin, so the date is probably mid-1850s. The use of large plate-glass windows supports this notion.

393. Villa near Ashby de la Zouch, Leicestershire

297

12.5 SCHOOL AND VICARAGE

The vicarage and the school, often also with the schoolmaster's house attached, was a development of the Picturesque cottage where the thatch and bargeboards of the 1840s were rejected. The other obvious features were a regular roof-line without overhangs, below which there was a random arrangement of windows, and the projection beyond or recession from the building line indicating the arrangement of the rooms. The overall plan was, however, usually simple – rectangular or L-shaped. Dormers were often hipped and there were retaining arches which could be rounded or pointed, grouped or separate. Chimneys were not stressed and the general impression was usually of neatness. Butterfield frequently worked in this way and was sensitive to textures. Colour also came into use as the decade advanced and, as Ruskin's ideas took hold, so it spread from the windows to other parts of the structure. His ideas on mass also began to enter architectural consciousness.

At Baldersby, in North Yorkshire, the Vicarage illustrates Butterfield's work in this type of building. Built of brick, it has Butterfield's typical half-hipped gables and must date from about 1858. There can be little doubt seeing this style of building how indebted to Butterfield Philip Webb was when he designed The Red House, at Bexleyheath, for William Morris in the following year. The school building, opposite the church in Baldersby, is also by Butterfield, and is in an irregular and Picturesque style.

The school at Inkpen, Berkshire, is by G.E. Street and

394. School and Master's House, Upton Magna, Shropshire

is a remarkably informal building for its date. Described in *The Ecclesiologist* in 1850, it is made of brick with tile-hung gables and blank pointed arches above the windows. In much the same manner is Street's Vicarage in Vicarage Lane, Colnbrook, Buckinghamshire. Dating from 1853, it is one of Street's earliest experiments with polychromy, being made of red and yellow brick. The building has half-hipped slate roofs, a Gothic entrance, a large chimney with a circular shaft, and coloured brick over some of the windows. Alas, the Vicarage has, at the time of writing, been unused for some time and it can only be hoped that a scheme of restoration will be put into effect without delay. At Colnbrook Street was also responsible both for the original school and for the

Headmaster's house, which are in the same style, although a little later.

At Upton Magna, in Shropshire, Street repaired the church of St Lucy in 1856 and, as we have already seen (12.1), built the Rectory, which stands close by, at more or less the same time. Behind the Rectory, but facing on to the village street, is the school and master's house **(Plate 394)**, also by Street, and all three buildings must originally have formed a picturesque group.

At Adderbury, in Oxfordshire, the school is by J.C. Buckler, and is dated 1854. Very much in the Gothic style, it has trefoiled windows and a small belfry. The headmaster's house next door is in a similar style and is probably by the same architect **(Plate 395)**.

395. The Old School and Master's House, Adderbury, Oxfordshire

396. *14 Holland Park Road, Kensington, London*

12.6 TOWARDS THE QUEEN ANNE REVIVAL

The thirty years of the Industrial Revolution between 1790 and 1820 created more wealth than any other event since the Dissolution of the Monasteries, three centuries before. The success of the railways in the decade after 1840 added to this and accordingly the Great Exhibition could justly celebrate the material success of Britain in the first half of the nineteenth century. The inevitable reaction can be seen in Dickens' approval of hard-working clerks whose virtue lay in improving their lot in life. Thackeray described the acceptable alternative in the concept of the gentleman who embodies cultivated tolerance and good manners as opposed to the greed and vulgarity which was how the intellectuals of the last quarter of the century saw the activities of their parents' generation. It should, however, be commented that it was the hard work and fear of failure of that earlier generation which provided their descendants with the unearned income to study art, collect Japanese ceramics, and argue the theories of art and architecture.

In the seventeenth century it was the object of the builder to construct soundly; in the eighteenth century it was necessary to abide by the Classical rules and to build well enough to last for a reasonable period; in the nineteenth century the aesthetics had to be right and the structure sound. The problem was in deciding which set of aesthetic principles to follow. Millions of words, many of them contradictory, were expended on the subject.

To the young artistic intelligentsia of the decade after 1850 it was easier to see what to avoid than what to do. Clearly Gothic was out. Municipal buildings and banks were being built with coloured bricks and with Gothic detailing. For the same reason the classical was to be avoided, though large houses and offices all covered with stucco in imitation of stone were springing up, covered with flattish roofs, wide eaves, curly brackets around windows and other classical decoration. The Battle of the Styles was over. The Picturesque style too had been developed to its limit, but it did still show the merits of English architecture during the period 1690-1740. It was the quiet sash and the red brick building with dormer windows that caught the eyes of the young architects who tramped rural England in search of ideas. But getting away from the Gothic proved not to be easy, and the first efforts at the Queen Anne Revival showed it.

14 Holland Park Road, in Kensington (**Plate 396**), was built by Philip Webb for the painter Val Prinsep in 1865. It has two distinctions: it is one of the first houses to revive the use of brick for London houses and it is a very early artist's house in the capital. Webb returned in the 1870s and in the 1890s to enlarge the property and so it is now difficult to visualise the fairly simple façade it had originally. However, the high gables clearly express the Gothic, a feeling which is enhanced by the height of the building and emphasised by the towering chimneys.

12.7 FRENCH GOTHIC

The middle of the nineteenth century saw a vogue for French Gothic interpreted with typical *elan* by the High Victorians. The most striking elements were steep roofs with cresting in iron, tall polygonal chimneys breaking the skyline, crockets and pinnacles, but with a symmetrical façade and a plan based on an E. An early example of this style is Westholme House *(Plate 397)*, today the Lincolnshire Library Service and Adult Education Centre, at Sleaford, Lincolnshire. Designed in 1850 by Charles Kirk the Younger, most probably for his partner, Thomas Parry, it is an extravagant version of fifteenth century French Gothic. Inside the steep-roofed structure the staircase hall extends to the full height of the house, the stairs themselves being supported by an arcade.

An expression of these principles can also be seen in a country house of moderate size – Knightshayes Court, near Tiverton, in Devon *(Plate 398)*. Designed by the arch-Goth William Burges for Sir John Heathcote-Amory, it was built between 1869 and 1874 in the early French Gothic style on a high terrace overlooking fine gardens. A far cry from Burges' much wilder medieval Cardiff Castle and Castell Coch, Knightshayes is quite restrained with a nearly symmetrical arrangement of the main block flanked by two projecting gabled wings. The stone is a local red Hensley with Ham Hill dressings and, when you look carefully at the

397. Westholme House, Sleaford, Lincolnshire

façade, plate tracery windows, chamfered mullions and transoms become apparent. The dormer gables are steep, there is a corbelled-out oriel on the first floor and also crenellated chimneys and gargoyles. Burges saved his most flamboyant designs for the interiors, but the owner lost his nerve and more restrained schemes were undertaken by J.D. Crace. But Knightshayes Court, now owned by the National Trust, remains an exciting house to visit.

398. Knightshayes, Tiverton, Devon

399. *Bestwood Lodge, Bestwood, Nottinghamshire*

12.8 VICTORIAN 'BRUTALISM'

Bestwood Lodge, at Bestwood, Nottinghamshire, is one of the most notable examples of a High Victorian country house of modest size. Designed in 1862-1865 by S.S. Teulon for the 10th Duke of St Albans, the house *(Plate 399)* is of brick of many colours with stone dressings and in the Gothic style. What is truly remarkable, however, is the skyline where there is no evidence of symmetry or balance. Admittedly some of this is due to later alterations, but the overall effect is jarring, while the porch has flying buttresses and carvings of the heads of Robin Hood and his Merry Men.

At Bearwood, in Berkshire *(Plate 400)*, the brutalism lies largely in its overwhelming size. Now a school, the house was designed in 1864 by Robert Kerr and built by 1868 for John Walter III, owner of *The Times*. Of red brick with stone dressings, its style would now be called

Jacobean but with French overtones, and Kerr himself said that it was 'of the irregular or non-Classical type'. The entrance façade is actually symmetrical and the two most striking elements are the huge tower incorporating the main stair to the left of the entrance and the large *porte cochère* in front of its own rather Flemish gabled tower. The main part of the house incorporated Dining Room, Drawing Room, Morning Room, Library and a large Picture Gallery. Accommodation for the many unmarried visitors was organised in separate corridors of Bachelors' and Young Ladies' Rooms, while the immense east part of the house and much of the upper floors was given over to the servants, with Robert Kerr using his best endeavours to keep men and women servants apart and to provide separate rooms for every domestic function that he could think of. Truly Bearwood was a Leviathan of a house.

400. Bearwood, Berkshire

12.9 RUSKIN'S INFLUENCE

Grittleton House, in Wiltshire **(Plate 401)**, illustrates well the change in thinking caused in the middle of the nineteenth century by the writings and lectures of John Ruskin. Begun in 1842 by Henry Clutton for Joseph Neeld, MP, it was still unfinished when the owner died in 1856. By that time the architect had been replaced by James Thompson and the task of construction was finished in 1870 to the commission of Neeld's brother. Here we have a large mansion at first designed for a man who had inherited a million pounds left to him by his great-uncle, Thomas Rundell, of the royal silversmiths, Rundell, Bridge and Rundell, who married the daughter of Lord Shaftesbury and who went into Parliament.

Without looking too closely at the detail, it is obvious that the house started as a 'Jacobean' mansion with shaped gables, tall chimneys and a tower, all symmetrically presented. This was standard design for the 1830s and 1840s, as we have already noted when discussing 'Jacobethan', though, in this case, it is clearly more 'Jacobean' than 'Elizabethan'. A more detailed consideration provides further evidence of Jacobean motifs. The decoration on the tower and pediments, the small oriel window in an ostentatious half-round form, and fretted-out decoration over the bay windows all show this. But there are other elements of decoration. To the right of

the *porte cochère* there are, on the first floor, pairs of round-headed windows in blank top arches separated by pillars headed with naturalistic carving. Below are more pairs with similar carving, and to the right, instead of the mullions and transoms one would expect in a bay window of this style, one finds a row of thin columns headed by more round arches with carved capitals, above which is an odd row of wedge-shaped mouldings. These are described by Pevsner as 'Veneto-Byzantine'. Ruskin's *Stones of Venice* appeared between 1851 and 1853 and, as the house was still not finished at this time, it is a fair assumption that the windows were redesigned to accommodate the new ideas on plate tracery and Venetian Gothic.

12.91 HIGH VICTORIAN HOUSES

There are a number of examples from mid-century that illustrate how the High Victorian motifs and decoration could be applied to existing forms. The half-circle arch is often used to cover two windows divided by a column, the Romanesque form as used in the Italian style. Although the shape of the windows is entirely different from the Georgian rectangular sashes, their symmetrical position in the façade continues the tradition. More artistic buildings might have rows of arches in homage to Venetian warehouses.

402. Engraving of Crown Life Insurance Office, New Bridge Street, London, from Building News 1858

A drawing from the *Building News* of 1858 *(Plate 402)* shows the Crown Life Insurance Office in New Bridge Street, London, built in 1855 by Benjamin Woodward, which has now, alas, been destroyed. It is relevant because it is set between two late Georgian buildings which are offices, but could just as well have been houses, and illustrates the changes brought about by Ruskin and the High Victorian movement. The naturalistic carving over the first-floor windows is by the O'Shea brothers whom Ruskin championed. The arches above are polychromed, there is a broad, decorated cornice, and further above two timber, decorated dormers in the arch. The accent is on the horizontal and it takes little imagination to visualise this decoration reduced to provide the miles of street houses in the 1880s.

St Martin's Villas, 43-44 Billing Road, Northampton, also illustrate this characteristic. Built by E.W. Godwin in 1865, they are cottages that could well have been symmetrical, late Georgian, were it not for the form and size of the fenestration. Indeed, the small openings under the roof are positively Palladian. Here too the horizontal is stressed both by a stringing line, which on the ground floor exaggerates the capitals at the expense of the arch, and the projecting line of the front door which supports the window sills. Relief carving depicting episodes in the life of St Martin, especially the cutting of his cloak to provide clothing for a beggar, decorates the façade. The windows are small, which emphasises the relative size of the building.

Sunnymead, in Chislehurst, Kent, is a typical High Victorian house of medium size *(Plate 403)*, formerly occupied by the Bromley Borough Education Department and now the Chislehurst Business Centre. Dated 1875, it is of red brick with bands of black brick, with stone around the windows, and polychromy in the tympana above them. The other conspicuous elements are the gables and large bargeboards.

403. Sunnymead, Chislehurst, Kent

404. *Estate cottages, Ilam Hall, Staffordshire*

12.92 ESTATE COTTAGES

Ilam Hall, in Staffordshire, was rebuilt by Jesse Watts Russell in the 1820s to the designs of John Shaw (see Plate 346). This large Gothic mansion with its battlements and turrets stands in the magnificent Manifold Valley and much of the village is made up of estate housing built by the family in the 1850s. Both the cottages and the school are striking in their use of tile-hanging (something normally associated with the Home Counties) and steep gables with bargeboards and some half-timbering *(Plate 404)*.

12.93 DOUBLE-BAY VICTORIAN VILLAS

Built symmetrically in red brick with a central entrance, these villas might have bay windows confined to the ground floor or, in the more expensive version, the bays might extend to the first floor as well. They were built in their thousands by speculative builders who effectively continued to build the Georgian house, but added on the bays.

Where there was money for decoration, it might be used to provide a Gothic pointed arch or a round-headed window, or perhaps even small pairs of windows in the rural Italian manner. The capitals which made up the front windows might also have a touch of naturalistic carving, following the dictates of Ruskin, or the builder might use different coloured bricks (polychromy). The Picturesque effect could be achieved by a curly bargeboard, or Olde English by nailing an arrangement of old floorboards to the gable end.

A nodding reference to Ruskin's views on light and

405. *Tiverton Villa, Burford, Oxfordshire*

shade could produce some inset of, for instance, flints. The builder himself might even have taken up Ruskin's idea that he should be encouraged to think up his own decoration, in which case any motif might be added so

406. *Houses in Aldersmead Road, on the Cator Estate, Beckenham, Kent*

long as it did not add materially to the cost. By the end of this period, however, bays tended to get smaller, squarer and more pinched-looking.

Illustrating this type of building is Tiverton Villa *(Plate 405)*, situated right in the middle of Burford, in Oxfordshire, but dating from the 1880s. The bays that have been described are very obviously flanking a central porch, but the balconies are striking, and it might be thought that the bargeboards are somewhat *passé* by the end of the 1880s.

12.94 VICTORIAN POLYCHROMY

References have already been made to polychromy as a result of the ideas of Ruskin, but the number of areas of housing where the style can be seen are relatively few. Aldersmead Road, at Beckenham, in Kent, was part of the Cator Estate which was laid out in 1864, and still has some of its original houses *(Plate 406)*. These buildings are tall and coloured yellow, and have somewhat tentative polychromy.

12.95 THE BEGINNINGS OF THE OLD ENGLISH STYLE

By the 1860s the development of the railways had made it possible to live in the Home Counties and to have easy access to London. J.C. Horsley, a character painter of historical scenes like *Rent Day at Haddon Hall in the Time of Queen Elizabeth*, and the brother-in-law of the great engineer, I.K. Brunel, lived among a group of artists at Cranbrook, in Kent. Here architects and artists, with their mutual interest in Gothic and vernacular buildings in their natural surroundings, mixed socially, particularly if, like Richard Norman Shaw, they were competent at both.

The house which Shaw altered for Horsley in 1865 is today the Willesley Arms Hotel, at Willesley, Cranbrook, Kent *(Plate 407)*. At the rear of the building we see features crowded together by the enthusiastic young architect which, in more subtle forms, were to appear time and again in his later work. Dominated by a massive

407. Rear view of the Willesley House Hotel, Willesley, Cranbrook, Kent

408. *Lea Wood, Dethick, Derbyshire*

and tall chimney, this elevation has a small hipped gable with decorated plaster below which appears the inscription 'Unless the Lord build the house, they labour in vain that build it'. A corner window has fish-scale tile-hanging above coving, while on the ground floor two small windows stand on either side of what in the Dining Room inside is Shaw's first inglenook fireplace, that popular feature of Victorian domesticity. Windows run under eaves and a satisfying pyramidal shape is achieved by the grouping of small roofs and chimneys on the centre right. There is even half-timbering with an extravagantly curved wind brace on the left next to a bay window with leaded lights and a conical roof. Inside the building there is a two-storeyed Great Hall.

Lea Wood, at Dethick, Derbyshire *(Plate 408)*, was built from 1874 by W. Eden Nesfield shortly after the termination of his partnership with the young Norman Shaw. It is a delightful house with its mixed materials, timber bays, fancy tiling, and coving with incised patterns, including the lily in the pot. The half-timbered gables, entrance porch and tall brick chimneys set the pattern for a generation of prosperous houses.

CHAPTER 13

1870-1915

13.0 INTRODUCTION

It is probably unique for a style of building to retain its popularity throughout the following century. That the Arts and Crafts movement did so is, perhaps, due to its looking back to a time before classical influences dominated architectural thinking. Instead it looked to the manors and farmhouses of the seventeenth century and earlier, to the stone houses and the half-timbering of the south-east, and from these examples built houses in materials that were traditionally associated with the countryside. The Arts and Crafts architects took an interest in the old techniques of building and in the quality of workmanship. For this reason it was common for them to spend time working in the builder's yard rather than studying the Italian and French Gothic styles that they needed to know in order to pass their exams.

The roots of the Arts and Crafts movement can be traced to Pugin's insistence on honest construction, the Picturesque movement, particularly as it can be seen in Salvin's Scotney Castle, in Kent *(Plate 409)*, and Philip Webb's new approach to the Gothic. The stress that Ruskin laid on the importance of light and surface texture was also influential. This was underlined by a growing awareness and love of the beauty of the English countryside and of the relationship of the house to its site and its surroundings. Expression was given to this in the watercolours of Helen Allingham *(Plate 410)* and of the hundreds of mainly amateur followers who painted idyllic views of timbered cottages with cherubic children, set in timeless sylvan settings. The educated and artistic upper middle class had had enough of the polychromed Victorian villa and what they termed 'the broken-down picturesque', and they turned to architects who had spent time in the builder's yard, understood traditional techniques, and whose designs derived from the long-standing heritage to be found in the countryside. As behoved a style that followed and rejected the excesses of High Victorianism, there had to be restraint in the Arts and Crafts.

Ruskin's view of the architect as artist influenced William Morris. His view was that 'the most important side of art [was] the decoration of utilities by furnishing them with genuine artistic finish in place of trade finish' and this was linked to his Socialist distaste for the damage done to both man and art by objects being tastelessly mass-produced by the machine. The irony of this was, of course, that machine production cut prices so that the less well-off had a chance to buy, whereas Morris made pieces which only the well-off could afford. By the end of the period some artists were designing for mass production rather than condemning machines.

But ideas in architecture go nowhere unless they attract clients. Here the Arts and Crafts movement was fortunate in its timing, for the development of the railways had reached the point when it became practical to commute daily into most of the large cities. This enabled the rich company director not only to escape the smoke and grime of coal-heated London or Manchester, but to aggrandise himself by emulating the traditional land-owning gentry. He could live in a house which derived its form from a similar source to their own and surround himself with his own acres, because by the 1870s agriculture was in deep depression and land was cheap. Within a generation many families had made the transition from industry or commerce to being landed gentry, albeit with no economic dependence on the land. Seaside holiday homes for the rich were also popular, as the railway system expanded to its maximum in the 1890s and the motor car came into general upper-class use by the end of the period.

But this was also a time when Britain went into economic decline. The effects of bad harvests after 1875 were exacerbated by the arrival of cheap American wheat grown on the newly cultivated prairie lands and carried by the new railways. American industry had learned from the embryonic mass-production methods used during the Civil War and started to underprice sections of British industry.

409. *Scotney Castle, Kent*

With the slump in wheat prices land was put down to grass, but by the 1880s meat was being imported from South America more cheaply than it could be produced in this country, and this depressed beef prices. So, from the 1870s, ownership of land, which had underpinned social and political power since the early Middle Ages, was no longer the vital constituent of British society.

No political action was taken because Free Trade was the basis on which industry exported and, on the positive side, cheap food kept manufacturing costs down, an important factor at a time when the unions were gaining strength. But, equally, the colonies were becoming stronger and less dependent on Britain, the price of cotton rose and industry slumped. As the economy worsened, an increasingly nostalgic love of the countryside developed. An interest in health and sport grew and the new bicycle of the late 1880s provided not only unchaperoned adventure for the young, but also opened up rural England to a generation whose grandparents or great-grandparents had had to desert the country for

the town. An enthusiasm for the open air also meant that a number of houses were built with sleeping balconies.

As the slow decline continued, so domestic architecture, based on the past, flourished to provide the expanding middle classes with reassuring pictures of their national past.

410. Cottage at Brook, Witley, Surrey *by Helen Allingham (detail)*

411. *Lowther Lodge, Kensington Gore, London*

Richard Norman Shaw's 'Olde English' style proliferated, and it even came to Town at Lowther Lodge, in Bayswater *(Plate 411)*. The Queen Anne Revival offered the more artistic professional classes a red-brick, white-timbered flavour of the early eighteenth century, which for their children appeared in Kate Greenaway drawings.

The Arts and Crafts movement provided both the intellectual base and the practical knowledge that enabled the best architects of the period to produce their greatest work. Men such as C.F.A. Voysey built memorable houses and set the path for the future. He was, however, at pains to make clear that he was not an Art Nouveau designer, considering the style to be 'of an aggressive and self-advertising originality, showing no respect for the virtues of reticence and the sense of fine proportion'; nor would he allow the Modern movement to claim him as a progenitor. Sir Edwin Lutyens also constructed a large number of wonderfully inventive vernacular houses steeped in the traditions of the Arts and Crafts, many of them set in gardens designed by Gertrude Jekyll. It should not be thought that the perspective is uniformly backward-looking, as both

Voysey and Lutyens, as well as E.S. Prior, experimented with advanced ideas, including the butterfly-plan house which was a way of introducing the most light and heat into a building.

Perhaps the most fundamental difference between this generation of designers and the previous one lies in their craftsmanship. When Ruskin attempted to make a column, it had to be disassembled and reconstructed by a craftsman. When an Arts and Crafts architect gave instructions, the builder would know that he was talking to a man who, often as not, could do the job just as well himself. One frequently reads of an architect of this period whose brother is a master-craftsman in building, stained glass or plasterwork. If a gentleman could be a craftsman, why could a gentleman not live in such a house? The outcome was that the hierarchy of decoration, which was part of the strict early Victorian class system, began to disappear to be replaced by a high degree of sensitivity to textures and balance of building.

But there is also a moral dimension which could be expressed as: 'Belief in the sacredness of home life…itself a religion pure and easy to believe'; and a foreign observer

412. Peabody flats behind Wild Street, Covent Garden, London

noted: 'The Englishman's love of his home has become proverbial'. It was this moral dimension of the home which persuaded William Morris, Philip Webb and other intellectual Socialists that the stability and well-being of society would best be served if the benefits of home could be extended down the social scale and be enjoyed by everybody. Clearly the best location was the country and not the smoky, overcrowded city, and so the idea of the Garden City was born. Bedford Park was the precursor in the 1870s, Letchworth started in 1904, and Hampstead Garden Suburb shortly after. The object was to provide simple, inexpensive housing for a socially mixed society.

Further down the scale, hanging on to the bottom rung of the middle-class ladder, was the army of clerks required to handle the paperwork needed to service an industrial colossus and its sprawling empire. The blind affection for home, family and friends, seen through the fictional eyes of one such socially inept clerk, Charles Pooter, struck a familiar chord with the middle classes, so that George and Weedon Grossmith's *The Diary of a Nobody* was a best-seller for many years. Pooter's rented house is instantly recognisable.

The belief that the working classes would also benefit from having a home led to the charitable trusts establishing blocks of flats. Those erected by the Peabody Trust have been criticised as somewhat grim, but they nevertheless provided an invaluable service, and continue to do so today **(Plate 412)**.

413. Stoneywell Cottage, Leicestershire

13.1 THE PICTURESQUE CONTINUED

Lawrence Weaver wrote that 'an old inhabitant of the district, who had been absent some years, greeted Stoneywell Cottage on his return with the puzzled observation: "Odd that I should have forgotten this old cottage"'. But, as Stoneywell Cottage, near Ulverscroft, Leicestershire, was only built by Ernest Gimson for members of his family in 1897-1899, it is the skill of the architect in conveying an impression of age in his building that should be commented on rather than the defective memory of the 'old inhabitant'. It is inevitable that the Arts and Crafts movement which valued old techniques and local materials should produce men who continued the well-established English tradition of the Picturesque.

Built on the edge of Stoneywell Forest, the cottage follows a Z-plan around an outcrop of rocks of which the great chimney seems to be an integral part *(Plate 413)*. The roof was slated after a fire in 1938, but it was probably a combination of the great chimney and the original thatch which prompted the observation. The flat roofs of the two dormers strike a jarring note with the well-crafted slate roof. The effect of random change and progressive alteration is achieved by contrasting the monumental stability of the great chimney with increased detail as the building moves away to the right. Internal details like a bedroom approached by a stepladder and vast lintels add to the primitiveness and the Picturesque impression. Set in its wonderful spring woodland garden, well away from the road, Stoneywell ranks high in the list of fine English houses.

13.2 BUTTERFLY PLANS

House plans based on the shape of a butterfly's wings were much in vogue at the end of the nineteenth century. The idea was that, by bending the spine of the house to create an oblique angle, one could increase the number of rooms that trapped the sun or made the best use of a spectacular view. Not only did this principle chime well with the greater priority being given to health and the outdoor life, but the consequential importance that such a design gave to the entrance hall satisfied the demand for a large room to be made available for the two sexes to meet with propriety.

The first time that this design was used in a substantial country house was in 1891 at Chesters, in Northumberland, by Richard Norman Shaw, but the layout was soon adopted by E.S. Prior at The Barn, Exmouth *(Plate 414)*. Built for Major Weatherall in 1896, the Barn, which is today a hotel, has overhanging gables at the centre, so that both the entrance and the garden façades seem to embrace the visitor. The stonework incorporates a number of local materials and the chimneys are large and rounded. Originally thatched, the roof was slated after a fire in 1905, and the interior has been largely remodelled.

Lutyens used the butterfly plan in two houses, one of which, Papillon Hall, in Leicestershire, has extraordinarily been demolished in spite of its singularly appropriate name. The other is Greywalls, alongside Muirfield golf links at Gullane, in East Lothian. Today this beautiful building

414. The Barn, Exmouth, Devon

415. *Greywalls, Gullane, East Lothian*

416. *Happisburgh Manor, near Cromer, Norfolk*

417. *Voewood, High Kelling, Holt, Norfolk*

(Plate 415) is a hotel, but it was built for Alfred Lyttelton, one of Lutyens' most faithful patrons, in 1898. Here the entrance front is elliptical with high chimneys at either end and the walls are of a rich cream-coloured rubble, the roof grey Dutch pantiles, the windows white casements, and the main doorcase in the Georgian style. In this lovely setting on the banks of the Forth, Lutyens has kept the building appropriately low, creating an idyllic composition.

Detmar Blow attended the Kensington School of Art at the same time as Lutyens in the 1880s, and he designed Happisburgh Manor **(Plate 416)**, now called St Mary's, at Happisburgh, on the North Sea coast of Norfolk, for Albemarle Cator in 1900. Not only Blow's first major work, but perhaps his best, St Mary's might be called X-plan, with a rectangular centre containing the main rooms with four wings projecting diagonally. Local materials fascinated Blow, as they did Lutyens, and here he used flint, pebbles and thatch. The windows were leaded casements, and in each of the four gables one word of the motif 'Ave Maria Stella Maris' appears. Both the entrance and the garden fronts also have gables, and there are a number of tall chimneystacks.

Prior was to make another contribution to the list of butterfly houses with Voewood, at Holt, in Norfolk, in 1903-1905 **(Plate 417)**. Commissioned by the Revd Percy R. Lloyd, Voewood has been called Home Place, Kelling Place, and Thornfield Residential Home, but, now back in private hands, it has reverted to its original name. The construction, which was supervised by Detmar Blow, was both lavish and highly idiosyncratic. The walls are made of mass concrete faced with

pebbles and some brick and stone, giving the building a very pleasing colour. The main front has a colonnade of stone columns, the ends of which are canted with gables and chimneys set asymmetrically, while in the middle there is a loggia of three bays made up of stone columns.

13.3 SURREY VERNACULAR

It is significant that these two examples of simple Arts and Crafts vernacular buildings should have been by architects for their own occupation, and in Surrey. The idea of unaffected quality craftsmanship and careful use of local materials was basic to the beliefs of the Movement, but it was also significant that both houses were within commuting distance of London where both architects had business interests. This tradition of building was responsible for many comfortable, un-assertive houses that were built over the next half century, houses that tend to melt into their surroundings to give the impression of timeless stable anonymity.

Writing about Westbrook, near Godalming, Surrey, in *Country Life* magazine in 1912, Sir Lawrence Weaver had this to say: 'Simple, unaffected, owing nothing, or at least singularly little to the spirit of the Renaissance, it shows what can be done by using local materials in a straightforward yet thoughtful manner'. The house was built in 1899 by and for H. Thackeray Turner, Secretary of the Society for the Preservation (now Protection) of Ancient Buildings (SPAB) for a quarter of a century before

418. Banney Royd, Edgerton, Huddersfield, Yorkshire

the First World War. The SPAB, which was founded by William Morris in 1877, still today plays a major part in making the public aware of buildings in danger.

Westbrook was built of Bargate sandstone by a local firm with the plasterwork done by the architect's craftsman brother. It would be easy to mistake this house for an L-shaped farmhouse that had been extended over the centuries. As Pevsner says: 'It is a house as comfortable and free from period allusion as anything Lutyens or Voysey were building at the time, with in addition a distinctive masculine rough-hewn overtone which makes Lutyens seem a little fussy'. Even the porch and the loggia with short fat columns suggesting an interest in the classical look as though they had arrived at a later date.

Vann is also near Godalming, in Surrey, and was designed by W.D. Caroe after 1908. This is a larger and more rambling house based on an early timber farm-house, which had itself developed over the centuries, and a large barn. All these elements were connected by timber and tile-hanging to produce an impressive asymmetrical house of near-medieval appearance. Like all the best Arts and Crafts architects, Caroe had a sensitivity to local materials which gives his buildings a timeless feel. He himself was particularly interested in the craft of working in lead.

13.4 NORTHERN VERNACULAR

On the Halifax Road out of Huddersfield, in West Yorkshire, is a remarkable house by a remarkable architect *(Plate 418)*. At first glance one might take Banney Royd, at Edgerton, for a seventeenth century house in the Calder Valley, which is, after all, only twenty miles away, but the distance in time is a quarter of a millennium. It is typical of the Arts and Crafts movement that respect for the vernacular was not confined to examples of building from the south of England, but embraced this quintessentially northern form where several gables are grouped and capped by heavy forward projecting stones.

Here we also see black sandstone has been cut into blocks of varying sizes, so that the courses run true, but vary considerably in depth. Tall stone mullions and transoms with leaded glass add to the sense of age. From the exterior only the broad segmental arched entrance and the splayed pillars suggest that we are looking at a late Victorian product with a hint of the Art Nouveau. Like so many Arts and Crafts architects, Edgar Wood, from Manchester, was a practical man skilled as a craftsman and with a thorough understanding of what he was asking the builders to do.

419. Glen Andred, near Groombridge, Sussex

13.5 RICHARD NORMAN SHAW

In the last quarter of the nineteenth century the architects who counted most in the domestic revolution that was taking place were William Eden Nesfield, Richard Norman Shaw and Philip Webb. We have encountered all three before, but it is helpful in looking at the buildings that they designed to know something of their backgrounds. Nesfield was not only the nephew of Anthony Salvin, in whose office he worked for three years, but also socially well connected. Shaw came from the business world, as his brother was the founder of the shipping line, Shaw, Savill and Co., and he had worked for William Burn, as also had Nesfield, before he entered the office of G.E. Street. Webb, the son of a country doctor and the brother of a clergyman, also worked for Street, though he and Shaw hardly overlapped there.

Nesfield set up practice in 1860 and Shaw joined him three years later; they remained in partnership until 1868, although they continued to share an office until 1876. Doubts continue to this day over who influenced whom and it has been suggested that their relationship was not dissimilar to that between Vanbrugh and Hawksmoor. Certainly the aesthetic direction of the partnership was set by Nesfield when he produced half-timbered and plastered cottages at Hampton-in-Arden, in Warwickshire, and referred to them as in the Old English style. As we have seen, this term had been used earlier in the century to cover neo-Tudor-Gothic and neo-Elizabethan houses, and it was used by Shaw at Willesley, in Kent, for J.C. Horsley, the painter.

Another charming house by Shaw, which follows the same style, is Glen Andred, near Groombridge, just over the

county boundary in East Sussex. Dated 1867, Glen Andred **(Plate 419)** was made for another painter, E.W. Cooke, and is in brick with much tile-hanging with, on the entrance side, three gables with plaster decoration in imitation of Elizabethan geometrical patterns, and a pointed Gothic porch. The garden front is quite asymmetrical with a tall brick chimney at the middle and an oriel window high up under the roof. In this relatively early commission we see Shaw consciously using the appropriate local materials.

Leys Wood, also at Groombridge, has, unfortunately, now been largely demolished. It was designed originally in 1869 for J.W. Temple, Managing Director of the Shaw, Savill Line, and the appearance of a drawing of the house in the Royal Academy **(Plate 420)** caused a sensation

420. Drawing of Leys Wood, Groombridge, Sussex

421. South front of Cragside, Northumberland

and the building made Shaw's name. Unlike previous country houses, Leys Wood was not set in extensive grounds, but on the edge of both a wood and of a rocky fall in the land, and consisted of a number of building elements of differing heights set around a courtyard. There were Gothic arches and a porch, Tudor windows and seventeenth century chimneystacks, half-timbering and tile-hanging. In stylistic terms it was indeed eclectic.

Both the setting and the style of Cragside, in Northumberland, are dramatic *(Plate 421)*. Shaw was actually enlarging a modest shooting box for Sir William Armstrong, later the 1st Lord Armstrong, scientist, inventor and armaments manufacturer, after the owner of the estate had decided to move his permanent residence twenty miles away from his shipyards at Newcastle upon Tyne to Rothbury. The woodland site is high on the east side of the Debdon Burn in the centre of an estate of 14,000 acres (5,500 hectares) and, although the enlargement of the house was carried out in three campaigns in 1870-1872, 1872-1877 and 1883-1885, Shaw claimed to have sketched out the final layout of the mansion in one day in 1870. In origin the style of Cragside is neo-Tudor and undeniably Picturesque, and the entrance front has, on the left, two levels of stone with timber-framing on top, while, beyond the tower under which an archway gives access to the court-yard and wings added in the 1890s, is Shaw's stone Drawing Room wing of 1883-1885 built straight on to the sandstone crag at second-floor level. The main west front overlooking the Debdon Burn is asymmetrical.

Inside, it seems probable that more of the original shooting box was retained than appeared from the outside, but Shaw's Library has good William Morris glass in the upper parts of the windows, and his Dining Room has a splendid inglenook. At this level there is also the entry to a remarkable Turkish Bath suite of rooms. The staircase is modest, but it leads to the Gallery which gives access to the large Drawing Room which is top-lit and dominated by an enormous marble chimneypiece designed by W.R. Lethaby in the Mannerist manner and employing decorative motifs that recall Hardwick Hall. Due to Armstrong's lifelong interest in electricity, Cragside became the first house in the world to have lighting produced by hydro-electric power.

No. 114 Shortlands Road, Beckenham, Kent *(Plate 422)*, was built by Richard Norman Shaw in 1868-1869 as The Corner House, for the novelist, Mrs Craik. This is in the designer's early tile-hung style, with the Gothic confined to the entrance arch. Red brick walls, steep roofs and prominent chimneystacks combine to create the impression of homeliness.

No. 6 Ellerdale Road, Hampstead, London *(Plate 423)*, was built in 1875 by W.H. Lascelles to Shaw's designs for the architect himself to occupy, and he did, in fact, live in it from 1875 until 1912. It comes from the especially innovative period of Shaw's career when he was building not only in north London but also in Kensington. The house is tall, to make good use of the views to the south, and the four-storeyed front elevation is asymmetrical, even

423. 6 Ellerdale Road, Hampstead, London

422. 114 Shortlands Road, Beckenham, Kent

though the designer seems to have contemplated symmetry and then backed away from it. The windows on the left of the façade are rather stern, while that on the right is an 'Ipswich' window with Queen Anne treatment of the coved cornice, pargeting and the use of small-pane leaded lights. The long central windows cannot all light the same staircase and, indeed, only one does. The sense of informality is heightened by the small oriel window high up in the centre with cornice and breast-front decoration. Here we can see an architect designing for himself, having

fun with the sloping site to provide a large inglenook in the Dining Room on the left and smaller rooms on the right.

Built for Mrs Christie, the wealthy widow of a manufacturer of hats (the remains of whose business continued until the 1990s in St James's Street, in London) and her daughters in 1879, Adcote, in Shropshire, is a mature Shaw design, this time using an Elizabethan style *(Plate 424)*. A conventional gabled frontage is given a horizontal emphasis by the large area of mullioned and transomed windows and verticality by the towering

424. Adcote, Shropshire

425. 15-17 Woodstock Road, Bedford Park, London

426. Tile-hanging at the corner of Woodstock and Rupert Roads, Bedford Park, London

chimneys which imperceptibly change from cool, grey stone to red brick There is very little timber-framing in this smooth, timeless house. The Hall is supported by immense buttresses with castellation and vast windows giving the impression of a chapel. Internally, the house is clearly organised with lavish hospitality as its main objective, and the Hall is treated like a medieval Great Hall. Today this is the Assembly Hall of a well-maintained girls' school.

Bedford Park, at Turnham Green, in west London, is probably the best-known Victorian suburb in the London area. Jonathan T. Carr, a cloth merchant, bought 24 acres (nearly 10 hectares) of the area in 1875. His first architect was E.W. Godwin, but he was replaced in 1877 by Shaw who was estate architect until 1880, then consultant until 1886. It was his thirty standard forms of houses that determine the appearance of the estate today. The young G.K. Chesterton met his future wife, Miss Frances Blogg, in Bedford Park, that Kate Greenaway picture-book of winding tree-lined roads which strove to create an idealised countryside within easy commuting distance of central London. He wrote about it: '...it was evening, and I think it was then that I saw in the distance of that grey landscape like a ragged red cloud of sunset,

the queer artificial village of Bedford Park'.

The revival of interest in Queen Anne, hitherto confined to larger single houses, moved in the mid-1870s towards modestly priced standard red-brick designs, with much woodwork painted white. They contrasted strongly with the surrounding dull sea of dirty stucco and grey brick and attracted world-wide architectural interest. It was the first modern new town on a green-field site.

In Bedford Park Shaw employed the full Queen Anne vocabulary of ornament: windows of all types – with small and large panes, with round ones, oriels and Ipswich style; and with Dutch gables, hanging tiles, deep coving, labelling under the windows and dentil moulding; all cleverly arranged to give each house individuality. In Woodstock Road the full range of Shaw's designs from 1878-1879 can be seen, with, on the east side, semi-detached houses such as this one **(Plate 425)** with bay windows and wooden balconies. Further on, at the corner of Rupert Road, are detached houses with tile-hanging **(Plate 426)** and then at Nos. 24-34 Shaw's first terrace design, clearly looking back to the seventeenth century, with roughcast overhanging gabled bay windows and small dormers above.

427. Chesterfield Villas, Cromer, Norfolk

13.6 'OLD ENGLISH' IN FLINT

Promoted by his highly professional drawings of 'Old English' which appeared regularly in the professional magazines, Shaw's ideas attracted a great deal of architectural interest. For an architect to study regional architecture, design freely, and then present his ideas to a landowning client steeped in the traditions of his estate must have been a delight for the potential client after the tyranny of formal style dictated by Classical or Gothic, Italian or Tudor. The north Norfolk coast is one of the flint areas of Britain and Cromer developed as a bracing seaside resort for the Norfolk aristocracy, a position which was further enhanced with the arrival of the railway.

Chesterfield Villas, Cromer *(Plate 427)*, were built around 1879 by the owner of Cromer Hall when he was having work done on the Hall. The flint was laid as far as possible in rows, which gives a neat and tidy appearance to the building. There is also generous use of stone trimmings, particularly in the kneelers which support the gables, while the feeling of the Gothic comes from the low-pointed arches over the simple casement windows. Apart from the extension on the

left, the design of the main group almost tries to be symmetrical, but finally avoids it by the use of details such as the oculus, or round window, in the left-hand gable.

The low half-timbered central section crouches below the Old English chimneys, but the thin timbers, the fussy oriels, and the improbable Gothic wind-braces echoing the windows are, by contrast with the rest of the structure, weak. It could not fairly be described as twee, but it comes close. One can see why local government describes them as '*cottage orné* style'. The roof, by contrast, is of simple peg tiles. On the right you can see part of the French Gothic pyramid roof of the tower belonging to the last house in the group. There is a heavily hipped gable, but the same flint and timber arrangement of the wall. The design is undoubtedly Old English, but it looks back to the earlier Gothic of Ruskin with a touch of Butterfield, alas let down by the same weak timbering and decoration. Overall, the Villas are a very pretty group typical of the period and with a sense of the traditions of the area.

428. *Munstead Wood, near Godalming, Surrey*

13.7 LUTYENS AND THE ARTS AND CRAFTS

About a mile south-east of Godalming, in Surrey, stands one of the most important houses of the end of the nineteenth century. Munstead Wood **(Plate 428)** was created in the Arts and Crafts style by the young Edwin Lutyens for Miss Gertrude Jekyll, a working gardener of genius, in 1896, and the house in its setting remains to this day the very epitome of Edwardian sophistication. The Jekyll family came to Munstead in 1877, with Gertrude Jekyll and her mother living in Munstead House, built on open heathland for them by J.J. Stevenson. Miss Jekyll had studied painting at the Kensington School of Art, where her theories of colour harmony first began to take shape, but it was in 1881 that her experiments in gardening began on a 15 acre (6 hectare) site on the opposite side of Munstead Heath Road from the family house.

With the death of her mother in 1895, Gertrude Jekyll's brother, Sir Herbert, took over Munstead House, and she needed a house of her own. For this it was understandable that she should turn to the twenty-seven year old architect who had already constructed a picturesque cottage called The Hut for her to build a \more substantial property in her already fully mature garden. Writing in *Home and Garden*, Gertrude Jekyll makes clear that the plans for the house had long been germinating in her mind and the wonder of Munstead Wood is not only that Edwin Lutyens was able to bring into physical reality the ideas of a strong minded, fifty year old woman to her complete satisfaction, but that he was able to secure her agreement to moving the site of the new house to the south of the prepared garden, bringing it close up to an existing chestnut copse. This reinforced the impression that Munstead Wood had been built in a clearing in the wood with only glimpses of the building being possible, even of the main south façade.

This Picturesque quality must have appealed to the artist in Gertrude Jekyll and, although more insensitive souls have since cut back the trees on this side of Munstead Wood, the Arts and Crafts principles which guided both gardener and architect at this stage of their careers are still apparent in the design and construction of the house. In plan the house is U-shaped with an entrance arch piercing an extended wall leading into a cloister in front of the main door. The main garden court made of Bargate sandstone has square ponds on two levels, but more remarkably a half-timbered, cantilevered gallery across its end. There is also an enclosed kitchen court approached beneath a timber arch. Internally, the main sitting room faces south and the door which leads

429. *Orchards, Munstead, Surrey, from the south-east*

to the terrace was doubtless used by Gertrude Jekyll as her main approach to the garden. On the first floor Lutyens has created a spectacular Gallery with a barn roof behind the half-timbering.

Part of the timeless quality of Munstead Wood comes from the close relationship between house and garden; both seem to have been created together at some distant point in the past. Writing about the building of her house in *Home and Garden*, Gertrude Jekyll says that the whole 'gives the impression of a comfortable maturity of something like a couple of hundred years', but points out that there is nothing of spurious antiquity about it. Although not the copy of any specific house, it does embody the characteristics of ancient structures in the district. The Bargate sandstone of the walls, the local red tiles, the brick chimneys, and the oak beams that give the building stability are all local materials, and the building of the house itself and the preparation of the internal fittings was done largely by Surrey craftsmen. The tall chimneys and the half-timbering look back, perhaps, to Richard Norman Shaw, but the simplicity of the two southern gables speaks of a level of sophistication remarkable in an architect who has never before built on this scale. Munstead Wood is a masterwork, both by

Gertrude Jekyll and Edwin Lutyens, and it points the way to even greater houses in the Arts and Crafts manner.

Only half a mile further up Munstead Heath Road is Orchards (*Plate 429*). Built in 1897 for Sir William and Lady Chance, respectively a writer and a sculptress, this was the first occasion on which architect and gardener could combine their talents on an entirely new project, and it was, perhaps, the close involvement of Gertrude Jekyll that made the design of the whole complex the very epitome of the Arts and Crafts. Orchards is, like Shaw's Leys Wood, a courtyard house, but Lutyens quite deliberately arranged the approach to the main door on the northern side of the house as a series of spatial surprises, the finest being the first sight of the simple doorway with its gable and the tall, grouped brick chimneys breaking the long line of the roof. A line of windows under the overhang of the roof gives light to a generous bedroom corridor, while on the east side a cloister joins Sir William's study with his wife's studio.

The garden façade of Orchards is, perhaps, the best Arts and Crafts work that Lutyens was to produce. The Bargate sandstone of the walls is enlivened by the use of tile set on its edge, the roof tiles being local, as is the brickwork of the chimneys, and, although the garden

430. *Deanery Gardens, Sonning, Berkshire*

forms a series of compartments, it does seem to encroach on and soften the south terrace and the loggia on both ground and bedroom floors. The steep pitch of the roof, the line of windows and the skilful placing of the simple windows in the gables combine to give the impression of timelessness which was so much the essence of the best house-building of this period. Vernacular simplicity is the root of the Arts and Crafts movement, and in this façade of Orchards the strong impression is conveyed that the house has simply grown out of the ground.

Deanery Gardens **(Plate 430)** stands encircled by a high and ancient wall in the middle of Sonning, in Berkshire. It was built in 1901 by Lutyens for Edward Hudson, proprietor and founding editor of *Country Life* magazine, probably the architect's most admiring and devoted patron. The entrance is directly off the street and, as he did not want to break through the wall, Lutyens arranged for the entrance to be through a small, arched doorway leading into a covered passageway approaching the front door, with an inner courtyard on the right. The main front of Deanery Gardens is to the south and its most wonderful feature is the tall bay window to the Living Hall which projects on to the terrace by three lights and has a six-light width. To the right of this bay the main house passage emerges in a deeply moulded round-headed arch, with, beyond that again, a chimneystack with three flues set diagonally on to the edge of the terrace. The brick of the main building, the timber of the bay window and the tiled roof combine to create one of Lutyens' most exciting as well as most secret façades.

13.8 LUTYENS AND THE NEW ARCHITECTURE

There has long been the belief that Lutyens' career moved in a consistent fashion from the early Arts and Crafts buildings to the classicism of houses such as Heathcote, in Yorkshire, The Salutation, at Sandwich, Kent, and Viceroy's House, now the President of India's Palace, in New Delhi. But this is clearly not so when buildings such as Fulbrook House, near Elstead, in Surrey, and The Pleasaunce, at Overstrand, in Norfolk, are examined **(Plates 431 and 432)**. He worked in a number of styles in around 1897, and it is, perhaps, not coincidental that Charles Rennie Mackintosh built the Glasgow School of Art and decorated several of Miss Cranston's Tea Rooms at that time. Moreover, Lutyens' commission to make additions to the Ferry Inn at Roseneath, Dunbartonshire, for Princess Louise took him to Glasgow when the debate about the new architecture was at its height.

Fulbrook is less eccentric than The Pleasaunce and has some of the qualities of the Surrey vernacular about it. The client was Mrs Gerard Streatfeild, the daughter of Richard Combe for whom Shaw had built Pierrepoint, a house that Lutyens much admired. Built on top of a south-facing ridge, Fulbrook has magnificent views towards the Devil's Punch Bowl, and the design of the house takes full advantage of them. But it is the entrance front which prompts a sharp intake of breath. As you approach the courtyard, the left-hand gable sweeps almost to the ground, while beyond the gabled porch a further gable terminates rather abruptly in another sweeping roof, but the design is given real delight by

431. Fulbrook, Elstead, Surrey

the little tile-hung turret projecting over the garden door. It is ironical that this *coup-de-theatre* is believed to be an afterthought and encloses an additional lavatory.

It is beyond the charming turret that the design becomes eccentric. The roof-line is higher than for the rest of the house and the hipped roof turns the corner above a pair of large bay windows which even run around to the south front. From here the south wall recedes and advances to produce two balconies to the first floor under a substantially over-hanging roof. Four slim bracket-pieces made of oak, or, perhaps, just a wall of window glass, seem to support the main roof, and the consequent absence of structural honesty contradicts both the vernacular tradition and the work of Norman Shaw which is apparent in other parts of Fulbrook's design. An architectural trick has been played on the observer and it has not come off entirely.

The Pleasaunce, now the Christian Endeavour Holiday Home, at Overstrand, in north-east Norfolk, was made from two red-brick seaside villas for Lord Battersea in 1897. The house is approached through what one can only call a Mannerist pedestrian gate, leaving the stables and a white-painted Voysey-like clock tower on the opposite side of a public road. Above the Ionic columns and pilasters of the doorcase is a somewhat pompous cartouche displaying the arms of the newly ennobled owner. Once inside the front door it is clear that you are walking along a covered passage supported by columns of Art Nouveau design. The garden elevation has a similar restlessness with the various elements moving back and forward, so that it becomes quite difficult to know whether the façade consists of six or nine bays. There is tile-hanging, a high Surrey hipped gable roof with oriels turning the corners, and a diagonally projecting wall that terminates in one of two octagonal summer houses. In lesser hands this diversity would just produce a jumble, but Lutyens was an architect who fully understood how to achieve balance, and this he did at the Pleasaunce with a panache which speaks of a new approach to architecture.

432. The Pleasaunce, Overstrand, Norfolk

433. *Exbury House, now Waterside Hotel, Westgate-on-Sea, Kent*

13.9 SEASIDE QUEEN ANNE

Ever since the Brighton Pavilion had been built between 1815 and 1822, there had been an excuse for flamboyance in seaside architecture. The development of the railways had opened up areas of coast to holidaymakers, who at the turn into the twentieth century sought the cold bracing winds of the British coast, just as we today head for the sun. The architecture tended to be more relaxed and rules were bent in order to give as good a view of the sea as was possible. The half-timbering of the Gothic Revival was popular and often mixed with the jolly white wood and red brick of the Queen Anne style to provide houses with plenty of accommodation and balconies from which the benefits of the ozone could be enjoyed.

Exbury House *(Plate 433)*, now the Waterside Hotel, at Westgate-on-Sea, Kent, might be called a 'seaside cottage'. Dated 1880 and the work of Ernest George and Peto, it has a wide gable facing the sea with Norman Shaw's fish-scale type tiles. Just as typical of Shaw is the small gable placed within a wide and higher one, which in turn meets the balcony, though, in this case, it is irritatingly a few inches too high to give a real sense of balance. There is a lot of spindly white woodwork with the fence echoing the balcony rails and the pattern of the glazing bars taking up the horizontality of the connections across the thin balcony supports. This element makes a delicate reference to Japanese design, which was so much a feature of the Aesthetic Movement.

13.91 THE BUNGALOW

The word 'Banggolo' was the eighteenth century's name for the peasant hut of rural Bengal. Its characteristic features were a pyramidal sloping roof which swept beyond the walls to form a verandah, and its construction above ground level to avoid flooding. The bungalow became the word for accommodation provided for the European administrators in India, some of them palatial, and so carrying the prestigious connotation of a house for foreigners.

In the search for novel *cottage orné* designs, John Plaw had published one in 1795 in the form of an Indian bungalow, but it was not until the three elements of the Indian Mutiny of 1857, the return of retired East India officials, and a new interest in the beneficial properties of salt water came together that the bungalow suggested itself as suitable seaside accommodation. The railway reached Westgate-on-Sea in Kent in the late 1860s and the first English bungalow development was started in 1869. Only a few of those built by J.P. Seddon, in Spencer Road, Birchington, in the 1870s now remain *(Plate 434)*, and these have sweeping roofs, verandahs, and were decorated between the half-timbering. However, their main distinguishing feature was a stocky tower with a low-pitched projecting roof.

In the 1880s and 1890s the bungalow was built to provide a second home, at first by the seaside, but later in the countryside. Reaction against the claustrophobic clutter of the High Victorian style of the 1850s resulted in an interest

434. Bungalow on
the corner of
Spencer Road,
Birchington,
Westgate-on-Sea,
Kent

in health and in the outdoors, creating a demand for 'a quiet weekend far from the madding crowd to strengthen us for the next week'. In 1887, two miles north of East Grinstead at what is now called Dormans Park, Surrey, a development of forty bungalows called 'Bellagio' was established. Here, typically, the new pastimes of cycling, amateur photography and croquet were popular, as well as other time-honoured activities which have given the decade the name of the 'Naughty Nineties'. Today the area has been redeveloped to provide large houses in wooded surroundings.

Until the 1900s 'away from it all' developments had only

been practical where there was railway development. Between 1900 and 1912, however, the number of motor-car registrations increased from 800 to 80,000 and consequently there was an expansion in the rate of building. Bungalows were cheaper than converting cottages, while prefabricated structures had been available since the 1880s as a by-product of work on instant buildings undertaken during the Crimean War, and in 1910 asbestos tiles reduced roof costs by as much as forty per cent. Perhaps more importantly, these prefabricated bungalows could be built by a practically minded occupier.

435. A more
elaborate design,
also in Kent

437. St Paul's Studios, 137-141 Talgarth Road, London

Below. 436. The Arab Hall, Leighton House, Kensington, London

13.92 ARTISTS' STUDIO HOUSES

Hard as it is to imagine today, West London had a thriving artistic community in the late nineteenth century. Leighton House, No. 12 Holland Park Road, is now a museum, but was built for the painter Lord Leighton in 1866 by his friend George Aitchison. The house has quite a reticent exterior, but inside it must be one of the most colourful of artists' houses. To the west of the winter studio added in 1889 is Leighton's Arab Hall, dating from 1877-1879, which is a small domed chamber intended to house the owner's Eastern collections **(Plate 436)**. These included the remarkable group of Middle Eastern tiles from the thirteenth to the seventeenth centuries which now cover the walls, while the mesh over the windows is musharabiyeh work from Cairo and the coloured glass in the dome is Damascene.

Edward Burne-Jones lived in North End Road and those travelling along Talgarth Road, close to the western approach to the Hammersmith Flyover, will know Nos. 135-149 **(Plate 437)** on the south side, built in 1891 as St Paul's Studios by Frederick Wheeler. Buff-coloured and decorated with terracotta, this picturesque group of tall houses was built as studios for bachelors, each with a large arched window facing north on the first floor, and with rooms for a housekeeper in the basement. No. 151 was built in 1885 for Sir Coutts Lindsay who founded the Grosvenor Gallery.

438. Houses in New Earswick, York, for the Rowntree Trust

13.93 GARDEN CITY HOUSES

The Garden City movement traces its origins to the middle years of the nineteenth century with the construction of Saltaire, near Shipley, in the West Riding. The mill-owner, Sir Titus Salt, moved out of the centre of Bradford and built a model village of about 700 houses for his workforce, combining the growing concern over working-class accommodation and the development of socialism with a degree of self-interest. This initiative was followed by William Hesketh Lever, later Lord Leverhulme, in the late 1880s when he provided houses for his soap workers at Port Sunlight, and from 1898 by the Quaker Cadburys at Bournville, in Birmingham, where every house had a garden.

This environmental strand, deriving from Bedford Park, in London, was to be important in the layout of New Earswick, north of York, from 1902 *(Plate 438)*. In this case the development was undertaken not by the chocolate firm, Rowntree's of York, but by Joseph Rowntree Village Trust, and was not only for Rowntree employees. The planners and architects for the Garden Village were Barry Parker and Raymond Unwin, and they began a series of experiments which were profoundly to affect the development of the movement. Each house was to have a garden and a view, but, in order to reduce the consequently expensive roads, they altered the traditional cottage layout by abolishing the back parlour and creating a living space which ran from front to back of the house. This enabled the houses to be built in terraces, but also to attract the sunlight whichever way the building was turned, and avoided the squalid back-to-back housing that so disfigured the industrial cities of the nineteenth century.

The idea of the garden city was first put forward by Ebenezer Howard, a non-architect theorist. He wanted to create new standards of civilisation based on service to the community in which every Arts and Crafts building should relate to its site, and the size of the community would be determined by economic research. His influential book, *Tomorrow: A Peaceful Path to Real Reform*, of 1898, revised and republished in 1902 as *Garden Cities of Tomorrow*, brought together philanthropy, socialism, practical social reform and economics.

The first Garden City was to be at Letchworth, in Hertfordshire, and the master plan for the layout was again developed by Parker and Unwin who defeated W.R. Lethaby and Halsey Ricardo in a competition. Here Ruskin's vision of 'a belt of beautiful gardens and orchards around the walls of the community' found expression in a large agricultural belt

439. Houses dated 1907 in Gernon Road, Letchworth, Hertfordshire

around the town. Estate ownership and leaseholds were adopted and individual groups of houses were built by Ricardo, Unwin and Baillie Scott. Professional people dedicated to the simple life were attracted to Letchworth and, although the smock-wearing and the Letchworth Morris Men were ridiculed, the city flourished and so did its inhabitants.

At Letchworth 3,826 acres (1,550 hectares) were purchased by the joint stock company, of which 1,300 acres (525 hectares) were given over to the city and the remainder to the encircling agricultural belt. The plan of the city was circular, having more than a passing resemblance to the diagram for the ideal city which accompanied Ebenezer Howard's thesis, with public buildings in the centre, surrounded by a park, and then by rings of houses and gardens. Railway lines and factories then ran between the houses and the agricultural belt. The design of houses varied considerably from terraces of simple gabled houses to more substantial properties, frequently

440. Houses in North Central Square, Hampstead Garden Suburb, London

441. *9 Willifield Way, Hampstead Garden Suburb, London*

442. *Waterlow Court, Hampstead Garden Suburb, London*

roughcast and painted white **(Plate 439)**, including those for members of the Parker and Unwin families.

Raymond Unwin had a further chance to put his ideas into effect when in 1905 he was appointed planner to the Hampstead Garden Suburb Trust. The concept of the Suburb originated with Mrs Henrietta Barnett, wife of an Anglican clergyman and lifelong worker in the slums of the East End. The extension of the underground railway line made possible the development of the northern approaches to Hampstead Heath and Mrs Barnett was determined to build for working men, but also to preserve some of what was at the time open countryside.

The final plan of 1912 provided for a fan of roads radiating out from the Central Square, where Lutyens was commissioned to build Anglican and Free churches as well as an Institute for community use and a number of large houses **(Plate 440)**. On the slope to the west the houses were built along curving, tree-lined streets; to the north,

across Lyttleton Road, there was an area of semi-detached workers' houses in cul-de-sacs; while on the strip of land alongside the Heath Extension the cul-de-sacs were given courtyards at the end, thus preserving the link between the Heath and the courtyard garden. The most complete of these is Waterlow Court by Baillie Scott **(Plate 442)**.

The name 'Suburb' was deliberate, as the layout did not have the urban amenities of the Garden City and was designed by Unwin so that there should be no more than twelve houses to the acre. This figure, he argued, wrongly, was the point at which the cost of roads began to outweigh the saving in the cost of land, except where land was unusually expensive. Hampstead Garden Suburb is not lived in today by the socio-economic group that Mrs Barnett intended, but it is an Arts and Crafts village of great character and beauty, close-knit to form a community, but full of trees and flanked by the countryside of the Heath.

444. Mrs Winthrop's Garden, Hidcote, Gloucestershire

13.94 HOUSE AND GARDEN UNITED

The interest in the open air which encouraged the development of seaside resorts and the bicycling craze of the 1890s had its effect on the house and garden. The sharp distinction between the two was blurred by devices such as recessing the ground floor from the building line to provide a loggia, as at Orchards, near Godalming, or, upstairs, a balcony on which to sleep in the open. An interesting example of this is Rodmarton Manor, in Gloucestershire *(Plate 443)*, which was built by Ernest Barnsley from 1909 for the Hon. Claud Biddulph, and has such a sleeping balcony. Huts and shelters offering varying degrees of protection from the weather were

made in the garden and these were often linked to the house by paths covered with skeletal structures such as pergolas which supported climbing plants.

Hermann Muthesius accurately expressed this Arts and Crafts attitude by writing in *Das Englische Haus*: 'the garden is seen as a continuation of the rooms of the house, almost a series of outdoor rooms…Thus the garden extends the house into the midst of nature…This means that the regularly laid-out garden must not extend merely to one side of the house, but all the way round it.'

Typically, the house would stand on high ground, if this was available, and the garden was approached by steps leading to a series of 'rooms', the enclosure of which was contrasted with carefully contrived vistas. In this way a

Opposite. 443. Rodmarton Manor, Gloucestershire: garden front

335

445. *View of the Rose Garden at Sissinghurst Castle, Kent, from the tower*

new twist was given to the old rules of the Picturesque which required close views to be set against distant ones. Furnishing the garden was achieved by walls, topiary and trellage, and where water was available the effect was enhanced. Two such gardens, Hidcote, in Gloucestershire **(Plate 444)**, created after 1907 by Lawrence Johnston, and Sissinghurst **(Plate 445)**, made by Vita Sackville-West from the 1930s, are world famous.

Yet what gave the Edwardian garden its unique quality was a combination of a formal layout with exuberant informal planting. This naturalistic approach came from professional gardeners led by their publicist, William Robinson, of Gravetye Manor, in West Sussex, who believed that gardens were the preserve of the plantsman rather than the landscapists, many of whom were architects. One such was Reginald Blomfield, who in his first book, *The Formal Garden in England*, attacked the landscape style of gardening which he believed deprived a house of its proper setting. Robinson joined issue with this in his *Garden Design and Architects' Gardens*, saying that 'there are lessons innumerable both in wild and cultivated Nature which will guide us well if we understand them simply', and in a later edition of his definitive book, *The English Flower Garden*, he adds that 'design can only imply formality'.

Robinson was essentially against excessive stonework in gardens and both protagonists were against the bedding out of annuals in the Victorian manner. As Robinson himself demonstrated at Gravetye, some formality should be retained near to the house and nature allowed to reign beyond. Robinson's most influential follower was Gertrude Jekyll, who it should always be remembered trained as a painter, spending hours in the National Gallery examining Turner's landscapes, and who also studied the theories of colour harmony enunciated by the French chemist,

Michel Chevreul. She and Lutyens collaborated on about one hundred gardens to houses that he was building from 1896 until the First World War, and here the character of the buildings was offset by the studied naturalness of the garden and the textures of the house were complemented by the subtle harmonies of the planting.

The gardens respected the geometry of the house and its site as well as the materials in which it was built, and terraces, paths and steps were softened with simple planting – roses, peonies, bergenias, santolina, lavender, pinks, valerian, iris, lilies and hollyhocks – set against clipped yew, and employing water wherever possible. The two designers visited the gardens together only at the beginning of the partnership and Miss Jekyll's blurred vision meant that Lutyens acted as her eyes, giving her the layout of house and garden, the type of soil, the aspect and the countryside surroundings, and she produced the planting plan, most usually at Munstead Wood.

The skill with which this was done can be seen clearly at Little Thakeham, near Pulborough, Sussex, where the partners were working for a keen gardener, Ernest Blackburn, in 1902. In this case the pergola divides a wide garden into two parts. At Abbotswood, near Stow-on-the-Wold, in the Cotswolds **(Plate 446)**, Lutyens was making additions in 1901-1902 to a nineteenth century manor house owned by Mark Fenwick, while, at Hestercombe, Kingston Tarrant, Somerset, the work for the Hon. E.W. Portman, later Lord Portman, was confined to the garden, and the spectacular rills running away from the house lead to a wide plat **(Plate 447)** and the garden is terminated by a pergola weighed down with roses. For many people the combination of such gardens by Gertrude Jekyll allied to a house by Edwin Lutyens makes an ideal ensemble and there can be little doubt that the gardens which Miss Jekyll designed continue to influence English gardening even today.

446. *The Paved Garden at Abbotswood, Stow-on-the-Wold, Gloucestershire*

447. *The Plat and the Pergola, Hestercombe, Kingston Tarrant, Somerset*

448. *South front of Standen, near East Grinstead, Sussex*

13.95. FROM WEBB TO MACKINTOSH: IS THERE A GOLDEN THREAD?

The apostolic succession of Arts and Crafts architects from G.E. Street is clear, and it consisted of William Morris, Philip Webb and Richard Norman Shaw. From these principals we can trace their pupils as being W.R. Lethaby, E.S. Prior, Ernest Newton and Mervyn Macarthy. But does C.F.A. Voysey fit into this pantheon, and what of M.H. Baillie Scott and Charles Rennie Mackintosh?

Philip (or more correctly Philippe) Speakman Webb was older than the others, having been born in 1831, and he was also the designer of one of the earliest and most important Arts and Crafts houses – the Red House, at Bexleyheath (see Plate 389). But, even if he helped to

light the lamp, it can be clearly seen at Standen, near East Grinstead, in Sussex, that thirty years later he was still holding firmly to the Movement's principles. Built between 1892 and 1894 for a prosperous London solicitor, James Beale, Standen remains today a testament both to the Arts and Crafts movement and to the skills and passions of its architect. Webb loved craftsmanship and the proper use of materials and persuaded his client to keep the existing old buildings on the site and to allow the new house to nestle into the hillside rather than dominating the spectacular south-facing views.

The approach to the front courtyard is equally modest,

but the south front *(Plate 448)*, built of brick above the stone, housing the Sitting Room and the adjoining Conservatory, surmounted by five gables, is one of the most lovely elevations of the period. Sandstone quarried on the property is set off by local brick, tile-hanging and weatherboarding. Inside the house Webb exercised the same level of care, providing a series of light rooms with simple panelling which are further embellished with Morris and Co. wallpapers and furniture made by the company, and by art pottery of the period.

C.F.A. Voysey was born in 1857, the son of an Anglican clergyman who, in one of the great ecclesiastical scandals of the nineteenth century, was dismissed from the Church and formed his own Theistic Church. The son was strongly religious, a devotee both of Pugin and Ruskin, but, although he was articled to the architect J.P. Seddon, it was the work of George Devey that most influenced him. In 1888 Voysey contributed a design for a cottage to *The British Architect* and in this design the basic theme of Voysey's architecture can be seen, best summed up as one-room-and-a-corridor-deep in the Arts and Crafts manner, together with the use of buttressing and cat-slide roofs.

In 1898 Voysey was commissioned by A. Currer Biggs to build Broadleys, overlooking Windermere *(Plate 449)*. This house, which is now the headquarters of a motor-boat club, is an enlarged version of that early cottage design, but its garden elevation consists of three bays of sandstone set into roughcast and rising above

449. Broadleys, Windermere, Cumbria

eaves level, which are quite spectacular. Not far away, but with a wonderful view of Cartmel Fell, is Moorcrag *(Plate 450)*, which Voysey built in the same year for J.W. Buckley. Again the house is roughcast and a cat-slide roof comes almost to the ground, the whole conception being anchored to the soil by a strong chimneystack.

450. Moorcrag, Cartmel, Cumbria

451. *South-west front of Blackwell, Cumbria*

If Voysey found his inspiration in the founding fathers of the Arts and Crafts movement, Pugin and Ruskin, M.H. Baillie Scott undoubtedly owed much to Voysey. Perhaps his grandest work is Blackwell, near Bowness, Cumbria, which he built in 1898-1899 as a holiday home for Sir Edward Holt, a Manchester brewer who had twice been the city's Lord Mayor. The house **(Plate 451)** stands high above Windermere, roughcast painted white, with stone-mullioned windows and a slate roof with high gables. Inside, the architect created a 'living hall', modelled on the medieval Great Hall, which, when examined carefully, reveals itself to be a series of spaces.

452. *The Reception Hall looking to the Dining Room, of Blackwell*

On the west side is the welcoming, white-painted Drawing Room; a Minstrels' Gallery with a half-timbered front approached from the landing of the main stair overlooking the Main Hall; while on the east is the darker panelled Dining Room **(Plate 452)**. Although they were not used at Blackwell, Baillie Scott had previously designed folding screens which could be swept back to enlarge the Living Hall, a device which was to have profound effects on twentieth century houses. Perhaps the most spectacular element at Blackwell is the giant inglenook which is beneath the Minstrels' Gallery, lighted by a south-facing window. After years of being used as a school, Blackwell has been superbly restored and is now owned by The Lakeland Arts Trust.

F.H. Newbury, Principal of the Glasgow School of Art when Charles Rennie Mackintosh was a student there, and who recommended him as designer of the School's new building in 1896, considered that Voysey was Mackintosh's main inspiration, and indeed there are striking similarities in Mackintosh's domestic work in elements such as his tall, tapering verticals. Voysey, however, disliked the work of the Glasgow artists, referring to them as the 'Spook School'.

Similar connections between Mackintosh and Baillie Scott are better documented. Both architects entered a competition in 1901 run by a German magazine for the design of an Art-lover's House and, although no first prize was awarded, Baillie Scott was given second prize and Mackintosh received a special prize. Baillie Scott's designs have a close resemblance to his Blackwell interiors, while

453. Windyhill, Kilmacolm, near Glasgow

Mackintosh's drawings are more in the style of the Art Nouveau than the actual houses he was to build.

In 1899 Mackintosh built Windyhill near Kilmacolm **(Plate 453)**, to the west of Glasgow, for one of his most important patrons, William Davidson. Here the inspiration was a subtle mixture of the traditional and the new, as the house is built of whinstone with brick around the windows and doors and the whole roughcast and painted grey. Little about the exterior challenges the principles of the Arts and Crafts and indeed the slate roof is what one would expect, but the generous D-shaped staircase and the flat-roofed bay window on the south side both enliven the design.

Two years later Mackintosh was commissioned to build a more substantial house for the publisher, W.W. Blackie, at Helensburgh, on a south-facing slope overlooking the Firth of Clyde. The Hill House **(Plate 454)** strikingly combines elements of the traditional Scottish tower house with the new architecture. The tall, circular stair tower with its conical roof, placed at the junction of two wings of the house, looks back to the sixteenth century, while the D-shaped stair, bay window to the Drawing Room, and projecting windows, one set above the main door and the other in an unexpected semi-circular extension to the Master Bedroom, are in the new style of architecture. The tapering chimneystack is made to appear even taller than it is by the white roughcast on the house, and the design of The Hill House speaks of sculpture rather than architecture. The entrance hall beyond the simple post-and-lintel door has a strong Japanese flavour, which was popular at the turn of the century, while the Drawing Room and the Master Bedroom are two of the loveliest rooms that one is likely to see. Beauty of design and a personal internal vision rather than style is what links the work of these four architects.

454. South front of The Hill House, Helensburgh

CHAPTER 14

1915-1940

14.0 INTRODUCTION

It is often thought that few substantial houses were built after the First World War, but, as will become apparent in this and the next chapter, such a view is only partly true. Certainly, a different group of people was building and their objectives were quite distinct from the traditional patrons. The new builders did not come from landed families, but had made fortunes in commerce. Gledstone Hall, at Skipton, in Yorkshire, for instance, was financed, by profits from synthetic textiles, while Castle Drogo, in Devon, was built on food retailing and Rodmarton Manor, in Gloucestershire, on banking. Some of the new money also came from foreign investments, from South African gold mines and Brazilian railways. None the less, until the war broke out, locally generated money was plentiful. In the first thirteen years of the new century, Britain's gross national product doubled to £635 million, and much of the expenditure was on sport – hunting, shooting and racing in particular.

For the first time in the nation's history, however, the new house was not the hub of a great estate. Polesden Lacey, in Surrey *(Plate 455)*, was one of the greatest social magnets of these years, patronised by everyone from King Edward VII downwards, and it had an estate of only 1,000 acres (405 hectares). The depression in farming at the end of the nineteenth century, and the arrival of cheap American corn, had destroyed the profitability of land and an estate had now to be financed from investments. The war brought a change in the social use of great houses, not only in the loss of life among the younger property-owning classes, but because the servants, on whom the running of the Victorian and Edwardian houses depended, had largely vanished. The very grandest houses were still built, as Middleton Park, in Oxfordshire, makes clear *(Plate 456)*. Here the client was the Earl of Jersey and the architect Sir Edwin Lutyens, assisted by his son, Robert, but the completion date was not propitious, as it was 1938. The most

extraordinary change here, however, was the quite substantial separate house that had to be provided for Lord Jersey's butler. Today Middleton Park is divided, sensitively, I am glad to say, into a series of separate residences.

This period is also dazzling for the new architectural style that arrived in this country from Germany. Launched here by F.R.S. Yorke in his book *The Modern House* (1934), the Modern movement in houses owes much to the influence of Walter Gropius and the Bauhaus, and it is ironic, to say the least, that the introduction to Yorke's book was written by W.R. Lethaby, a committed Arts and Crafts designer. Indeed, however strange it may seem to us today, these white concrete-and-glass buildings which sprang up between 1930 and 1960 were seen by the architectural followers of William Morris to be the fulfilment of the work of the Arts and Crafts.

And, socially, to some extent they were. The shortage of servants has already been commented on, but the 1920s and 1930s saw a greater emphasis placed on social housing and projects such as schools rather than on individual houses for the wealthy. And it was no coincidence that these clean, cool boxes were not built in any numbers again after the Second World War because of their association in the public mind with Germany. The Modern movement houses were also seen as test-beds of steel and concrete construction and, although neither material was new to Britain, buildings using concrete had previously most usually been faced with brick. The cry also went up from architects and commentators that an honest use should be made of the materials, with overtones of the words of Ruskin and Morris. The functional nature of the rooms also recalled the Arts and Crafts, but in practical terms expandable spaces needed central heating to make them successful as living environments, and this continued to be rare in Britain until the 1960s.

455. Polesden Lacey, Surrey

456. Garden front of Middleton Park, Oxfordshire

457. A courtyard at Bailiffscourt, Climping, Sussex

14.1 NEO-MEDIEVALISM

One effect of the horrors of the Great War was to inspire houses which in their style seemed to recall the idyll of the pre-Industrial Revolution age. The nostalgia which had so characterised the Edwardian period was even more pronounced in the 1920s and buildings in the Tudor taste were especially admired. Wyke Manor, Worcestershire, is an example of this. It was altered in 1924 as a memorial to the owner's son, Lieut. Alban Hudson, who had been killed in the Battle of Messines in 1917, from a plain Georgian box to what from the outside is a quite convincing version of a sixteenth century yeoman's hall house. The architect was Cecil G. Hare who incorporated two of the original rooms of the Georgian house in the neo-Tudor structure, but the planning seems deliberately inconvenient and the staircase excessively narrow.

Bailiffscourt, at Climping, in Sussex (**Plate 457**), is so named because it was originally the house of the bailiff of the abbey of Seez, in Normandy, and the simple rectangular late thirteenth century chapel is the only part of the structure which dates from these early times. The rest of the extensive building dates from 1931-1935 and was designed by Amyas Phillips for Lord Moyne. In this case the main part of the house is constructed of limestone with a

roof of Horsham slate and consists of an irregular quadrangle. The greatest care was taken in the carving, the materials and the textures, and also in the medieval arrangements, so that the resulting appearance of the house, or more accurately houses, could hardly be more authentic. And yet it is not. The patina of the late fifteenth century has been applied as one might apply paint and the very expertise with which it has been done must heighten, in the purist's mind, the notion that this is a pastiche. The interiors incorporate several medieval roofs, there are several authentic thatched cottages and a complete gatehouse in brick and half-timbering. The whole has been done not only with expertise but with love, and Bailiffscourt consists of buildings that seem to be at home in their new setting and, indeed, in their function today as a hotel.

The wording of the famous cablegram sent by William Randolph Hearst in 1925 is now part of this nation's architectural history: 'Want buy castle in England'. The castle he bought was not even in England, but when he eventually saw St Donat's (**Plate 458**), in the Vale of Glamorgan, three years' later he was entranced and as a result of a very brief visit was able to write a detailed letter of restoration instructions to his architect, Sir Charles Allom. The castle

458. *North range and the inner gatehouse of St Donat's Castle, Glamorgan*

stands on the coast overlooking the Bristol Channel, two miles from Llantwit Major, and is now occupied by Atlantic College. A motte-and-bailey was most probably raised in the early twelfth century, but the earliest features of the castle that we can recognise today date from 1300, and this was the time when Sir Peter Stradling married the heiress of St Donat's, Joan de Hawey, establishing a dynasty which was to last until the eighteenth century. Inside concentric walls a dry moat surrounds the inner bailey and the heart of the castle is now a peaceful Tudor manor house.

Hearst imported many old items, including the roof of the Prior's Lodging of the ruined Bradenstoke Priory, in Wiltshire, which dates from about 1320 and is incorporated into the largest space at St Donat's *(Plate 459)*. As it stands between the inner and outer curtain walls on the west side, it is behind the original Great Hall. On the other side of the inner court, the College's Dining Hall, once Hearst's Banqueting Hall, has a late medieval hooded fireplace from Beauvais, in Normandy, bearing the Valois coat of arms with three fleurs-de-lis. The Perpendicular screen probably

459. *The medieval roof of Bradenstoke Hall, at St Donat's*

345

460. *Entrance front of Castle Drogo, Devon*

comes from a Bridgwater house and the ceiling is late sixteenth century Flemish work which was originally the nave roof of St Botolph's church, Boston, in Lincolnshire.

The Society for the Preservation (now Protection) of Ancient Buildings was outraged and questions were asked in Parliament as to whether American millionaires should be allowed to confuse important items of the national heritage in this way. Hearst got some of his own way in that these historic items were incorporated into St Donat's, while the medieval Bradenstoke barn vanished entirely, and no one to this day knows what happened to it. Hearst altered the rooms on the north side of the courtyard, but even here something of a muddle was made, as its eighteenth century panelling originally came from the north wing and it was these apartments that the owner used when he paid his rare visits to St Donat's. It is true that parts of some of the medieval buildings that he had acquired were eventually returned to this country, but it seems impossible to me to see how any of those involved in this famous dispute emerged with any lasting credit.

However much he might have altered St Donat's Castle, William Randolph Hearst was buying not only a building but a dream of medieval romance, and the same can be said of William Waldorf Astor at Hever Castle, in Kent. Both Julius Charles Drewe and his architect, Sir Edwin Lutyens, were also romantics, but the result of their dreams was to be Castle Drogo, Drewsteignton, Devon, a completely new granite castle, standing on an exposed outcrop on the edge of Dartmoor *(Plates 460 and 461)*. Drewe was a typical product of Victorian enterprise and energy. After spending some years as

a tea-importer in China, he had opened his first Home and Colonial store in Liverpool at the age of twenty-two and within eleven years had made a fortune large enough to enable him to retire and take up the life of a country gentleman.

In 1910, when Drewe's commission for Castle Drogo was received, Lutyens' career was beginning to flourish and two years later he was to become involved in the greatest British building project of the twentieth century – the Imperial capital at New Delhi. But Lutyens had a gift of being able to realise the dreams for houses of his clients and instinctively he understood how much the nation had changed in the first decade of the new century. The entrance front of Drogo is undeniably a castle, but it no longer speaks of feudal authority, rather of generous hospitality. Lutyens expressed this change of attitude in a letter to his wife, Lady Emily, in 1910, in which he said that the great house should be 'the centre for all that charity that should begin at home and cover henwise with wings of love those all near about her that are dependent, weaker and smaller'.

Julius Drewe had £50,000 to spend on the house and £10,000 on the garden, sizeable sums at any time, but riches indeed for an architect who thought that his ideal client should have just £6,000 for house and garden together. But the client was insistent that the great stone walls should be authentically solid, and in places this meant up to 6ft. (1.8m) thick. This, and the onset of the Great War within four years, led to the size of Castle Drogo being reduced by two-thirds from what was originally conceived, and to the re-siting of the Dining Room below the Drawing Room when the

461. *Chapel and south tower of Castle Drogo*

architect had intended them to be on the same level.

Julius Drewe spent considerable time researching his ancestors. Links between the site and a medieval Drogo de Teign, who gave his name to Drewsteignton, are recorded in Lutyens' symbolic lion who stands grandly over the door and portcullis accompanied by the motto 'Drogo nomen et virtus arma dedit', that is 'Drewe is the name and Valour gave it arms'. After the walls of the entrance tower have risen vertically by about 9ft. (3m) they begin to lean away from you, enhancing the impression of great height, a skilfully executed batter, while the mullioned window above the lion sets the tone of the relationship between window and wall at Drogo, which recalls the true medieval castle of Haddon Hall and of Elizabethan Hardwick, both in Derbyshire.

The most exciting spaces in Castle Drogo are the stairways and corridors, especially the one which leads from the light and tranquil Drawing Room, with its views east towards Exeter and south towards Teignmouth and the sea, to the Dining Room on the floor below. The ceilings are heavily ribbed in granite; where corners are turned, strongly articulated classical circles are used; while, in a consciously theatrical gesture, the ceiling level is maintained above the staircase so that, when the Dining Room is reached, a mullioned bay window 27ft. (8.2m) in height lights both the lower stair and the Drawing Room above. As a result of the reduction in size of Castle Drogo, the foundations of the unexecuted Great Hall were used by the architect for the granite chapel, the apse of which projects from the south wall giving the structure the appearance of a crypt. Its simple bell-tower makes the whole conception seem abstract and suggests the designer Le Corbusier rather than Lutyens.

Castle Drogo was not completed until 1930 and Julius Drewe died in the following year after only a few years' enjoyment of the remarkable building he had created. His eldest son Adrian, who had helped to decide on the precise siting of the building and the line of its long drive, had died in the Great War. In spite of some melancholy aspects of its construction, not least the loss in the trenches of almost all the stone masons who first worked on it in 1910, Castle Drogo is one of the great buildings of the last century. Like many such works of genius it still polarises argument about the nature of modern architecture and about its place in that pantheon. It is certainly not a building that will leave you indifferent.

462. *Garden front of Heathcote, Ilkley, Yorkshire*

14.2 LUTYENS AND 'WRENAISSANCE'

Although Lutyens has been presented here as a remarkably ingenious architect, he did not move quickly and decisively from his early Arts and Crafts manner to what he himself called his 'Wrenaissance' style. What he and other architects such as Sir Reginald Blomfield meant by the term was the seventeenth century classicism of Sir Christopher Wren. The simple elements of this great master's work stimulated Lutyens' passion for geometry, and with it came a lightness of touch and a sense of proportion. Two Yorkshire houses bear out this progression – Heathcote, at Ilkley, and Gledstone Hall, in Skipton.

The first is hardly a country house at all as it is really a suburban villa, set in King's Road, Ilkley, and today the headquarters of a commercial firm. The client was Mr Ernest Hemingway and the date an early one for this classical building – 1906. The main entrance is on the north and the circular courtyard is approached through a semi-circular wall and gateway, with the main façade consisting of a two-storeyed house rising to three storeys in the recessed centre, the roof hipped with a dominant and symmetrically placed chimney. The simple detailing of the

north face has a feeling of Vanbrugh about it, but the garden (south) side is altogether livelier *(Plate 462)*. Here the two-storeyed elements are more clearly articulated with circular windows on the first floor and the ground-floor windows framed by Doric columns. The three-storeyed centre has a round-headed frame to a rectangular window on the first floor and a carved stone garland above that, giving the whole conception an Italianate feeling.

Gledstone Hall, at Skipton *(Plate 463)*, was built for Sir Amos Nelson between 1925 and 1927 and is one of Lutyens' best later houses. Classical in style and modest in size, it is built of ashlar with a hipped slate roof. On the entrance side it has been given a giant Ionic portico, while on the garden (south) side two wings project forward slightly, and there are one-storeyed colonnades with bedrooms above framing a central bay. Shutters on the windows combine with these other features to give the impression of French rather than British classicism. The focus for the garden is a long canal terminating in a half-recessed lily pond below the central bay, and its planting was designed by Gertrude Jekyll, who was by this time about eighty years old.

463. The canal and garden façade of Gledstone Hall, Skipton, Yorkshire

Ednaston Manor, in Derbyshire **(Plate 464)**, was built for W.G. Player between 1912 and 1914. Its plan, which is H-shaped, is Lutyens at his most lucid, and the style certainly classical, though perhaps more Queen Anne than 'Wrenaissance'. The entrance front is curved, its five bays in two-storeyed brick divided by stone pilasters. The garden front has two projecting wings, but here the pilasters of the recessed middle section are irregularly placed and the doorcase is surmounted by a decorated triangular pediment. The two garden pavilions at either end of the terrace have Tuscan columns, as used in classical Roman garden buildings. It is a garden front of great style and harmony.

464. Ednaston Manor, Derbyshire

465. 'Homes fit for Heroes' in Benenden Road, Biddenden, Kent

14.3 SUBSIDY HOUSES

The Great War left Britain exhausted in every sense. Building materials were in short supply and yet the demand for houses was strong. To encourage the building of smaller houses, the Government paid a subsidy of £260 for new houses with a maximum floor-space of 1,400sq.ft. (130sq.m). This more limited area led to a rethink of the use of space and the enlargement of the living room at the expense of the dining room and the larder. As families were having increasingly to do without servants, the kitchen was also made smaller.

The house plan most frequently adopted was in the economical rectangular form, and within this shape one might have a living room 21ft. by 14ft. (6.5m by 4.25m), an 11ft. (3.4m) square dining room and a kitchen 14ft. by 10ft. (4.25m by 3m). Upstairs there would be four bedrooms. The subsidy stopped in July 1921, but the idea of a more compact house had been implanted in the public mind and the new form continued to be demanded. It is also true that a disproportionate number of subsidy houses were built for employees of large estates.

Little Orchards, at Denham, in Buckinghamshire, is an example of this economically sized house. Hand-made roof tiles and quality Crowborough bricks were used, and this doubtless derived from the Arts and Crafts Movement, but steel-framed windows ensured that money was saved on joinery. Here, too, the idea of having fewer, larger rooms is carried to its logical conclusion by installing folding doors which could be opened up between the dining room and the living room to create a space 29ft. by 14ft. (9m by 4.25m) which stretched right across the front of the house. Upstairs there were four bedrooms of which the smallest was 10ft. by 8ft. (3m by 2.5m). The roof space at the rear of the house was lighted by glass tiles so that not an inch of space was wasted.

14.4 'HOMES FIT FOR HEROES'

At the end of the Great War the nation faced acute social problems. A large army returned to an uncertain future and many younger members of the gentry who might have been expected to provide employment had died in the Flanders battlefields. Agricultural depression reduced the value of land and it soon became clear that the fabric of Edwardian society had been irretrievably destroyed, with little to put in its place. Discontent became apparent and in 1919 King George V made it plain to his ministers that, 'If unrest is to be converted into contentment, the provision of good houses may provide one of the most potent agents in that conversion'.

In response to this concern Lloyd George made the suggestion on behalf of the Government that every returning soldier should be given a smallholding consisting of a modest dwelling on three acres (1.2 hectares) and a cow. This was the first time that the British Government started building houses in a serious way, and on a nationwide basis, and it was to lead to the more extensive provision of council houses in the 1930s, especially after the Second World War. Housing estates were constructed serving new industries, while speculators offered small houses for sale at low prices with mortgages that were within the means of newly married men returning from the War.

Farmers too joined in the Government's initiative by selling plots of their land adjoining access lanes to returning soldiers. Inevitably many of these 'Homes for Heroes' have now been swamped by more recent development, but one of these simple homes (**Plate 465**) can still be seen on the Benenden Road at Biddenden, in Kent, which was built on land once owned by Lord Randolph's Farm. Similar 'Homes for Heroes' were

466. Royal British Legion cottage in the Preston Hall Colony, Aylesford, Kent

constructed at Blacon and at The Lache, on what was then the outskirts of the City of Chester. The Sunray Estate, on Herne Hill, in south London, is perhaps one of the best-known examples of this initiative. Built in 1920-1921, the houses' construction was uniquely organised by the Office of Works on direct labour and building guild lines, and so efficient was the operation that the estate, which used to be known as the Casino Avenue Estate, was completed quickly and to a high standard of design. The houses were carefully sited and had steeply pitched roofs and plain rendered walls. Just as well organised was an estate of bungalows built by the British Legion for returning soldiers at the Preston Hall Colony at Aylesford, Kent (**Plate 466**), in 1923. In the case of the single-storeyed buildings (**Plate 467**), it is striking how similar they were to the pre-fabs that were built after the Second World War.

467. Cottage in Glanvilles Wootton, Dorset

468. *House at Woodville, Derbyshire*

14.5 ARTERIAL ROAD HOUSES

Writing in *Here of All Places*, Osbert Lancaster had this to say about Arterial Road Houses: 'It is sad to reflect that so much ingenuity should have been wasted on streets and estates which will inevitably become the slums of the future'. He had bestowed the title 'By-Pass Variegated' on a group of houses which it is impossible to ignore, and it is a pity that this great writer and illustrator should have made in this case one of his rare and ill-founded predictions. In fact, the reason for the success of these buildings is that, whatever their decorative shortcomings, they had sufficient character for the owner, or more commonly the mortgagee, to see that his property was a home rather than a house, on which he would be prepared to spend time and money ensuring its good condition.

There is a positive infinity of examples of these houses with many different motifs and in many different styles, but the task of assessing each one is the same: 'Within the limits of this group of houses, how successful is this individual one?' On the A50, halfway between Burton upon Trent and Ashby de la Zouch, at Woodville, in Derbyshire, there is a group of houses built in 1932 *(Plate 468)* which makes an effort to produce a bold roof mass, but somehow fails. We should ask how they would have looked with thirty more courses of bricks on their chimneys. That might have had the effect of producing a definite architectural statement recalling the work of Richard Norman Shaw. Or would the miserable little hip at the base of the chimneys still have made them a design failure?

The predominantly suburban character of Hendon, in north London, was broken up in the 1920s when the A1 was made into a by-pass, creating Hendon Way and Watford Way as an alternative to the old Great North Road and the North Circular Road, which was made into a dual carriageway in 1935. The flows of fast-moving traffic inevitably give the houses along Hendon Way a feeling of insecurity, but the owners of many of them have, over the years, endowed these perfectly acceptable buildings with their own identities, which may seem eccentric, but which still indicate the affection in which they are held.

To the west of London an arterial road was created for slightly different reasons, but with much the same effect. The Great West Road was constructed in 1920-1925 to provide an alternative route to the west to the congested Brentford High Street, and within ten years the 'golden mile' of factories had been constructed along the road with houses continuing the line out to Hounslow. It is, perhaps, ironic that, at the beginning, many of the factories were in some way or another connected with the motor trade and, until the 1980s when the M4 was built, it was the car that made the ribbon development of houses to begin with accessible and then unbearable to live in. Like Hendon Way, the Great West Road has its own suburban character, however, and, now the road is quieter than it was, owners have stamped their houses with their idiosyncrasies.

14.6 STOCKBROKER TUDOR

It was again the great Osbert Lancaster who invented the term 'Stockbroker Tudor' in his *From Pillar to Post*, published in 1938. He intended to lampoon the bourgeois suburb and the epitome of this class-conscious style was the thatched garage. The derivation of the style is surely Richard Norman Shaw, with references to Lutyens' vernacular designs, but the original conceptions of these two architects became clichés in the hands of high-quality builders who were seeking a distinctive character for roomy, prosperous family houses.

In London most houses continued to be built during this period in the traditional materials of the Thames Valley – brick and tile – but the Victorian preference for half-timbering continued and it can still be seen today in the houses designed by E.G. Trobridge, at Kingsbury. Trobridge's patent system of wooden buildings was first introduced at the Daily Mail Ideal Home Exhibition in 1920 (itself an indication of the growth in demand for private housing), and his proclaimed intention was to build 'rural cottages in which ancient construction is modified to meet modern needs'.

Tile-hung gables, panels with nogged brick or pebble-dashing, and leaded windows were all used to create the impression of continuity and the principle of tradition worked its way through the whole range of house and cottage types, so that, as Osbert Lancaster said in *From Pillar to Post*, 'the passer-by is a little unnerved at being suddenly confronted with a hundred and fifty accurate reproductions of Anne Hathaway's cottage, each complete with central heating and garage'. It is easy to snigger at the false antiquity, but, at a time of social and economic uncertainty, the values of past ages do offer both aesthetic security and comfort.

14.7 THE MODERN HOUSE

For a brief but dazzling period of twenty or thirty years the modern house offered a new approach to the social and architectural history of Britain. Although never large in number, and in general terms confined to England rather than other parts of the United Kingdom, these steel and concrete buildings with their large areas of glass and interior open-planning had an influence not only on design but on the way that houses were used. The influence was from the Continent, and from Germany in particular, and indeed many of the early designers of the modern house in this country were those who escaped from Germany in the 1930s and either settled in England or used it as a transit point on their way to the United States.

Walter Gropius was the first director of the most advanced architecture and art training establishment in Europe – the Bauhaus – and until Hitler closed the School in 1935 it was the power-house of the Modern movement in architecture The twentieth century, it argued, was the age of the machine and architecture should fit in with the needs of the factory. Just as Pugin had expounded the central importance of function in design, so the Modern movement did likewise, though it did not adopt the same level of decoration. The thinking as it was translated to houses produced the concept that the house was merely a machine for living in and that anything added to this was unnecessary.. The clean straight lines and the lack of clutter had an appeal, as had the fact that costs could be kept to the minimum by the use of machine-made components, such as metal windows, and the use of shuttered concrete walls.

There are a number of fallacies in this argument. People are not machines, they have a strong aesthetic sense and want to surround themselves with objects precious to them and with decorations whose familiar presence heightens their sense of well-being. Just as striking in the context of this country is the fact that many of the early modern iconic buildings were steel-framed, but clad in traditional brickwork, while some of the most influential of the designers were not only brought up in the Arts and Crafts traditions, but believed that their designs were the logical fulfilment of Arts and Crafts principles.

In 1934 a very influential book, *The Modern House* by F.R.S. Yorke, was published in England, illustrating fifty-seven modern houses from fourteen countries. To those of his less well-travelled colleagues it was an eye-opener and certainly caught the mood of the time among the better-off patrons. Within four years the few English examples included in the first edition had become a flood and the names of the designers of modern houses read like a roll-call of the most distinguished architects of the time in England: Gropius himself with Maxwell Fry, Berthold Lubetkin, Mendelssohn and Chermayeff, Wells Coates, and Connell, Ward and Lucas.

Many of these houses were quite large, but the shortage of servants after the Great War meant that living patterns had to be more flexible, and so did the interior disposition of living rooms. It is interesting that the modernist style did not catch on in the same way after the Second World War, partly because of anti-German sentiment, but also because of the general hardship of the post-war years and the essential preoccupation with large-scale housing schemes and the need to work at a more economical scale. Gropius certainly saw the modern house as a test-bed for steel and concrete construction, and for Crittall windows, and although, as we have seen, neither material was new to British building, it had previously been faced with brick. Also, flowing spaces needed central heating and this was rare in Britain until the 1960s except in 'social housing'.

Cohen House, in Old Church Street, Chelsea *(Plate 469)*, was built for Dennis Cohen, himself an émigré, in 1935-1936 by Mendelssohn and Chermayeff, a partnership of a distinguished foreign architect and an English practitioner born in Russia. The cool, white façade fits in well with the Chelsea street scene, as does the conservatory by Norman Foster, but it was a house intended to be run by servants. There is a two-storeyed hall incorporating the staircase and a run of Drawing Room, Library and Dining Room facing away from the road.

One of the most stunning statements of the Modern movement is High and Over, in the Chilterns near Amersham on the Hill, Buckinghamshire *(Plate 470)*. Built in 1929-1931 by Amyas Connell, at that time of A.D. Connell and S. Lloyd Thomson and later of Connell, Ward and Lucas, for Bernard Ashmole, Professor of Archaeology at London University, it consists of three wings radiating out from a central, hexagonal, double-height hall. This creates a Y-shaped plan facing south and west and is reminiscent of the sun-trap houses of the 1890s, but High and Over was none the less the first example in this country of Le Corbusier's early villa style. The essence is of stark, white walls with cut-in horizontal windows and, once again, although the house has a concrete frame, rendered brick for the walls.

469. *The Cohen House, Church Street, Chelsea, London*

470. High and Over, Amersham on the Hill, Buckinghamshire

The Hopfield, at Platt, in Kent *(Plate 471)*, was designed by Colin Lucas, before he joined Connell and Ward, as a weekend cottage for himself and his family. The date was 1933 and the size of the house not very large, even allowing for the two-storeyed extension to the north. But the white-painted reinforced concrete structure with its long upper window and the projecting balcony and exterior stair are all typical elements of the Modern movement.

Torilla, near Hatfield, in Hertfordshire, is F.R.S. Yorke's first important house, and its construction in 1934 coincided with the publication of *The Modern House*. This charming building *(Plate 472)*, which fits so well into its natural setting, has a number of Continental antecedents,

but is not especially Le Corbusier in style. It consists of a large central hall and a first-floor terrace, and was somewhat extended two years after it had been built by Yorke and Marcel Breuer. Although it came near to being demolished in the 1990s, Torilla has now been sensitively restored by John Winter for an enthusiastic owner.

Hampstead is just the sort of place to find avant-garde houses, and this was as true of the 1930s as it is today. In Frognal Way, E. Maxwell Fry built the fine Sun House *(Plate 473)* in 1934-1935 which clearly owes much to Mies van der Rohe. The façade harmonises with its surroundings whilst still possessing a character of its own. Set in white, rendered walls, with three levels of horizontal windows of varying heights, together with a

471. The Hopfield, Platt, Kent

472. Torilla, Hatfield, Hertfordshire

473. The Sun House, Frognal Way, Hampstead, London

357

474. The Wood House, Shipbourne, Kent

large first-floor balcony on thin steel supports, the house still provokes a surprised reaction from the observer.

A contrast to the white reinforced concrete houses of the Modern movement is provided by Gropius himself. At Shipbourne, in Kent, is The Wood House **(Plate 474)**, completed by Maxwell Fry after Gropius left for the United States. There seemed to be an inevitability about white concrete and Gropius wanted to turn back to natural materials. Consequently the structure is faced with cedar weatherboarding, while the projecting eaves are painted white. It is a simple and coherent design and its date, 1937, underlines why its design successors lie across the Atlantic rather than in this country.

There is another modern house in Hampstead, though it has a very different character from The Sun House. 1-3 Willow Road **(Plate 475)** is by the Hungarian-born

Erno Goldfinger, No. 2 being occupied by the architect himself, and this house is now owned and opened by the National Trust. Built in 1937-1939 to the accompaniment of much local hostility, the three houses have different internal plans, although all three have stylish spiral staircases, but the design was deliberately made capable of extension into a continuous street frontage. The Willow Road façade is of three storeys, but the garden façade is of four, the main living level being marked by larger windows, and the ground floor taken up with garage and services. Although the structure is of reinforced concrete with columns supporting the first floor, brick is used to face the walls, and it is now hard to see why this quiet and elegant design caused so much upset in the 1930s, and was even considered to require defending as late as 1952.

475. 1-3 Willow Road, Hampstead, London

476. *Gardnor Mansions, Church Row, Hampstead, London*

14.8 APARTMENT BLOCKS

Flats probably have their origins in the seventeenth century and in the accommodation enjoyed by Charles II when he was in exile on the Continent. The term means no more than a series of rooms on one level making up a residence, and in the great French houses the *appartement* consisted of an *antéchambre*, a *chambre* and a *cabinet* occupied exclusively by the owner of a house or his principal guest. This plan derived ultimately from Italy and, with variations, was adopted in the Low Countries, Germany and Spain. The French arrangement was broadly employed by Charles II after his Restoration, and by his returning courtiers, and the implications for

existing houses can be clearly seen at Ham House, in Surrey, while Chatsworth, in Derbyshire, rebuilt later in the century employed the same arrangement. The degree of public access allowed in the individual rooms of these apartments or lodgings was strictly controlled, but broadly the more important a visitor the further he would be allowed to progress towards the Cabinet or Closet.

It goes without saying that the same rules applied to great houses in the towns and cities, but the pressure on space in London soon led to the relaxing of the restrictions and the renting either of single rooms or a number of rooms in other people's houses. It was a short

477. Vernon Court, Hendon Way, Cricklewood, London

step from this to the construction of blocks of flats, either for the luxury end of the market, such as Gardnor Mansions in Church Row, Hampstead **(Plate 476)**, of 1898, or for independent social housing typified by the Peabody Estate flats, for instance those near Bow Street, in London's Covent Garden, which have already been noticed (see 13.0). Cheapness of construction was the impetus behind the tenement buildings of Glasgow and other industrial centres in this country, while the shortage of land which gave rise to New York's apartment blocks must also have influenced the thinking of public and private authorities and their architects at the end of the nineteenth century.

But in the 1930s the development of blocks of flats also had a philosophical motivation. Suburban sprawl was seen as an evil in itself; architects like Le Corbusier and his disciples advocated the value of vertical living with the fine views that went with it, and to which the airy, clean style of the Modern movement was particularly suited, while a new group of busy professional people grew up needing serviced *pieds-à-terre* and quick access to the City.

It is interesting to compare Vernon Court **(Plate 477)**, on Hendon Way, Cricklewood, in north London, which has a half-timbered façade, surely a hang-over from the suburban houses of the end of the preceding century, with Highpoint 1, in North Road, Highgate, London. The first of these blocks was built in 1930 in the neo-Tudor style,

478. Highpoint, North Road, Highgate, London

while the distinguished Highpoint 1, by Berthold Lubetkin and Tecton, of 1935, was inspired by the work of Le Corbusier and is very much a product of the Modern movement. The rendered construction is of reinforced concrete with a bulge in the middle which contains the hall, staircase and lifts, but also a winter garden and, projecting from the garden façade, a brick-built tea room. The client of Highpoint 1 was Sigmund Gestetner, who had first intended to build flats for his employees, but who finished by building luxury flats which, in the manner of the time, required a series of maids' rooms at the back of the ground floor. Although the plan appears complicated, it is basically a double cross with eight flats on each floor consisting of two living rooms and three bedrooms.

Highpoint 2 was built three years later, and by this time the architect had understood the disadvantages of a cement-rendered façade in the English climate, so it was built of brick with tile infilling. The flats are also bigger, having three living rooms and four bedrooms, arranged in the jig-saw fashion favoured by Le Corbusier, so that the living spaces could be double height. Perhaps the most sophisticated aspect of Highpoint 2 is the use of caryatids copied from the Erechtheum on the Acropolis to support the entrance canopy, but from the point of view of the role of flats in the urban scene, it is the subtle placing of both blocks on high, well-treed land that was to be most influential *(Plate 478)*.

479. *Trent Park, Middlesex*

480. *Garden front of Hinton Ampner, Hampshire*

14.9 1930s GEORGIAN

In spite of this, the main theme of domestic architecture between the wars was neo-Georgian in a romantic rural setting. So far as country houses are concerned, the most extreme form of this traditionalism was Trent Park, at Enfield *(Plate 479)*, built in 1926-1931 by Philip Tilden for Sir Philip Sassoon of materials gathered from other demolished buildings. Today Trent Park is used by Middlesex University and the grounds are now a country park. From a small villa built in 1777 by Sir Richard Jebb in an enclosure of part of Enfield Chase, Trent Park grew both at the end of the eighteenth century and again in 1894 until a symmetrical composition in the Georgian style with projecting wings was created for Sassoon by the architect who had already worked for the Member of Parliament at Port Lympne, in Kent. The whole building was cased in red brick and given a balustrade around the roof. Inside the house has lost most of its original furniture and decoration, though there are fireplaces by William Kent which must have come from the demolished Devonshire House in Piccadilly, and there are murals by Rex Whistler.

Hinton Ampner, in Hampshire *(Plate 480)*, has all the serene characteristics of the perfect Georgian manor house, though only the cellars are original. The house was reduced by Ralph Dutton from what he called 'the

exceptional hideousness' of the large Victorian structure to neo-Georgian scale in 1936, and was then rebuilt and refurnished after a disastrous fire in 1960. In 1982 Ralph Dutton succeeded his cousin as the 8th Lord Sherborne, and four years later the estate was bequeathed to the National Trust. Today Hinton Ampner appears to be a house of about 1800 with a fine country house collection of pictures and furniture, set in gardens of exceptional beauty. The work of reduction was carried out in 1936 by Lord Gerald Wellesley, later Duke of Wellington, and his partner, Trenwith Wills, but the rebuilding, again by Trenwith Wills in 1960, was carried out largely in replica, although the attic storey was removed. The Adam ceiling of the Dining Room, which came in 1936 from 38 Berkeley Square, London, also survived the fire.

Although, as we have seen earlier, the style of most of the original houses in Hampstead Garden Suburb was 'picturesque vernacular' established by Sir Raymond Unwin, the larger properties built between the wars followed Lutyens' buildings in the Central Square in adopting a Neo-Georgian style. The first house in this style seems to have been No. 19 Wellgarth Road by C. Cowles-Voysey, of 1910, but it was followed by many others, mainly in the outer areas of the Suburb where the Trust had little or no control, certainly of variable quality. Quite restrained houses in the Neo-Georgian style can be seen in Fairway Close, with No. 3 *(Plate 481)* of 1929 being occupied by their architect, C.H. James, while Nos. 1 and 2 Bunkers Hill were built in 1928-1929 by C. Cowles-Voysey, one of them again for his own occupation. All these Neo-Georgian houses were of brick, and usually had doorcases which were decorated with pediments or brackets, and sash windows, with the occasional brick pilaster.

In the London Borough of Merton the Douglas Haig Memorial Homes at Morden unite the Homes Fit for Heroes Campaign with Neo-Georgian design. These houses were designed by Grey Wornum in 1929 to house disabled servicemen from the Great War and, as a constant reminder of the sufferings on the Western Front, terracotta roundels with Field Marshal Haig's portrait are included on the façades. Care was taken to maintain the dimensions of true Georgian windows with sashes and glazing bars and rather Art Deco architraves.

481. 3 Fairway Close, Hampstead Garden Suburb, London

14.91 THE BUNGALOW BETWEEN THE WARS

The single-storey house must be the most primitive form of shelter, which, depending on the materials used for its construction, has a degree of permanence about it. In this sense, such building styles can be traced back to the earliest times, but, as has been noted before, the bungalow has a specific origin in India. Peacehaven, in Sussex, has often been referred to, disparagingly, as a rash on England's countryside. Dating from the period after the First World War, it is famous for its individual houses, many of them bungalows *(Plate 482)*, on their own plots of land, stretching as far as the eye can see. Its name is obscure,

though the first part of the name must surely refer to the Peace of Versailles of 1919, but the 'haven' remains mysterious. The generous consumption of land for the development suggests a colonial suburb rather than an English one, and, indeed, when it was first built it was called New Anzac on Sea. The two Witterings at the end of the Selsey peninsula to the south of Chichester sum up the different social levels of the house and the bungalow. West Wittering is full of posh houses in moderate sized gardens, while East Wittering has unending avenues of bungalows and chalets, with caravans nearest to the beach.

482. Bungalows at Peacehaven, Sussex

CHAPTER 15

1940-2000

15.0 INTRODUCTION

The story of the house in Britain since the Second World War demonstrates a co-relation between design and the strength of the national economy. That is not only to say that in times of hardship cheap public housing was preferred to the construction of substantial mansions, but that, at all levels of society, the quality of design depended on investment of time and money. The style in which houses and flats were built during this period seemed to matter little, although there continues to be a strong preference for the classical style, particularly at the upper end of the housing market. Even here, however, what mattered most was the accuracy with which the classical vocabulary of motifs was used, perhaps more so than it had been in earlier times, and suggesting, maybe, a lack of certainty among designers as to the direction architecture was going in.

What has developed steadily during this half-century is the technology of building, not so much in making discoveries as in the refinement of the innovatory ideas of the early part of the century. Reinforced concrete has changed dramatically, as has the steel space-frame leading to a three-dimensional system where the loads could be distributed in all directions. Traditional structures had also been altered to resist the effects of wind at high levels, using stiff cores for a building, which, combined with cross walls and a braced outer skin, created a type of cantilever.

Just as important was the improvement of the services inside a building, not only heating, but also air-conditioning and acoustic control. When these factors were combined with tinted glass, a new dimension in flat-building had obviously been created. Tall blocks of flats use great amounts of energy and it has now been accepted that they create social problems for those who live in them, but it was also the oil crisis of 1973 that saw these blocks lose much of their appeal.

Three other factors influenced the development of housing during the last fifty years. At the end of the war there was a chronic shortage of accommodation in London, partly as a result of the Blitz. To begin with new public housing was in the hands of the London County Council whose architects imposed what might be called a 'house style' for new building where good design was insisted on. In spite of shortage of materials, large numbers of houses were built both inside the London area and in what were called 'out-county' developments, such as those at Harold Hill and St Paul's Cray, but all too often it was simply houses that were built rather than self-sufficient communities.

The New Towns were also built around London in accordance with Professor Abercrombie's *Greater London Plan*, but, although this was the ultimate in state planning of communities in this country, the progress was slow and the towns themselves were built at relatively low densities on land which it had been intended would be protected from development to act as lungs for London. They were, of course, mixed developments along the lines of the Lansbury Estate *(Plate 483)* at Poplar in east London, which had been designed as part of the Festival of Britain in 1951.

The careful siting of houses and flats in the landscape was pioneered with great effect at the Alton Estate, in Roehampton, between 1952 and 1960, but the use of the environment in this way was not confined to public housing schemes. In a number of beautiful houses such as Stratton Park, at East Stratton in Hampshire, the garden was brought inside, with the designers making use of the new building technology to overcome intrinsic problems like the misting of large glass windows. Just as important during these years was the conservation of the envelope of historic buildings and those that played an important role in the local environment, such as churches, warehouses, mills and barns, and their skilful adaptation to domestic use.

15.1 THE 'PRE-FAB'

Towards the end of the Second World War there had been serious shortages of materials and this had led to the Temporary Housing Programme of 1944. As Minister of Works at the time, Lord Portal, who had already been responsible for the experiments made by his ministry's Building Research Station into standardised houses using traditional materials, produced a model steel bungalow,

483. Flats and maisonettes on the Lansbury Estate, Poplar, London

named after him, which was exhibited outside the Tate Gallery. Ironically, this structure never went into production, but, instead, eleven different designs prepared by private firms were licensed for production by the government, all of them covering 645sq.ft. (60sq.m) and consisting of two bedrooms and a standard kitchen and bathroom unit.

The pre-fabs were supposed to last only for ten years, but, in spite of the methods of their construction, their small size, and the fact that they were built very often on temporary sites, they came to be regarded with great affection by many of their occupiers, so that some are still lived in today. Nearly 8,000 pre-fabs were supplied to the London County Council and the metropolitan boroughs received a further 7,300. In 1967 these houses passed into local authority ownership and in cities such as Bristol there have been campaigns for these properties to be improved rather than replaced; this is due, in

part at least, to memories of the poor housing conditions that their occupiers had known during the war and the intimacy of the small garden layouts where they were built. The sense of community, so strong in pre-war neighbourhoods, had been miraculously preserved, and it has to be acknowledged that the facilities in the pre-fabs were much better than anything their tenants had previously enjoyed.

In the London area the largest surviving group of pre-fabs is the Downham Bungalow Estate in Baudwin Road, Lewisham. Between 1945 and 1947 some 187 Uni-Seco dwellings were built along roads named after King Arthur's Knights of the Round Table. It is remarkable to think today that in 1961 the London County Council launched a second building programme for pre-fabs. These adopted the same space criteria as those from 1944, although they had strong timber frames and flat roofs.

484. 'Pre-fabs' in Persaut Road, Lewisham, London

485. Ashdale House, on the Woodberry Down Estate, Stoke Newington, London

15.2 THE COUNCIL HOUSE

It is a truism that the style of the council house is as varied as the district and the year in which it was built. A further complication arises when it is remembered that, as the result of the legislation that enabled tenants to buy their council houses, what once was a local authority property is now quite likely to be privately owned. The changes that owners make to their houses can be quite profound and will certainly affect the appearance of a group of similar properties.

Looking at the development of council housing in London over five decades certainly demonstrates a diversity of architectural styles, as well as illustrating changing social attitudes. In the introduction to this chapter, the Lansbury Estate, at Poplar in east London,

was held out as the pioneering mixed development which incorporated both high flats and houses of varying sizes with shops and other services needed to create a real community. Another early mixed estate was the Woodberry Down Estate at Stoke Newington (**Plate 485**). Designed in the 1940s by the Architects' Department of the London County Council under J.H. Forshaw, it was completed in 1954 and had a real heart with its own health centre, school and library, as well as flats and houses with gardens for families. The eight-storey blocks of flats enabled a high density of 178 persons per acre to be achieved, and the effects of this were mitigated somewhat by a picturesque arrangement of the blocks which, at the time, was pioneering town planning not only in Britain. A later development allowed for bungalows to be introduced into the layout to accommodate old people.

In 1963 Sir Colin Buchanan's seminal report, *Traffic in Towns*, was published offering an authoritative guide to planning the inter-relationship of the living areas of towns and the road network that serviced them. In some places blocks of flats were deliberately built with their backs to the roads to cut down the damaging effects of vehicle noise, but at Thamesmead the proximity of a new motorway and local flood restrictions led to a network of footpaths and cycle-ways being built at first-floor level to connect the houses and flats. Binsey Walk *(Plate 486)*, of 1969, was the only part of the plan to be constructed as intended and it featured long blocks of houses and flats which were to become such a feature of public housing in the following decade.

The damaging effect that tall blocks of flats could have on the environment was recognised early on, but it was not until Sir Leslie Martin was appointed to the newly created chair of architecture at Cambridge University in 1957 that experiments with low-rise housing were undertaken first in Cambridge and later in London. Although not the first to be built in this manner, Lillington Gardens, in Pimlico, by Darbourne and Darke, was successful. The subject of a competition in 1961, the scheme was finished in 1972. The architects used reddish-brown, load-bearing brick for the terraces of flats and maisonettes. No effort was made to build in straight lines and the random shapes of the layout were something of a relief after the formality of the blocks of flats.

In the 1960s the then Ministry of Housing and Local Government researched what the users of public housing wanted of their new accommodation, and the model for compact, low-level planning which proved to be most influential had recently been built at Siedlung Halen, outside Berne, in Switzerland. Two low-rise, high-density schemes inspired by this prototype were built in the

486. Binsey Walk, Thamesmead, London

487. *Flats and maisonettes at Alexandra Road, Camden, London*

Borough of Camden – the Alexandra Road Estate of 1972-1978 **(Plate 487)** and its contemporary, Branch Hill, in Hampstead **(Plate 488)**. Designed by Neave Brown, of the Camden Borough Architects' Department, the Alexandra Road maisonettes and flats recall a Georgian terrace facing on to a walkway rather than a road, with the housing set progressively back. This arrangement has the additional advantage of forming a baffle against the noise of the railway line which runs behind.

The architects for the Branch Hill development, Gordon Benson and Alan Forsyth, had to cope with restrictive covenants on the land which insisted that development must be of only two storeys and semi-detached.

Consequently there are narrow paths between the houses and the design allows for the garden of one house to form the roof of the one below, with small courtyards bringing light into the lower level of the upper house.

The Byker Wall, in Newcastle upon Tyne **(Plate 489)**, was also a milestone in the development of community architecture. From its inception in 1969, the architect, Ralph Erskine and his project leader, Vernon Gracie, set out to consult the 3,000 people who would occupy the new homes. They also set themselves the task of protecting the dramatic topography of the Tyne Valley by ensuring that the materials and textures of the new development were sympathetic to the area, and that the

488. *Houses at Branch Hill, Hampstead*

489. *The Byker Wall, Newcastle upon Tyne*

building followed the flow of the contours, rising to a single wedge-shaped block at the west and creating a wall of flats along the northern ridge. The high wall itself is largely blank, with the exception of small windows to the less important rooms, to act as a baffle to the traffic noise from the Byker bypass (now completed), and on the south side there are timber balconies to the flats which also have fine views over the river. Below the Wall there are small houses in terraces linked by steps and pathways which have been built to replace the steep streets of brick houses that were there before, and this more conventional urban arrangement contrasts with the Byker Wall itself.

490. *Alton West flats on Tangley Avenue, Roehampton, London*

15.3 STREETS IN THE SKY

Hermann Muthesius, writing in *The English House* in 1904, had this to say about flats: 'If the influence of the metropolis is dulling in itself, to allow children to grow up in urban, multi-storeyed buildings can only intensify the influence, for it cuts people off from their rightful world as unnaturally as a cage does an animal from its home in the wild'. The logic of the Modern movement in architecture led to the conclusion that, where space is expensive, one could always build upwards, as New York had done and as the post-war need for homes in London and in other British cities had made inevitable.

The point blocks, like Ronan Point, which were built after the war were designed and related to lower structures with their sculptural qualities very much in mind, but the views that the tenants had from their flats soon became a matter of concern, and the English designers readily adopted the notion enunciated by Le Corbusier that the flats should be seen as 'Streets in the Sky', and that the residents should take their garden spaces with them up to their flats. This necessarily laid stress on the space and the topography of the land between the blocks, and complex calculations were made to ensure that the optimum amount of open space should notionally be available to each flat, and the placing of the structures should respect the environmental quality of the area in which the estate stood.

In the 1960s and 1970s public housing schemes had a poor reputation, partly because of inadequate maintenance and also because of the collapse in 1968 of part of the Ronan Point flats in Newnham due to a gas leak. The imperative of accommodating the largest number of people in the smallest area, dominant in the 1950s, had to be revised, and the better quality of public housing built in the 1970s still awaits assessment, as by the end of that decade local authority house building largely came to an end and is only now being restarted in a different form.

One area where new housing could still be built in London in the 1950s was Roehampton, where a number of villas still stood in their own landscaped grounds. To begin with a series of point blocks (after the German *punkthaus*) were built on the Portsmouth Road, but by 1955, when these were finished, tastes favoured the slab blocks and five of these were built by the London County Council along Roehampton Lane in an estate now known as Alton West **(Plate 490)**.

The architects involved here were Bill Howell, John Killick, John Partridge and Stanley Amis, who subsequently formed a partnership. The inspiration for their design was the Unité d'Habitation at Marseilles, by Le Corbusier, and great design strength derives from the siting of the blocks on stilts (another Le Corbusier idea) into the slope of Downshire Field. Three original villas and their parkland were preserved, two groups of point blocks also constructed, and old people's bungalows inserted in the layout in a seemingly random manner. Although these five-storeyed slab blocks were not the first built by the LCC, Alton West displayed careful detailing and skilful siting which satisfies both environmental concerns and the need for generous and beautiful views from the balconies of the flats.

15.4 CONVERTED SCHOOLS

The implementation of the 1944 Education Act meant a reduction in the number of school buildings for teaching purposes, particularly in the countryside. Charming buildings of modest size dating very often from the middle of the nineteenth century that had previously accommodated infant schools were no longer economic to run. Some were put to inappropriate uses and gradually deteriorated until they were replaced, but some were converted into houses, especially during the 1970s. The most important action taken by the new owners and their architects was to preserve the exterior appearance of the buildings, especially the large windows which gave light to the main room of the original school.

Care has been taken in the conversion of this small, stone-built infants' school in Compton Dando, near to Bristol, in Somerset *(Plate 491)*. The date of the school building was 1870 and both the large west window and the main doorway speak clearly of the Gothic which was the inspiration of the first builder. A rather larger building, and this time in brick appropriate to its Suffolk location, is at Saxtead. Changes have not been made to the outer structure of the school, but the building's greater size has meant that it could incorporate not only a house, but a dance studio housed in the main room of the old school.

491. The Old School, Compton Dando, Somerset

15.5 CHURCHES INTO HOUSES

Converting churches into housing became popular in the late 1970s and 1980s, especially in the large towns and cities. Not only was space at a premium, but a less devout population, the movement of people and the amalgamation of non-conformist sects combined to create a surplus of religious buildings which almost always played an important townscape role in an urban area. The problem for the designers was not so much preserving the exteriors of such buildings as ensuring that they were converted internally in a way that did not compromise the integrity of the spaces, while still achieving the number of flats and maisonettes in the building that would produce an economic return.

One such scheme is in Cromwell Road, at its junction with Highgate Hill in north London *(Plate 492)*. The stone building dates from 1887 and was the former

492. Former Congregational Church, Hornsey Lane, Highgate, London

493. A former church near Coggeshall, Essex, now a house

Presbyterian Church which had amalgamated with the Union Church for Congregationalists in Pond Square, Highgate, and the two congregations needed only one church building for worshippers. A fine porch facing the Highgate Hill junction was added to the church by George Lethbridge in 1900 and the decorative detail of the original structure was retained in the conservation work. To a large degree the integrity of the interiors was retained by dividing the church horizontally, except where this meant inserting floors across the great west window. In that case the floor was taken back from the line of the window.

Another scheme of conversion involved a small thirteenth century Anglican church near Coggeshall, in Essex *(Plate 493)*. It had become redundant, but because of its modest size was suitable for making into just one residence. One lancet in the north vestry speaks of the

thirteenth century, while there are two south windows of two lights each which must have been made in the following century; the roof of the nave has a tie-beam with a king-post. These elements have all been kept in the conversion, as has the nineteenth century glass of the east window.

Rather than dividing up the nave and chancel space vertically, the new owners and their architect retained the integrity of the interior, accepting the heating and privacy problems that inevitably arose, while creating a second storey for bedrooms at the west end of the church, but with the floor kept back from the west window. The insertion of dormer windows to light these bedrooms has been done with modesty and charm, and the outside views of the building now have a Dutch appearance. It does show how a historic church can be given a new use when changes are both modest and sympathetic to the original.

375

494. Pear Tree Barn, Mount Bures, Essex

15.6 BARN CONVERSIONS

Barns are often the oldest surviving buildings in the rural landscape. Where the farmhouse has been substantially changed, perhaps on several occasions, barns have not been subject so much to the whims of fashion and have continued to perform their original function since, in some cases, the medieval period. In recent times, however, farming practices have changed fundamentally, and storing crops or equipment in large barns has been either reduced or abandoned altogether.

Finding new uses for what are often listed vernacular buildings in the countryside has become a growing problem during the last thirty years or so and in counties where there are large numbers of either wooden or stone barns, such as Essex and Gloucestershire, the planning authorities have had to take a view on what might be acceptable and what would certainly not be. In sensitive areas of both counties there is a presumption against the conversion of listed and unlisted barns to houses, but the pressure has been so great that many conversions to houses have taken place with

varying results. In Essex, for instance, the County Council received 220 applications for residential conversion of barns in the six years to 1989, of which roughly 150 were approved, and at least ninety of these were either completed or were at that time being converted.

Although there are brick and stone barns in Essex, the largest number of such structures is timber-framed and in the landscape their profiles appear as large, rectangular wooden boxes with steep roofs and without openings. Originally thatched or tiled, the roofs have in more recent times been given pantiles or natural slates, and these harmonise well so long as vernacular materials are used. Essex County Council has given advice on barn conversions in sensible Policy Guidelines which point out that, where the character of the listed barn dominates in its new role as a house, the number of window openings should be kept to a minimum, their frames painted black to relate to the tarred wood of most of the timber-framed barns, and the major glazing concentrated in the old cart entrances. Just as important externally is avoiding brick chimneystacks, using matt-surfaced metal flues instead, while care needs to be taken when replacing the wooden cladding to use materials with the same profile as the original. Some screening is almost always going to be needed to conceal those necessities of modern life such as washing lines, patios, gardens and swimming pools.

Inside every effort needs to be made to keep at least one large undivided space, ensuring that a simple staircase does not cross the glazing and leads to an upper floor that does not wrap around the side walls. It goes almost without saying that internal features such as studs, sole plates and roof braces should be retained, and only modestly restored, if necessary. Roof lights should be introduced only where there are no alternatives, and if a strip of long, shallow windows under the roof line can be used instead, these are, to my mind, preferable. A distinction can also be drawn between the public and the private side of a converted barn, perhaps retaining the original cart doors as exterior shutters. The design work on Pear Tree Barn, at Mount Bures, Essex (**Plate 494**), has been sensitively done, producing a most attractive house while respecting the essential qualities of the barn. It is also true to say that the guidelines for timber-framed barn conversions are, in general terms, equally applicable to stone structures.

15.7 WAREHOUSE CONVERSIONS

Changes in commercial viability as the result of ever-larger container vessels left many of the Port of London warehouse buildings redundant. Progress in changing the use of many fine nineteenth century warehouses has been predictably slow, especially when it is remembered that Ivory House, in St Katherine's Dock, Wapping, was restored and converted in 1973, while the houses and flats at The Lakes, at Norway Dock, Rotherhithe, were only completed in 1996.

Ivory House (**Plate 495**) was a prestigious work of conservation, with the Italianate building of 1854 by Thomas Aitcheson being made into shops on the dock level, offices on the mezzanine, and thirty-eight luxury flats on the top four storeys, by Renton Howard Wood Levin. Fortunately, much of the splendid iron-work, the vaulted brick ceilings and the flagstones of the old warehouse was kept.

Rotherhithe lies in the great bend of the Thames and being too wet for farming became the site for London's first wet dock. To begin with the area concentrated on shipbuilding and repair, but with the building of the Surrey Commercial Docks between 1801 and about 1864

495. Ivory House, St Katherine's Dock, London

the source of its trading wealth became apparent in the names of the docks along the peninsula – Norway, Greenland, Canada, Russia and Quebec. Today those names have been perpetuated in the flats which have been inserted into warehouses such as Canada Wharf *(Plate 496)*, in Rotherhithe Street, where fifty-seven apartments have been constructed by Michael Squire Associates in three buildings: a listed four-storeyed riverside warehouse with Islamic overtones, a similar one fronting on to Rotherhithe Street, and a third replacement building. Canada Wharf has no basements, but great voids, which made it one of the first silos for grain storage in England.

By contrast, the old Maltings at the southern extremity of Long Melford, in Suffolk, have been converted into flats and maisonettes during the past five years. The handsome early nineteenth century brick building *(Plate 497)* with stone dressings framing the original arched entrances has been carefully restored and converted, and now provides a striking entrance to the long village street.

496. Canada Wharf warehouse, Rotherhithe, London

497. The Old Maltings, Long Melford, Suffolk

498. *Span flats and maisonettes at Hallgate, Blackheath Park, London*

499. *Lakeside and The Cedars, Castlebar Hill, Ealing. London*

15.8 SPAN HOUSING

Lurking in the back of the minds of designers of this period were the merits of London's classical squares and terraces. The importance of these examples came late to public housing and much the same is true of private development. The firm which was to revive such layouts, and to create estates that are still admired today, was Span Developments Ltd. Founded by Geoffrey Townsend, an architect turned developer, with Eric Lyons, the main executive architect of the firm, Span was the first private developer in the country to turn away from the speculative and the mundane and to concentrate on the aesthetics of the houses, both inside and out.

Just as important for the future appearance of the Span estates was the decision to grant only leaseholds, so that the tenants' management committees could control the setting of the houses and flats and maintain the common parts of the development. The Parkleys Estate, on Ham Common, in the Borough of Richmond, was one of the earliest Span developments built between 1954 and 1956 and its appearance today sums up many of the company's achievements. The densely developed site was originally a nursery and the generous landscaping even now gives the two-storeyed ranges of flats set in courtyards, offset by four-storeyed blocks, a bosky, well cared for appearance. In 1958 Thurnby Court was built at the corner of Wellesley Road and Spencer Road, on Twickenham Green. It consisted of a quadrangle of twenty-seven flats, compact and tile-hung,

while at Fieldend, off Waldegrave Road in the same area, the layout was more generous with fifty-one weatherboarded terrace houses being built at a density of forty rooms to the acre. These houses, completed in 1961, had private back gardens arranged informally in an outstandingly sylvan setting, with a perimeter road for vehicles.

Eric Lyons saw his houses as essentially urban and his instinct for high-density building often brought Span into conflict with local planning officers, especially when the plan was for infilling, as it was at Hallgate, on the old nineteenth century Cator Estate, at Blackheath Park (**Plate 498**). It is on Blackheath that the greatest diversity of the work of Span Developments can be seen. The Priory (1954-1956) consists only of flats and is quite small, giving its arrangement a secluded intimacy, but a rather later scheme is Park End, of 1967, at the end of Blackheath Park, where the houses have split-level roofs and private gardens at both front and back. In the decade the Span houses became larger, as they are at Corner Keep (1979), often three storeyed, in a more angular style, and mostly of brick.

It is only fair to point out that the Span formula was much followed, not least by Wates. One of their best schemes is Lakeside, at Castlebar, Ealing (**Plate 499**). Built in 1966, it consists of three-storeyed houses with a tall block of flats, the whole layout sharing a mature landscape with a small pool which had been preserved from a nineteenth century villa on the site.

500. Ranch-style house near Sudbury, Suffolk

15.9 MEXICAN RANCH-STYLE HOUSES

By the 1960s, 'bungalow' had become a dirty word as these buildings had spread over the countryside or ribboned their way along the main roads going out of the large towns and cities. They were, of course, still built in the post-War period, but the Mexican ranch-style house, itself a single-storeyed structure, was promoted as a new and acceptable design to the bungalow. It could and still can be identified by the large stone chimney and French windows and often spreads out over a considerable area. The local planners saw it as an acceptable modern version of an old adversary because it did not break the skyline excessively and fitted into its surroundings no matter how spacious it might be.

This style of house can be found all over the country, but a striking example is this **(Plate 500)**, which is near Sudbury, in Suffolk. Equally interesting is this house at Bradenham, Norfolk **(Plate 501)**.

501. Mexican ranch-style: Mill Farm, Bradenham, Norfolk

502. Executive Neo-Georgian: Aylmer Road, Highgate, London

15.91 EXECUTIVE NEO-GEORGIAN

Before the Second World War post offices were built in a sparsely decorated mid-Georgian style which was christened 'Nudist Georgian' by contemporary architectural writers. Executive Neo-Georgian is often found on developments striving for superior effect at little extra cost, rather like those post office buildings seeking to give themselves airs and graces. Even allowing for the lack of weathering and the hard, unfriendly materials often used, most of these modern executive houses were clearly designed without reference to James Gibbs' method of achieving Georgian proportions by means of compass-drawn circles, as was described in 8.92.

The architects working in this style seem happier with the flat roof and their approach to Neo-Georgian was to use a few Georgian motifs, such as architraves incorporating mouldings over doorcases and glazing bars on the windows, to trick out a box-shaped structure. This economy of effort makes an interesting comparison with the care that was expended by architects designing Neo-Georgian buildings between the wars, as discussed in 14.9.

At the junction of the Great North Road and Aylmer Road, in north London, there is a group of Neo-Georgian executive houses built in the 1970s **(Plate 502)**. Without denigrating their design in any way, the standard is very much of the time, with Georgian features added to the basic box-shaped house.

503. The entrance front, Arundel Park, Sussex

15.92 NEO-PALLADIAN COUNTRY HOUSES

The relatively chaste style of Palladianism has continued to command its adherents into modern times. Arundel Park, in Sussex *(Plate 503)*, was built by the 16th Duke of Norfolk between 1958 and 1962 to serve as a Dower House in the Castle park and to be used in conjunction with Arundel Castle. The architect was Claude Phillimore and it might well be that the special appeal of the Palladian style to both architect and his client was the plan, which consists of a central block containing the main living rooms, and pavilions on each side, one accommodating the staff and the other the Duke's dependent family. In the centre of the house there is a double-storeyed living hall also incorporating the staircase, top-lit from a cupola in the manner of Sir John Soane. Also perhaps in the manner of the time, Arundel Park was decorated by John Fowler, of Colefax and Fowler, very much in his English country house style.

King's Walden Bury, Hertfordshire *(Plate 504)* is an exceptionally handsome Palladian building by Raymond Erith and Quinlan Terry. Dating from 1972, and replacing a neo-Elizabethan mansion of the 1890s, King's Walden Bury was built for Sir Thomas Milburne-Swinnerton-Pilkington, and in design terms derives from one of Palladio's villas on the Veneto. The main front is of two storeys and five bays, with the windows set under arches, and a pediment crowns the central three. The two-tier frontispiece is framed by Doric columns on the ground floor and Ionic above, and behind it there is a central living hall with a stone floor and a barrel-vaulted staircase. The two-bay wings with hipped roofs project forward and contain the four main rooms on the ground floor. Hand-made red bricks from Suffolk are used as facing material, with details in stone and in painted plaster, and the use of 3:2 in the proportions of the structure and the use of the Venetian foot, which is 14in. (35.5cm), ensures harmony in the design.

504. King's Walden Bury, Hertfordshire

505. *The forecourt, Dalton Hall, Cumbria*

506. *The Ionic Villa, Regent's Park, London, from the Regent's Canal*

Dalton Hall, in Cumbria **(Plate 505)**, was Sir Clough Williams-Ellis' last house, built in 1968-1971. The client was Mr Anthony Mason-Hornby and the new classical design replaced an earlier house. The restrained and symmetrical building with its sash windows has a three-bay, pedimented frontispiece on the entrance side, which breaks forward by a modest amount from the two bays on either side. Tuscan pilasters support the pediment, which has a cartouche over the door and a circular window in the pediment, sitting against a hipped roof of Westmorland slates surmounted by tall chimneystacks. The overall appearance of Dalton Hall is that of effortless confidence and security, a skilful re-interpretation of the essence of Palladian design.

Quinlan Terry continued Raymond Erith's practice after his partner died in 1973, and when he was appointed architect for the first three of a series of six new villas in Regent's Park in 1988 he was, in a sense, stepping into the shoes of John Nash. As mentioned in section 11.1, Nash's 1811 plan for Regent's Park had envisaged fifty-six villas, later reduced to twenty-six, although only six were actually built. Land became available in the north-west section of the Park and the Crown Estate decided to develop a series of grand houses informed by, rather than copying, Nash's original concept. The first three of the villas were named the Ionic, the Veneto and the Gothick. The entrance façade of the Ionic Villa, dating from 1989, consists of five bays, with the central three framed by four engaged Ionic columns surmounted by a pediment which carries a cartouche of the arms of the owner, Lord Bagri, together with supporters.

The first thing which strikes the observer is the exuberance of the design of this villa. This is due partly to the stucco which covers the load-bearing brick structure and also to the proportions and richness of the façade, and in particular the little cupola on the hipped roof. Perhaps this gives a clue to the restlessness of the design which is so apparent, as the Ionic Villa shows its origins in the Veneto, and especially in the Villa Ragona, designed by Palladio, but probably never built. Palladio's ideal domestic plan works well here, but some of the exterior design touches strongly recall the Baroque rather than the usual restrained Palladian style.

The garden slopes down to the Regent's Park Canal and from this side **(Plate 506)** the elevation of the Villa recalls those that you see along the Brenta Canal as it runs from Padua into the Venice Lagoon. Here Quinlan Terry has brought forward a three-bay element under a pediment, the surface of which is strongly rusticated. On the ground floor a loggia leads out on to a terrace with staircases panelled by flint leading down to the garden . The view from the canal is one of the most imposing to be had of a modern house in London. Since the Ionic Villa was built, the three remaining villas, named the Corinthian, the Tuscan and the Regency, have been built in 2001 and 2002 by the same architect.

383

507. 82 Swain's Lane, Highgate, London

15.93 METAL AND GLASS HOUSES

Houses built of metal and glass depend for their effectiveness on modern technology. To be acceptable even in our mild climate, the central heating has to be efficient and flexible, the large glass windows have to be capable of retaining a fair proportion of the internal heating and keeping out some of the more harmful rays of the sun. Very often, too, the notion behind such houses is to become as much a part of the natural environment as is possible, and overlooking by our fellow human beings must therefore not be a problem. All these characteristics can be seen in No. 82 Swain's Lane, Highgate, a house built by architect John Winter for his own occupation *(Plate 507)*. Constructed between 1966 and 1969 on the edge of Highgate Cemetery on three floors with a central service core, it is one of the most interesting of modern structures. The frame is made of Cor-ten steel, which weathers to a rusty brown colour, the first time the material was used in this country. The large glass windows of the top-floor living space offer spectacular views and the impression that you are part of

the wild-life that inhabits the Cemetery.

In 1978 John Winter also built No. 85 Swain's Lane, again with a steel upper floor, but this time cantilevered over a central concrete core and with a wall entirely glazed on the cemetery side. Just at the top of the hill in Pond Square, Highgate, another interesting modern house has been built. The architect of No. 16 Pond Square was Leonard Manasseh and in 1961 he built a house with the main living rooms on the upper floor with the services below.

15.94 A VERNACULAR REVIVAL?

The 1980s and 1990s have seen a renewed interest in vernacular styles, not only in housing but in public buildings as well. The imagery is that of pitched roofs, colourful and friendly tile and brick surfaces, symmetrically placed windows and doors and, in London especially, stucco on ground-floor walls. The term 'vernacular' implies the style of a local area, and also of a period, as

508. *Houses behind Finland Street, Greenland Dock, Rotherhithe, London*

reconstituted stone might be more appropriate in a district not noted for its brick, and Edwardian substantiality perhaps more familiar than small terraced houses.

A feeling of generous space is clear in the private housing scheme placed in a crescent around what remains of Norway Dock in the London Borough of Southwark *(Plate 508)*. By the beginning of the 1980s public housing was in the doldrums, with the local authorities having insufficient resources for house building and the then Conservative Government having vested control of the vacant Thames-side land in the London Docklands Development Corpora-tion. Many of the characteristics of this private development, designed by Shepheard, Epstein and Hunter and built between 1988 and 1996, recall London houses of the 1840s.

In Hackney, the Mothers' Square *(Plate 509)* consists of new and adapted buildings designed by the architects Hunt Thompson between 1987 and 1990 to provide housing, sheltered flats, a day hospital and a nursing home. The property was formerly used by the Salvation Army's Mothers' Hospital. The rectangle of terraced houses is built of coloured brickwork and the classical details are coarse, imitating the local builders' vernacular of the Victorian period.

509. *The Mothers' Square, Hackney, London*

15.95 NEW HOUSES IN THE COUNTRYSIDE

'An isolated new house in the countryside may exceptionally be justified if it is clearly of the highest quality, is truly outstanding in terms of its architecture and landscape design and would significantly enhance the immediate setting and wider surrounds…Proposals for such a development would need to demonstrate that proper account has been taken of the definitive characteristics of the local area, including local or regional building traditions and materials…'. These words come from an obscure but important document entitled Planning Policy Guidance No. 7, of February 1997, issued to local planning authorities by the Department of Planning and Rural Affairs and in the last eight years the surprise is that more advantage has not been taken of it.

One of the underlying assumptions of this book has been the importance of the English country house to the development of this nation's culture, and indeed to the progress of world aesthetics. The tale has not only been a tedious recital of architects' names and a succession of styles, but the recognition that, in the main, cultural initiatives, which we might take as read today, first made their appearance in our countryside. The Dissolution of the Monasteries in the sixteenth century, and the curbing of the power of the monarchy in the seventeenth, left the great landowners of the eighteenth century in possession of much of the nation's land, and they were not to be absentee landlords as their opposite numbers were in other countries. Much of their time was spent in London, of course, but it was their country estates that they called home, and it was there that they spent their ever-growing wealth in building and beautifying their houses.

The industrial moguls and entrepreneurs of the nineteenth century followed their lead and it was not until the beginning of the last century that the balance tilted in favour of the urban communities. Ever more restrictive planning controls have meant that few totally new country houses of architectural distinction were built in this country in the last quarter of the twentieth century. The emphasis was on replacement buildings or those of an earlier period altered by a skilful architect who could work with the local authority and government planners, and this at a time when many hundreds of country houses had been demolished, a haemorrhage which reached its peak in 1955. And, in terms of style, those that have been built have tended to be uncontroversial and timid Georgian boxes, although, as we have seen, there are exceptions to that rule, in particular the exuberant and scholarly houses of Quinlan Terry.

With PPG 7 this is, perhaps, set to change. Great fortunes are being made in the City of London and in industry, not only in this country, and it would be inspiring if some of the money were to be invested in new and inventive country houses. One great project is presently building in Hampshire at a contract price of about £3 million, designed by the architect, Robert Adam, and, if the style is predominantly classical, it is the Neo-classicism of the German architect, Karl Friedrich Schinkel.

Avant-garde architects are working in the housing field in Switzerland and Spain and some of these firms have done striking work in public architecture in this country. It is surely inevitable that a country house scheme will soon be submitted following the PPG 7 line which will place strains on the essential conservatism of our local planning process.

15.96 WHERE NEXT?

Good architecture has always tended to follow a prosperous economy. In recent years the money which has come from the Lottery Fund 'for good causes' has fuelled the illusion that the nation's economy is stronger than in truth it is, but it has also produced public buildings of high quality all over the country. As housing is outside the remit of the Lottery, this aspect of our environment has fallen behind, but there are indications that the nation might be on the edge of a Renaissance in the English house.

As has been suggested already, the relaxation in the planning controls for the new country house in its own extensive parkland envisaged by PPG 7 will surely produce a design either by one of the avant-garde firms of architects in this country or perhaps by the Dutch architect, Rem Koolhaas who has built a remarkable house in Bordeaux. Whether, if such a design is submitted, either our town planners and the members of their planning committees, or the planning inspectors, will make an aesthetic rather than a political judgement about it remains to be seen.

In recent years we have also seen a number of country houses of architectural distinction divided sensitively into flats and maisonettes, among them the late seventeenth century Burley-on-the-Hill, in Rutland. In such cases the key to good adaptation is to preserve the integrity of the main internal spaces and usually to subdivide vertically rather than horizontally, converting with perhaps a firmer hand within the envelope of the out-buildings.

Country houses such as these stand in their own land and skilful redevelopment tends to impinge rather less on the surroundings than would be the case, for instance, on the edge of a town. And, should we as a nation continue to place a blanket refusal of planning permission on proposals for new housing on a modest scale in former country house estates

510. Houses in Poundbury, Dorset

where, for instance, the house has been previously demolished? This book has noted a number of instances where this has been done in the past; the villas built in the grounds of Calverley Park, Tunbridge Wells, in Kent, spring to mind. What makes those villas acceptable today is the moderate size of the houses. This is the most important factor whether or not the development accommodates one or more units, or how informal the layout is, and equally significant is the preservation of the original landscaping. If what is needed to preserve the parkland setting of such an estate is the easing of the laws governing pension funds being able to invest in residential property for rental in a way that does not benefit the pensioner, his or her family or the Fund's associates, then surely this is a change worth examining.

So far as more modest houses are concerned, the key to acceptable development should be relating the buildings to the landscape setting in which they are to be placed. If the site is in or alongside existing buildings, the mixed development should be consciously urban in nature, whereas free-standing estates ought to be built at a lower density than at present. Here the solution is, perhaps, mixing houses with

flats and maisonettes in an informal manner which does not seem to be enslaved by the road engineer's requirements and which respects the natural flow of the topography. If the appearance of Toy Town estates is to be avoided, it is essential that the landscape should seem natural and not be an element that the developer has reluctantly added on to supplement the greenery of the private gardens.

And what of style? I do not believe that the architectural style of the new buildings is important as such. What is essential is that the materials and the way in which they are used should respect the traditions of the local area, and that there should be a consistency in the appearance of a group of houses. In this context, the new village of Poundbury, outside Dorchester, in Dorset *(Plate 510)*, has been skilfully executed, and investigates how classical motifs can be used to unite different sizes of houses, and commercial buildings as well, in a harmonious community. But, in its setting, cut off from Dorchester, it feels as foreign as does Clough Williams-Ellis' Portmeirion, in north Wales. When all is said and done, our houses should make us feel at home, and that is the true meaning of vernacular.

GLOSSARY

Ashlar – Blocks of cut, and squared stone prepared so that they can be laid in courses with sharp lines separated by mortar. Contrasted with rubble, where the stone is randomly used.

Bay window and bay – Modern domestic use is the projection from a house front that might be circular, rectangular or even canted, all forms being on plan. In the book, the term bay is also used to indicate the regular sub-division of the length of a house, by buttresses with windows inserted into the wall, by part of a medieval building between supporting timbers, or by the Classical Orders, and, more loosely, by the number of windows inserted into an 18th century façade. The reason why this is referred to as 'more loose' is that the façade windows should relate to the function of the room spaces behind and do not always do so.

Bow window – In the Regency period, a segmental bay projecting from a house front is defined as a 'Bow'.

Colonnette – A small column or circular shaft.

Corbel – Projection of stone or wood from a wall supporting a load which might consist of an arch, a truss, or a beam. A succession of such corbels could support a vault in medieval times.

Corps de logis – The main, usually hospitality, block of a country house, in design terms dominating subsidiary pavilions where the family lived, ate, and often worshipped.

Crocket – An ornament in the Gothic style and usually foliage placed regularly along a canopy or gable. The largest bunches might be placed at the top forming a finial.

Dentil moulding – Small stone blocks of differing lengths creating the impression of teeth. Used extensively in the cornices of 18th century houses, but deriving from Greek Classical times, when it was early used on the Caryatid porch of the Erechtheion in the 5th century BC.

Diocletian window – Semicircular window divided vertically by two mullion into three sections. Takes its name from the Baths of Diocletian, in Rome (AD306). Used extensively in Palladian and Neo-classical architecture at the end of the 18th century.

Elvan – Crystalline rock composed in part of quartz used as a building material in 16th century Cornwall.

Entablature – In Classical terms the stone or other material borne by the columns, but subsequently divided into the lintel, the frieze and the cornice. An important feature of the façade of a Classical 18th century country house.

Garderobe – In the medieval house the clothes would be stored in this room, but it came to be the latrine.

Impost – Elements projecting from both sides of an arch, often moulded, from which the arch springs.

In antis – In Classical architecture, where a portico was formed by having the side walls project beyond the columns, the design of the portico and columns is described as being in antis.

Ipswich window – A 17th century oriel window, of which a good example can be seen on Sparrowe's House, in the Buttermarket, Ipswich, with convex sides between the mullions and the wall, the transoms being two thirds of the way up the side-lights and with an arched central light. The window also has much decoration.

Kneeler – A large stone cut to a triangular shape at the bottom of a gable and following the line of the gable to secure it.

Lozenge – A parallelogram with the two opposing angles cut more acutely than the others, in the shape of a diamond or rhomboid. Frequently occurs in mouldings, in strapwork and in lead window-lights.

Mullion – Vertical member between window lights or a screen made of stone or timber and usually moulded.

Newel – The continuous vertical element of the axis of a circular stair.

Oriel – Large bay-window projecting from the wall of a building on the upper floor supported on brackets.

Outshut – Early medieval extension of living and storage space under the same roof frequently found in the wool areas of the Upper Calder Valley

Piano nobile – The main storey of a building containing the rooms of ceremony, hospitality and display usually set over a lower storey and approached from outside by a flight of steps.

Purlin – Horizontal timber beam carried on roof trusses to enable it to support the rafters.

Rustication – Stone cut to form a contrast between a roughened surface and dressed ashlars.

Sima recta moulding – Projecting moulding often found in Classical architecture with equal convex and concave arcs. The *Sima recta* is found at the top of a cornice, while the lower is called the *Sima reversa*.

Soffit – A ceiling or the visible underside of an arch.

Solar – Upper chamber private to the owner of a house often to be found in a cross-wing.

Strapwork – 16th and 17th century ornament cut to resemble leather thongs found frequently in northern Europe. Its influence came into this country from Flanders and especially from Fontainebleau.

Transom – Beam across a window usually found in Elizabethan and Jacobean houses where window lights were formed.

Triglyphs – Upright slots occurring on either side of a Doric frieze in Classical architecture recalling the ends of timber beams.

Tympanum – Triangular face of a Classical pediment often enriched with relief sculpture.

Undercroft – Space beneath a church or other building often vaulted.

Volute – Spiral scroll of stone or plaster of which there are usually four on an Ionic capital and eight on a composite one.

ACKNOWLEDGEMENTS

Michael Wright

In a book of this kind, the first and, indeed, greatest acknowledgement must go to the Buildings of England series of books written first by Dr Nikolaus Pevsner and subsequently by a long list of art and architectural historians, and published for many years by Penguin and now by Yale. The debt to their scholarship is profound and I am happy to acknowledge it. Both John Steel and I would also record that the inspiration for this book came from Hermann Muthesius' book also entitled *The English House*, published in 1904. Among the authors whose books I have read with great benefit, I would like to mention those of my former colleague at *Country Life* magazine, Dr Mark Girouard, and in particular his *Life in the English Country House* (Yale), *Sweetness and Light* (Oxford), *Robert Smythson and the Elizabethan Country House* (Yale) and *The Victorian Country House* (Yale). Also from *Country Life*, but of an earlier generation, I acknowledge my debt to Christopher Hussey's *Life of Sir Edwin Lutyens* (Antique Collectors' Club), while *Architecture in Britain 1530-1830* by Sir John Summerson (Penguin), *English Brickwork* by Nathaniel Lloyd (Antique Collectors' Club) and Osbert Lancaster's books, especially *From Pillar to Post* and *Here of All Places* (John Murray) have also been invaluable.

Nicholas Cooper's *Houses of the Gentry 1480-1680* (Yale) has proved a great resource, and *Early Georgian Interiors,* by my friend and colleague John Cornforth, published after his recent untimely death, has helped everyone interested in the field to understand how interiors were made to work in the early eighteenth century. *A.W.N. Pugin, Master of the Gothic Revival*, edited by Paul Atterbury (Yale), and Tim Hilton's two-volume biography of John Ruskin (Yale), Peter Davey's *Arts and Crafts Architecture* (Phaidon), *Anthony Salvin* by Jill Allibone (Lutterworth Press), *Richard Norman Shaw* by Andrew Saint (Yale), *C.F.A. Voysey* by Stuart Durant (Academy Editions, St Martin's Press) and *Docklands* by Stephanie Williams (Architecture Design and Technology Press) have all been of great assistance to me, while another former colleague, Clive Aslet's *The Last Country Houses* (Yale) and John Martin Robinson's *The Latest Country Houses* (Yale) have both helped to make the late nineteenth and twentieth centuries more revealing. In that context, F.R.S. Yorke's pioneering work, *The Modern House*, *The Modern House Today* by Kenneth Powell with pictures by Nick Dawe (Black Dog Publishing Ltd) and *London Suburbs* (Merrell Holberton) have made a complex story infinitely more understandable.

I am grateful to the Bridgeman Art Library for permission to reproduce Plate 385, and to Norman Scarfe for Plate 27.

Finally, I should like to express my thanks to the many owners whose beautiful houses have been photographed, for the universal welcome that they have given me and for the permission they have granted.

HOUSES BY COUNTY

Argyll and Bute
The Hill House, Helensburgh

Bedfordshire
Milton Ernest Hall
Old Warden
Woburn Abbey
Woburn High Street
Wrest Park, Silsoe

Berkshire
Bearwood House, Hurst
Coleshill House
Deanery Gardens, Sonning
Hinton House, St Nicholas Hurst
Inkpen School
West Woodhay House

Buckinghamshire
Harleyford Manor, Marlow
High and Over, near Amersham on the Hill
Little Orchards, Denham
Stoke Park, Stoke Poges
The Vicarage, Colnbrook
The Vicarage, Stoke Poges
Winslow Hall

Cambridgeshire
Fellows' Building, King's College,
Cambridge
St John's College, Cambridge
Wimpole Hall, Royston

Cheshire
Blacon, Chester
Cholmondley Castle, near Malpas
Churche's Mansion, Nantwich
Dorfold Hall, near Nantwich
The Lache, Chester
Little Moreton Hall, near Congleton

Conwy
Plas Mawr, Conwy

Cornwall
Caerhays Castle, St Michael Caerhays
Cotehele
Trerice, near Newquay

Cumbria
Belle Isle, Windermere
Blackwell, near Bowness
Broadleys, Windermere
Calder Valley, 17th century house
Dalton Hall
Grecian Villa, Cockermouth
Hodge Hall, Cartmel
44/45 Irish Street, Whitehaven
Killington Hall
Levens Hall
Longhouse, Hacket Forge
Moorcrag, Cartmel
Moresby Hall
Swarthmoor Hall, near Ulverstone
Townend, Troutbeck

Derbyshire
Barlborough Hall
Brizlincote Hall, Stapenhill
Calke Abbey
Chatsworth House
Ednaston Manor
Haddon Hall
Hardwick Hall
Kedleston Hall
Lea Wood, Dethick
The Little Castle, Bolsover
Prior Overton's Tower, Repton
St Anne's Terrace, The Crescent, Buxton
Sutton Hall, Sutton-on-the-Hill
Wolfscote Grange, near Hartington
Woodville, house on A50

Devon
The Barn, Exmouth
Castle Drogo, Drewsteignton
Devon Square villas, Newton Abbot
Endsleigh House, Milton Abbot
Holcombe Court, Holcombe Rogus
Kingsland House, Modbury
Knightshayes Court, near Tiverton
Luscombe Castle
Mothecombe
The Old Rectory, Clyst St Lawrence
School Street, Sidford
Shute Barton, Shute
Thatchways, Thurlestone
Walkey's Cottage, Clyst St Lawrence
William of Orange House, Strand, Topsham

Dorset
Abbey Street, Cerne Abbas
Abbot's Hall, Cerne Abbey
Anderson Manor
Athelhampton, near Dorchester
Chalmington, near Cattistock
Chantry, Trent
Chettle House
Clyffe House, near Tincleton
Eagle House, Blandford Forum
Encombe House, near Corfe Castle
Glanvilles Wootton cottage
Guest House, Cerne Abbey
Kingston Lacy
The Manor House, Sandford Orcas
The Manor House, Winterbourne Clenston
Poundbury, near Dorchester
Rampisham Rectory
Seaforth Cottage, Wool
Thornhill House
Woolbridge Manor, Wool
Yetminster

Dublin
Casino, Marino, Clontarf, Dublin

Dunbartonshire
Ferry Inn, Roseneath

East Lothian
Greywalls, Gullane

Essex
Audley End, Saffron Walden
Bocking, mansard roof
Castle Hedingham
Chapel Street, Steeple Bumpstead
Church Street, Saffron Walden
Coggeshall church conversion
Crown House, Bridge End, Stansted
Mountfitchet
Horham Hall, near Thaxted
Layer Marney
Moulsham Mill, Chelmsford
Paycocke's House, Coggeshall
Pear Tree Barn, Mount Bures
Rainham Hall
Sherman's, Dedham
Stansted House
Wanstead House

Glamorgan
St Donat's Castle

Gloucestershire
Abbotswood, near Stow-on-the-Wold
Ablington Manor, Bibury
Barnsley House
Clifton House, Chipping Campden
Daylesford House, Adlestrop
Dover's House, Chipping Campden
Gloucester Cathedral
Grevel House, Chipping Campden
Hidcote Manor, near Chipping Campden
The Old Rectory, Coalpit Heath
Rodmarton Manor
Seymour House, Chipping Campden
Sezincote, near Moreton-in-Marsh
Stanway House

Gwynedd
Penrhyn Castle

Hampshire
Highclere Castle
Hinton Ampner
Osborne House, Isle of Wight
Stratton Park, East Stratton
The Vyne, Sherborne St John

Herefordshire
Downton Castle
Eastnor Castle
Lucton School
Newhouse Farm, Goodrich

Hertfordshire
Ashridge, Little Gaddesden
Benington Lordship
Gernon Road, Letchworth
Hatfield House
King's Walden Bury
The Old Farmhouse, Wheathampstead
Theobalds Park, Cheshunt
Torilla, near Hatfield

Huntingdonshire
Manor House, Hemingford Grey
Northborough Manor House

Inverclyde
Windyhill, near Kilmacolm

Kent
Abbot's Fireside, Elham
Aldersmead Road, Cator Estate, Beckenham
Ashour Farm Lodge, Penshurst
Beckenham, 114 Shortlands Road
Benenden Road, Biddenden
Bentham Hill, near Southborough
Betteshanger House, near Deal
Biddenden
Brasted Place
Bridge Place
Broome Park, near Barham
Calverley Estate, Tunbridge Wells
Chafford Arms, Fordcombe
Cobb's Hall, Aldington
Danson Hill, near Bexleyheath
Exbury House, Westgate-on-Sea
Fairfield, Eastry
Finchcocks, near Goudhurst
Fleur-de-Lys, Canterbury
Godinton House, Ashford
The Grange, Ramsgate
Great and Little Pagehurst, near Staplehurst,
Groombridge Place
The Grove, Penshurst
Hammerfield, near Penshurst
Hawkhurst, gambrel roof near
Hever Castle
The Hopfield, Platt
Ightham Mote
Knole, Sevenoaks
Lee Priory
Maidstone, 78 Bank Street
Mereworth Castle
Nurstead Court
Old Post Office, Wickhambreux
Old Soar, Plaxtol
Penshurst cottages
Penshurst Place
Preston Hall Colony, Aylesford
The Salutation, Sandwich
Scotney Castle, Lamberhurst
Sissinghurst Castle
Spencer Road, Birchington, Westgate-on-Sea
Starkey Castle Farm
Sunnymead, Chislehurst
Swanton Street Farm, near Bredgar
Tenterden, 114-116 High Street
Willesley Arms Hotel, Willesley, Cranbrook
The Wood House, Shipbourne

Lancashire
Astley Hall, Chorley
Borwick Hall
Borwick village house
Rufford Old Hall
Samlesbury Upper Hall
Scarisbrick Hall
Whittington Hall

Leicestershire
Ashby de la Zouch, villa near
Manor House, Donington le Heath
Old Rectory, Church Langton
Papillon Hall, Lubenham
Sileby Road, Mountsorrel
Stoneywell Cottage, near Ulverscroft

Lincolnshire
Angel Hotel, Grantham
Belton House
Burghley House, Stamford

Doddington Hall
Gainsborough Old Hall
The Jew's House, Well Lane, Lincoln
Manor House, Boothby Pagnell
Tattershall Castle
Thorpe by Water, Lyddington
Westholme House, Sleaford
Woolsthorpe Manor

London
Alexandra Road Estate, Camden
Alton Estate, Roehampton
Asgill House, Richmond
Aylmer Road, Highgate
Banqueting House, Whitehall
Bedford Park, Turnham Green
Binsey Walk, Thamesmead
Bloomsbury Way
Branch Hill, Hampstead
1 and 2 Bunkers Hill, Hampstead Garden
Suburb
Camberwell Grove
Camberwell New Road
Canons, Edgware
Cator Estate, Blackheath Park
Chiswick House
Clarendon House, Piccadilly
Cohen House, Old Church Street, Chelsea
Congregational Church, Hornsey Lane,
Highgate
Covent Garden
Crown Life Insurance Office, New Bridge
Street
Crystal Palace, Hyde Park
Davidge Terrace, 154-158 Kennington
Road, Lambeth
Devonshire House, Piccadilly
Douglas Haig Memorial Homes, Morden
Downham Bungalow Estate, Baudwin
Road, Lewisham
Dulwich Mausoleum
6 Ellerdale Road, Hampstead
Eltham Lodge
Essex Street, Temple
3 Fairway Close, Hampstead Garden
Suburb
Finland Street, Greenland Dock,
Rotherhithe
Gardnor Mansions, Church Row,
Hampstead
'Goose-pie House', Whitehall
Great West Road
Grosvenor Square
Ham House
Hampstead Garden Suburb
Hampton Court
Hendon Way
Highpoint, North Road, Highgate
Holland Park Road, Kensington
Home House, Portman Square
Ionic Villa, Regent's Park
Ivory House, St Katherine's Dock, Wapping
Kew Palace (The Dutch House), Kew
Gardens
Kingsbury, Brent
The Lakes, Norway Dock, Rotherhithe
Lakeside, Castlebar, Ealing
Lansbury Estate, Poplar
Leighton House, 12 Holland Park Road
Lillington Gardens, Pimlico
Lindsey House, Lincoln's Inn Fields
Lloyd Baker Estate, Islington
Lowther Lodge, Bayswater
Marble Hill House, Twickenham
Montagu House, Bloomsbury
Montague Street, Bloomsbury
Mothers' Square, Hackney

Norway Dock, Southwark
Old Town, Clapham
Parkleys Estate, Ham Common
Peabody Estate flats, Covent Garden
Persaut Road pre-fabs, Lewisham
Pitzhanger Manor, Ealing
16 Pond Square, Highgate
Porchester Terrace, Bayswater
Queen's House, Greenwich
Red House, Bexleyheath
Regent's Park
Ronan Point, Newnham
St Paul's Studios, 135-149 Talgarth Road
Sekforde Street, Clerkenwell
Sherwood and Lydia Houses, Dartmouth
Grove, Blackheath
Soane Museum, Lincoln's Inn Fields
Somerset House
Strawberry Hill, Twickenham
Sun House, Frognal Way, Hampstead
Sunray Estate, Herne Hill
82 and 85 Swain's Lane, Highgate
Swakeleys House, Ickenham
Syon House, Isleworth
Thurnby Court, Twickenham Green
Tooks Court, City
Trent Park, Enfield
Vanbrugh's Castle, Greenwich Hill
Vernon Court, Hendon Way, Cricklewood
19 Wellgarth Road, Hampstead Garden
Suburb
Westminster Hall
1-3 Willow Road, Hampstead
Woodberry Down Estate, Stoke Newington

Monmouthshire
Chepstow Castle

Norfolk
Barningham Hall
Blickling Hall
Carrow Manor, Norwich
Chesterfield Villas, Cromer
Denver Hall
East Barsham Manor
Felbrigg Hall
Happisburgh Manor
Heydon Hall
Mill Farm, Bradenham
Holkham Hall
Houghton Hall
Kirstead Hall
Oxburgh Hall
The Pleasaunce, Overstrand
Raynham Hall
Sheringham
Voewood, High Kelling, Holt

Northamptonshire
Boughton House
Castle Ashby
16 Cobthorne, Oundle
Holdenby House
Kirby Hall, near Corby
Market House, Rothwell
The New Bield, Lyveden
St Martin's Villas, 43-44 Billing Road,
Northampton
Warrener's (Triangular) Lodge, Rushton

Northumberland
Cragside, Rothbury
Langley Castle
Seaton Delaval Hall

Nottinghamshire
Bestwood Lodge
Budby, estate house
Holme Pierrepont
Newstead Abbey
Normanton Prebend, Southwell
Radcliffe on Trent
Wollaton Hall, Nottingham
Worksop Manor

Oxfordshire
All Souls College, Oxford
Ashdown Park
Blenheim Palace
Broughton Castle
Burford High Street
Chastleton House
Ditchley Park, near Enstone
Great House, Burford
Heythrop House
Hill House, Burford
Middleton Park, Middleton Stoney
Natural History Museum, Oxford
Old Bull Hotel, Burford
Old Rectory, Burford
Old School and Master's House, Adderbury
Old Schools, Oxford
The Old Vicarage, High Street, Burford
Peckwater Quad, Christ Church, Oxford
Rousham House
St Winnow, Burford
Tiverton Villa, Burford
Tom Quad, Christ Church, Oxford

Peterborough
Thorney Abbey
Thorpe Hall

Powys
Church Street, Presteigne

Roxburghshire
Abbotsford, Melrose

Rutland
Bede House, Lyddington
Burley-on-the-Hill

Shropshire
Attingham Park, near Shrewsbury
Buntingsdale, Market Drayton
Condover Hall
Council House Gatehouse, Shrewsbury
Cound Hall
Cronkhill House, Attingham Park, near
Shrewsbury
Longner Hall, Uffington
Madeley Court
Stokesay Castle, Craven Arms
Warleigh Manor, near Bathford
Wilderhope Manor, Longville
Yeaton, farmhouse

Somerset
Adcote House, Little Ness
Albemarle Row, Hotwells, Bristol
Barrington Court
Blaise Hamlet, Henbury, Bristol
Chantry House, Mere
The Circus, Bath
Clevedon Court
Clifton Maybank, Yeovil
Combe Down, Prior Park, Bath
Cothay Manor
Gay Street, Bath
General Wade's House, Abbey Churchyard,
Bath

George and Pilgrim Hotel,, Glastonbury
George Inn, Norton St Philip
Glastonbury Abbey
Grammar School, Chard
Hatch Court, Hatch Beauchamp
Hestercombe, Kingston Tarrant
King's Weston House, near Bristol
Montacute House
The Old School, Compton Dando
Queen Square, Bath
Rectory, Upton Magna
Royal Crescent, Bath
Saltford Manor House
School and Master's House, Upton Magna
Sham Castle, Bathwick Hill, Bath
Tickenham Court, near Nailsea
Tintinhull House
Tyntesfield, near Wraxall
Vicars' Close, Cathedral Precinct, Wells
Windsor Terrace, Clifton

South Lanarkshire
New Lanark

Staffordshire
Barlaston Hall
Broadoak, Leek
Gothic Rectory, Chapel Street, Cheadle
Hales Hall
Harecastle Farm, Talke
Heron Court, Rugeley
Home Farm, Sandon Park
Ilam Hall
Orgreave Hall
Speedwell Castle, Brewood
Trentham Park, Stoke-on-Trent

Suffolk
Cupola House, Bury St Edmunds
Deanery Tower, Hadleigh
Greyfriars (Regency House), Southwold
Hemingstone Hall
Hengrave Hall
Heveningham Hall
High House, Huntingfield
Ickworth House
Little Wenham Hall
Mansard House, Bardwell
Melford Hall, Long Melford
Newe House, Pakenham
The Old Maltings, Long Melford
Otley Hall
Pentecostal Church, Churchgate Street,
Bury St Edmunds
Prince's Lodging, Newmarket
Rushbrooke Hall
Seckford Hall, near Woodbridge
Shire Hall, Woodbridge
Sparrowe's House (Ancient House), Ipswich
Sudbury, ranch-style house near
Tattingstone Wonder
Tide Mill, Woodbridge
Wolmers, Stonham Aspal

Surrey
'Bellagio', Dormans Park
Brook, Witley, cottage
Fulbrook House, near Elstead
Munstead Wood
Nonsuch Palace
Orchards, Munstead
Polesden Lacey, Great Bookham
Sudbrook Park, Petersham
Vann, near Godalming
Westbrook, near Godalming

Sussex
Alfriston Clergy House
Arundel Park
Bailiffscourt, Climping
Bodiam Castle
Brighton Pavilion
East Wittering
Glen Andred, near Groombridge
Gravetye Manor, near East Grinstead
Leys Wood, Groombridge
Little Thakeham, near Pulborough
Peacehaven
Petworth House
Regency Square, Brighton
Standen, near East Grinstead

Tipperary
Swiss House, Cahir

Tyne and Wear
Byker Wall, Newcastle upon Tyne

Warwickshire
Charlecote
Hampton-in-Arden cottages
Kenilworth Castle

West Midlands
Birmingham, Court 15, Hurst Street and
Inge Street

Wiltshire
Belcombe Court, Bradford-on-Avon
Biddesden House, near Ludgershall
Caen Hill Flight, Devizes, lock-keeper's
cottage
The Courts, Holt
Fonthill Abbey, Fonthill Gifford
Great Barn, Lacock
Great Chalfield Manor, near Melksham
Grittleton House
Lacock Abbey
Longford Castle, Bodenham
Longleat
Porch House, Potterne
St Marie's Grange, Alderbury
Salisbury, 68 The Close
Shane's Castle, Devizes
Stourhead, Stourton
Wardour Castle, Tisbury
Westbury House, Bradford-on-Avon
Wilton House

Worcestershire
Hagley Hall
Wyke Manor, Wick, Pershore

Yorkshire
Baldersby Vicarage
Banney Royd, Edgerton, Huddersfield
Burton Agnes Hall
Castle Howard
Fleece Inn, Westgate, near Elland
Gilling Castle
Gledstone Hall, Skipton
Heathcote, Ilkley
Huthwaite Hall, Thurgoland
Lazenby Hall, Danby Wiske
New Earswick, York
Nostell Priory
Rievaulx Abbey
Somerset House, Halifax
Wentworth Woodhouse
Wood Lane Hall, Sowerby
64-72 Lady Row, Goodramgate, York
48-60 Stonegate, York

INDEX

Page numbers in bold type refer to illustrations

THE ANTIQUE COLLECTORS' CLUB

Formed in 1966, the Antique Collectors' Club is now a world-renowned publisher of top quality books for the collector. It also publishes the only independently-run monthly antiques magazine, *Antique Collecting*, which rose quickly from humble beginnings to a network of worldwide subscribers.

The magazine, whose motto is *For Collectors-By Collectors-About Collecting*, is aimed at collectors interested in widening their knowledge of antiques both by increasing their awareness of quality and by discussion of the factors influencing prices.

Subscription to Antique Collecting is open to anyone interested in antiques and subscribers receive ten issues a year. Well-illustrated articles deal with practical aspects of collecting and provide numerous tips on prices, features of value, investment potential, fakes and forgeries. Offers of related books at special reduced prices are also available only to subscribers.

In response to the enormous demand for information on 'what to pay', ACC introduced in 1968 the famous price guide series. The first title, *The Price Guide to Antique Furniture* (since renamed *British Antique Furniture: Price Guide and Reasons for Values*), is still in constant demand. Since those pioneering days, ACC has gone from strength to strength, publishing many of today's standard works of reference on all things antique and collectable, from *Tiaras* to *20th Century Ceramic Designers in Britain*.

Not only has ACC continued to cater strongly for its original audience, it has also branched out to produce excellent titles on many subjects including art reference, architecture, garden design, gardens, and textiles. All ACC's publications are available through bookshops worldwide and a catalogue is available free of charge from the addresses below.

For further information please contact:

ANTIQUE COLLECTORS' CLUB

www.antiquecollectorsclub.com

Sandy Lane, Old Martlesham
Woodbridge, Suffolk IP12 4SD, UK   or
Tel: 01394 389950 Fax: 01394 389999
Email: info@antique-acc.com

Eastworks, 116 Pleasant Street – Suite 18
Easthampton, MA 01027
Tel: (413) 529 0861
Email: info@antiquecc.com